Kurdistan

The Quest for Representation and Self-Determination

LUNGTHUIYANG RIAMEI

Foreword by

Girijesh Pant

KNOWLEDGE WORLD

KW Publishers Pvt Ltd
New Delhi

ISBN 978-93-86288-86-8 Hardback
ISBN 978-93-86288-87-5 ebook

Published in India by Kalpana Shukla

KNOWLEDGE WORLD

KW Publishers Pvt Ltd
4676/21, First Floor, Ansari Road
Daryaganj, New Delhi 110002
Phone: +91 11 23263498/43528107
Marketing: knowledgeworld@kwpub.com
Editorial: jose@kwpub.com
Website: www.kwpub.com

Printed and Bound in India.

Cover courtesy: http://thechive.com/2015/12/18/isis-fears-female-kurdish-soldiers-36-photos-video/

Contents

Foreword vii

Acknowledgements ix

Preface xi

Acronyms xv

1. Introducing Kurdistan 1
2. Establishment of the Kurdish Regional Government in Iraqi Kurdistan 25
3. The Kurdish Conflict in Turkey 73
4. Political Situation of the Kurds in Iran and Syria 115
5. International Positions on the Kurdish Problem in the Middle East 163
6. The Question of Kurdish Self-Determination: Challenges and Prospects 203
7. Conclusion 237

References 251

Chronology of the Kurdish National Movement 281

Appendix 1 285

Appendix 2 288

Appendix 3 289

Index 291

Dedicated

To my father

Foreword

The 'Quest for Representation and Self-Determination', the theme of the book, by the Kurds began with the drawing of the political map of contemporary West Asia, following the end of the First World War a hundred years ago. The fragmentation and division of the Ottoman Empire into respective areas of influence by Britain and France led to a regional territorial map putting the Kurds under different political dispensations. Located in the divided territories of Turkey, Iraq and Iran with smaller parts in Syria, Armenia and Azerbaijan, the Kurds—known as the largest non-state nation—have been denied their rightful place in the respective political spaces. Known for their warrior temper, ironically they are on the receiving end in their locale—culturally, socially, economically and politically. No wonder that they are in adversarial relations with the ruling regimes. Their struggle for the recognition of their legitimate positioning in the power structure is seen as an act of hostility. Given the fact that through international agreement they are placed in different nations, it is obvious that their aspiration for nationhood contests the territoriality of the place of their location. Thus, the making of Kurdistan means territorial segregation from more than one nation. That complicates and makes the struggle more arduous. However, there is a view gaining strength that with the failure of the regimes in West Asia to script a stable and democratic order, a new regional political alchemy is in the making—one on the strength of popular assertion. Tunisia is the product of the new alchemy. Others too are engaged with it in their respective ways and modes. The processes unleashed by the US invasion of Iraq leading to the Arab uprising and the creation of the Islamic State of Iraq and the Levant (ISIS) are a pointer to the possibilities of the making of a new West Asia with shared traditions, culture, language and history underlined by the new alchemy of the struggles in the region. However, history does tell that many times a drift in popular movement leads to distortions. While it will be presumptuous to make any forecast on the makeup of the new regional profile, it is definite that the Kurds are going to have a more decisive say in its making.

This book provides an insightful account of the complex reality of the Kurdish aspirations in the emerging regional and global contexts. It recognises the virility of the Kurdish nationalism and its determination and makes a strong case for an inclusive autonomous space for the Kurds to empower their culture, language and citizenship. It is a rigorous attempt to analyse the subject with the support of theoretical constructs. While focusing on the Kurds in Iraq and Turkey it factors the role of a strong Kurdish diaspora in this study. Though it rightly concludes that a military solution is not the right choice, but in the times when the Kurds are fighting for their survival in Iraq and Syria, an armed struggle has become the necessity of the time not only for protection but also to bargain for a term of reference for a solution which is sensitive to their dignity not only as a community but as a legitimate member of the West Asian community. The author deserves complements for providing a rich commentary and analysis on the subject which by all accounts is going to figure prominently in the West Asian discourse in the coming times.

Prof. Girijesh Pant
Energy Studies, Jawaharlal University
Former Dean, School of International Studies
Jawaharlal Nehru University and
Former VC Doon University & GGD University

Acknowledgements

I express my heartfelt gratitude to Professor Gulshan Dietl, ICSSR Senior Fellow at the Institute for Defence Studies and Analysis (IDSA), for her invaluable guidance, encouragement and moral support for the book. Her constant assistance and advice enabled me to complete this book.

I am grateful to Professor Achin Vanaik, former Head of the Department of Political Science, Delhi University, Professor Navnita Behera Chadha, Delhi University and Professor Subrata Mukherjee, former Head of Department of Political Science, Delhi University, for introducing me into the world of academia. I would like to thank Professor Raj Rani, Department of Teacher Education and Extension, National Council for Educational Research and Training (NCERT) for her constant encouragement and moral guidance. Their diverse fields of specialisation inspire me to pursue further academic knowledge.

I am indebted to the late Air Commodore Jasjit Singh (Retd), AVSM, VrC, VM and former Director General, Centre for Air Power Studies (CAPS), New Delhi for highlighting and sharing his knowledge of his visit to Iraqi Kurdistan. His suggestions and inputs have been valuable in updating the content of my book. Associating briefly with the Centre for Air Power Studies has given me the wider range of ideas about academic research.

My sincere gratitude for the help and assistance rendered by the Librarians and the staff of the Jawaharlal Nehru University Central Library, Institute for Defence Studies and Analysis Library and the American Library. I would also like to thank the faculty members of the Centre for West Asian Studies, JNU, for their various insightful inputs. My heartfelt thanks go especially to the library and staff of the Centre for Air Power Studies (CAPS); Mrs. Sushma Zutshi, Mrs. Surbhi Sarin and Mr. Sunil for providing me the necessary information.

Special thanks are due to my friends Mr Aditya Sikder, Mrs Emeni Kayina, Akhailiu Rimai and (late) Ms Kiushingliu Golmei for their kind help in reading and editing the various drafts of the chapters. I also wish to thank the faculty members of the Department of Political Science, Janaki Devi Memorial College, Delhi University, for their moral support.

Most importantly, I thank my parents and dear ones for their best support in carrying out this book. I alone bear the responsibility for all the errors and shortcomings.

6th May 2015

Lungthuiyang Riamei
New Delhi

Preface

Looking from the Westphalian state perspective, the Kurds are ethnic minorities in Turkey, Iraq, Iran and Syria. Together with their sub-state identity, the Kurds have a pronounced supra-state identity as people. The Kurdish political movement was not enabled to seize the historic opportunity which presented itself during the brief period of political vacuum from 1918 and 1920, following the collapse of the Ottoman Empire. After the Second World War, the question of the colonies was settled more or less throughout the world. The end of the Cold War, the weakening of the Left and the process of globalisation have unleashed new forces in many countries. Of these, the return of Kurdish nationalism or resurgence of the Kurdish identity is quite notable. The Kurdish question consists of the desire of most of the Kurds to have cultural, linguistic and political rights that will protect their identity. Some Kurds also seek autonomy or independence from the countries in which they live; however, those states have denied such aspirations. The result has been a constant instability that promises to intensify as the Kurds become more and more politically aware and as their cause grows more visible to the outside world. The Kurds have inhabited the sprawling mountainous region lying amid the West Asian landmass that is roughly encompassed by the Black Sea, Caspian Sea, the Persian Gulf and the Mediterranean.

The book examines several models which have been advocated for a workable and acceptable solution to the Kurdish problem. Solving the Kurdish problem would be necessary for stability in the Middle Eastern region. This book evaluates how the decades-long experience of Kurdish self-rule in a democratic framework in Iraqi Kurdistan affects the debate over other Kurdish regions in Middle East. With Turkey's European Union accession process contributing to the opening of political space to ethno-nationalism, the study will analyse the need for a non-military solution to the Kurdish issue. The book also evaluates the role of the Kurdish diaspora which plays a significant part in placing the Kurdish question on the European political agenda.

The book also attempts to locate the issue within the state-system and the global system. The Kurds are the victims of a conservative 'world-system' that suffers from its own contradictions and its anachronistic structural limitations. The 'world-system' is an important tool of analysis in an investigation of the dynamics of political-social movements and struggles in the periphery. The owners of the means of production—the oppressors—utilise every means to maintain the status quo, ensuring their privileged position and the oppressed struggle to change it. The history of the colonial and neocolonial era provides evidence of the atrocities inflicted on humanity as the processes of domination and exploitation continue. The Kurds are an example of those who have struggled to liberate themselves from this process. The sense of an imagined community and nation has been a critical identity for the Kurds.

The establishment of a de facto state in northern Iraq under Western protection gave a new impetus to Kurdish nationalism and provided a logistical base for the Kurds in the Middle East. Saddam Hussein's overthrow has weakened the state of Iraq while strengthening Kurdish nationalism; thereby, jeopardising regional security. Saddam's defeat in the 1991 Gulf War led to the creation of a de facto state and government in northern Iraq. There is a developing relationship between Turkey and the Iraqi Kurds. Turkey is anxious that an unfriendly Iraqi Kurdish state might begin aiding the Kurdish Workers Party (PKK) or even make territorial claims on Turkey's Kurdish region. By supporting the Iraqi Kurds, Turkey can influence them to be pro-Turkish and thus help to solve its own Kurdish problem. On the other hand, the Iraqi Kurds need to access Turkey's territory for exporting the products from their booming oil industry.

The emergence of the modern nation-state system and the concomitant rise of secular nationalism in the Middle East have profoundly affected inter-ethnic relations in the region. A carefully crafted constitutional scheme leading to the establishment of a genuine pluralistic polity is the best means to promote Kurdish integration in Iran, Iraq and Turkey. Assimilation, which has characterised Turkey's Kurdish policy, may succeed in the short run in stemming the tide of ethno-nationalism. However in the long run, the human and material costs to the state of forced assimilation are likely to be quite high—resulting in the rise of armed resistance movements by the affected minority.

The Kurdish problems and the socio-economic conditions prevailing in the Kurdish areas have always ended in defeat and catastrophe for the Kurdish civilians. The West has been reluctant to intervene on the Kurds' behalf, viewing the Kurdish question as the internal affairs of Turkey, Iran and Iraq—particularly, to avoid upsetting the sensibilities of Turkey, a North Atlantic Treaty Organization (NATO) member. Prior to the 2003 invasion of Iraq, the US policies towards the Iraqi Kurds were based on benign neglect and political containment.

The Kurdish nationalists consider Turkey's integration into Europe as an obstacle to the achievement of their goal of a united Kurdistan. In contrast, moderate Kurds have enthusiastically supported the policy of the European Union, which provides a legal and economic framework for the protection of minority cultural and political rights. Many Kurds see this policy as a context within which they can achieve political accommodation within the Republic of Turkey. Kurdish nationalism was not just a challenge to the states itself but it was the basis of ethnicity that legitimised it. The threat of Kurdish nationalism throughout the 1980s and 1990s represented the greatest threat to the Turkish government; the threat continues even today.

Ethnic problems like that of the Kurds are not only an internal but also an international problem. The Kurds are divided across international borders like many other communities. The aspirations of a people in one country thus directly affect the aspirations and actions of the minority across the border. Any pretensions to ethnic unification therefore not only imply separation of territory from one country but also massive redrawing of the international boundaries in the region where the nationalities reside. However, for long the struggle for Kurdish self-determination in the Middle East has remained limited due to fractious ideologies, internal divisions, rivalries and ad hoc alliances.

The aftermath of the Arab Spring 2011 saw a sweeping change in the region which has had a major impact on the Kurdish demands for self-determination. Now, the Kurds maintain the strongest platform in the volatile region and they are battling the ISIS terrorists. Sitting in the mineral belt of the region, their assertion for a movement for independence is far more visible. The Kurdish movement has given an impetus for democratic decentralisation and to the struggle for self-determination. The emergence of an independent greater Kurdistan is the dream for millions of Kurds.

Acronyms

ARGK	People's Liberation Army of Kurdistan
BDP	Peace and Democracy Party
CETIM	Centre Europe-Tiers Monde
DDKO	Revolutionary Cultural Society of the East
DTP	Democratic Society Party
EU	European Union
ETA	Euskadi Ta Askatasuna
ERNK	National Liberation Front of Kurdistan
GoI	Government of Iraq
HADEP	People's Democratic Party
HROK	Kurdish Human Rights Organization
ICP	Iraqi Communist Party
IDP	Internally Displaced Person/People
IKF	Iraqi Kurdistan Front
ILP	Independent Labour Party
INC	Iraqi National Congress
IMK	Islamic Movement of Kurdistan
IMIK	Islamic Movement of Iraqi Kurdistan
INTP	Iraqi National Turkoman Party
INC	Iraqi National Congress
INGOs	International Non-Governmental Organizations
IIPF	Islamic Iran Participation Front
IRA	Irish Republican Army
ISIS	Islamic State of Iraq and Syria (al-Sham or Levant)
ITF	Iraqi Turkoman Front
KADEK	Kurdistan Freedom and Democracy Congress
KHRP	Kurdish Human Rights Project

KCP	Kurdish Communist Party
KDP	Kurdistan Democratic Party
KDP-I	Kurdistan Democratic Party-Iran
KDPT	Kurdish Democratic Party of Turkey
KHRP	Kurdish Human Right Projects
KIF	Kurdistan Iraqi Front
KLF	Kurdish Liberation Front
KNA	Kurdish National Assembly
KPE	Kurdish Parliament-in-Exile
KRG	Kurdistan Regional Government
KRP	Kurdish Revolutionary Party
KSDP	Kurdistan Socialist Democratic Party
KSP	Kurdistan Socialist Party
KTP	Kurdistan Toilers' Party
NATO	North Atlantic Treaty Organization
OSCE	Organization for Security and Cooperation in Europe
PASOK	Party of Socialism in Kurdistan
PLO	Palestinian Liberation Organization
PKK	Kurdistan Workers' Party (Partiya Karkeren Kurdistan)
PUK	Patriotic Union of Kurdistan
TIP	Turkiye Isci Partisi or Workers' Party of Turkey
UNSCR	United Nations Security Council Resolution
TAL	Transitional Administration Law
UN	United Nations
UNHCR	United Nations High Commissioner for Refugees
UNICEF	United Nations Children's Fund
UPK	Unity Party of Kurdistan
UK	United Kingdom
US	United States
WHO	World Health Organization
YPG	Yekineyen Parastina Gel (People's Protection Units)

CHAPTER 1

Introducing Kurdistan

Kurdistan, or the homeland of the Kurds, is a strategic area located in the geographic heart of West Asia. The Kurds are an ancient race that inhabited the contiguous mountain region that falls under the southeastern part of modern Turkey, the north and eastern part of Iraq, the northeastern part of Syria and the northwestern part of Iran for about 3,000 years (or longer, as some historians insist), retaining their own language, customs and culture. These parts were created on two different occasions: first in 1514 when Kurdistan was divided between the Ottoman and Persian empires following the battle of Chaldiran;[1] secondly between 1920 and1923 when Britain and France further altered the political contours of Kurdistan by dividing Ottoman Kurdistan among Iraq, Iran, Syria and Turkey (Meho and Maglaughlin 2001: 3). A fierce and independent collection of wild mountain tribes, they had ferociously defended their terrain and somehow managed to survive the succession of conquering armies including Assyrians, Persians and Greeks that marched and countermarched across Anatolia and Mesopotamia over the centuries. Prior to World War I, Kurdish territories were divided between the Persian and the Ottoman Empires. In order to maintain their exploitation in the colonised areas, the colonising powers, especially the British, resorted to the divide-and-rule strategy pitting one ethnic group against the other. This policy heightened ethnic conflict and fragmentation. The world system as an externally activating variable has played a critical role in politicising ethnic differences and the resulting political conflicts. The British imperialism provoked Kurdish nationalist aspirations for an independent Kurdistan but pitted Armenians and Kurds against each other to block its actualisation. Since the goal of imperialism was to appropriate the oil fields of the Kurds in the south, the creation of a centralised neo-fascist and imperial state was the critical solution.

Immediately after World War I, President Woodrow Wilson's support for the principle of national self-determination for the non-Turkish nationalities living under the Ottoman Empire gave impetus to the Kurds. The Versailles Peace Conference of 1919 provided the first forum where Kurdish national aspirations were acknowledged by the international community; but, this acknowledgement proved to be short-lived. Upon the breakup of the Ottoman Empire, an ancient race composed of tribes, tribal confederations and feudal groups with martial traditions were promised for the first time in their long history an independent state in their own mountainous homeland under the Treaty of Sevres of August 10, 1920 (Eagleton 1963: 11-12; Chaliand 1980: 8-10). However, a vigorous nationalist uprising under the Turkish leader Mustafa Kemal Ataturk forced the Allies to accept a revised agreement—the Treaty of Lausanne 1923—which omitted all references to an autonomous or independent Kurdish state. The Sevres–Lausanne period presented what might be called a tragic incident in the Kurdish struggle and aspirations. Moreover, the Treaty of Sevres and the creation of new boundaries leading to the distribution of the Kurds among several countries—Turkey, Iran and Iraq—further complicated Kurdish plans. As a result, the Kurds became a stateless minority in the region.

Traditionally, Kurdish life was nomadic, revolving around sheep and goat-herding throughout the Mesopotamian plains, the highlands of Turkey and Iran. Although the Kurds lived in Kurdistan for centuries, they never had a state of their own nor had formed an independent political entity. In the modern times, they achieved two short-lived semi-independent entities: the Kingdom of Kurdistan in Iraqi Kurdistan under Sheikh Mahmoud (1922–1924) and the Mahabad Republic under Qazi Mohammed (January–December 1946), which is now Iranian Kurdistan. Throughout their history they have been ruled by outsiders including Armenians, Persians, Byzantines and later the Turks and Arabs.

Since the end of the First World War, when the great powers imposed their ill-suited solutions to the problems of West Asia, the Kurdish people have constantly suffered from various forms of national oppression in each of the newly constituted states. In some cases this oppression was brutal, as in Kemalist Turkey, while in others it was cunning, like the suppression in Iran. Iraq, on the other hand, has allowed the existence of a Kurdish nationality; it has allowed a limited use of Kurdish language and provided for at least a nominal degree of autonomy to the Kurdish-inhabited areas which also has included a policy of Arabisation involving the mass deportation of Kurds and implantation of Arabs on their lands.

Origins of the Kurds

One of the first mentions of Kurdistan in the historical records appears in cuneiform in the Sumerian and Assyrian inscriptions of 2000 BC, which refer to it as the 'land of the Karda' in the Zagros-Taurus Mountains of the northern and northeastern parts of Mesopotamia. The Babylonians called the inhabitants of 'Karda' as 'Gardu' and 'Qarda'. In the neighbouring area of Assyria to the south, they were known as 'Qurti' or 'Guti'. When the Greeks entered this territory, they referred to these people as either 'Kardukh', 'Carduchi' or 'Gordukh'. The Armenians called the Kurds 'Gortukh' or 'Gortai-kh' and the Persians knew them as 'Gord' or 'Kord'. In Hebrew and Chaldean languages they were respectively referred to as 'Qardu', 'Kurdaye' and 'Qurdaye' (Izady 1992: 31). The modern form 'Kurd' first appeared in the Arabic writings of the ninth century AD with the plural form 'Akrad' (Elphinston 1946: 92).

In the sixteenth century, after prolonged wars, Kurdish-inhabited areas were split between the Safavid[2] and Ottoman Empires. A major division of Kurdistan occurred in the aftermath of the Battle of Chaldiran in 1514 and was formalised in the 1639 Treaty of Zuhab (Somel 2003: 306). As a result, western Kurdistan became part of the Ottoman Empire while eastern Kurdistan became part of Iran. However, prior to World War I most Kurds lived within the boundaries of the Ottoman Empire in the province of Kurdistan.

Many Kurdish historians, anthropologists and scholars assert that the Medes[3] are the ancestors of the Kurds. Scholars are on unsure ground when trying to establish the definite early origins of the Kurds. There are two favoured hypotheses: either the Kurdish people have sprung from the Iranian tribes that had immigrated into the Zagros mountains in the pre-historic times and had established themselves there or from those Iranian tribes migrating west that had imposed themselves on an autochthonous people and have exploited them ever since (Pelletiere 1984: 20-21).

Many Kurds are the descendents of several ancient peoples, mainly Iranian. They include Caucasian strains in the north and some Semitic strains in the south. They are however, bound together by a purely Kurdish influence which probably derives from the original mountain tribes which have inhabited these regions from the earliest times.

Kurdistan's Physical Geography

Kurdistan lies at the mountainous transition belt of the Fertile Crescent with the Taurus and Zagros mountains forming an arc encircling the Mesopotamian region. The mountain chains of Iraqi Kurdistan run in a northwest to southeast direction along the border territories with Iran and Turkey. The territory of Kurdistan has no recognised international boundaries and even internal administrative boundaries within states are sometimes controversial and commonly ephemeral. This problem was compounded by the normative viewpoints of neighbouring states refusing to acknowledge the existence of a contiguous Kurdish geographical entity or as in the case of Turkey, the denial of the existence of Kurds as a distinct and discrete people and culture. The Kurds have a legitimate and possessive claim to a vast homeland that consists of roughly 2,00,000 square miles—an area equal to France, or slightly smaller than the state of Texas (Manafy 2005: 5).[4] Figure 1.1 illustrates the Kurdish areas in West Asia.

Fig. 1.1 Kurdish Areas

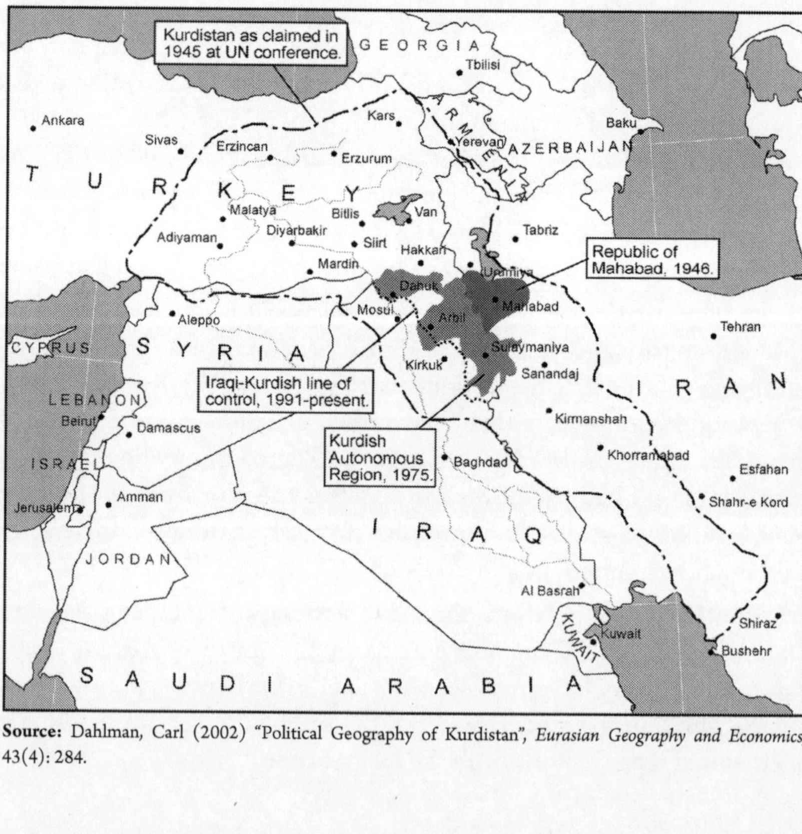

Source: Dahlman, Carl (2002) "Political Geography of Kurdistan", *Eurasian Geography and Economics,* 43(4): 284.

Kurdistan is an oasis in a water-starved region. The abundant rainfall, which is common over the Zagros and Taurus mountains, has made Kurdistan one of the few watersheds of West Asia; it is home to the source of two major river systems in the world—the Tigris and Euphrates.

Economy

Kurdistan is known to be very rich in its natural resources. Not only oil and water, but also copper, chromium, iron and sulphur are found in abundance in the Kurdish soil. Kurdistan's wealth of high-grade pasture lands has long made it suitable for a pastoralist economy, but it is equally suitable in many areas for intensive agriculture. The rich pastures have always ensured that in all historical periods, regardless of how dominant the agriculture sector may have been, there have been nomadic herdsmen exploiting them to their fullest.

Despite the huge economic production of Kurdistan whether from its natural resources or agriculture goods, only a small portion of its benefits is geared towards the local population. Moreover, modern heavy industries in Kurdistan are almost non-existent. After the fall of Saddam Hussein, Iraqi Kurdistan has attracted foreign investment especially in the oil sector (Torchia 2007). It is true that oil is produced in abundance from the Kurdish areas; nevertheless, skilled labourers are entirely non-Kurds. Kurdistan has among the largest oil reserves in West Asia. According to various studies, Kurdistan sits on 43.7 billion barrels (bb) of proven oil and 25.5 bb of potential reserves. In addition, the majority of the estimated 200 trillion cubic feet of gas in Iraq is reported to be in the Kurdistan region.[5] However, both in Iran and Iraq, the oil and gas sub-sectors were particularly hard-hit by the war, with much of the infrastructure destroyed. These sub-sectors were and are the primary source of the income from foreign exchange.

A special factor of the Kurdish economy is that it does not constitute one entity but is split among several countries. The individual parts are isolated from one another and each part is dependent on the economy of its ruling state. Nevertheless, the mountainous borders of Kurdistan are practically beyond control, and for this reason, contraband trade is widespread—particularly between the Iranian and Iraqi Kurdistan. The countries controlling Kurdistan are economically linked to the industrialised countries and the different parts of Kurdistan are in turn dependent on their respective central governments—a unique situation which might explain why economic progress is so irregular and disproportionate. Kurdistan constitutes the marginal areas of these countries; therefore, it is also underdeveloped. Looking at vital statistics, it is always what the central government wants the people to know, which is not always the reality. Healthcare, educational facilities and last but not the least, job opportunities are not available to their Kurdish minorities unless they go through the assimilation process. In Turkey, everything is dependent on how well a Kurd is assimilated in the political economy (Leezenberg 2000: 3).

Kurdish Population, Society and Stratification

Stephen C. Pelletiere asserted that in Kurdistan, tribalism and nomadic life have been largely replaced by a growing feudalism and a semi-capitalistic development. However, the *Aghas*, who were encouraged by the British to secure and privatise tribal lands, still command Kurdish loyalty in some parts of Kurdistan and in the remote and primitive regions of Kurdistan tribalism still persists (Pelletiere 1984: 18). Kurdish society is highly stratified, where tribal elites dominate the settled peasants. Conflicts between the tribes and exploitative relations between the dominant and subject strata have long divided Kurdish society. Conflicting interests have always prevented collective action. Furthermore, there are various non-Kurdish minorities living among the Kurds and tied to them by intricate networks of social and economic relations. In terms of numbers, the estimates of Kurdish population vary (see Table 1.2 for population estimates). Kurdish nationalists are tempted to exaggerate the number; governments of the region minimise it. Although there are no official censuses regarding the number of the Kurds, most sources agree that there are more than 30 million Kurds and at least one-third of them live outside Kurdistan because of war, forced resettlements or economic deprivation.

Pelletiere (1984) approximates the Kurdish population in Turkey, Iran, Iraq, Syria and the former Soviet Union to be between 7 and 7.5 million. A breakdown of this figure illustrates the following: 3 million in Turkey, approximately 2 million in Iran and 2 million in Iraq and a very small number of Kurds in Syria and the former Soviet Union. See the distribution of the Kurdish population:

Table 1.2 Population Estimates for Kurds, 1991*

Country	Percentage	Total Population	Kurds
Turkey	19%	57,000,000	10,800,000
Iraq	23%	18,000,000	4,100,000
Iran	10%	55,000,000	5,500,000
Syria	8%	12,500,000	1,000,000
USSR	NA		500,000
Elsewhere	NA		700,000
Total			**22,600,000**

*Estimates in round numbers

Source: Adopted from McDowall, David (1992), *The Kurds: A Nation Denied*, London: Minority Right Publications, 2.

Fig. 1.3 Kurdistan Identified by Population Distribution

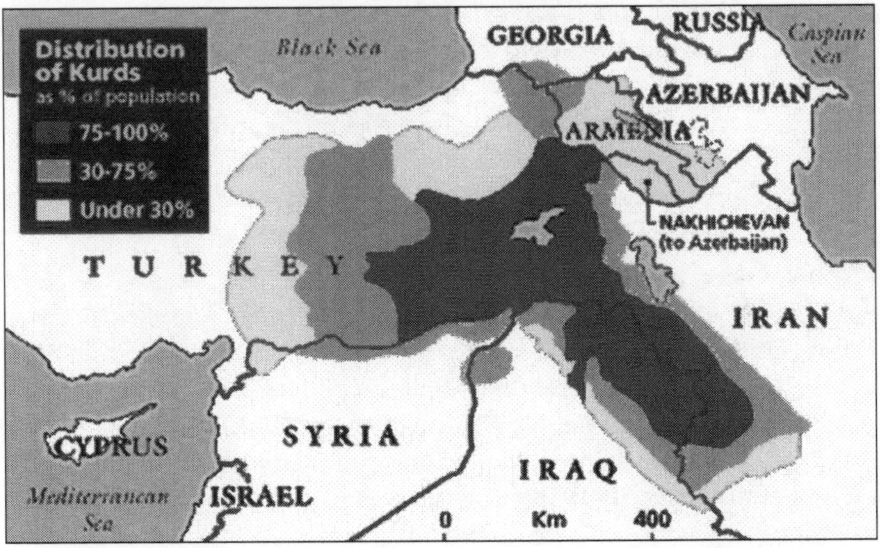

Source: http://www.iranreview.org/content/Documents/Kurds-A-Comman-Issue-for-Iran-Turkey.htm

Yavuz and Gunter (2001) approximate the Kurdish population in Turkey as 7 million (making up between 12 to 15 percent of the population), 6 million in Iran (11 percent), 3 million in Iraq (between 20 to 23 percent) and 8,00,000 in Syria (7 percent). There are also large concentrations of Kurds in Germany (over 50,000), Israel (over 1,00,000) and Lebanon (75,000–1,00,000). Australia, Canada, England, Finland, France, Greece, Sweden and the United States each have a Kurdish population of over 10,000 (Meho and Maglaughlin

2001: 3). The Kurds are largely Sunni Muslims divided tribally, geographically, politically, linguistically, religiously and ideologically. However, the accuracy of the Kurdish population estimates is difficult to determine. They are the third largest ethnic group in the region after the Arabs and Persians.

Several factors have contributed to the Kurds' isolation in the mountainous terrain that formed a geographical and cultural barrier between them and their neighbours. These factors include their ferocity in defending their own territory and their largely self-sufficient economy which reduced their dependence on outsiders. The fact that most Kurdish areas are remote and inaccessible has fostered the independence of even the small villages. The scarcity of arable land and pastoral range lands increases the struggle for water and pasture. The village isolation in their tribe-oriented and class-ridden society has remained very strong despite modern influences. The Kurds lived in a variety of settings as urban dwellers but the vast majority lived in small villages. The numbers of nomads and semi-nomads steadily decreased; although, that way of life still exists. Small working class and middle-class groups have begun to emerge in the cities but in most rural areas the basic form of social and political organisations are still based on descent, clans and ownership of land. In the villages, leaderships are divided between the *mir* or *beg*, who leads the tribe (or the *agha* who leads one of the clans that form a tribe) and the sheikhs or mullahs who are the religious leaders.

There were other major divisions within Kurdish society. A basic distinction was between tribal and non-tribal Kurds. In principle, most Kurds belonged to one or the other of the many tribes, defined by Chaliand as 'a territorially fixed social and economic unit founded on real or imagined blood ties which give the group its structure.' But not all were tribal by the twentieth century; many lived in towns or had become tenants or labourers on land in the plains. By 1918, many Kurds had chosen to live in Kurdistan having taken service with the Ottoman government in the army or civil services (Chaliand 1994: 19). For sheer survival, smaller tribes had to ally themselves with larger ones or with each other or enter into federations which in turn dissolved or changed in composition dictated by the fortunes of war and other circumstances. Tribes were subdivided into clans and groups of families; each always being on the defensive— even suspicious of the others. Each man owed complete allegiance to his family and tribe and to the tribal sheikh, who settled disputes in accordance with the Islamic and tribal laws and Kurdish customs.

The cohesion of the Kurdish tribe is based on a mixture of blood ties and territorial allegiances associated with strong religious loyalties. Beyond the tribe, many Kurds, especially those who lived in the rural areas, occasionally showed loyalty to a nation, state or any other entity. The socio-economic and political changes that most Kurds have witnessed since the 1960s, such as the mechanisation of agriculture, industrialisation, subsequent revolts, rural–urban migration, emigration, political mobilisation in party politics, the expansion of public education and mass communication have weakened the tribal structure of the Kurdish society and provided an impetus for developing a larger Kurdish nationalism (Meho and Maglaughlin 2001: 5).

In Kurdistan, feudal relations of production suffered major setbacks, largely due to peasant uprisings and later due to land reforms initiated by the central governments. A visible change in the Kurdish society in this period was the rise of the urban population due to land reform and the wars in the countryside. Newly-freed peasants moved into Kurdish cities where the lack of industrial enterprises seriously hindered their transformation into wage labourers. While some rural migrants engaged in seasonal or temporary construction work (contractual or wage labour), others ended up in street-vending activities. Some migrants maintained their village ties by working in towns while continuing to farm for family consumption. The differentiation and specialisation in urban economies introduced new social strata. A small Kurdish working class formed in the oil industry, construction industry and a few factories. Small workshops required auto mechanics, electricians, printers, mechanics, plumbers and painters, while services and transport employed many others. A modern bourgeoisie emerged, comprised mainly of professionals rather than entrepreneurs—doctors, nurses, engineers, teachers, bank managers, lawyers and journalists. Migrant labourers travelled as far as Ankara, Baghdad, Istanbul, Tehran, Isfahan and Europe (Hassanpour 1994: 4-5). Becoming aware of the great disparity between their impoverished lives in Kurdistan, Kurdish emigrants became more socially and politically conscious and their awareness of their Kurdish identity and ethnic solidarity was strengthened.[6] The traditional intelligentsia, mainly the *ulama* and the educated landed notables, was displaced by a growing modern intelligentsia. The social and economic negligence of Kurdistan by the local governments and the protracted cultural and political repression exercised against the Kurdish populations became decisive factors in fostering Kurdish nationalism.

Another feature of changing social relations was the increasing access of urban women to education and their participation in social, economic, political and cultural life outside their homes. These transformations left their impact on the nationalist movement, expanding its social bases and increasing political, ideological and organisational tension. The urban intelligentsia eventually made its presence felt in the countryside, the traditional domain of the landed aristocracy, not as nationalists who sought protection but rather as political and military leaders. This also marked the beginning of a bitter struggle within the autonomist movement (Hassanpour 1994: 5).

The vertical stratification of Kurdish society was consolidated and even reinforced by the central governments. The Ottoman and Persian Empires and their successor states were never strong enough to directly control all of Kurdistan. Various forms of indirect rule therefore developed in which tribal chieftains were left in control of large areas in exchange for formal allegiance and symbolic taxes or members of the tribal elite were given bureaucratic and military functions. Traditionally, Kurdish tribal leaders have necessarily been guided in their politics by the conflicting balance of power among the neighbouring tribes and with the government of the region.

Kurdish Religious Minorities

Kurdistan has a history of religious diversity with a fairly large Christian minority. The majority of Kurds follow Sunni Islam, while the remaining are divided between Shi'a, Alevi (strong in Central Anatolia), the Ahl-i-Haqq and Yezidi. But, most of the Kurds with whom the British and Baghdad regimes had to deal with in post-1920 Iraq were Sunnis or Yezidis with a smaller intermingling of other Islamic groups (Edmonds 1957: 34). The Sunni Kurds differ widely in degree of their devotion and in ritual practices. Traditional religious education in the *madrasas* was rather widespread and may have contributed to the Kurdish self-awareness. In Turkey, *madrasas* are banned as being obstacles to modernisation and Westernisation. The oppression of religious expression and of Kurdish ethnicity strengthened the association of Kurdishness with Sunni Islam. Though never banned in Iran and Iraq, the *madrasas* have a marginal functionality (Bruinessen 1992: 36). But in all parts of Kurdistan, secular education has by and large replaced traditional religious education.

There are numerous heterodox minority groups and sects among the Kurds. A quite significant minority known as Alevis are found in Turkish Kurdistan. Under the reign of the Ottoman Emperors, the Alevis were often persecuted both for their heterodoxy and because they were suspected of pro-Iranian sympathies. The Alevis are either defined as a heterodox Islamic sect and community or as the continuation of pre-Islamic Zoroastrian. Owing to the difference in definition, the term is best described as a 'blanket' describing a large number of groups with heterodox beliefs, rituals and practices (Bruinessen 1996: 7). The Alevis have generally supported the Turkish Republic whose official secularism promised a certain protection for the heterodox groups. However, throughout the existence of the Turkish Republic, the importance and strength of the Alevi identity decreased which led in the early 1980s to speculation about the disappearance of Alevism as a community (Hirschler 2001: 157).

Another syncretistic sect, even further removed from orthodox Islam, is that of the Yezidis who are often correctly or incorrectly called as 'devil worshippers'. The origin of this sect appears to have been Sunni Islam, which had progressively incorporated elements of other regional religions including Paganism, Zoroastrianism, Manichaeanism, Judaism, Nestorianism and Christianity among other Islamic features (McDowall 1992: 13). The Yezidis worship the sun and believe in reincarnation. They believe in God as the Creator of the world, which He placed under the care of seven holy beings or angels, the chief of whom is *Mele Taus*[6] (the Peacock Angel). One of the key creation beliefs of Yezidism is that all Yezidis are descendants of Adam rather than Eve. They speak Kurmanji, but some of the more pious Muslims nevertheless refuse to recognise them as Kurds because of their religious peculiarities. In the seventeenth century, the Yezidis were numerous but their numbers have dwindled due to physical oppression, forced conversion and emigrations (Bruinessen 1992 a: 38). There are four major regional clusters of the Yezidis: in the Kurd Dagh (Kurdish mountain) district of Aleppo in Syria, in the Sinjar mountain on the Syrian–Iraqi border, in the Shaykhan district north of Mosul and in the southwestern Caucasus (Andrews 1989: 118-9). In the past, the Yezidis have faced persecution at the hands of their Muslim neighbours. However in the 1990s, the situation seemed to improve although some have sought refuge in Germany.

The Ahl-i-Haqq is a sect found in south and southeastern Kurdistan. Its central belief is in seven successive manifestations of the Divinity. Although

Ali, Prophet Mohammed's son-in-law, is venerated the focus of the sect is the founder of the Ahl-i-Haqq, Sultan Sahak (McDowall 1992: 13). From the Ahl-i-Haqq point of view, the universe is composed of two distinct yet interrelated worlds: the internal (*batini*) and the external (*zahiri*); each having its own order and rules. Although humans are only aware of the outer world, their lives are governed according to the rules of the inner world. Among other important pillars of their belief system, two are that the Divine Essence has successive manifestations in human form (*mazhariyyat,* derived from *zahir*) and the belief in the transmigration of the soul (*dunaduni* in Kurdish). The Ahl-i-Haqq do not observe Muslim rites and rituals (Mir-Hosseini 1994: 267-268).

The two most distinctive non-Kurdish minorities are the Turkomans and the Christians. The Turkomans share the same religious beliefs as the Kurds but the Christians display a different religion as well as a different ethnic origin. The largest Christian community used to be the Armenians but after assimilation into the surrounding people in the region and conversion to Islam, the development of a Kurdish identity in the late nineteenth century and the mass deportation and massacres of Armenians in the Kurdish region in 1915, there are only a few Armenians left (Bruinessen 1992b: 6).

Language Diversity

The degree of a shared language has long been identified as a key indicator of the development of an ethnic consciousness and ethno-consciousness (Entessar 1992: 4-5). Unlike many other minority groups in West Asia, the Kurds failed to adopt a lingua franca. With Kurdistan being a land of high mountains with a difficult communication system and the Kurds never having enjoyed the political unity that might have given them a common literature, it is not surprising that local dialects within groups have varied widely. This hindered inter-Kurdish communication. It also reduced the importance of language as a symbol of ethnic identity for the Kurds. Kurdish belongs to the family of Iranian languages and, like other Iranian languages, has an Indo-European origin. It is fundamentally different from Semitic Arabic and Altaic Turkish. Kurdish is therefore more akin to Persian than to Arabic. Modern Kurdish is divided into major groups supplemented by scores of sub-dialects. In brief, the three major languages are

- *Kurdi,* which includes the *Gurani* and *Sulaymani* dialects. *Gurani* is spoken mostly by the Kurds in Kermanshah (Bakhtaran) in Iran and is very similar to *Lori,* an Iranian language spoken by the Lors, who along with the Kurds constitute the two major ethnic groups in Kermanshah. *Kurdi* is also spoken by some Iraqi Kurds. The *Kurdi* is spoken by about 3 million Kurds.

- *Kurmanji* is spoken by the largest number of Kurds, especially those in Turkey. It is, for all practical purposes, the literary language of the Kurds and as such is considered the most prestigious of all Kurdish vernaculars. *Kurmanji* is divided into North and South *Kurmanji.* The former dialect is spoken by most Kurds living in the Caucasus region of the former Soviet Union, while the latter is spoken by the people of central Kurdistan. It is spoken by about two-thirds of the Kurds.
- *Zaza* dialect predominates in the north and northwest sectors of Kurdistan. It is also used by some Kurds in the Iranian province of Western Azerbaijan and Central Turkey. *Zaza* is the least developed Kurdish literary language[8] (Entessar 1992: 5). The dialect is spoken by at least 3 million Kurds.
- The southern dialect, often called *Sorani,* with about 6 million speakers, is in fact a grouping of many dialects. *Sorani* is considered to be the classical Kurdish language. This dialect is spoken in southern Kurdistan, including most of the Iraqi and Iranian Kurdistans (Stansfield 2003: 37).

The very existence of linguistic differences has had an inhibiting impact on the development of a common Kurdish identity. Religion also was not a uniting factor. The plurality of Kurdish dialects creates the problem of intelligibility, which undermines the creation of national solidarity based on a politicised identity. Kurdish dialects have not been protected or enriched by scientific and literary efforts. Since the Kurds are often deprived of reading and writing in their own mother tongue, a unified or unitary dialect has not been established. The absence of a strong, centralised administrative structure to unify rival Kurdish groups encouraged the development of diverse languages among the Kurds (Entessar 1989: 87). The high impassable mountains, the remoteness of the Kurdish rural areas from one another, the lack of transportation and communication systems among different tribes and constant isolation of one group from another have led to the development of different dialects. More importantly, attempts at

Arabisation, Turkification or deKurdification by the states in the region have further exacerbated the problem (Chaliand 1980: 149). The influence of the states which have fragmented Kurdistan into various parts and placed the Kurds under the jurisdiction of countries which themselves have displayed linguistic diversity has also added to the problem. The different educational systems of these countries have inevitably left deep imprints on the Kurdish culture as well.

The Rise of Kurdish Nationalism

Nationalism is a method whereby consciousness is raised—a consciousness of a people's political identity; of their very existence. The belief on the part of a mass of people that they are distinctive from their fellows and by virtue of their distinctiveness are entitled to a state of their own is not something that arises spontaneously or is something that individuals are born with. People assign their primary loyalty to a tribe or a village of a sect quite naturally. The appeal of nationalism is based on a more mature awareness and it proceeds from the recognition that a unit of protection greater than any tribe or village or sect is an absolute necessity (Pelletiere 1984: 24-25). The formation of a national identity is not only limited to the content of the respective identity but also the boundaries of the relevant group play an equally important role (Hirschler 2001: 156). The concept of national identity could be different in its multidimensionality and could encompass language, sentiments and symbolism. The twentieth century's two world wars, the imperatives of globalisation and the need for economic, political, environmental and military cooperation have given rise to collective identities. For example, the European states are coming together and have developed a continental identity (collective identity). Since then, the devolution of power to its sub-national units has accentuated the regional and weakened the national identity. However, some ethnicity-based nationalities like the Basques, Kurds, Kashmiris and Tamils form a clear national/sub-national identity even without a state of their own; recognition of which contributes to turmoil and conflict (Smith and Julia 1993). In some parts of Africa and Northeast India, tribe is the primary basis of self-determination and the tribal identity carries greater weight than the national one. The chances of a nation without a state to promote its own national identity depends on the nature of the state within which the nation is included—in particular, its attitude towards internal diversity. However, national identity reflects the sentiment of belonging to the nation regardless of whether it has or does not have a state of its own.

'National identity,' according to Anthony Smith, involves some sense of political community, history, territory, patria, citizenship, common values and traditions. He argues that nations must have a measure of common culture and civic ideology, a set of common understandings and aspirations, sentiments and ideas that bind the population together in their homeland. For Smith, national identity or the membership of a political community is an important and a valued part of individual identity (Smith 1991: 11). Members of the political community are likely to have lived in it for generations and their history and individual memories are bound up with it. It provides a home—a place they call their own—and whose membership of it generally cannot be taken away from them. They grow up and are educated within it; they are deeply shaped by its values and ethos. Being territorially bounded, the political community also creates a structured space that gives intensity and depth to their relations with each other and forges common bonds. Their personal and collective security is also bound up with it and creates the ties of common interest. Their daily involvement in the common life of the state such as voting in elections, forming and expressing opinions on national issues and feeling angry or proud at what is done in their name, reaffirm their national identity (Parekh 2008: 56).

Kurdish nationalism emerged as an ideology long before the formation of the Kurds as a nation not in a middle-class milieu but in a largely agrarian society with a powerful tribal component. From the sixteenth century to the mid-nineteenth century, much of Kurdistan was under the rule of independent and autonomous Kurdish principalities that produced a flourishing rural and urban life. Kurdish destinies changed radically when the Ottoman and Persian Empires divided Kurdistan into their own spheres of influence. In order to protect their sovereignty, the principalities supported one or the other power. A prevailing war destroyed the agrarian system, devastated villages and towns, precipitated massacres and led to the forcible migrations of Kurds and their consequent settlement in parts of Kurdistan (Hassanpour 1994: 3). All of this inhibited further growth of urban areas and settled agrarian production relations thus reinforcing tribal ways of life.

Nationalism is always constructed by the cultural elite and shaped by the political context. The major difference between Turkish, Iranian, Iraqi or Syrian nationalism and Kurdish nationalism is the presence of the state. Since Kurdish nationalism in Turkey, Iraq, and Iran has evolved in response to modernising nation-states, it constantly stresses its ethnic difference and has used it to historicise itself. Although the Kurdish cultural elite tend to identify Turks as their other half in the construction of Kurdish nationalism, major tribal, linguistic, religious and regional fissures exist within the Kurdish identity itself. The Kurds are a nation in formation at the crossroads of the Arab, Iranian and Turkish Worlds. The sources of these divisions are socio-historical and have prevented the emergence of a full-fledged Kurdish identity (Yavuz and Gunter 2001: 33). By the early 1920s, the political geography of the Kurdish areas had begun to assume the general shape that it has today with the Kurds divided among the states of Iran, Iraq, Syria and Turkey. Their policies towards the Kurds were extremely repressive. All the rebellions were put down with great ferocity (Sluglett and Sluglett 2001: 25-26).

The Kurds have never been aggressively nationalistic. Kurdish life remains tribally structured in most areas and is based on local, tightly-knit rural communities under a tribal–religious leader known as sheikh or *seyid*. Traditionally, local power in northern Iraq had been wielded by the tribal chiefs or *aghas* and to a lesser degree by the Muslim sheikhs (Prince 1993: 18). For them, the effective unit of allegiance has remained the tribe. A tribe is a community, or a confederation of communities, that exists for the protection of its members against external aggression and for the maintenance of the old customs and standards of living. This tribal structure has played a dual role: impeding the formation of Kurdish unity by keeping the Kurds fragmented and in preserving a heightened Kurdish attitude toward the Turks, Iranians and Arabs. The tribal structure has constituted the core depository of Kurdish identity, has facilitated mobilisation against centralising governments and has also kept a modern concept of nationalism from developing until the mid-twentieth century (Yavuz and Gunter 2001: 33-34).

In many parts of the world the tribe has died out, but it has persisted in Kurdistan because of the extremely rugged mountainous terrain that has often separated one community from another and also from those of the Arabs, Iranians and Turks. But in recent times, the tribal system has been largely undermined by a penetration into Kurdistan of the concept of private property. The British and the Turks before them made it possible for the tribal chiefs to take legal possession of land in that free-holding tribesmen became tenants. Later on, many of these tenants were driven off the land. Thus, by the early part of the twentieth century when the whole Kurdish society came under assault by the Turks and later by the Arabs, and to a certain degree by the Iranians, the society was already in disarray. To withstand the assaults upon it, the Kurds needed a mobilising idea and this was what Kurdish nationalism was meant to be (Pelletiere 1984: 25). Besides, diverse Kurdish dialects have dominated the regions and until recently, sub-ethnic identities have been more powerful than a Kurdish consciousness.

The Concept of Identity and Representation

Identity is a distinctive characteristic belonging to any given individual, or shared by all members of a particular social category or group. Identity may define one's consciousness of oneself and others' perception of one's individuality. It refers to social categories and to the sources of an individual's self-respect or dignity. Identity is about how individuals or groups see and define themselves and how other individuals or groups see and define them (Fearon 1999: 2-3). In other words identity is the people's concept of who they are, of what sort of people they are and how they relate to others. Identity is formed through the socialisation process and the influence of social institutions like the family, the education system and the mass media. Students of political science, for instance, find the concept of 'identity' at the centre of debate in every major subfield. Identity is sometimes used to refer to a sense of integration of the self in which different aspects come together in a unified whole. Researchers in social science have devoted research to the 'identity politics' of caste, religion, gender, race and ethnicity. In comparative politics, 'identity' plays a central role in any work on nationalism and ethnic conflict (Smith 1991). In international relations, the idea of 'state identity' is at the heart of the constructivist critiques of realism and analyses of state sovereignty (Wendt 1992: 391). In political theory, questions of identity mark numerous arguments on gender, sexuality, nationality, ethnicity, and culture (Young 1990). Globalisation challenges these traditional identities—be it national, ethnic, cultural or religious.

In contemporary times, a common use is identity politics, where the reference is typically to different political positions that are staked out by members of ethnic and nationality groups. Ethnicity is a sense of ethnic identity, which has been defined by de Vos as consisting of its subjective, symbolic or emblematic use by 'a group of people... of any respect of culture, in order to differentiate themselves from other groups (Vos 1975: 16). Ethnicity or ethnic identity also involves, in addition to subjective self-consciousness, a claim to status and recognition either as a superior group or as a group at least equal to other groups. Ethnicity is to the ethnic category what class consciousness is to class (Brass 1991: 19). Identifying with others can be extremely important for living in a society. Therefore, the Kurds' separate ethnic identity is authentic and different from those of the Arabs in the region.

Practically, all identities go through a process of enumeration as the inevitable accompaniment of European colonisation—the factual counting of the census and the emergence of a fundamentally different world of counted and mapped identities (Taylor 1989). If people become dissatisfied with modern nation-states, they immediately have available to them a whole range of different identities. Democracy is seen as a logic of self-determination. A whole range of identities might wish to assert their complex rights to self-determination. For instance in India, the identities offered are both traditional and modern. There is a large and impressive philosophical literature which argues that the advent of modernity brings in with itself a new notion of self (Sandel 1984: 81-96).

In participatory democratic institutions, citizens develop and exercise capacities of reasoning and discussion. Modern democratic institutions are closely bound to the idea of representation. Democracy is based upon the claim that politicians serve as the people's representatives. In politics, representation suggests that an individual or group somehow stands for, or on behalf of, a larger collection of people. Political representation therefore acknowledges a link between the two otherwise separate entities—government and the governed—through which link the people's views are articulated or their interests are secured (Heywood 2004: 222-223). Therefore, a representative is not a person acting on behalf of another but one who is typical or characteristic of a group or society.

To be representative in this sense, it is necessary to be drawn from a particular group and to share its characteristics. A representative government would therefore be a microcosm of the larger society; containing members drawn from all groups and sections of society in terms of social class, gender, religion, ethnicity etc. and in numbers that are proportional to their strength in the society at large. This theory of representation is based upon the belief that only people who are drawn from a particular group can genuinely articulate its interests. To represent means to speak for, or on behalf of others, something that is impossible if the representatives do not have intimate and personal knowledge of the people they represent (Heywood 2004: 238). Kurdish representation in the political system varies in the state of Iraq, Iran, Syria and Turkey.

Theoretical Analysis of the Kurdish National Movement

Since the establishment of the state system in the Middle East, the Kurds have effectively been located geographically in the sensitive boundary regions of Iran, Iraq, Turkey and Syria which has resulted in their being pawns in a geopolitical arena which is home to a multitude of other states' interests. As such, analyses of Kurdish politics have often focused upon the relation of the Kurds as a minority people with the state/external involvement in their political development. The reasons for the Kurds occupying such a prominent position in the foreign policies of various states can be traced to several interrelated factors such as the Kurdish region being resource-rich—particularly, oil being located in an area of immense geo-economic significance.[9] Therefore, theories of international relations have a crucial role in developing an understanding of the Kurdish region but have limited utility in analysing the Kurdish political development.

However, since 1991, geopolitical realities have promoted a further development of the Kurdish situation. The change in the global and regional geopolitical systems at the beginning of the 1990s and the fall of Saddam Hussein in 2003 presented an unprecedented opportunity for the Kurds. Further, globalisation[10] has created conditions in which both territorial states and ethno-territorial entities must manoeuvre within a global context. This certainly enables ethno-territorial discourses to become internationalised more effectively and to escape the nation-state's hegemony. Globalisation has also created unambiguous conditions in which military superiority does not guarantee political legitimacy anymore but participation to the globalised world does (Akcali 2009). Therefore, actors involved in any ethno-territorial conflict as first, second or third parties are well-aware of these conditions and take their actions accordingly.

The 'world system' approach provides a theoretical framework to analyse the ethno-territorial conflict in West Asia. The Kurds are victims of a conservative world system that suffers from its own contradictions and anachronous structural limitations. The 'world system' approach gave to an analysis the dynamics of political and social movements and the struggle at the periphery. The world system is divisive. The owners of the means of production—the oppressors—utilise every means to maintain the status quo for insuring their privileged position and the oppressed struggle to change it (Amin 1980: 109). The history of the colonial and neocolonial eras provides evidence of the atrocities inflicted on humanity and the process of domination and exploitation still continues. The Kurds are an example of a group that has struggled to liberate itself from this process; a realisation which has been impeded by the world system of domination and exploitation.

Immanuel Wallerstein has developed a theoretical framework for understanding the historical changes involved in the rise of the modern world. The modern world system, essentially capitalist in nature, followed the crisis of the feudal system which helps explain the rise of Western Europe to the world system supremacy. For Wallerstein

> "a world-system is a social system, one that has boundaries, structures, member groups, rules of legitimation and coherence. Its life is made up of the conflicting forces which hold it together by tension and tear it apart as each group seeks eternally to remold it to its advantage. It has the characteristics of an organism, in that it has a lifespan over which its characteristics change in some respects and remain stable in others... Life within it is largely self-contained, and the dynamics of its development are largely internal" (Wallerstein 1974: 347).

He attempts to explain why modernisation had such wide-ranging and different effects on the world. He shows how political and economic conditions after the breakdown of feudalism transformed northwestern Europe into the predominant commercial and political power. The geographic expansion of the capitalist world economy altered political systems and labour conditions wherever it was able to penetrate. Wallerstein (1974) proposed four different categories into which the world could be placed:

- **Core:** These societies dominate and exploit the weak. Technology is a central factor in the positioning of these countries. These core states promote capital accumulation internally through tax policy, government purchasing, sponsorship of research and development, financing infrastructural development and maintaining social order to minimise class struggle. It is the economic, political and military power of the core that allows significant capital to be accumulated into the hands of the few; the capitalist world-system that produces and maintains the gross economic and political inequalities within and between nations.

- **Semi-Periphery:** Being exploited by the core, they assume their role in the exploitation of the peripheral areas. In the recent past, they have been expanding their manufacturing activities particularly in products that core nations no longer find very profitable.
- **Periphery:** Lack strong central governments or are controlled by other states; export raw materials to the core and rely on coercive labour practices. Unequal relations exist between the periphery and the core.
- **External:** Maintain own economic system; remain outside the modern world economy. For example, Russia (USSR) (Wallerstein 1974: 349-50).

The core region always benefits at the expense of the periphery and that has brought about a skewed development in which economic and social disparities between sections of the world economy have increased instead of providing prosperity to all.

For Wallerstein, nation-states are variables elements within the world system. States are used by class forces to pursue their interest, as in the case of core countries. Imperialism refers to the domination of weak peripheral regions by strong core states. Hegemony refers to the existence of one core state temporarily outstripping the rest. Hegemonic powers maintain a stable balance of power and enforce free trade as long as it is to their advantage. However, hegemony is temporary due to class struggles and the diffusion of technical advantages. And finally, there is a global class struggle.

The global capitalist economy imposes concrete restrictions or dictates prescriptions for the peripheral countries and these conditions lead to identity transformations or sometimes de-territorialisation and re-territorialisation as foreign policy articulations. Peripheral states and people are more compelled to redefine identities, in order to adapt to the global change and attract the help of trans-national organisations. They can also resist by developing even more rigid identities and consolidating or defending their territorial claims. However, they are usually the vulnerable sides of the world's system. Core states are more able to maintain their rigid identities and firm geopolitical and foreign policy articulations of their economical and technological advantages (Akcali 2009).

The 'world system' has betrayed the Kurdish cause. President Wilson promised the Kurds some form of statehood at the end of World War I but when the British and French governments learnt that the proposed area for the

Kurdish state contained oil, they moved to block it. In order to participate in the colonial competitions and gains, the Soviet Union supported the Iranian Kurds in their struggle to create their own state at Mahabad, the capital and headquarters of the Kurdish movement. This short-lived state collapsed in 1948. The leaders of the countries where Kurds lived have often sponsored Kurdish rebellions in neighbouring countries while massacring Kurds in their own territory. Syria does not tolerate any expression of the Kurdish identity within its borders but shelters and equips a large force of Kurds fighting against Turkey. Turkey denies its own Kurds cultural and identity rights.

In the aftermath of the 1991 Gulf War, the United States created a neutral no-fly zone in both northern and southern Iraq. The objective was the defence of the status quo oil-producing countries. In the south, the policy aimed to contain Saddam Hussein's ambitious plan of developing nuclear weapons. In the north, 'Operation Restore Hope' initiatives were adopted to protect the Kurds from Saddam Hussein's brutality. The policy helped the Kurds and was welcomed, especially by their leader Massoud Barzani, but the policy contained other objectives. The Kurds were seen as agents for capital accumulation and used to balance the region's power configuration. The Kurds of Turkey provide the empirical evidence supporting this thesis. The American foreign policy does not support Turkish Kurds and advocates Turkey's Saddam-style assault on the Kurds in the country's southeast (Manafy 2005: 34-35). The centre of the world system, the United States of America, along with the Turkish government considers the Kurdish struggle as a form of terrorism. Such a contradictory stand is based on a self-interested selective perception. Turkey is an ally; Iran is not. Iraq allied with the United States against the Iranians with the objective of containing the Iranian Revolution which was followed by economic sanctions. When the goal was accomplished, the alliance relationship was abandoned. When the policy shifted in favour of the Kurds, they were utilised to undermine the internationally recognised sovereign states in the region.

The Kurds have been used by both regional and international powers and are abandoned after the goals of these political powers are achieved. Neither the world system nor the regional powers are genuinely concerned about the Kurds. The Kurds are critical factors when they can be used as the agents for capital accumulation and as instruments in a regional balance of power. The concept of capital is divisive; the resulting conflict is indicative of the structural crisis of the system of accumulation. As Rosa Luxemburg argues, the West takes into account only one aspect of economic development—the realm of peaceful competition—but fails to acknowledge the realm of violence that arises from the capital accumulation process. Violence and destruction are seen as independent of the realm of the accumulation process, hence, incidental to foreign policy and both are structurally linked (Luxemburg 1964: 452). Accumulation at the global level means conflict and divisiveness. The realisation of the Kurdish political and human rights cannot be attained under the arrangement of the existing world system, which chooses the capital's rights over human rights. Hence, the Kurds have been victims of the hegemonic powers who were working for their own political gain.

Conclusion

The history of Kurds is known for destruction and displacement. The emergence of the modern nation-state system and the concomitant rise of secular nationalism in West Asia have profoundly affected inter-ethnic relations in the region. The rise of centrally controlled and highly stratified states has not accommodated the demands of ethnic nationalism. The Kurds have waged a long struggle to develop and sustain an identity of their own. Though often described as harsh, convulsive rebels, they are one of the oldest communities in West Asia. Because of their readiness to revolt against chastisement, regional and international powers have exploited them habitually and incited them to assume a militaristic role in destabilising regional regimes. Kurdish rebellions, whether tribal or nationalist, became common place in Iraq, Iran, Syria and Turkey, with all of them being successfully repressed. Military attacks by state authorities against the Kurds were combined with policies of assimilation and/or suppression to weaken the Kurdish nationalist movement. The state that emerged in the individual nations tended to ignore ethnic diversity and structured the political system to the benefit of the dominant ethnic group.

For most of the twentieth century, different nation states with 'troublesome' Kurdish minorities on the peripheries managed to control them through a combination of repression (occasionally large-scale killings and deportations) and co-optation. In addition to the partitions imposed by international boundaries, the Kurds were also divided among themselves often unable to coalesce around single leaders or movements. However after 1991, an opportunity was given to the principal political groupings of the Kurds to present themselves as organisations capable of mobilising widespread popular support. The Kurdish ethno-nationalism although unique in many respects, represents dilemmas and faces multi-ethnic societies in terms of conflict management and resolution. The Kurds face a new challenge after the Arab Spring where the newly floated Islamic State of Iraq and Syria (ISIS) is destabilising the region.

Notes

1. The Battle of Chaldiran occurred on August 23, 1514 and ended with a victory of the Ottoman Empire over the Safavid Empire of Persia. As a result, the Ottomans gained immediate control over eastern Anatolia and northern Iraq.
2. The Safavids were one of the most significant ruling dynasties of Iran. They ruled the greatest Iranian empire since the Islamic conquest of Persia.
3. One of the Indo-European peoples, related to the Persians, who entered northeastern Iran probably as early as the 17th century BC and settled in the plateau land that came to be know as Media. For details see "Encyclopaedia Britannica", (Online: web), Accessed 14 July 2010, URL: http://www.britannica.com/EBchecked/topic/372077/Mede
4. Also see, Washington Post Company (1999), *Who are the Kurds?* (Online: web), Accessed 30 October 2005, URL: http://www.washingtonpost.com/wp-srv/inatl/daily/feb99/kurd profile.htm
5. For details see, "Kurdistan's Economy: Its Potential and its Challenges", (Online: web), Accessed 5 July 2010, URL: http://www.krg.org/articles/detail.asp?lngnr=12&smap=02010200&rnr=73&anr=31571. Also see, "Kurdistan Region Economic Development Assessment", Final Report December 2008, Local Government Project. The publication was produced for a review by the United States Agency for International Development. It was prepared by RTI-International.
6. Bruinessen, Martin van (1992) "Kurdish Society, Ethnicity, Nationalism and Refugee Problems", in Phillip Kreyenbroek and S. Sperls (eds), *The Kurds: A Contemporary Overview*, London: Routledge, pp 48-54.
7. The Yezidis consider this benevolent angel as an emanation of God. Some Christians, Muslims and others identify this angel with Lucifer or Shaytan (Satan). The Yazidis have a cultural prohibition against uttering the word "Shaytan" as it is considered offensive and blasphemous.
8. Bruinessen, Martin van (1992) "Kurdish Society, Ethnicity, Nationalism and Refugee Problems", in Phillip Kreyenbroek and S. Sperls (eds), *The Kurds: A Contemporary Overview*, London: Routledge, p.3.
9. For analyses of the relationship between secessionist minorities and external involvement, see, Heraclides, A. (1991), *The Self-Determination of Minorities in International Politics*, London: Frank Cass.
10. Globalisation can be defined as the new hegemony of transnational capitalism. This hegemony has not changed the nature of ethno-territorial conflicts in the sense that such conflicts are still based on ethnic and territorial claims.

CHAPTER 2

Establishment of the Kurdish Regional Government in Iraqi Kurdistan

The concept of autonomy is seen as a solution to the political problems of minorities seeking socio-political and economic justice within multi-ethnic societies. David Held defines the concept of autonomy as

> Persons should enjoy equal rights (and, accordingly, equal obligations) in the framework that generates and limits the opportunities available to them. That is, they should be free and equal in the determination of the conditions of their lives, so long as they do not employ this framework to negate the rights of others (Held 1991: 228).

The right to participate in the process of collective political decision-making should not be limited by distinctions of creed, political persuasions, colour, sex or minority status (Manafy 2005: 128). However, autonomy is based 'on the deliberations of all'. It is crucial to distinguish between state sovereignty and popular sovereignty. Advocates of state sovereignty vest ultimate power in the state to determine the normative code of behaviour and define for citizens their rights. The supporters of popular sovereignty assign to the state the role of class mediation and its crucial function is to implement the "will of all" (general will). In fact, both these approaches involve tyranny and jeopardise individual autonomy and liberty. Hence, both must be integral to each other. The supremacy of one or the other can pose a threat to democratic ideals (Held 1991: 227-232). Government (or power) and freedom do not mix; one is the anti-thesis of another. Yet, both are critical values for human interaction: a government that is effectively in control and a government that is effectively controlled. Increase in one will come only at the cost of the other. Government control would be legitimate only if people in turn controlled the government (Bramsted and Melhuish 1978: 274-277). Thus, for democratic autonomy to be realised, it has to be enshrined in a legitimate framework that enables and limits the sovereignty of the state and its citizens. The survival of civil society can only be ensured within a constitutional system with a bill of rights, free and competitive elections and a constitutionally limited freedom of democratic states (Held 1991: 232). Autonomy without democracy cannot be realised. Fragmented traditionalistic political culture, tribal affiliations, informal group politics and conservative mode of thinking undermined the realisation of the Kurds' desire for autonomy. The most debilitating contradiction between the Kurdish traditionalistic leadership and the desire to liberate the Kurdish society from externally created internal domination was the Kurdish dependence on imperial forces for liberation; a reliance on the oppressors. This logic prevented the development of Kurdish class solidarity and political consciousness for a long time. The Kurdish quest for political autonomy and self-determination, especially in Iraq, had been consistently reactionary. This mode of behaviour and political factionalism had played a key role in defeating the idea of political autonomy for the Kurds.

Since 1991, the Kurdish region had enjoyed de facto autonomy within an area defined by the 36th Parallel. The election on May 19, 1992 was the first free and fair parliamentary election in the history of Iraq. Voter turnout was very high and the elections were deemed to be free, fair, and democratic by international observers. After decades of dictatorship, the people in Kurdistan were able to choose their representatives. This regional election led to the formation of the first Kurdistan National Assembly (later renamed the Kurdistan Parliament) and the establishment of the KRG. The leadership and the people of the Kurdistan region decided to remain part of Iraq and to adopt and abide by all national laws except for those that violated human and universal rights. The use of chemical weapons against the population of Halabja in 1988, which killed 5,000 people, embodied Saddam's policy of annihilation of the Kurdish people.[1]

The fall of Saddam Hussein's regime in 2003 brought about numerous changes for the Kurdish Autonomous Region. The military intervention by the Coalition forces in 2003 marked a turning point; while maintaining these trappings of autonomy, the Kurds also benefited from their robust inclusion and participation in the Iraqi central government and brought into the public domain the repression being suffered by them over decades. By remaining under the control of the Iraqi state, the Kurds have avoided foreign intervention by Iran and Turkey, gained the gratitude of the United States, secured key positions in the central government (including the presidency) and gained access to revenue and resources.

The 2003 war on Iraq solidified the Kurds' international visibility. The United States, having failed to obtain the Turkish Parliament's consent to open up a second front against Saddam Hussein, had to rely extensively on Kurdish paramilitaries to maintain order in the north. The Kurds were the only ones to regard the US occupation of Iraq as liberation. The Kurdish-controlled areas became Iraq's most stable and prosperous regions. Kurds also took an active political role in Baghdad. In 2005, one of the two Kurdish leaders, Jalal Talabani, the Head of the Patriotic Union of Kurdistan (PUK), assumed the presidency of Iraq and proved to be an able politician in building consensus in Baghdad. Massoud Barzani, the Head of the Kurdistan Democratic Party (KDP), assumed the mantle of President of the KRG. Manoeuvring in the post-Saddam political struggles, the Iraqi Kurds won the argument with their rivals over the redrawing of provincial boundaries in order to reverse decades of ethnic cleansing and gerrymandering at their expense. Baghdad also agreed to their demand for a referendum on Kirkuk's fate, which, they have argued, represents the Kurds' Jerusalem.

While the Kurdistan Regional Government (KRG) took the lead in this new era for the region, 2003 saw the beginning of a large-scale and hugely lethal conflict in the rest of Iraq which submerged the country in a spiral of violence. Since then, including the attacks against the US military forces, there have been attacks between the Sunni and Shi'a communities and later against the Christian community in parallel with actions by the al-Qaeda, the Iraqi army and international troops' 'counterinsurgency' activities and other destabilising elements. Combined together, they have created one of the biggest humanitarian crises in the world with two million people already seeking refuge in other countries, principally Syria and Jordan, and two million more having fled to other parts of the country, many of them to Kurdistan (Tomas and Villellas 2009: 5).

The Physical Geography of Iraqi Kurdistan

Kurdistan in Iraq is often referred to as Southern Kurdistan but in fact, it occupies a more or less central position in the Kurdish territories. It is the link between what is variously known as Turkish, Northern or Western Kurdistan to the north and northwest and the so-called Eastern or Iranian Kurdistan to the east and southeast and also borders Kurdish areas of the Syrian Jezireh. This part of Kurdistan is a rich country which extends over a partly wooded region of mountainous terrain curving from the river Zagros in Iranian Kurdistan to the mountains of Turkish Kurdistan. Iraqi Kurdistan is well endowed with a broad spectrum of natural resources—in particular, oil and water. However, the control of such resources, whether in terms of dams, oil refineries or mines has rarely been in the hands of the Kurds. The people of Kurdistan have never directly benefited from the exploitation of the resources but have only received its benefits indirectly through the Government of Iraq.

Figure 2.1 The Iraqi Kurdistan

Source: htm//www.iran-daily.com/New/155384.html

The area of northern Iraq where the Kurds predominate is a region about 83,000 square kilometres to the north of the Hamrin Mountain (see figure 2.1). The area is roughly the size of Jordan or Austria. Smaller ethno-linguistic communities of Assyrians, Chaldeans, Turkomans, Arabs and Armenians are also found in Iraqi Kurdistan. The Turkomans share the same religious belief as the Kurds, but the Christians display a different religion as well as being of a different ethnic origin. The largest Christian community is that of the Assyrians. The other Christian community includes the Chaldeans. Both of these speak the Aramaic language and have a strong cultural identity. There are about 3.7 million Kurds in the Kurdish northern safe-haven area and between 1 and 2 million in the rest of Iraq. That comprises roughly 16 to 20 percent of Iraq's population (Yavuz and Gunter 2001: 36). Kurdistan sits on some 45 billion barrels of oil reserves and more than 110 trillion cubic feet of gas. Since 2003, it has granted oil and gas concessions to some of the world's biggest energy companies including ExxonMobil, Gazprom Neft, Total and Chevron.[2]

The Gulf War and the Kurdish Uprising

On August 2, 1990, Iraqi forces invaded Kuwait after several weeks of acrimonious charges by Saddam Hussein against the rulers of Kuwait for overproducing oil and lowering prices, thus "impoverishing" Iraq which needed higher oil revenues to finance reconstruction projects after eight years of war with neighbouring Iran. After occupying Kuwait, Saddam Hussein revived the old Iraqi claim to Kuwait and declared it to be the nineteenth province of Iraq. For Saddam, the Gulf War was an opportunity to solve his pressing economic problems and become master of 40 percent of the world's oil reserves while staking an old claim for leadership of the entire Arab world (Mazarr et al 1993: 1-2). For George Bush Sr. Saddam's aggression created a clear need to respond to an unprovoked aggression and in doing so, to begin the redefinition of the US role in the world in the aftermath of the Cold War; a necessary exercise for which the admininistration was ill-prepared. President George Bush ordered the deployment of a large number of US air, naval and ground troops in and around Saudi Arabia under Operation Desert Shield. When Operation Desert Shield was transformed into Operation Desert Storm with the start of the Allied war against Iraq in January 1991, the United States had deployed over 500,000 troops in the Arabian Peninsula. The Iraqi regime, which had been courted and supported by the

United States throughout the 1980s was turned overnight into a demonic entity with superpower ambitions. Reports of Iraq using chemical weapons against the Kurds and Iranians, which had been ignored, were publicised in US print and electronic media as if they were novel revelations (Entessar 1992: 145).

Following Saddam's defeat in the 1991 Gulf War and their own failed uprising that had ensued, Iraqi Kurds nevertheless began increasingly to move toward the creation of a de facto state and government in northern Iraq. This was accomplished under the protection of the US-led Allied forces stationed in south-eastern Turkey (northern Iraq) and a United Nations presence sanctioned by the Security Council Resolution 688 that condemned the repression of the Iraqi civilian population.[3] The economic blockade Baghdad began imposing against the Kurds on October 1991 ironically had the effect of hardening rather than weakening the Kurdish revolt. In the political environment of Iraqi Kurdistan, the development of the KRG cannot be separated from the status of the relationship between the KDP and PUK. The election held in May 1992 led to the formation of the KRG which encompassed the geographically and politically divided cities of Arbil and Suliemaniyah; mirroring the division of the KDP and PUK respectively.

The success of Operation *Al-anfal*[4] led the Kurds to change their strategy in the period falling between the end of the Iran–Iraq War and Iraq's invasion of Kuwait. Along with a number of smaller Kurdish groups, the PUK and KDP formed the Iraq Kurdistan Front (IKF) to better coordinate their activities and their demands in dealing with Baghdad. The IKF stressed autonomy for Kurdistan within the framework of a democratic Iraq as their goal. The Kurds did this in order to allay the suspicions of other Iraqi opposition groups with whom they were seeking closer relations for the first time (Cordesman and Hashim 1997: 76). With the Allied Forces attacking Iraq, the Kurds feared that they might become the victims of war. The IKF moved cautiously once Iraq invaded Kuwait. It was aware that international pressure against Iraq was mounting, but it also realised that Saddam would have no qualms about using troops and chemical weapons against any rebellion. Notwithstanding Massoud Barzani's initial hesitation to open a second front against Saddam Hussein, the Iraqi Kurds revolted in March 1991 after the defeat of Saddam's military at the hands of the US-led forces in southern Iraq. The Central Intelligence Agency (CIA)-run radio (The Voice of Free Iraq) operating from Jeddah, Saudi Arabia, had been encouraging a Kurdish revolt and the Kurds were led to believe that they would receive outside assistance if they led an uprising against the Iraqi government.[5]

The Impact of Desert Storm

The Coalition's massive air bombardment of Iraq aimed not only at the Iraqi military, its oil supply pumps and its communications lines but also at a wide array of economic and industrial targets. The bombing amplified the economic impact of sanctions, incited the Iraqi people to oppose Saddam Hussein, degraded Iraq's ability to sustain itself as an industrial and military power and created a leverage over post-war Iraq in that it would not be able to repair extensive damage without outside help (Hashim 1992: 13-14). Iraq suffered particularly extensive damage in critical areas such as the national electric power grid, telecommunications and the oil industry.

The Allied Campaign against Iraq, following its invasion of Kuwait, provided the Kurds with yet another opportunity to press their claims against the Iraqi Government. Both Sunni and Shi'ite Muslim leaders associated themselves with the Iraqi opposition group formed in Damascus, Syria, in December 1990. The unified Kurdish forces launched a more organised revolt that achieved unprecedented success, albeit briefly.

The IKF took the risk of creating a new uprising after Saddam's shattering defeat in the Gulf War and the uprising soon became a mass movement. The Kurds had little military strength, but they were able to take advantage of the paralysis of the Iraqi Army and the disorganisation within the security services. In fact, the various pro-government tribal militias often persuaded the Iraqi Army in Kurdistan to leave virtually without a fight. As a result, the Kurdish revolt rapidly expanded to cover most of the rural and urban areas with large Kurdish populations. Neither Barzani nor Talabani were fully prepared for the scale and success of this uprising, but they acted quickly to take control of an inchoate rebellious mass and engaged their veteran *peshmerga* guerrillas who took over several major urban centres including the oil-centre of Kirkurk. In the process, they defeated ill-motivated troops who surrendered in droves, joined the guerrillas or fled south. Large quantities of heavy military equipment including several tanks, helicopters, anti-aircraft guns, artillery and mortars fell to the rebels. By mid-march, the IKP declared that 75% of Kurdistan was in their hands (Cordesman and Hashim 1997: 77). The group rapidly moved to restore essential services and civil administration in the "liberated" areas. This Kurdish success, however only occurred because of the power vacuum created by the Gulf War.

On April, 1991, Baghdad accepted the terms for a permanent ceasefire in accordance with UN Security Council Resolution 687, which stipulated continuing an arms embargo for the indefinite future; UN supervised destruction of all chemical and biological weapons, long-range ballistic missiles and nuclear infrastructure; Iraqi compensation to Kuwait and other countries for damages incurred during the war; an unequal demilitarised zone along the border with Kuwait extending 6 miles into Iraq and 3 miles inside Kuwait to be patrolled by UN observers and UN demarcation of the border between the two countries (Hashim 1992: 11).[6] Controversially, the Coalition did not take steps to dismantle the Saddam Hussein regime. This vague and inconclusive end to the 1991 Gulf War proved tragic for the people of Iraq—in particular, for the Kurds in the north of Iraq and for the Shi'a population in the south of Iraq.

Depopulation of Kurdish Areas

Initially, the Kurds gained control of a few cities, but they were driven back by the Iraqi forces attacking them from air and land. Neither the IKF nor the international community had expected what actually happened as the revolt collapsed. As a consequence, Kurdish villages were devastated once more and another mass exodus of Kurdish refugees started. When the Republican Guard proceeded, well over a million Kurds fled in unprecedented numbers to the Turkish and Iranian borders. An estimated 500,000 Kurds fled to Turkey and 1.5 million to Iran when they realised that they were defenceless. Thousands of people died because of the cold weather or lack of food as they escaped to the safety of Iran or Turkey. The exodus may have been prompted by a fear of reprisals by government forces including the possibility that chemical weapons might be used as in 1988.[7] In addition to terrorising the civilian population, Saddam Hussein's crackdown on the Kurdish uprising left deep rifts in the opposition. Some members of the Kurdish opposition made matters worse when they began to harass and threaten Kurds who worked for the government as civil servants or those who worked in the oil refineries. In any case, the effectiveness of the Iraqi forces in putting down the Kurdish rebellion and the plight of the refugees compelled the two leading groups within the Iraqi Kurdistan Front, the PUK and KDP, to seek peace with the Iraqi regime (Entessar 1992: 147).

Many Kurds felt that with a defeated Saddam Hussein, the time was right to sign an agreement that would maximise their prospects of gaining autonomy within a federated Iraqi state. Furthermore, the Kurds reasoned that if another person or group came to power in Baghdad, there would be no guarantee that they would not behave the same way toward the Kurds as Saddam Hussein. Without a peaceful settlement, some Kurdish leaders also thought that there would be a permanent refugee problem creating a fertile ground for outside powers to exploit the Kurdish situation and "for all sorts of negative tendencies" to develop within the refugee population (Lahoud 1991: 18). Another impetus for an Iraqi–Kurdish rapprochement was the high price Kurdish soldiers had paid by serving in the Iraqi Army during the Gulf War. According to one estimate, two hundred thousand Kurds were members of the Iraqi occupation army in Kuwait. Although no casualty figures are available, it is safe to assume that they were among the several thousand Iraqi soldiers who died during the saturation-bombing runs of Iraqi targets during the war.

The first round of the Iraqi–Kurdish talks was held in late April 1991 in Baghdad between Ba'athi authorities and a team of Kurdish negotiators representing the IKF headed by Jalal Talabani. The other members of the Kurdish team included Rasoul Mamand, Secretary General of the Kurdish Socialist Party, Sami Abdul Rahman, Secretary General of the People's Party of Kurdistan, and Nashirawan Barzani, a nephew of Massoud Barzani, representing the KDP. The inclusion of the representatives of various Kurdish groups as members of the negotiating team was intended to demonstrate that the Kurds were a united front (Entessar 1992: 148). The Talabani-led team of Kurdish negotiators did not sign an agreement with the Iraqi government. However, another round of Iraqi–Kurdish talks began in June 1991. This time, the negotiations were led by the KDP's Massoud Barzani, whose talks with Saddam generated optimism that peace was at hand when the KDP announced the impending signing of an agreement on Kurdish autonomy. The status of Kirkuk which had derailed many previous negotiations remained an unresolved issue causing opposition to the impending deal with Saddam Hussein. However, Talabani's PUK rejected Barzani's plan. Instead, Talabani made a surprising announcement from Turkey proposing that Turkey take a more active role in solving the Iraqi Kurdish problem (Entessar 1992: 149).

In July 1991, talks on Kurdish autonomy were moved from Baghdad to the Kurdish city of Arbil where Kurdish leaders met with Izzat Ibrahim, Saddam

Hussein's second-in-command in the ruling Revolutionary Command Council. In addition to the autonomy demands made in the previous talks, the Kurds put forward a new proposal for establishing democracy in Iraq that would involve the oppressed Shi'ite majority (Muir 1991: 8). Although no agreement was reached, the Iraqis, perhaps by default, allowed more armed Kurds in the region including the major cities of Arbil and Sulaymaniyah.

Sanctions and Humanitarian Intervention

The damage Iraq suffered in its war with Iran between 1980 and 1988 pales in comparison with what it has suffered as a result of sanctions, the allied air campaign and the insurrections. The trade sanctions that the UN approved on August 6, 1990, seriously affected food stocks. Economic sanctions had a severe impact on local industry, which relied heavily on foreign suppliers for spare parts, raw materials, machinery and expertise. By the end of 1991, the private sectors suffered from shortages of materials and goods. According to the head of the Iraqi industrial association, 16,000 private ventures were either working at reduced capacity or on the verge of halting operations (Hashim 1992: 13).

The social impact of the Iraqi crisis revealed a shocking human tragedy. Hundreds and thousands of people died prematurely from the health disaster that swept Iraq in the wake of war and during the more than eight years of comprehensive sanctions (Cortright and Lopez 1999: 744). Sanctions targeted the weakest and the most vulnerable members of Iraqi society—the poor, the elderly, the newborn, the sick and the young. Many equated sanctions with violence. Sanctions, coupled with the pain inflicted by the US and UK military attacks, reduced Iraq's infrastructure to virtual rubble. Water sanitation plants and hospitals remained in dilapidated conditions. Surveys by the United Nations Children's Fund (UNICEF) and the World Health Organization (WHO) noted a marked decline in health and nutrition throughout Iraq. The UNICEF reported in 1996 that 4,500 children under the age of five were dying every month in Iraq from hunger and disease (Arnove 2003: 85). The situation in northern Iraq became worse with double sanctions by the Saddam regime.

The economic and military situation of Iraqi Kurdistan became steadily grimmer and became more involved in the fighting between the Kurdish factions. Many foreign relief workers were forced to leave Iraq. In August 1992, relief workers in the north continued to be harassed. The Iraqi regime maintained an ongoing internal embargo over the north which included necessities such as food, medicine and other humanitarian supplies. After August 1993, the embargo also included massive electric power cut-offs in specific areas, causing the spoilage of medicines, breakdown in local water-purification systems and the loss of certain hospitals (Leezenberg 2005: 636). A disaster was averted only by the prompt action of the United Nations and donor governments, which imported and installed temporary generators to alleviate the crisis. The embargo of the north had an impact on the Kurds and various other minorities such as the Turkomans who lived in the area.

Kurdistan became an economic shamble as a result of the civil conflict and the internal embargo imposed by Baghdad which cut off the north from the markets. Supplies from the centre and south of Iraq were prevented from entering the Kurdish-controlled territories. The region had no viable commercial or financial infrastructure. The only source of revenue came from the import/export custom duties imposed on goods coming from Turkey on their way south to Mosul and the rest of the country or on Iraqi oil smuggled out via the KDP-controlled territory. But, this revenue was more of a bane than a benefit to Kurdistan as the KDP and the PUK fought and quarrelled over the control of the customs points and the division of revenue. Nor did the Kurds use this revenue to build up their administrative infrastructure. This helped the semi-permanent state of militarisation in the Kurdish enclave because the largest and the best-equipped militias belonged to the KDP and PUK and represented the only major source of large-scale employment for young Kurdish men (Cordesman and Hashim 1997: 86-87). The Government of Iraq's economic blockade of the Iraqi Kurdish region was an attempt to force the Kurds into considering a political settlement.

The oil-for-food programme (the UN Security Council Resolution 986) that began functioning in 1997 continued to provide to the region substantial resources from Iraq's public oil wealth.[8] The KRG directly cooperated with thirteen UN agencies in the region including ten which were involved in the management of the oil-for-food programme. At its own expense, the KRG supported the programme by providing the services of thousands of government staff (teachers, health workers, electricity staff, water and sanitation workers etc). The KRG also provided warehousing and other building facilities as well as transport, security and telecommunication services. In managing the programme, the UN literally ran on the KRG-built and maintained roads. KRG funds were obtained from unstable sources, mostly road taxes, and taxes levied on imports.[9]

Iraqi officials opposed the oil-for-food programme as overly intrusive and a violation of national sovereignty. They rejected the programme because they saw it as providing the basis for the United Nations sanctions indefinitely. The Iraqis insisted that the only proper humanitarian response was to lift the sanctions and allow the country to repair its oil industry, resume trade and re-build its shattered economy and society. But, had the oil-for-food programme been accepted when first proposed in 1991, much of the suffering of the Iraqi people in the intervening years might have been avoided (Cortright and Lopez 1999: 744).

There was a serious problem with landmines in Iraqi Kurdistan despite the fact that the KDP and PUK stated irrevocably that they were against the use of landmines. Landmines killed up to 3,000 people from 1991 and casualties remained high. Furthermore, in mid-2000, the UN reported that there were instances of freshly laid mines being found in previously cleared minefields. The landmines also prevented agricultural activities in large swathes of the country and prevented displaced families from returning to their homes. About 80% of the population in Iraqi Kurdistan was unemployed and chronic malnutrition remained a serious problem. It was estimated that there were around 6,00,000 displaced people; 1,00,000 of whom had been expelled from government-controlled areas. Many of these people lived in tents, open spaces, or unheated public buildings (Carver 2002: 78-79). It should be noted that many Kurds who sought asylum in Europe actually came originally from areas not inside the 'safe haven'.

Iraqi Kurdistan existed under a kind of double rule: a weak Kurdish Regional Government and a collection of international relief agencies. Donor states continued to deal with Kurdish administration in so far as necessary to clamp social unrest and prevent the refugee problem. Given the deepening economic crisis and growing interference of the neighbouring states, the situation of the Iraqi Kurds did not differ substantially from that of the Kurds in Turkey whose oppression continued with the knowledge and even support of the leading NATO states (Ofteringer and Backer 1994: 41).

International NGOs (INGOs) had been operating in Iraqi Kurdistan since 1992. The Kurdistan Regional Government had cooperated with these organisations as much as possible to benefit from their experience and assistance. There were about 28 INGOs operating in the Kurdish area from eleven countries such as Save the Children or Help Age International from the UK, Qandil from Sweden and Emergency from Italy which were involved in all types of projects. The emergency situation had settled down and humanitarian needs were being largely looked after under the UNSCR-986 programme. Many were also involved in various construction projects such as IDP housing, water projects or access roads funded under the UN programme. The Ministry of Humanitarian Aid and Cooperation was responsible for overseeing the activities of the INGOs operating in the region.[10] The Ministry aimed to have a better coordination of services, less duplication of projects and easier operation in the area for the INGOs.

The comprehensive embargo on Iraq had a major effect on food availability, nutrition and health—especially for children. This remained true even after the implementation of the oil-for-food resolution. The Western media frequently ignored or downplayed the many accounts of major nutritional problems. Even when consideration was reluctantly given to the human costs of sanctions, attention was often diverted by claiming that deaths and deprivation in Iraq were caused not by United Nations actions but by the Iraqi government (Arnove 2003: 198). A country that once profited from its great oil wealth and talented, skilled and well-educated people was devastated by years of war and economic sanctions. Iraq was self-sufficient in agriculture and proud of its modern health and educational systems but after the sanctions, the Iraqis were unable to send their children to school or treat all sick people. It was the capital of the Arab-Islamic empires during the Golden Age of the Abbasids, when Arab culture, science, medicine, literature, mathematics and philosophy flourished from the eight to the thirteenth century (Yaphe 2003: 7). Iraq could have been a model for the more equitable distribution of resources to its people in a region known for its profligate spending; instead, it became a model for a republic of fear. Iraq proved to be a failing state.

Russia, China and France were resentful of the American and British use of the sanctions to continue pressure on Iraq until Saddam fell from power. Hoping to rebuild their lucrative political and economic relations with Iraq and unable to understand the American concept of Iraq as a 'rogue' state, these countries insisted that the Security Council should acknowledge the increase in Iraqi cooperation and that it should be rewarded by easing or lifting sanctions (Hashim 1996:12).

Sanctions were designed to produce deprivation and poverty; hence, it was not surprising that they brought about widespread malnutrition and increased mortality. Sanctions had not succeeded in their stated aim of overthrowing the regime. Indeed, they probably strengthened the position of Saddam Hussein not only within Iraq but throughout the region.

Functions of the Kurdistan National Assembly (Kurdistan Parliament)

The Kurdish National Assembly is the Kurdistan Region's democratically elected parliament. The main functions of the KNA are to examine proposals for new laws, to scrutinise government policy and administration. The founding principles of the KNA are liberty, pluralism, accountability, openness and the representation of all peoples in the Kurdistan Region.[11] The Kurdish parliament chose

> "the federalism formula… as an ideal solution for the ethnically pluralistic Iraqi society that would safeguard its unity and would… satisfy the legitimate aspirations of the people of Iraqi Kurdistan as this formula will guarantee their participation in the making of decisions while protecting the integrity and unity of Iraq" (Gunter 2005: 50).

On October 4, 1992, the parliament of the de facto Kurdish state in northern Iraq declared Iraqi Kurdistan a constituent state in a federal Iraq (Gunter 2005: 47-48). Both the two main Kurdish leaders Massoud Barzani and Jalal Talabani endorsed the concept. The democratically elected Kurdistan Regional Government exercises executive power according to the Kurdistan Region's laws as enacted by the Kurdistan Parliament. However, Iraq's lack of a democratic culture since its inception would make actual federalism difficult to implement.

Structure and Programme of the Kurdistan Regional Government

The government coalition consists of several political parties. The coalition reflects the diversity of the region's people who are Chaldeans, Assyrians, Turkomans, Yazidis, Kurds and others living together in harmony and tolerance.

The KRG determined to establish strong constitutional institutions to support the democratic process in Iraq. Its main task is to form a system of good governance through the participation of all groups with transparency and accountability which means a modern professional government. The cabinet worked at all socio-economic levels of the Kurdistani society. The KRG looked forward to a democratic federal system in Iraq, based on agreement and respect for all nationalities and religions.[12] It therefore, supported democratic consensus in the political process. The Kurdistan Parliament has passed several laws that have contributed to the Region's social and economic progress. These include

- passing a modern and open investment law
- passing a progressive hydrocarbons (oil and gas) law for the Kurdistan Region
- significantly increasing the prison sentence for those committing the so-called honour killings which were previously given minimum sentences
- Strict limits on the practice of polygamy
- The Kurdistan Parliament approved by a large majority a constitution for the Kurdistan Region and intends to put it to a referendum in the future.[13]

Parliamentary Elections

Elections for the Kurdistan Parliament are held at least every four calendar years (as stipulated in Article 8 of the Kurdistan Electoral Law). Anyone aged 18 or over who is a citizen of the Kurdistan Region is eligible to vote in a direct, universal and secret ballot. Elections for the Kurdistan Parliament are based on a closed party-list proportional representation system. Electors vote for a party's list of candidates, rather than for an individual candidate. After the election results are announced, each party is allocated seats in proportion to the number of votes it received, using the ranking order of candidates on its list.

Powers of the Kurdistan Parliament

As provided in the Federal Constitution of Iraq, the Parliament has considerable power to debate and legislate on policy in a wide range of areas: health services, education and training, policing and security, the environment, natural resources, agriculture, housing, trade, industry and investment, social services and social affairs, transport and roads, culture and tourism, sport and leisure, and ancient monuments and historic buildings. The Kurdistan Parliament shares legislative power with the federal authorities. Priority is given to the Kurdistan Parliament's laws: customs, electric energy and its distribution, general planning and internal water resources.

In addition, under Article 121 of the Iraqi Federal Constitution[14] the Kurdistan Parliament has the right to amend the application of Iraq-wide legislation that falls outside of the federal authorities' exclusive powers.

The Kurdistan Regional Government, 1992–1996

In the absence of a negotiated autonomy agreement with the Iraqi Government, the KIF (Kurdistan Iraqi Front) organised elections to a 105-member Iraqi Kurdistan National Assembly. Both Talabani and Barzani hoped that the elections would result in the establishment of a legitimate, constitutional and legal entity embodied in a council that would represent the Kurdish people and would be the political decision-making body in the Iraqi Kurdistan. Kamal Fuad, the official in charge of foreign relations in the PUK, added that "the only solution to Iraqi Kurdistan is through parliamentary elections for the people of Kurdistan. The Kurdish parliament will form the civil administration and will act as the Kurdish northern government" (Gunter 1993: 297). Faced with an administrative vacuum and a double embargo, the Kurdistan Iraqi Front—an alliance of diverse political groups in the Kurdistan region—held a general election. The internationally supervised election was held on May 19, 1992 in which virtually an estimated 1.1 million-strong electorate participated in the Kurdish areas. Their goal was to establish an administration to provide for essential public services and to meet the basic needs of the people. The people expressed a strong desire to choose their representatives. Men and women over the age of 18 were eligible to vote. The legislative candidates had to be citizens and residents of Kurdistan for at least 30 years. Barzani and Talabani were the two leading candidates for the supreme leadership position. However, the election for an overall Kurdish leader was inconclusive; Massoud Barzani, the leader of the KDP, received 50.22% of the votes cast and Jalal Talabani, the leader of the PUK, 49.78%.[15] This regional election led to the formation of the first Kurdistan National Assembly and the establishment of the Kurdistan Regional Government. The leadership and the people of Kurdistan decided to remain part of Iraq and adopt and abide by all national laws except for those that violated human and universal rights. After decades of dictatorship, the people in Kurdistan were able to vote for their representatives.

The two socialist parties, the Kurdish Socialist Party (KSP) and the Party of Socialism in Kurdistan (PASOK), both of which called for an independent

Kurdish state, ran on the same ticket in the 1992 elections garnering 2.6 percent of the total vote; they did not win any seats in Parliament since a party must receive 7 percent of the vote to be represented. A few months after the polling, the parties merged with Abdulrahman's Kurdistan Popular Democratic Party (KPDP) to form the Kurdistan Unity Party, under the leadership of Abdulrahman and Mahmoud Osman. The Islamic Party of Kurdistan which believed that Iraq should become an Islamic state captured 5.1 percent of the votes in the elections and sent no members to the Parliament. The northern branch of the Kurdish Communist Party received 2.2 percent of the votes. The number of Christian Assyrians in northern Iraq was in dispute, but to forestall international criticism and local disapproval, the Iraqi Kurdish Front allocated the Assyrian Democratic Movement five seats in the Parliament regardless of the party's electoral showing; theoretically these were the swing votes in the body (Prince 1993: 19). Apparently, only seven of the eight reputed members of the Iraqi Kurdistan Front participated in the elections.

On the other hand, the Iraqi National Turkoman Party (INTP), which was not a member of the Kurdish Front, decided not to participate in the elections (Gunter 1993: 298). None of the smaller Kurdish parties achieved representation. After much negotiation, the Kurdish Front decided that the KDP and the PUK would be given 50 (fifty) seats each in the National Council. The remaining five would be given to the Christian minority with four of them going to the Assyrian Democratic Movement. The elections contributed to the KDP and PUK working even closer together. As a part of the agreement, it was decided that the Chairman of the National Council would be from the KDP, while his deputy would be from the PUK. Conversely, the Chairman of the Executive Council would be from the PUK and his deputy from the KDP. The design adopted effectively divided all executive and legislative positions equally with real power being unofficially vested in the political bureaus of the PUK and KDP and became known as the 50: 50 system (Stansfield 2003: 145).

The Establishment of The Power-Sharing System

In order to alleviate the ever-present tensions apparent in the political arena, the 50: 50 system was dependent upon the goodwill and support of the sources of the tension. The aim of the system was to achieve, at least on the surface, an even division of power between the KDP and PUK in all government offices throughout the territory. Such a balance was deemed to be particularly appropriate as the two leaders of the parties remained out of the official government equation, postponing dealing with the most problematic of who was to be President. The Presidium of KNA was divided between KDP and PUK personnel, with Jawher Namiq Salim of the KDP becoming the Speaker, and Mohammad Tawfiq his deputy. An identical division was then applied to the cabinet, with the minister being from one party and the deputy from the other. However, the decision-making process of the administration was still ultimately dominated by the PUK and KDP, thereby preserving the influence of the party elites (Stansfield 2003: 146). Hence, the power-sharing system perhaps acted as catalyst rather than a constraint.

At the ministerial level, the deputy enjoyed the same power and influence as the minister for he needed the support of the other to advocate policies and important programmes, with each possessing veto. This typology of division existed throughout the governmental structures from the cabinet to the town councils which also included schools, health facilities and internal-security positions.

The First Cabinet of the KRG

The first cabinet of the KRG (See Appendix 1) was presented with the unenviable task of attempting to govern the newly formed de facto state. Within the territory, UN sanctions and the GOI embargo were creating immense socio-economic problems in addition to the unease created by the tense political environment. Furthermore, the first Cabinet had managed several internal and structural problems.

The first Cabinet targeted the problem of the massively over-staffed and under-skilled personnel in the administration. However, its achievements have often been overlooked due to the subsequent breakdown of inter-party relations and the formation of the second Cabinet under the premiership of Kosrat Rasoul of the PUK. The greatest problem the first Cabinet presented to the decision-making process was the equality of power which existed between ministers and their deputies, creating an administration effectively hamstrung by the contrary political motivations of its highest executive members. The actual decision-making process of the Cabinet therefore appears to have been managed by some form of coordination between the two political bureaus. However, there was a problem with achieving a balance within the governmental structure with regard to the inclusion of civil servants trained by the GOI and those Kurds who had spent their lives fighting in the *peshmerga* brigades (Stansfield 2003: 149). The attempts at achieving a balance between these two groups created the first signs of tension between the KDP and the PUK, with both sides accusing the other of placing *peshmerga* personnel into positions which required technocrats.

The Second Cabinet of the KRG

Towards the end of 1992, the first Cabinet of the KRG became increasingly embattled. Faced with increasing partisan problems caused by the seemingly inextricable difficulties of revenue control, the leadership of the Cabinet attempted to become more technocratic in the face of the politicisation of the governmental structures by the KDP and the PUK. In March 1993, the Kurdish Cabinet elected in 1992 was dismissed by the Iraqi Kurdistan National Assembly for its failure to deal effectively with the crisis in the region. An important shift in government positions saw the PUK place some of its senior leaders into the Cabinet. Kosrat Rasoul Ali, a leading member of the PUK politburo, replaced Faud Massoum who was more of a technocrat as the Prime Minister. Tension began to rise as the government became more partisan. Moreover, in the summer of 1993, Sami Rahman's Kurdistan Unity Party—an alignment of three smaller parties that had previously all been members of the Iraqi Kurdistan Front—joined the KDP (Gunter 1996: 232). The change in Kurdish politics in favour of the KDP sent shock waves in the PUK camp.

The second Cabinet of the KRG included members from the KDP and the PUK only and one Christian. There was no representative from the newly combined three leftist parties (SPKI, KPDP and PASOK—a group that began as the 'Unity Party of Kurdistan') because they had unsuccessfully demanded one of the three main ministries—namely, Interior, *Peshmerga* Affairs and Humanitarian Aid as well as one governor, several districts officers and sub-district directors (Gunter 1996: 302).

The partisanship of the governmental structures was considered a primary reason of the subsequent fall into conflict which occurred in 1994. As a renowned *peshmerga* commander with an infamous fighting reputation, Kosrat Rasoul remained an easy target for members of the KDP to describe as uneducated and volatile. However, he proved able in mobilising public support behind his Cabinet and his premiership far more effectively than the more technically minded Faud (Stansfield 2003:150-51). But, the KDP had deep-rooted feelings regarding Kosrat and attributed much of the failures of the 50: 50 system of the government to him.

The Eighth Cabinet of KRG 2014

The eighth Cabinet of the Kurdish Regional Government (see Table 2.2) was sworn into office on June 18, 2014. The new government is a broad coalition consisting of all parties that are represented in the Parliament. It reflects the inclusion of all political, ethnic and religious groups in the governance of the Kurdistan Region. For the past decades, the KRG has dedicated its efforts to decreasing the gap in living standards between rural and urban areas and in modernising the health system. The eighth Cabinet has committed itself to the achievement of a continuous economic growth by diversifying sources of income and encouraging the private sector.[16] of the eighth Cabinet is to maintain security and stability in the Kurdish region.

Table. 2.2 The Eighth Cabinet of the Kurdish Regional Government (18 June 2014)

Ministries and Departments	Minister
Prime Minster	Nechirvan Idris Barzani
Deputy Prime Minister	Qubad Jalal Talabani
Ministry of Agriculture and Water Resources	Abdulstar Majeed
Ministry of Culture and Youth	Khalid Doski
Ministry of Education	Pishtiwan Sadiq
Ministry of Electricity	Salahaddin Babakir
Ministry of Endowment & Religious Affairs	Kamal Muslim
Ministry of Finance & Economy	Rebaz Mohammad
Ministry of Health	Rekawt Hama Rasheed
Ministry of Higher Education & Scientific Research	Youshif Mohammad
Ministry of Housing and Reconstruction	Darbaz Kosrat Rasul
Ministry of Justice	Sinan Abdulkhaliq Chalabi
Ministry of Interior	Abdulakarim Sultan Sinjari
Ministry of Labour and Social Affairs	Mohmoud Haji Salih
Ministry of Municipalities and Tourism	Newroz Mawlood Amin
Ministry of Natural Resources	Abdullah Abdulrahman Abdullah (Ashti Hawrami)
Ministry of *Peshmerga* Affairs	Mustafa Sayid Qadirof
Ministry of Planning	Ali Sindi
Ministry of Trade and Industry	Samal Sardar
Ministry of Transport and Communications	Jonson Siyawash

Minister of State (Parliamentary Affairs)	Mawlood Murad Mohyeldhin
Minister of State (Environmental Affairs)	Abdulrahman Abdulrahim Hama Reza
Further Posts with Ministerial Rank	
Chief of Staff, Kurdish Region Presidency	Fuad Hussein
Department of Foreign Relations	Falah Mustafa Bakir
Department of Media & Information/ Govt. Spokesperson	Safeen Muhsin Dizayee
Presidency, Divan of the Council of Minister	Nechirvan Ahmed

Source: "Kurdistan Regional Government", *Ministries and Departments,* URL: http://www.krg.org/p/p.aspx?l=12&s=030000&p=228, Accessed 31 July 2014.

Civil War within the Kurdish Enclave

The KRG formed in 1992 after the Gulf War was weakened from its inception by Masoud Barzani's and Jalal Talabani's decision not to participate. This denied the government valuable credibility and left it in the hands of mere lieutenants of the KDP and the PUK. By 1993, the 50:50 principle that split power between the two parties in each ministry had further paralysed its initiative while fuelling partisanship (Gunter 1996: 302). In May 1994, supporters of the PUK clashed with supporters of the KDP, leaving 300 dead. Relations among the groups soured in March 1995 when the KDP backed out of an attack on Saddam's frontlines led by the Iraqi National Congress. A new burst of Kurdish infighting erupted in August 1995 when the PKK suddenly attacked the KDP because the KDP, as part of a deal United States was trying to broker, had agreed to police the border to prevent PKK (Kurdistan Workers' Party) raids from northern Iraq into Turkey.[17] Syria and Iran covertly supported the PKK in attempting to prevent the United States from gaining further influence in the area, while the PUK supported the PKK in an attempt to open a second front against the KDP (Yavuz and Gunter 2001: 38). Clashes between the PUK and KDP were matched by a vitriolic war of words, heightened by PUK accusations that the KDP received arms from Baghdad in order to tilt the military balance of power in its favour. The suspicions between these two largest Kurdish factions did not dissipate and Iraqi Kurdistan's socio-economic situation and stability showed no sign of improvement (Hashim 1996: 14).

On the other hand, the Iraqi National Congress (INC)[18] had achieved its moment of maximum success and popularity when it had acted as a mediating force between the warring Kurdish groups. It was only after Saddam made an offer of mediation that both sides decided to accept a ceasefire brokered by the INC which called for a return to the status-quo ante in Arbil (i.e. cessation of fighting) and a separation of the forces of the two rivals by the INC militia (Cockburn and Cockburn 2000: 239). A tenuous ceasefire between the KDP and the PUK was held until April 1995, although minor clashes took place. This ceasefire broke down when Turkish forces advanced into Iraq. The Turkish attack on the PKK triggered a fresh wave of fighting between the two factions, and this resurgence in intra-Kurdish fighting virtually paralysed the Kurdish Regional Parliament in Arbil, whose mandate was due to expire in early June 1995 (Cordesman and Hashim 1997: 82). The conflicts converged in November 1996 when the Turkish paramilitary joined the KDP to force the PUK and the PKK to return to the established intra-Kurdish ceasefire line.

The United States tried to mediate between the two groups in a series of talks conducted in Drogheda, Ireland from August 9–11, 1995. These talks were aimed at resolving the deep-rooted differences between the two leading Kurdish groups (Barkey 1997: 2). The Iraqi National Congress participated and Turkey sent observers. The two agreed to cease media attacks against each other, to respect the rights of the other followers and to release detainees captured during the hostilities between them.[19] Despite the accord, the situation continued to deteriorate in late 1995 and early 1996. The agreement seems to have unravelled before it was even implemented. The crisis that exploded in 1996 began in 1994 when Barzani's KDP refused to hand over to the Kurdish government custom revenues from the Turkish–Iraqi border point. These revenues, estimated at US$ 35 million annually and the chief source of Kurdish government revenues, were collected at the Ibrahim al-Khalil checkpoint near Zakho—a KDP stronghold. The KDP argued that they were retaliating for the disappearance of some US$19 million from the coffers of the Central Bank of Kurdistan under the direction of the PUK. Following several bouts of fighting in the period between May 1994 and July 1995, Barzani came to control around one-third of Iraqi Kurdistan's territory and population. The PUK's two-thirds included the major cities of Arbil and Sulaymaniyah leaving Barzani with only Dohuk and the less-developed western part of the region (Al-Khafaji 1996: 36). The situation further degenerated in August 1996 when the PUK began to use arms received from Iran to threaten the KDP's existence. The desperate Barzani did the unthinkable and invited Saddam Hussein to intervene in the war. Saddam sent at least 30,000 troops into the UN-protected Kurdish region and recaptured the KDP stronghold of Arbil. The KDP was immediately installed in power, again (Cordesman and Hashim 1997: 88). Turkish forces entered Iraq several times during the year to combat the PKK.

The ceasefire sharply reduced the number of civilian casualties and the use of torture on those detained or arrested. Northern Iraq, as a result was further divided between a KDP-controlled northern zone and a PUK-controlled southern area. The stalemate between the two Kurdish rivals also created opportunities for Iran, Iraq and Syria to jockey for influence with the KDP, PUK and other smaller Kurdish militias further aggravating the divisions among the Iraqi Kurds.

The fighting left over a thousand people dead and forced thousands of civilians from their homes. The KDP estimated that 58,000 KDP supporters were expelled from Suleimaniyah and other PUK-controlled areas from October 1996 to October 1997; the PUK said that more than 49,000 of its supporters were expelled from Arbil and other KDP-controlled areas from August through December 1997. The UN reported that more than 10,000 persons were forced from their homes when fighting broke out between the Kurdish factions along their ceasefire line in October 1997. It also documented over 16,000 cases of disappearance of persons in the Iraqi sector of Kurdistan.[20] The euphoria of 1992, when the Kurds engaged in free and democratic elections had given way to despair and a desire on the part of young Kurds to escape from Kurdistan. Clearly, the PUK–KDP fighting presented a serious setback for democracy in the Kurdish region of Iraq.

The Division of Iraqi Kurdistan

In August 1996, the combined forces of the KDP and GOI invaded Arbil, expelling the PUK from the city. A further round of serious fighting took place in 1997 before a ceasefire was reached and the division between the KDP and PUK reverted to the status quo ante. Particularly after the 1997 conflagration, the two political areas of Iraqi Kurdistan developed into two administrative zones; one dominated by the KDP in the Arbil and Dohuk Governorates. The PUK administered in Suleimaniyah and New Kirkurk Governorates (See Figure 2.2). Both sides claimed legality for themselves and scorned the legality of the other with the political system of Iraqi Kurdistan becoming characterised by two separate, almost identical, political and administrative systems (Stansfield 2003: 153-54).

This system proved to be a stable alternative to the previous power-sharing arrangement. It managed to preserve the influence of the political elite of both the parties and allowed governance and administration to take place with less consideration for party politics than when all political groupings had been located in Arbil. Furthermore, the divide in the system implied that the overt potential for the de facto state becoming more institutionalised was somewhat diminished—thereby, reducing the necessity for neighbouring states to promote stability within a unified structure. However, it was argued that the cabinets of the divided administration were the most effective of the Kurdish political institutions formed since 1991. The ability of the two main factions to dominate the administrations within their strongholds enabled both entities to relax somewhat and promote a more effective system of governance.

Iraqi Kurdistan was therefore divided geographically and politically between a KDP-dominated axis of Arbil–Dohuk and a PUK-dominated axis of Suleimaniyah–Kirkurk. The creation of this system enabled smaller parties to enjoy more political power as both the KDP and PUK realised the dangers of being seen as too overly dominant—both to the Iraqi Kurdistan populace in particular and the international community in general. Whilst the administration remained divided between Arbil and Suleimaniyah, the judiciary remained unified and was headed by the Supreme Court of the Iraqi Kurdistan region based in Arbil (Stansfield 2003: 155). It was the presence of this unified institution and an unwritten agreement not to alter the interim status of the position of the President that seemed to exist between Talibani and Barzani, which provided a small degree of unity to Iraqi Kurdistan.

The emergence of Kurdistan's de facto autonomy forced the Kurds to set up their own administrative and legislative organs to avoid chaos and a further decline in public security. But, the Kurdish experiment in freedom has revealed deep-seated differences and splits within the Kurdish movement and attracted the intervention of their Turkish and Iranian neighbours (Hashim 1996: 13).

Fig.2.3. Division of Iraqi Kurdistan: KDP and PUK

Source: https://commons.wikimedia.org/wiki/File:Iraq_kurdish_areas_2003_vector.svg

Islamic Movement of Iraqi Kurdistan (IMIK)

Iraqi Kurdistan was predominantly Islamic, so it should not be surprising that Islamist political parties have steadily developed. Some of these were formed as early as the 1970s, benefiting from the presence of the Islamic Republic of Iran, and fought against Saddam's regime during the 1980s. However, it was the development of the de facto Iraqi Kurdish state and its instability in the mid-1990s which gave the Islamist parties the space and opportunity to become a force in the region. The most popular was the Kurdistan Islamic Union led by Salahadin Baha'adin. Part of the Muslim Brotherhood, it had no militia and enjoyed good relations with the KDP and the PUK (Stansfield 2003: 11). As a non-combatant party, it had a great deal of support among the people of Iraqi Kurdistan.

Established in 1978, the Islamic Movement of Iraqi Kurdistan (IMIK), another Islamist party differed from the PUK and KDP in its fundamental goal which was not the creation of a Kurdish state but the replacement of the Iraqi regime with an Islamic regime. IMIK was led by Mulla Ali Abd al-Aziz and Mulla Ali Bapir's Islamic Group of Kurdistan (IGK). As part of a coalition agreement with the PUK brokered by Iran, IMIK controlled an enclave between Halabja, Tawela and Panjwin in the southeast of Suleimaniyah, near Iran. It was politically close to the Iranian government and received support from Iran to extend Islamist influence. In late December 1993, an armed conflict was reported to have taken place between fighters of the PUK and the Islamic League of Kurdistan (ILK, also known as the Islamic Movement of Iraqi Kurdistan or IMIK). The two parties were reported to have signed a peace agreement in February 1994, following mediation by the INC. In June 1995 the IMIK withdrew from the INC, accusing its leadership of incompetence and corruption. In 1996, the IMIK began to enforce Islamic Punishment Law within the enclave. Islamic dress codes were strictly observed, even a car carrying a foreign female aid worker who did not have her hair covered was shot and all residents were forced to attend the mosque on Fridays (Stansfield 2003: 12; Carver 2002: 72).

Both KDP and PUK were keen to clamp down on Islamic activity. Within the city of Arbil (in the KDP-controlled areas), several new groups and Islamic charities had been formed. The relationship between these groups and the KDP had steadily deteriorated. Heavily influenced and financed by the al-Qaeda organisation, a militant breakaway faction of the IMIK known as the *Fund-al-Islam* (soldiers of Islam) began fighting the PUK in September 2001. The *Fund-al-Islam* took control of the Iranian border regions of Tawela and Biyara, and attacked several non-Muslim settlements.[21] But by mid-October, the PUK had regained control of the region and a ceasefire was declared.

The Kurdish Islamic Group, which won two seats in the January 2005 elections in Iraq, joined the Kurdish Alliance[22] to form a 77-seat bloc in the 275-member Parliament. They supported the demands of the Kurdish Alliance concerning the federal system and reintegration of Kirkuk and other towns into Kurdistan as well as for a fair share in the country's natural resources. They also opposed the separation of state and religion.[23] However, the mainstream Kurds have rejected the idea of an Islamic republic in Iraq following the victory of a conservative Shi'ite in the polls.

The Washington Agreement of 1998

In January 1998, the PUK leader Jalal Talabani proposed peace and reconciliation and the establishment of a transitional government, in which both the PUK and KDP would be represented to assume sole responsibility for custom duties on the cross-border trade. However, the KDP did not respond following its military success against the PUK. Iran continued to offer some support to the PUK, but appeared unwilling to become more directly involved in the Kurdish enclave.

Under the auspices of the Ankara peace process, the two parties met again. The first meeting took place on February 12, 1998 in Shaqlawa (territory controlled by the KDP). The KDP delegation was led by Sami Abdul Rahman and also included Jawher Namiq Salim (Speaker of the KNA), and Bruska Nuri Shawaise (Central Committee). The PUK delegation was led by Kamal Fuad and also included Omar Sa'id Ali and Arsalan Bayaez (all Political Bureau members). This meeting formulated confidence-building measures including the enforcement of ceasefire, the ending of media attacks, release of prisoners, ending of expulsions, establishment of a joint committee to ensure the implementation of UNSCR 986 and the promotion of an increased coordination between public service ministries. The specialised sub-committees formed for coordinating the public service sector proved to be reasonably successful and resulted in the reduction of checkpoints between cities and the easing of travel restrictions between Arbil and Suleimaniyah (Stansfield 2003: 100). By mid-1998, the fragile peace process between the PUK and the KDP appeared to be holding and after a number of meetings between representatives of the two factions, agreement was reached on the exchange of prisoners and the establishment of a joint committee to promote cooperation in public health, education and energy. Meanwhile, the issue of KDP control over customs duties on cross-border trade from Turkey which had thwarted previous attempts to reconcile the rival factions remained unresolved. Nevertheless, the two factions continued to hold regular meetings and both parties pledged to cooperate to secure a permanent settlement with Baghdad leaders and stated that all Kurdish factions were prepared to make peace with the Government of Iraq. The US spearheaded negotiations that culminated in the September 1998

'Washington Accord'[24] reached between Barzani and Talabani which halted their infighting and obligated both to prevent the PKK from using northern Iraq as a base from which to attack Turkey. The Iraqi Kurds conceded to the accord because they needed Turkish acquiescence for their own local administration (Gunter 2001: 609; Katzman 2009: 2). The United States' support gave the Kurds increased security against potentially destructive policies of the governments of Turkey and Iraq. The agreement was expected to draw the two political parties into closer cooperation and in the formation of an interim administration in Arbil followed by multi-party elections to unify the KNA and the KRG. An interpretation of the agreement included potential areas of coordination in public service ministries, followed by a joint national assembly—possibly of a unified regional executive. It was endorsed when the Kurdish Parliament reconvened in 2002, by which time the Kurds and other oppositionists had prepared to overthrow Saddam Hussein. However, Washington's interest in Iraqi Kurdistan derived from Kirkuk's oil.

Reconvening of the Kurdish National Assembly

A major step in the implementation of the 1998 Washington Agreement was taken on October 4, 2002, when all the members took their seats in the Iraqi Kurdistan National Assembly in Arbil for the first time since 1994. Roj Nuri Shawaise, President of the Parliament, opened the session. Massoud Barzani and Jalal Talabani addressed the Parliament where both stated in clear and unequivocal terms their total commitment to make the Iraqi Kurdistan National Assembly function for the benefit of all the people in the region. New Members of Parliament were sworn in during the session. Members unanimously voted to accept the terms of the Washington Agreement. They reaffirmed their position on the future of Iraq. All parties remained in agreement that Iraq should be a free, democratic, federal and pluralist country.

Free and fair local elections were held in dozens of municipalities in the KDP-administered areas in May 2001. According to KDP sources, to select 571 officials, KDP candidates received 81 percent of the votes cast and the rate of voter participation was recorded at 79 percent. A second session of the Assembly was held on October 8, 2002 in Suleimaniyah; further strengthening solidarity and unity. Government and party officials of KRG remained very positive and people in the local community were very pleased that the Parliament was unified again. More steps were taken and aimed at normalising the situation in the Kurdish area. At a further session held on November 12, 2002 a joint committee was established with the aim of preparing for parliamentary elections scheduled to be held in Iraqi Kurdistan within nine months. However, these elections were postponed following the US-led campaign to oust the regime of Saddam Hussein (O'Leary 2002: 3).[25] The reconvening of the KNA was a clear indication of the growing cooperation between the KDP and the PUK. In particular, the KDP and PUK were unified in asserting the Kurdish right to self-determination in a democratic Iraq in future.

Despite various internal difficulties and constraints, including a strong opposition of neighbouring countries and both external and internal embargoes on the region, all basic public services were again provided. Freedom of speech and free movement was respected. According to the Human Rights Watch, the leadership of the region made notable progress in promoting and protecting the basic rights of the people.

The Kurds in Post-Saddam Iraq

On March 19, 2003, the United States launched a war on Iraq which quickly drove Saddam Hussein from power. Its goal was to gain access and control of the region's vast petroleum and natural resources with the complicity of a clutch of UN collaborators (Clairmmont 2003: 3983). Many Arabs considered the Kurds traitors for having supported the United States in the 2003 war. On the other hand, many Kurds saw the Arabs as chauvinistic nationalists who opposed Kurdish rights because they would end up detaching territory from the Arab partrimony (Gunter and Yavuz 2005: 122). The fall of Saddam's regime in April 2003 gave the displaced Iraqis an unprecedented opportunity to return to their places of origin, particularly in northern Iraq. Saddam's authoritarian regime and its policies of ethnic cleansing were responsible for huge numbers of internally displaced persons (IDPs). The Arabisation programme and the *Anfal* campaign thus had led to the greatest numbers of Iraqi IDPs and refugees in the country's history accounting for the majority of the 70,000 estimated IDPs in northern Iraq (Bruinessen 2000a).

The US-led war to depose Saddam Hussein, the criticism of its legality and justification notwithstanding, allowed for an organised programme anchored within a humanitarian approach. The ponderously legal return process, along with inter-communal tensions and the uncertain political future of Iraq derailed the entire programme. At the same time, unregulated and rushed returns in the wake of the war of March 2003 created a new group of IDPs which gradually increased in number (Romano 2005: 430-431). But, the 2003 war did not produce vast numbers of displaced persons and the humanitarian catastrophe that many analysts had predicted—little had transpired to rectify the IDP and refugee problem that had existed before the war. Although, thousands of IDPs had returned to their general areas of origin, most of the 'returnees' were living under difficult conditions (Baker 2004). In November 2003, Refugees International described the situation as follows:

> Iraq remains volatile. On 14 November, UNHCR recommended that host countries continue to ban forced returns of Iraqis to their homeland and continue to provide temporary protection to Iraqi refugees. A lack of law and order in many regions, a high rate of unemployment, a housing shortage and inadequate basic services make return inadvisable for many refugees.[26]

Faced with harsh realities, the Iraqi Kurds turned to federalism as their best realistic hope in a post-Saddam Hussein Iraq. Turkey, however, saw federalism as simply another step towards Kurdish independence. The Kurds who had enjoyed a de facto government since the establishment of the northern no-fly zone have been adamant in demanding a democratic Iraq with a federal system of government (Dawisha and Dawisha 2003: 38). Federalism was seriously broached as a solution to the Kurdish problem in Iraq following the Gulf War in 1991.

Significantly, an unambiguous Kurdish challenge to regional security did not emerge for over a year following the US invasion in 2003. Concerns that the Iraqi Kurds would use the downfall of the Iraqi government to immediately declare independence proved unfounded, as the PUK and KDP emphasised their commitment to keep Kurdistan part of Iraq and remained engaged throughout 2003–2004 in efforts to reconstitute a central Iraqi government (Gunter 2003: 9-10; Bengio 2003: 46-47). After the invasion, the KDP and the PUK placed their enmity aside and presented a unified front to the American-led Coalition and the rest of Iraq in order to legalise their autonomous status and consolidate their position at the national level. The two main political parties have stopped hostilities and have agreed to the control of their autonomous regions throughout Kurdistan (Khalil 2009: 21). The KRG region in Northern Iraq has demonstrated that they govern the most peaceful, democratic and affluent area of Iraq. In September 2006, Iraqi flags were taken down in the northern part of the country, replaced with the official Kurdish one (Rubin 2007). A non-binding bi-partisan US Senate resolution was passed by a vote of 75–23 in early October 2007, calling to establish a decentralised and federalised Iraq with three states (Karadaghi 2007). The KRG's support for the Senate resolution sparked indignation from Arabs both inside Iraq and across the region, and has compounded the long-held impression by some Arabs that Kurds are divisive and deceptive and outsiders to the region (Ridolfo 2007). The Arab League deemed it a calamity for the entire Arab and Islamic world.

Kurdish Role in the Iraqi Constitution

The constitutional process in 'post-conflict' Iraq was begun by the Coalition Provisional Authority (CPA) under Ambassador Paul Bremer[27] in August 2003, following the formation of the Iraqi Governing Council (IGC) in July. The IGC appointed a 25-member Constitutional Preparatory Committee (CPC): 12 Shi'ite Arabs, five Sunni Arabs, five Sunni Kurds, one Turkoman, and one Assyrian (Christian). Only three women were included (one Turkoman and two Shi'is). The CPC was vaguely mandated to start consultations with community leaders and others.

The United Nations (UN) Resolution 1511[28] of October 16, 2003 called on the IGC to set a timetable and programme for drafting the Constitution and holding elections. The United States and its Iraqi allies reached an agreement in November 2003 that an interim constitution—a 'Transitional Administered Law' (TAL)—should be drafted and signed before Iraq were to regain its sovereignty in June 2004. The TAL, signed March 8, 2004, laid out a political transition process as well as the citizens' rights especially for the Kurds. The TAL defined the foundations of liberal, consociational[29] and federal polity. The TAL also established for a democratic, federal and decentralised state structure with human rights protection. The UN Resolution 1546[30] endorsed the transitional procedure as stipulated by the TAL, strengthening international support and internal legitimacy. The Kurds supported the constitution because it met most of their significant demands. However, the TAL did not give the Kurds control of Kirkuk (Tamin province)—instead, setting up a process to allow the Kurds expelled from Kirkuk by Saddam to reclaim their homes (Kaztman 2009: 3).

The Constitution not only retained substantial Kurdish autonomy but also included the Kurdish insistence on federalism or de facto or formal creation of its own regional government. The Constitution recognised the three Kurdish provinces of Dohuk, Arbil and Sulaymaniyah as legal 'regions' (Article 113). The KRG was given the power to amend the application of national laws not specifically under national government purview, to maintain internal security forces and to establish embassies abroad (Article 117). Several provisions of the TAL ensured the Kurds' autonomy:

- The Kurds maintain their autonomous 'Kurdistan Regional Government' (KRG) but the TAL disallows changes to the boundaries of Iraq's 18 provinces. This provision, at least for now, denies the Kurds control of the city of Kirkuk, the capital of Tamim province.
- Arabic and Kurdish languages were deemed 'the two official languages of Iraq.' Islamic principles are to be considered 'a source', but not only or the primary source of law. Most Kurds are secular and differ with the philosophy of Iraq's Shi'ite Islamist leaders that Islamic law be paramount in Iraq.
- The KRG was given to alter the application in Kurdish areas of those Iraqi laws that do not relate to foreign policy, national security, national budgetary matters and control of Iraq's natural resources including power to "impose taxes and fees within the Kurdistan region." The KRG retains "regional control over police forces and internal security," thereby allowing the *peshmerga* to legally continue operation (Katzman and Prados 2005: 3-4).

The Kurds worked for the constitutional process that culminated in the October 15 referendum.[31] Their role in advocating for federalism and other issues particular to their minority status and interests had an effect given the very limited participation by Sunnis in the Constitution-drafting process. The draft constitution put to voters on 15 October was essentially a Kurdish-Shi'a pact on power sharing. It called for federalism with strong powers to the regional constituent provinces. The regions retained their sectarian or ethnicity-based militias, which function as a national guard, distinct from the Iraqi military forces and police. They retained the right to have a regional parliament in the region. On the identity issue, the Kurds won recognition of Kurdish as one of the two official languages of the Iraqi State. Turkoman and

Assyrian are to be additional official languages in areas where those groups are numerous (Barkey and Laipson 2005: 66-67). The only principle the Kurds wanted that did not make it to the draft was the right to secede from the Iraqi state. Also, the Kurds did not achieve anything on the status of the oil-rich city of Kirkuk.[32]

Kurdistan National Assembly Election 2005

The provincial elections for the Kurdistan National Assembly (KNA) were held along with the Iraqi national elections (for an interim government) on January 30, 2005. The primary goal of the 2005 elections was to end party-rule in Iraqi Kurdistan and unify the two major parties (KDP and PUK) that had fought a civil war in the mid-1990s over territorial disputes and control of the Kurdistan region.[33] Previously, the region was divided into administrative provinces that were under control of either the KDP or the PUK. In 2004, the two parties created one unified list called the Democratic Patriotic Alliance of Kurdistan which included smaller parties. The alliance achieved 104 of the 111 seats in Parliament. The majority voted for the alliance (an overwhelming 90%) allowing the KDP and PUK to effectively divide key positions in the government. After a series of negotiations, on May 29, the KNA appointed the leader of the KDP, Massoud Barzani, as the president of the Kurdistan region. In 2006, Nechervan Idris Barzani was selected as Prime Minister. On January 21, 2006 an agreement was reached for the joint administration of the KRG. Under the agreement, Nechirvan Barzani from the KDP was retained as Prime Minister (Kaztman 2009: 3). PUK's Adnan Mufti was appointed as Speaker of the KNA. Furthermore, a new post of Vice-President was established and filled by the PUK Politburo executive chief Kosrat Rasul Ali.[34] The Vice-President served as the Deputy Commander-in-Chief of the *Peshmerga* Forces of the Kurdistan Region.

The seat of the KRG is in Arbil. According to the new power-sharing agreement, the KDP headed the KRG Ministries of Finance, *Peshmerga* Affairs, Higher Education, Agriculture, Martyrs, Culture, Electricity, Natural Resources, Municipalities, Sports and Youth as well as the Ministry for Extra-Regional Affairs. The PUK oversees the Interior, Justice, Education, Health, Social Affairs, Water Resources, Transportation, Reconstruction, Planning and Human Rights Ministries. The Kurdistan Islamic Union, the Kurdistan Islamic Group as well as the Turkoman and Chaldo-Assyrian parties are heading the remaining ministries.[35] All the security, intelligence and armed forces are united under the two ministries of the Interior and *Peshmerga* Affairs.

The *peshmerga* primarily remain in Kurdish areas to protect Kurdish inhabitants there; but, some have joined the Iraqi Security Forces (ISF) and have served mostly in northern Arab cities such as Mosul and Tal Affar and also in Sunni areas and in Baghdad. Given the effectiveness of the *peshmerga* in maintaining peaceful conditions in Iraqi Kurdistan, the past experiences of the PUK and KDP in administering the KRG and a 2003 agreement between the PUK and KDP designed to settle outstanding political differences and to provide for a joint PUK–KDP administration of the KRG, the KRG emerged as one of the areas of Iraq where the US troops were neither needed nor present to provide for the security of the population. On May 30, 2007, formal security control over the three KRG provinces was handed from the US-led coalition in Iraq to mostly Kurdish ISF units (Kaztman 2009: 3; Shifrinson 2006: 3).

The KRG has assumed the role of government in a federal region of Iraq. As stipulated by the Iraqi Constitution, Iraq is divided into federal regions that handle their own domestic affairs while the Baghdad central government deals with external affairs (Gunter 2005: 50). In the wake of the ratification of the Iraqi Constitution in October 2005, Iraqi Kurdistan reconstituted itself as a federal region under the new constitutional framework.

Kurdistan Referendum Vote

The Kurds had accumulated political momentum as a result of the national assembly and provincial elections as well as in the municipal elections in Kirkuk city. The Kurds' desire for an independent state also gained credibility as a result of the vote in the Kurdistan Referendum Movement (KRM) which was also unofficially conducted on January 30, 2005. The referendum asked voters to choose one of the two options: One, "I want Kurdistan to stay a part of Iraq"; and two, "I want Kurdistan to be independent". Out of a total 1,998,061 ballots cast, 1,973, 412 people voted for independence; 19,650 voted for Kurdistan to remained as a part of Iraq. Thus, 98.5 percent of the people who voted, voted for independence (Berawri 2008: 892-98).

Kurdish Participation in the Central Government

Over the years, Baathist Iraq had countenanced a wide range of attitudes toward the Iraqi Kurds vis-à-vis the rest of Iraq (Bengio 1998: 120). The

Baathist regime spoke about the Kurds as a nation (*qawm*) possessing national rights and aspirations; they were careful to declare that these rights were given to the people and not to the territory which implied secession. In addition, these rights were given by proclamation (*bayan*) rather than agreement (*ittifaq*). The designation "Kurdistan" was also seldom used by the Baathists. Instead, the Baathist regime used terms such as 'region', 'zone', 'northern region', 'our north' or 'the autonomous area' (Gunter and Yavuz 2005: 123-124). But, the Kurds have strongly objected to the concept of Iraq being part of a pan-Arab union because this reduces them to being an obscure minority. The Kurds managed to establish fledgling democratic institutions which are functioning very well for their uniquely Westernised Kurdish autonomous state within Iraq. In addition, since the formation of Iraq's new federal governing system based on its permanent Constitution approved by the Iraqis in the Constitutional Referendum of October 2005, the Kurds are able to hold some key Iraqi governing posts and legalise their strife over the contested oil-rich regions.

Iraqi Kurdistan is recognised as a federal region in the Iraqi Constitution under Article 117, consisting of the three provinces of Dahuk, Arbil and Sulaymaniyah. The Kurdish Regional Government, led by Nechirvan Barzani since 2005, exercises legal supremacy and financial autonomy, including taxes and grants, within Kurdistan. There is a Kurdish National Guard made up of *peshmerga* forces and Iraqi Kurdistan has exclusive ownership of its own resources. Essentially, the KRG has its own ministers who do not report to Baghdad, their own economy, their own internal border. More importantly, the Kurds have their own foreign policy and their government is internationally recognised.[36] The Kurdish region fully participated in the Iraqi elections of 2005. The KDP and PUK allied in the national elections of 2005. In the January 2005 elections, their Alliance won about 26% of the vote, earning 75 National Assembly seats out of 275.[37] Because of a boycott of the elections by most Sunni Arabs, the Kurds also won control of the provincial council of Nineveh Province which is mostly inhabited by Arabs (Kaztman 2009: 4). The Iraqi Kurds not only came to possess their most powerful regional government since the creation of Iraq but also played a very prominent role in the Iraqi government in Baghdad. Kurds held important portfolios including the post of President (Jalal Talabani), Deputy Prime Minister (Barham Salih), Foreign Minister (Hoshyar Zebari) and six other Cabinet positions (Fawzi Hriri—Industry, Latif Rashid—Water

Resources, Bayan Dazee—Housing and Construction, Narmin Othman—Environment, Assad Kamal Mohammed—Culture and Ali Mohammad Ahmed—Minister of State). The dual government role stands in a marked contrast to the situation that had existed before the events of 1991 and 2003, when the Kurds were treated as second-class citizens (Gunter 2006: 3). Many Arabs resented the Kurdish claim to autonomy as a challenge to the Arab patrimony and a federal state for the Iraqi Kurds within Iraq as simply a prelude to secession.

The Kurds, thus, play a critical role in the Iraqi national policy and retain their own relationship with the outside world. Relations with Washington remain the Kurds' top priority. The Kurds became Washington's primary ally in Iraq in the 2003 war. The relationship intensified when the Turkish Parliament turned down the US request to open a second front in the north against Saddam, and the Kurds became more critical partners, working alongside American forces in the capture of key northern towns. The population in the Kurdish areas wholeheartedly embraced the arrival of American troops. Support for the United States has also meant that Kurdish areas have been largely devoid of violence and Washington has relied on the *peshmerga* forces to maintain security there. In many counterinsurgency actions, Kurdish forces have served on the frontline, often earning the enmity of the Sunnis, especially in places such as Mosul and Fallujah (Barkey and Laipson 2005: 69). Kurdish leaders have been among the primary interlocutors with Washington. In October 2005, Massoud Barzani in his capacity as President of the Kurdish Regional Government reassured the Kurds of their special status for American leaders. He thanked the Americans for their sacrifices "to advance the banner of freedom and democracy" (Barzani 2005).

But, relations with Washington have also been subject to occasional rough spots since the fall of the Saddam regime. The Kurds at various times began to feel neglected, as American policy makers, struggling to keep other major groups engaged in the rebuilding of Iraq, courted Shi'a leaders. Some American experts were worried that Kurdish assertiveness during the constitutional debates made it even harder to persuade the Sunnis to participate. Human rights activists and democracy promoters are not entirely comfortable with the Kurdish-style democracy. There are also worries about Kurdish behaviour towards Arabs in Kirkuk (Barkey and Laipson 2005: 69).

The Economy Post-2003 War

Since the 2003 Iraqi war, international humanitarian relief has encouraged greater economic and political autonomy in Iraqi Kurdistan. With the transition of the remaining UN oil-for-food account ($1.5 billion) to the Kurdish Regional Government in November 2003 and a Baghdad-approved regional budget, the KRG has obtained much-needed revenue to increase salaries for civil servants and implement economic development programmes. This financial injection into the Kurdish political economy as well as international investment from private companies has created new linkages among the Kurdish nationalist elite, the KRG, local institutions, private contractors, diasporic communities, and the US-led reconstruction of Iraq (Natali 2005: 168). The per capita income in the KRG is estimated at the equivalent of $3,500 per year and the GDP at a growth of 7 percent (Cagaptay 2008: 8).

The Kurdish region has attracted lots of foreign investment. On July 7, 2006, the KRG Parliament unanimously approved a new foreign-friendly investment law to attract more foreign capital to the region. Under the new legislation, foreign firms are permitted to hold up to 100 percent of a company.[38] Since there was a security problem in the south, many foreign investors were attracted to the Kurdistan region. Among them were the Turkish firms, which have been heavily involved in projects such as building international airports in Arbil and Sulaymaniyah as well as cement plants and others. Despite the lack of any comprehensive agreement, the KRG has moved forward in developing its energy sector. The KRG has signed numerous development deals with foreign firms under its own law adopted in August 2007; even though Iraq's Oil Minister Hussein Shahristani has called the deals 'illegal'. Deals so far are with Genel (Turkey), Hunt Oil (US), Dana Gas (UAE), BP (Britain), DNO Asa (Norway), OMV (Austria), SK (South Korea), Talisman (Canada), Addax (Switzerland) and several others (Hasan and Ben Lando 2007). The oil deal attracted controversy because of the firms' leaders' ties to the Bush Administration officials and the perception that it contradicted the US commitment to the primacy of the central government (Kaztman 2009: 8).[39] Iraq has warned all the foreign oil companies which have signed deals with the autonomous Kurdish Regional Government. A report by the Swiss Refugee Council, July 10, 2007, stated that

> "The economic situation in the KRG area has improved markedly. For the general public, salaries have risen and employment opportunities in the private sector have been enhanced. Thanks to investments by the KRG in local development and to international companies attracted by the liberalised policies, the relative stability and the security offered in the KRG area, the private sector in the KRG-area is being boosted especially by construction projects. 'Around three quarters of the work force comes from other areas of the country, such as central and southern Iraq. Whilst the average salary for a construction worker in Baghdad is US$ 12 they can make up to US$ 20 a day in Iraqi Kurdistan...' reported a Kurdish construction supervisor in Erbil. Likewise, an array of public sector posts has been created, to such an extent that one out of three inhabitants is employed by the KRG. For instance, the police force in Sulaimaniyah province has increased considerably since April 2003, rising from about 7000 members to some 20000 at the end of 2005"(Gerber 2007: 2-3).

Iraqi Kurdistan sits on an oil reserve of thousands of barrels. This vibrant region has taken production of 250,000 barrels a day in just over 5 years and has the capability to export over 1 million barrels by 2015. In all Kurdish exports, 83% of the revenues are forwarded on to the Iraqi Federal Government—in line with the Iraqi Constitution. Based on this legal and constitutional framework, the Kurdish authorities continue to call on the Iraqi Government to pay the oil and gas companies the costs and profits. The Kurds have welcomed Baghdad's involvement in the development of the region's hydrocarbon industry, but the Iraqi authorities have flatly rejected the involvement of the international players to development in the region. The long-standing power struggle over authority has forced the Kurdish government to explore other revenues, including ways of breaking away from financial dependence on Baghdad (Dosky 2013: 6).

Socio-economic and political transformations have also affected identity politics. Autonomy from Baghdad has invigorated the Kurdish sense of nationhood with a positive development in the form of autonomy and governmental institutions. The popular discourse in Kurdistan rapidly became dominated by notions of Kurdishness, Kurdish nationalism and, even more, the right to statehood possessed by all Kurds in the region. Kurdish ethno-nationalism remains significant and distinct from an Iraqi identity. It has changed to accommodate the economic constraints and opportunities that have shaped the region over the past decade, particularly after 2003. The KRG's self-confidence is boosted by international oil magnates rushing in to explore and produce Kurdistan hydrocarbons—bringing with them not only the technological inputs but also the much needed legitimacy for the quasi-independent Kurdish entity (Candar 2015).

The Status of Kirkuk

Kirkuk's citizens—specifically its Kurds and Turkomans—had been victims of an ethnic cleansing, expulsion, and 'Arabisation' campaign carried out by the Baathist regime during the three and a half decades of its absolute rule. Under Saddam's dictatorship, enforcing Arab supremacy became government policy. Kirkuk suffered numerous mass expulsions, destruction of its rural areas and agriculture and the seizure and diversion of the revenues from natural resources to no benefit of the local peoples. No reliable population census has been taken in Kirkuk since 1957. This census, by the Iraqi Ministry of Interior, recorded language-speakers according to mother-tongue. It showed that Kurds were the largest ethnicity (48 to 49 percent) in the Kirkuk governorate in 1957 (O' Leary 2005: 83-87). Kirkuk has been ignored by the central government in Baghdad; neither has it benefited from the economic boom in the north.

In April 2003, Coalition forces and the Iraqi Kurdish *peshmerga* liberated Kirkuk from Baathist control. The liberation of Kirkuk has encouraged thousands of Kurds to return to their original lands which has led to new territorial conflicts between Kurds, Arab and Turkoman populations (Talabany 2007: 77). Since the US invasion, Kirkuk is the only large city that has been contested by the KRG and the rest of Iraq. As in Mosul, the Kurds established control over Kirkuk in 2003. The two Kurdish parties spearheaded a military push toward Kirkuk and encouraged residents expelled by Saddam's Arabisation policies to return (Cagaptay 2008: 14). Turkomans and Arabs have interpreted the Kurds' behaviour as a land grab at their expense. The Kurds' demand for the "normalisation" (the redrawing of boundaries and resettlement of previous residents) of Kirkuk province, as stipulated by Article 140,[41] to be followed by a census and a referendum on the city's future, constitutes the core of the conflict. Kirkuk was the scene of enormous crimes and injustice. For this reason, and in the light of the acknowledgment of these crimes against humanity, Article 140 of the Iraqi Constitution (approved by 79% of Iraq's voters) made provision for reparation for the citizens of Kirkuk who had been victims of the former regime. Article 140 of Iraq's constitution, enacted in 2005, provided that a referendum on Kirkuk would be held no later than December 31, 2007 (Washington Kurdish Institute 2007: 4-7). However, the referendum has been delayed because of the lack of necessary preparations. The KRG faces opposition from Arabs and Turkish-speaking Turkomans and from neighbouring countries, especially Turkey. The Turkomans, supported by Turkey, argue that Kirkuk is historically a Turkoman city. The Kurds claim the Kirkuk province based on their majority status in the Province before Saddam's campaign of deportation and his alteration of provincial boundaries to emphasise Kirkuk's 'Arab' character.[42] The dispute centres on the potential for Kurdish independence and also on answering the question of 'who will control the oil'. Many Iraqis as well as neighbouring states do not want the city of Kirkuk and its adjacent oil fields, the second largest oil producing region of Iraq (10% of Iraq's overall oil reserves of about 112 billion barrels), to be incorporated into the KRG. They worry that oil wealth and autonomy would create further momentum for independence (Katzman 2009: 7).

US officials estimate that after the fall of Saddam, as many as 3,50,000 Kurds moved into Kirkuk to strengthen the Kurds' vote there. In addition, there is a substantial Turkoman minority in Kirkuk which has claims to the city. Turkey is said to be seeking protection of the Turkoman minority and also the denial to the Iraqi Kurds the control of the city; a result which could give the Kurds enough economic strength to support a drive for outright independence (Kaztman and Prados 2005: 6). At present, the Kurds make up a little over 50 percent of Kirkurk population, while Sunnis account for 32 to 35 percent and Turkomans have 13 to 14 percent (Ignatius 2015). The Kurds regard Kirkurk as part of their ancestral homeland.

Problems arose in 2007 between Barzani and the Turkish President Recep Tayyip Erdogan over the issue of Iraq's oil-rich city of Kirkuk, which is viewed as an economic and political stronghold for Iraqi Kurdistan. According to an article in the *International Harald Tribune*, Barzani issued warnings to Turkey not to get involved in discussions over the future of Kirkuk. Any such involvement, Barzani said, and Iraqi Kurds would interfere in the Kurdish areas of southeastern Turkey. These threats were not well received by Erdogan who suggested that there would be a price to pay if Iraqi Kurds were to involve themselves in southeastern Turkey.[42] Turkey, a diehard opponent of any move to extend Kurdish autonomy, has kept up its pressure on its US ally for the city's status to be left unchanged.

Unless a legitimate solution is formulated by the Iraqi government, together with the United States and the UN, Kirkuk stands ready to explode into inter-ethnic conflict (Paley 2008). But for the Kurds, seizing Kirkuk from ISIS gives opportunity to regain access to significant oil resources. It also put an end to years of dispute with the central government of Iraq over the implementation of Article 140 which seeks normalisation for Kirkurk's multi-ethnic population (Kajjo 2014). Securing the annexation of this oil-rich region would put the KRG in a more powerful position.

The Kurdistan Regional Government's Call for Referendum

No other region in the Middle East has experienced more profound and positive changes in recent history than the Kurdish region of northern Iraq. The Kurds have been fighting for autonomy for most of their existence; their issues are quickly gaining more recognition on the international stage. The region has seen several major advances as regards their cause and now maintains an autonomous government in northern Iraq while becoming an important player in regional affairs (Dosky 2013: 1).

The Arab Spring, 2011, has realigned political balance and has enhanced the Kurdish nationalist movements. The conflicts in Iraq and the rise of the Islamic State of Iraq and al-Sham (ISIS) which occupies a large area of Iraq poses a threat to the KRG. The existence of international oil companies has also put the Kurdistan Region on the radar of global politics. Oil has raised Kurdistan's international political and economic standing. With Iraq mired in unprecedented turmoil, which has seen swathes of territory fall to the ISIS, the Kurds in northern Iraq have expressed deep disappointment about Baghdad's move.

The President of the KRG in July 2014 has called on the Kurdish Parliament in Arbil to work on fixing a date for a referendum on independence (Salih 2014). According to Barzani, United Sates and Turkey are unlikely to oppose the declaration of an independent Kurdish state. The veteran Kurdish leader said that the Baghdad government of Prime Minister Nouri-al-Maliki was largely to blame for the crisis in Iraq and that it had ignored the KRG warning about the rise of the ISIS.[43] The referendum would be held in areas contested by both the Kurdish and the Iraqi governments on whether the local populations wanted to join Kurdistan or be under the federal government's control in Baghdad. Then in the next phase, a general referendum on independence from Baghdad would take place in areas under the Kurdish government's control. Disputed areas include large swathes of energy-rich land that spreads across four northern and central provinces in Iraq including Kirkurk (Salih 2014). However, Iraqi Prime Minister Nouri al-Maliki is against this attempt by the KRG to hold the independence referendum saying that the move is unconstitutional. The Iraqi premier has emphasised that the Kurdish region is part of Iraq and must act within the boundaries of the country's constitution.[44] The KRG move for referendum on independence was supported by Israel. On June 29, 2014, Israeli Prime Minister Benjamin Netanyahu expressed support for the creation of an independent Kurdish state describing the Kurds as a fighting people who have committed themselves to political moderation (Tripathi 2014). Israel is the only democratic state in the region and an independent Kurdistan would create a balance in favour for Israel's geopolitical dynamics in the region.

Kurdish Regional Government and the ISIS

Like other nation-states in the region, Iraqi Kurdistan was borne out of conflict. The Kurdish Regional Government is a parliamentary democracy within the Federated Republic of Iraq. The KRG has jurisdiction over three provinces, Erbil, Duhok and Sulaymaniyah. After the collapse of the Iraqi Army security in the region and the current occupation by ISIS forces, the KRG gained de facto jurisdiction over an additional three provinces--Diyala, Nineveh and Kirkurk.[45] With the ISIS invasion and occupation of large swathes of land in Iraq as well as in Syria, KRG has been defending against ISIS's intention to establish an "Islamic Caliphate" in the region. KRG is providing its Peshmerga's with sufficient resources and training to defend Iraqi Kurdistan. ISIS is also facing airstrikes by the US- led coalition and by Russia, which has sent warplanes to support the Syrian government. Iraq's armed forces recapturing the western city in December 2015 paved the way for an assault on Mosul, ISIS de facto capital in Iraq. ISIS oil export routes are closed denying the group of a crucial source of income and foreign currency. The ISIS's future in its self-proclaimed "Caliphate" over the few years might depend on whether it can put forward its strategy from moving westward into regime-controlled areas in Syria as it loses momentum in Iraq especially in Kurdish dominated areas. Iraqi Kurdish Peshmerga emerged as strong force fighting the ISIS. ISIS lost many of its "control zones" along the Syrian-Turkish border in 2015 that came at the expense of the region's highly capable YPG. In Iraq, ISIS was expelled from Mount Singjar in the country's north, cutting off the group's supply line between Iraqi and Syrian Kurdish areas. ISIS has lost territory around Tikrit and Kirkurk, the two crucial cities in eastern Iraq. Counter offensive by Iraqi and Kurdish armed forces supported by the US-led coalition, and by Iran-backed Shiite militias have forced ISIS militants out several cities including Tikrit, north of Baghdad, Ramadi, and to the West of Iraq (Rosen, 2016). On 25 May 2016, ISIS militants lost control of the city of Fallujah but might be able to launch spectacular attacks in Lebanon and on the Jordan border. Iraqi Security Forces (ISF) cleared the city of Fallujah with support from coalition airstrikes (Forrest, 2016). Gradually, ISIS's ability to make strategic influenced lessen losing its vital territory in the region. There is possibility that ISIS will look to gain a foothold in Lebanon, a perennially unstable country with a weak state and no majority religious groups. With the offensive from Kurdish forces led by US airstrikes and Russian strategic support, ISIS is gradually losing its control in the West Asian region.

Conclusion

The Kurds had lived in and successfully governed an autonomous 'safe haven' in northern Iraq for more than a decade. The Kurdistan Regional Government (KRG), a unified organisation at the beginning of the 1990s, could not sustain and was divided in two separate systems. The joint system of the first and second cabinets brought together two political parties which were separated by the quest of power. Furthermore, the joint system was of concern to neighbouring states as the de facto state also possessed a structure of governance which had the potential to promote the Kurdish national movement in a unified manner. This was unappealing for Turkey, Syria and Iran as well as for Iraq itself. The result of the collapse into conflict in 1994 was a direct manifestation of the internal and external factors. However, the divided system of government which characterised Iraqi Kurdistan since 1996 was responsible to a significant degree for the maintenance of a fragile peace. In addition, the socio-political tensions created by having both sides could address the domestic affairs of the de facto state in more efficient way, without worrying about the activities of their counterparts. Active mediation by the United States and other outside parties helped keep the two main Kurdish parties working together for their shared goal of ousting Saddam Hussein despite occasional setbacks and outbreaks of intra-Kurdish violence.

Since 2002, Iraqi Kurdistan has benefited from the establishment of a unified system of governance. The credit for the progress enjoyed by the people of Iraqi Kurdistan was shared between the international community and the Kurdistan Regional Government. The creation of a protected, autonomous region encouraged the transfer of peoples' ideas and resources to Iraqi Kurdistan—all of which helped advance the notion of Kurdish self-rule. The Kurdish region has a complex and rich political culture, but its politics is also bound to its relations with Baghdad and the outside world. Since the fall of the Saddam regime, Kurdish politicians have also been well-represented in the various transitional governments. The Kurds played a critical role in the Iraqi national policy and retained their own relationship with the outside world. Despite a recent past marked by the state violence of the Saddam Hussein regime against Kurds and other communities as well as an internal civil war (1994–1998), the Kurdish region has optimistically undertaken a rapid process of social and political normalisation. The KRG made a notable progress in addressing the critical needs of its people. The public interest remained the KRG's primary preoccupation. The development of the political party system in Iraqi Kurdistan is best described as being characterised as a punctuated equilibrium, with the steady development of the system being changed by extraordinary events. The election of a Kurd as the new Iraqi President and the establishment of a federal government in Iraqi Kurdistan have implications for regimes throughout the Kurdish regions—endorsing the feasibility of peaceful, state-based solutions to the Kurdish issue and challenging the legitimacy of the repressive policies practised against the Kurds by Iran, Syria and Turkey. Peaceful co-existence amongst the communities in Kurdistan strengthens democratic experiments as well. There is a genuine freedom of religion and movement throughout the region, making for a truly unique experience. Thus, the Kurdish political histories, which may be termed as guerrilla movements, have developed to political groupings which have become a successful democratic political movement. The KRG with its own parliament, army, flag, language and economy (with a big wealth of oil wells) is likely to hold a referendum for independence.

Notes

1. See the 'Washington Kurdish Institute' website <http://www.kurd.org/> for links to human rights organisations that have documented the ethnic cleansing, Arabisation campaign against the Kurds of Iraq as well as the Anfal campaign and the use of chemical and biological weapons on Kurdish towns and villages, including Halabja. See also "The March 16 Chemical Attack on Halabja", (Online: web), Accessed 13 May 2010, URL: http://hrw.org/reports/1993/

iraqanfal/ ANFAL3.htm. Also see, "Genocide in Iraq: The Anfal Campaign Against Kurds" (July 1993).

2. See, "Kurdish Independence from Iraq in Five Years, KRG Advisor Says", RUDAW, 25 January 2014, URL: http://rudaw.net/english/kurdistan/25012014, Accessed 28 July 2014.
3. For detail of the UNSRC 688 see, United Nations (1996), *The United Nations and the Iraq-Kuwait Conflict: 1990-1996*, Department of Public Information Vol. 9, New York: 199. Also see UNSRC 688(1991), Adopted by the Security Council at its 2982nd meeting on 5 April 1991, (Online: web), Accessed 2 June, URL: htt://www/fas.org/news/un/iraq/sres/sres0688.htm
4. The word is religious in origin; it is the name of the eighth *sura*, or chapter of the Koran. In this *sura* the Arabic word '*al-anfal*' means 'spoils' as in the spoils of war. It was the code name given by the Iraqi government to its policy of ethnic cleansing in the three northern governorates of Iraq in 1987–88.
5. *Iran Times*, April 12, 1991, cited in Entessar, Nader (1992), *Kurdish Ethnonationalism*, Boulder: Lynne Rienner Publishers, 146.
6. For details of the Resolution 687 (1991), 2 March 1991, see Weller, M (ed.) (1993), *Iraq and Kuwait: The Hostilities and Their Aftermath*, Cambridge International Document Series, Cambridge, Grotius Publications Ltd. Vol.3, 7-12.
7. For details see, Bengio, Ofra (1998), *Saddam' World: Political Discourse in Iraq*, Oxford: Oxford University Press.
8. For details of the UNSRC 686 see, United Nations (1996), *The United Nations and the Iraq-Kuwait Conflict: 1990-1996*, Department of Public Information Vol.9, New York: 182-183.
9. For details see, Kurdistan Regional Government (4 July 2005), "A Brief History of Iraqi Kurdistan: The Kurds and Kurdistan", (Online: web), Accessed 22 October 2006 URL: http://www.krg.org/articles/article_detail.asp?
10. For details see, "Kurdistan Regional Government" (15 October, 2002), *Kurdistan Today*, (Online: web), Accessed 8 June 2007, URL: http://www.old.krg.org/docs/KT021015_full.asp
11. For details see, "Kurdish Regional Government" (21 May 2009), *UK Border Agency*, Country of Origin Information.
12. See, Kurdistan Regional Government (KRG), "About the Kurdistan Regional Government", (Online: web), Accessed 5 June 2007, URL: hhtp://www.krg.org/articles/article_detail.asp?RubricNr=93&AricleNr=48&LangNr=12&L....
13. See, " Kurdish Regional Government", URL: http://dfr.krg.org/p/p aspx?p=88&l=12&s=030400&r=403, Accessed 28 July 2014.
14. See, *Constitution of Federal Republic of Iraq*, Official Documents, (Online: web), Accessed 11 July 2010, URL: http://www.krp.org/eng/documents/default.aspx?gid=1&sm=7
15. For details see, Kurdistan Regional Government (4 July 2005), "A Brief History of Iraqi Kurdistan: The Kurds and Kurdistan", (Online: web), Accessed 22 October 2006, http://www.krg.org/articles/article_detail.asp?
16. For details see, "The Kurdish Inauguration of Eight Cabinet 26 June 2014, URL: http://www.krg.at/en/achtes-kabinett-angelobt/, Accessed 31 July 2014.
17. PKK (Kuridistan Workers Party) was founded by Abdullah Ocalan. The policies of the Turkish military, regional developments in Iraq and Iran which consolidated Kurdish separatism led

to the PKK launching an armed uprising to defeat the Turkish state in 1984. The PKK's main goal was to destabilise Turkey and create an independent Kurdish state.

18. An opposition political party in Iraq. It was a multi-party coalition-based political party. Ahmad Chalabi was its President. The INC played a crucial role in toppling Saddam Hussein.
19. For details of the agreement see, Cordesman and Ahmed (1997), *Iraq: Sanctions and Beyond,* Boulder: Westview Press. pp. 82-83.
20. For detail see, Military, "Kurdistan Democratic Party (KDP)", (Online: web), Accessed 27 February 2007, URL: http:// www.globalsecurity.org/military/world/para/kdp.htm/
21. Human Rights Watch, March 2002, as cited in Natasha Carver (2002), "Is Iraq/ Kurdistan a State such that it can be said to Operate State Systems and thereby Offer Protection to its 'Citizens'?" *International Journal of Refugee Law,* 14 (1):72.
22. Kurdish Alliance was made up of the two main Kurdish parties: the Patriotic Union of Kudistan and the Kurdish Democratic Party.
23. See, "Iraq's Kurdistan Islamic Group to Join Mainstream Kurdish Bloc", (Online: web), Accessed 7 June 2010, http://www.mowr.krg.org/article/detail.asp?lngnr=12&smap=02010200&rnr=73&anr=1278
24. For details of the Agreement see, Stansfield, Gareth (2003), *Iraqi Kurdistan: Political Development and Emergent Democracy,* London: Routledge Curzon, p.100-102.
25. Also see, "Kurdistan Regional Government" (15 October, 2002), *Kurdistan Today,* (Online: web), Accessed 8 June 2007, URL: http://www.old.krg.org/docs/KT021015_full.asp
26. See, Refugees International (21 November 2003), "Iraq: A Status Report on Refugees and Displaced Persons, (Online:web), Accessed 11 June 2010, http://www.refugeesinternational.org/content/article/detail/1552/
27. The US Administrator to Iraq charged with overseeing the country's reconstruction after the 2003 invasion.
28. For details of the resolution see, UNSC Resolution 1511(2003), adopted by the Security Council at its 4844th meeting on 16 October 2003: New York, URL: http://www.un.org/Docs/sc/unsc_resolutions03.html
29. It refers to the inclusion of representatives of all ethno-religious groups and the creation of mutual checks and balances to avoid the tyranny of large ethnic or majority groups. For a detailed analysis of the Consociational theory see, Lijphart, Arend (1969), "Consociational Democracy", *World Politics,* 21(2): 206-225 and Lijphart, Arend (2003), "Consociational Democracy" in Robert Dahl et al (ed), *The Democracy Source Book,* Massachusetts: MIT Press,142-146.
30. For details of the Resolution see, UNSC Resolution 1546(2004), Adopted by the Security Council at its 4987th meeting, on 8 June 2004, New York, URL: http://www.un.org/Docs/sc/unsc_resolutions04.html
31. The Independent Electoral Commission of Iraq announced the official results of the referendum on October 25, 2005. 78.59 percent of the voters voted for the Constitution. The Sunnis voted overwhelmingly against, but did not meet the two-thirds 'no vote' in the three provinces necessary for defeating it.
32. Article 58 of the Transitional Administrative Law (TAL) contains provisions regarding the future of Kirkuk that were maintained in the new constitution. The text of the TAL can be

obtained from the CPA website: http://cpa-iraq.org/government/TAL.htm. The final status of the city and its possible incorporation into the Kurdish federal area was to be determined by the end of 2007.

33. "Kurdistan Regional Government, Kurdistan Regional Government Unification Agreement", 21 January 2006, (Online: web), Accessed 15 June 2010, URL:http://www.krg.org/articles/article_detail.asp?LangNr=12&RubricNr=107&ArticleNr=8891&LNNr=28&RNNr, Also see, Kurdistan Regional Unification Agreement, 21 January 2010, (Online: web), Accessed 15 June 2010, http://www.unhcr.org/refworld/docid/469cdd7a2.html
34. "Kurdistan Regional Government", (Online: web), Accessed 15 June 2010, URL: http://www.worldlingo.com/ma/enwiki/en/kurdistan_Regional_Government#KRG_role_in_Iraq
35. For details see "Members of the Kurdish Regional Government" (Online: web) Accessed 15 June 2010, URL: http://www.krg.org/articles/detail.asp?rnr=159&lngnr=12&anr=10938&smap=04060000. Also see "The Members of the Previous and Fourth Cabinet, Which was in Office from 1999 to Early 2006". (Online: web) Accessed 15 June 2010, URL:,n http://www.krg.org/articles/detail.asp?rnr=159&lngnr=12&anr=10938&smap=04 060000 For list of the Cabinet see, Appendix 1.
36. Elgebeily, Sherif, "Kurdistan: Federalism, Sovereignty and Independence", Interview by Leonhardt van Efferink, September 2009, (Online: web), Accessed 7 June 2010 ,URL: http://www.exploringgeopolitics.org/Interview_Elgebeily_Sherif_Kurdistan_Sovereignty_Independence_Kurdish_Regional_Government_Federalism_Constitution.html
37. "Kirkurk: Kurds' Bottomline in Coalition Talks", *Middle East Online*, (Online: web), Accessed 14 June 2010, http://www.middle-east-online.com/english/?id=12896.
38. For details see, "Kurdish Regional Investment Law (July 2006)", (Online: web), Accessed 15 June 2010, URL: http://www.krg.org/articles/detail.asp?lngnr=12&smap=04030000&rnr=107&anr=12626.
39. Also see, Hasan, Omar and Ben Lando (16 November 2007), "Iraqi Kurds Oils Deals Provoke Conflict with Baghdad", *Middle East Online*, (Online: web), Accessed 13 June 2010 URL: http://www.alternet.org/world/68140/
40. For details of Article 140, see Appendix 2.
41. See, "Kirkuk: Kurds' Bottomline in Coalition Talks", *Middle East Online*, (Online: web), Accessed 14 June 2010, http://www.middle-east-online.com/english/?id=12896.
42. See, "KDP", (Online: web), Accessed 23 December 2010, URL: http://www.globalsecurity.org/military/world/para/kdp.htmrkey. Accessed 15 June 2010.
43. For details see, "Barzani: America, Turkey will not Block Kurdish Independence", RUDAW, 6 July 2014, URL: http://rudaw.net/english/kurdistan/060720141, Accessed 28 July 2014.
44. For details see, "Kurdistan Independence from Iraq Illegal: Analyst", 31 July 2014, URL: http://www.presstv.com/detail/2014/07/05/369954/iraq-kurdistan-separation-illegal/, Accessed 31 July 2014. Human Right Watch and Middle East Watch, Report: New York, Analyst", (Online: web), Accessed 31 July 2014, URL: http://www.presstv.com/detail/2014/07/05/369954/iraq-kurdistan-separation-illegal/;
45. See, "KRG: Kurdistan Regional Government" *The Kurdish Project*, URL: http://thekurdishproject.org/history-and-culture/kurdish-democracy/krg-kurdistan-regional-government/, Accessed 20 August 2016

CHAPTER 3

The Kurdish Conflict in Turkey

Turkey remains the most interesting country from a Kurdish point of view. The Kurdish question is arguably the most serious internal problem in the Turkish republic's history and certainly the main obstacle to its aspirations of full integration with the European Union. It is the only country which has a relatively open political process; although, limited and precarious. Most Westerners define the problem simply as a matter of oppression and denial of rights of an ethnic minority (the Kurds) by a majority (the Turks). The civil war in southeastern Turkey is viewed as a national liberation movement and enjoys widespread sympathy both in the West and in the Third World. The Turkish political elites promote an entirely different view of the problem, which is often misunderstood and ridiculed in the West. In the official Turkish discourse, there is no Kurdish problem but rather a socio-economic problem in the southeastern region and a problem of terrorism that is dependent upon external support from foreign states and aimed at weakening Turkey. In reality, neither the official Turkish view nor the dominant Western perception holds up to close scrutiny (Cornell 2001: 31). A deeper study of the problem reveals its extreme complexity with a number of facets and dimensions that tend to obscure the essentials of the conflict. David Laitin who has analysed ethnic and national group identity formation argues that people's identities become prone to shifts; they become especially responsive to state policy and discourse; to the identity strategies or projects offered by competing socio-political leaders; to the political-economic advantage of different identity strategies and to in-group and out-group social pressures (Laitin 1998).

The Kurdish population is estimated in the range of 10 to 20 percent. This puts them in a stronger position than other minorities to maintain their language and culture (Smith 2001: 46). However, Turkey has severely repressed cultural and linguistic expressions of the Kurds. Turkey appears to have a more complex political and economic structure than Iraq, Iran or Syria. The Kurdish areas have consistently lagged behind the rest of Turkey in terms of economic development, largely due to the preservation of the tribal structures and negligence by the central government. The Kurds have entered the Turkish society at many levels. In an electoral system, the numerical potential of the Kurds has acquired great importance. However, the pressure on the ruling authorities engendered by political participation including parliamentary representation as well as external pressures from the Western world with respect to human rights has led to a weakening and subversion of the rules denying the Kurds their identity.

The end of the Cold War renewed the attention on Turkey's role as a democratic model, forcing a succession of Turkish state representatives into the awkward position of trying to explain to the international community why Turkish democracy necessitated a repression of the Kurdish political identity. The Kurdish problem with the rise of the PKK in the aftermath of the Gulf War adversely affected Turkey's relations with a host of states in the region as well as the EU. Domestically, reconciling an espousal of democratic principles with the suppression of the Kurdish political and social expression also became increasingly difficult (Watts 1999: 635). During the 1990s, Turkey witnessed the rising consciousness and politicisation of the Kurdish identity; the surging visibility of the Kurdish category within the mainstream public political discourse. The failure to accommodate Kurdish ethnicity and culture has been an important fact that has led to the deaths of thousands of civilians and the displacement of people as well as several hundreds of human rights violations. This failure has also caused many governments and international political actors to be drawn into the conflict between Turkey and the Kurds. As a result, the Kurdish question has become internationalised and has come to dominate a significant proportion of Turkey's foreign policy with issues such as Turkey's membership of the European Union (EU) and its regional implications. The ascent of Turkish nationalism is viewed as the major antagonist by the Kurdish rebel movement, the Kurdistan Workers' Party (PKK) in particular and by the Kurdish nationalists in general (Bruinessen 2000c: 91-95).

The Origins of the Kurdish Problem in Turkey

Kurdish nationalism first began to stir with the collapse of the Ottoman Empire at the end of World War I and the emergence of modern Turkey under Mustafa Kemal Ataturk. The Lausanne Conference of 1923 not only established the present boundaries of the Turkish republic, but also settled the ethnic problem once and for all by permitting a special status to non-Muslim minorities. The concurrence of the politics of Westernisation and that of nationalism culminated in the gradual erosion of the role of Islam in the organisation of Ottoman politics and administration (Yegen 1999: 559). When Kemal Ataturk first began to create a Turkish nation-state after World War I, it was not clear what constituted a Turk. Ismet Inonu's[1] initial formula for a modern Turkey consisted of a homeland of "Kurds and Turks" (Harris 1977: 115). However, the creation of a secular and purely Turkish state was nurtured on the Kemalist ideology of republican Turkey's national unity and territorial integrity which sprang from the trauma of the gradual disintegration of the Ottoman Empire (Brown 1995: 117). The Kurdish contributions to the War of Independence are well-known. In the Kurdish inspired Kocgiri revolt of 1920–22 against the Kemalist forces, the leader of the revolt was Alisan. The revolt's aim was to create a Kurdish state in the areas where the Kurds were a majority. Ataturk at first tried to co-opt the rebellion, but the revolt was suppressed (Barkey and Fuller 1997: 62). Kurdish troops played an indispensable role in the over-all nationalist victory. Following the nationalist victory, a series of steps were taken in an attempt to eliminate the Kurdish presence in the new republic of Turkey through legal fiat and gradual assimilation. For example in March 1924, a decree banned all Kurdish schools, organisations, publications and *medresses*, which were a source of education for most Kurds (Gunter 1997: 5). The Turks fiercely and successfully refused to extend minority status to any part of its Muslim population which included the Kurds (Gunduz 2001: 25). Between 1925 and 1937, the Kurds launched three rebellions against the autocratic regime of Ataturk. The Kurdish uprising in 1925 under Sheikh Said[2] led to Ankara's reinstatement of independent tribunals, which gave enormous powers to the local military and other state officials to judge and execute dissidents or rebels. These tribunals were also used to eliminate some of the potential Kurdish opposition. The revolt was suppressed; Sheikh Said and many others were sent to the gallows. The state's reaction to this revolt was repeated in the subsequent and more serious revolts of Agri (Ararat) from 1926–30 and Dersim (Tunceli) in 1937, as well as in numerous other lesser but almost endemic rebellions. Deportations of Kurds to the West began after the Sheikh Said rebellion was crushed in 1925 (Barkey and Fuller

1997: 63). The process of assimilation gained momentum after the revolts of 1925. The government forbade the use of Kurdish language in public places. The Turks were resettled in Kurdish areas. The purpose was to dilute the Kurdish population in order to facilitate its assimilation. However, a lack of resources hampered Ankara from fully carrying out the government's policy of assimilation. The Kurdish areas were declared a military zone forbidden to foreigners (Bruinessen 1992a: 281). The Republic of Turkey had become an authoritarian, one-party regime. There was no cohesive Kurdish leadership that could exert significant pressure on Ankara. However, there are debates whether uprisings were religious or ethnic as the nature of the revolt included both religious and ethnic characteristics (Gurbey 1996: 13; Gunter 1997).

During the 1930s the basic principles of Kemalism were laid down: republicanism, secularism, nationalism and populism. A personality cult began to grow around Ataturk that presented him as the father, saviour and teacher of the nation. An extreme form of Turkish nationalism with its associated historical myths developed that had no place for Kurdish awareness. During the 1937 rebellion, the Kurds attacked several key military posts and killed hundreds of soldiers and the Turkish state erased the villages of the province Dersim from the map and renamed it Tunceli. These three rebellions against the young and inexperienced republic created a cumulative image of the Kurdish people as socially tribal, religious, fanatic, economically backward and most important—a threat to the national integrity of the Turkish state (Yavuz and Gunter 2001: 34). The Turkish republic did not deny the existence of the Kurds but instead developed a new discourse to speak of them without pronouncing the word 'Kurd' in the ethno-national sense.[3] The concepts of 'Kurd' and 'Kurdistan' were abolished from the Turkish vocabulary and the use of Kurdish words was prohibited. The Kurds were referred to as 'Mountain Turks' (Chaliand (ed) 1980: 68).

Throughout the Kemalist period, political space became ethnically restricted. The Kurds, could not speak their language, celebrate national holidays or mobilise as an ethnic group. After Ataturk ethnicised and liberalised the Turkish state, instead of trying to create a sense of Kurdish–Turkish partnership, the then Prime Minister Adnan Menderes, leader of the Democratic Party, made no changes in the official ideology of Turkish citizenship. He emphasised Turkish greatness in his campaign and upheld the fight against subversive ideologies such as communism which was linked to Kurdish nationalism. However by the 1950s, Turkey turned toward the West and engaged in a democratisation process which resulted in a more expansive political space. In February 1956, the Grand National Assembly ratified laws that called for secret ballot elections, political party representation and an independent judicial system. Interest groups became active giving rise to a Turkish civil society. An increased complex space created greater diversity in the manifestation of Kurdish political identities including nationalism (Natali 2005: 97). The Kurdish identity itself was secularised and transformed within the broader leftist movement in Turkey in the 1960s and 1970s. With the spread of universal education and the socio-political liberalisation introduced by the 1961 Constitution, modern intellectuals rather than tribal and religious leaders began to shape the Kurdish identity. Besides Turkey's official ideology, Kemalism remained a set of eclectic principles and aspirations aimed at legitimising the hegemony of the Turkish republican elite. Kemalist nationalism has served the dual function of forging a nation-state out of the multi-ethnic remnants of the Ottoman Empire and combating all claims of disparate ethnic identities (Kurkcu 1996: 3). Republican Turkey's Kurdish policy was outlined by Ataturk, the nationalist founder of a modern Turkey, and has been followed by his successors. In their quest to build a 'modern state' the Kemalists[4] decided to emulate the 'homogeneous' states of the West. They were more interested in building the centre at the expense of the periphery. The Kurds as a result, were regulated to the minor role of errant Turks. Expressions of Kurdish nationalist thought as well as language and culture were severely repressed (Barkey and Fuller 1998: 11-12). In fact, no country has been as preoccupied with the eradication of Kurdish national identity as Turkey.

In 1965, the Kurdistan Democratic Party of Turkey (KDPT), an explicitly Kurdish organisation, was formed in Diyarbakir. The KDPT programme included an explicit demarcation of 'Kurdistan' with Kurdish as the official language, an exclusively Kurdish government bureaucracy, proportional Kurdish representation in Turkey's parliament and economic investment. Another major development was the establishment of the Revolutionary Cultural Society of the East (DDKO was its Turkish acronym) in 1969—the first organisational attempt to raise the consciousness of the Kurdish population by stressing Turkey's uneven economic development. The other path of Kurdish political engagement was through the leftist Workers' Party of Turkey (*Turkiye Isci Partisi* or TIP). The Turkish government's alarm at the revival of Kurdish nationalism increased following the March 1970 autonomy agreement between Baghdad and the Kurdish Democratic Party led by Mustafa Barzani (Kutschera 1994: 13). Between 1971 and 1973, diverse Kurdish cultural associations such as the Revolutionary Democratic Cultural Association organised regular teachings to raise Kurdish nationalism and mobilised youth in the name of social justice and identity (Yavuz and Gunter 2001: 35). This mobilisation polarised society and led to communal violence. To stop the violence, the Turkish military carried out a coup in 1971. The coup identified Kurdish nationalism, along with radical Islam, as a divisive force and banned all forms of cultural expression. The military government proceeded to outlaw leftist Turkish as well as Kurdish organisations including the TIP and DDKO and imprison many of their cadres. The prisons functioned as schools and the period spawned explicitly Kurdish leftist groupings including the Socialist Party of Kurdistan in Turkey. In their monthly bulletin, the DDKO wrote mainly about the economic problems of eastern Turkey, the oppression of Kurdish villagers by Kurdish landlords and tribal leaders and the brutal violent behaviour of the Turkish army units in Kurdish villages. The 1970s and early 1980s were also a period of ferment in which Kurdish leftist-nationalist formations experienced factionalisation (Bruinessen 1984: 8; Kutschera 1994: 13).

The policy of forced assimilation remained as a basic Kemalist policy until 1991 (Kurkcu 1996: 3).

Turkey's policies toward the Kurdish nationalist movement became more discernible in the aftermath of the Gulf War, for Turkey

- Supported the KDP and PUK in northern Iraq;
- Compelled the KDP and PUK to stop all support of the PKK and other Kurdish nationalist organisations in Turkey;
- Separated the Kurdish nationalist groups of Turkey and Iraq as much as possible, even to the extent of creating *cordon sanitaria* by demolishing and evacuating a Kurdish village close to the Iraqi border. This no-man's land would be similar to the one Iraq created along its Turkish and Iranian borders in the 1980s;
- To use whatever military force was necessary for eliminating the PKK in northern Iraq and within Turkey;
- To provide political avenues to the Kurds in Turkey to create political parties and to participate more fully in the political process;
- To marginalise the Kurds as much as possible within the political system after they had agreed to accept its legitimacy;

- To allow a continued emphasis on Islam in order to co-opt part of the Kurdish population and to reduce the appeal of the leftist parties to its legitimacy;
- To improve the standard of living of the Kurds in south-eastern Turkey through increased industrialisation (Olson 1991: 496).

The Rise of the Kurdish Workers' Party

Kurdish rebellions before World War II had a strong tribal and religious character that often overshadowed the national component, but in the postwar period this pattern underwent a significant change. Turkey held its first multiparty election in 1950, resulting in the electoral defeat of Ataturk's Republican People's Party and a transfer of power to the centre-right Democratic Party. The new government allowed exiled sheikhs and *aghas* to return (Mcdowall 2000: 396-400). The strengthened position of the tribal leaders gave further impetus to the migration of Kurds to the urban areas of western Turkey, where many of them benefited from the increasingly market-oriented economic policies of the government. After the military coup in 1960, a new and more liberal constitution was adopted that included substantial protections for democracy, freedom of expression and human rights. Indeed, the 1961 Constitution (which was superseded in 1982) was the most liberal one that Turkey has ever had. These freedoms led to a mushrooming of leftist activity among Kurds in Turkey. During the 1970s, leftist radicalisation intensified as migration to the urban areas of western Turkey continued and enrolment in higher education increased. These parallel processes heightened an awareness of the economic and political disparities between the southeast and the rest of the country and the Kurds became socio-economically predisposed to be absorbed into the leftist climate. Gradually, the Kurdish leftists became alienated from their Turkish colleagues and formed separate political movements. Although more radical groups with various Marxist–Leninist affiliations emerged, the most prominent of them was the Workers' Party (PKK), whose public statements called attention to an oppressed Kurdish minority (Cornell 2001: 38-39). Meanwhile, the increasing stature of Mullah Mustafa Barzani and his Kurdish Democratic Party (KDP) in northern Iraq and the rise of Kurdish nationalism in Iraq had a profound effect on the more right-wing Kurdish activities in Turkey.

The PKK grew out of the anarchy and turmoil of the 1970s when a number of radical left-wing Turkish groups had emerged (Barkey and

Fuller 1998: 22-23). Abdullah Ocalan's political vision led to the creation of the Partiya Karkari Kurdistan. The emergence of the Kurdish Workers' Party (PKK, Partiya Karkari Kurdistan), also known as Apocus (after Apo, the short form of their leader Abdullah Ocalan's name), in 1974 as a revolutionary organisation in the quest for Kurdish independence marks a major phase in the evolution of the Kurdish national movement entering a stage of sustained armed struggle. The military regime which seized power in 1980 instituted some of the most regressive and repressive policies towards the Kurds including the broadening of the language restrictions. In the 1960s and 1970s, the Kurds demanded economic aid and cultural rights either through pro-Kurdish parties or by pro-Kurdish media (Krisci and Winrow 1997: 108). The PKK emerged as a well-organised force which used violence and this led to an upsurge in the fight with the government forces. This small group emerged in Ankara from the Dev Genc[5] branch and left the capital for revolutionary agitation in Kurdistan.

The 1980s' Military Rule and the Resurgence of Kurdish Identity

The 1980s represent a critical turning point because they witnessed the re-emergence of Kurdish nationalism with an unexpected strength and vehemence. The military regime which seized power in 1980 instituted some of the most regressive and repressive policies towards the Kurds. The lack or inability of political and legal institutions to secure their functioning through the established principles and within the framework established by the constitution in Turkey opened the ground for the armed forces to intervene in politics (Konuralp 2009: 102). The 1980 military coup was directed not just at the Kurds, but also at the proliferating left-wing groups which had wrought havoc on the Turkish politics. A significant segment of the leftist core, however, was made up of Kurdish activists who had made common cause with the Turkish left in the belief that the socialist revolution would free both peoples from the yoke of imperialism and repression. Not only the revolution took place but also a ferocious counteraction to the left emerged. Thousands were imprisoned and many sought refuge in the West. The Turkish left was not sympathetic to the Kurdish cause. Their disillusionment with the left and the impact of the coup convinced the Kurdish activists to start a revolution. The army underestimated the strength of and support for the PKK. Having ostracised the country's civilian policy-makers, the military views automatically became state policy.

The onset of the Iran–Iraq War (1980–1988) and eventually the Gulf War in 1991 provided the PKK with strategic depth in its confrontation with the Turkish government. In the first instance, the regime in Baghdad was forced to reduce its troop concentrations significantly in the north, creating a power vacuum. Similarly, during the much shorter Gulf conflict, Iraqi troops were thinned out of northern Iraq; a de facto Kurdish autonomous zone emerged under the protection of the US, Britain and France. The PKK benefited from the absence of a military presence which could impede its activities. On the other hand, the Turkish assumption that the Iraqi regime would be sympathetic to Ankara turned out to be negative. To impede the PKK's freedom of movement in northern Iraq, Turkey has mounted numerous military operations—land or air—across the international border (Barkey and Fuller 1998: 22-23). The organisation's ability to profit from geopolitical changes and its resilience on the ground have clearly touched a nerve within Turkey. Whether the organisation survives or not in the longer run, the fact remains that it has managed to change Turkey's foreign and domestic politics.

PKK's Goal

The Party's programme was a curious brand of Marxist–Leninism and ultra-nationalism, with the ultimate aim of establishing an independent, united Kurdistan (i.e. including the parts presently in Iran, Iraq and Syria) and thus made no secret of its pan-Kurdish aspirations. The PKK claimed that armed struggle was the only way to achieve independence (Bruinessen 1984: 11). The main agenda of the leftist Kurds was socio-economic restructuring of the southeast into a more equitable society through the dismantling of tribal institutions and the creation of a socialist system. This agenda was naturally anathema to the right-wing groups, which were closely linked to the tribal hierarchy (Cornell 2001: 39). The revolutionary goal of the PKK included a two-phased strategy in enabling the Kurdish people to realise their national and democratic rights. The first dimension of the national phase would establish an independent Kurdistan, critical for the realisation of ideals of liberation. The democratic phase or the second dimension was devised to solve the contradictions dominating the Kurdish society which include "..feudal and comprador exploitation, tribalism, religious sectarianism and the slave-like dependence of women" (Gunter 1990: 59-60). The PKK with its political agenda has divided itself into three elements: The PKK is the foremost organ. In 1985, it created the second element of National Liberation

Front of Kurdistan (ERNK) to bolster its recruitment, provide intelligence and engage in propaganda activities in Turkey and abroad. And the third element, People's Liberation Army of Kurdistan (ARGK), was formed in 1986 (Gunter 1997: 23-25). The PKK is distinguished from other Kurdish political parties by its social base which includes a sizable portion of workers and peasants. It has been open to women's participation and now claims to have thousands of women in its ranks (Hassanpour 1994: 7). Although the Party has benefited from some Syrian aid[6], it has effectively relied on the organised support of the Kurds in Kurdistan and in the diasporas.

The PKK has, since its foundation, gone through a series of tactical transformations. From the proclaimed aim of an independent, unified Kurdistan, via the aim of an independent Turkish-Kurdistan, it turned in the 1990s to the aim of establishing autonomy within the Turkish state. The PKK's intrinsic weaknesses shrank its base of popular support. In the early 2000s, the PKK declared that it was abandoning the armed struggle in order to attempt resolution through democratic means and be recognised as a political movement (Hirschler 2001: 160-161). In April 2002, at its Eighth Party Congress, the PKK changed its name to the Kurdistan Freedom and Democracy Congress (KADEK) and proclaimed a commitment to non-violent activities in support of Kurdish rights. However, the PKK/KADEK spokesman stated that its armed wing, the People's Defence Force, would not disband or surrender its weapons for reasons of self-defence[7].

Military Operations against the PKK

PKK's primary focus has been the Turkish military presence in the southeast. Using at first standard insurgency tactics against the military which was unprepared and untrained to confront such a challenge, the PKK achieved impressive results. It even engaged the Turkish military in large skirmishes, but suffered heavily. The brutal conflict led to the destruction of thousands of villages and hamlets and an internal flow of refugees. Since 1984, the struggle between the PKK and Turkey has resulted in the deaths of 37,000 people mostly in the southeastern Kurdish provinces (Barkey 1997: 4). An enormous mobilisation since 1992, costing nearly 10 billion dollars per year, has enabled the Turkish armed forces to take control of major Kurdish population centres. However, fighting the Turkish military and surviving against the efforts to eradicate it made the PKK popular among the Kurdish masses. But, the situation began to change in the mid-1990s. The

Turkish army, having apparently realised the importance of not alienating the civilian population, emphasised discipline within the ranks and initiated a public relations campaign that included the introduction of health and educational facilities for the population in the southeast. Meanwhile, the Turkish military adapted eventually and successfully to guerrilla warfare and gathered enough strength to strike the problems at its roots in northern Iraq. According to the army sources, nearly 8,000 PKK fighters were killed in 1994 and 1995 (Bozarslan 1996: 16). Since 1995, regular and massive troop incursions (sometimes involving up to 35,000 troops) and the establishment of a security zone have caused the PKK's position in northern Iraq to wither away. By 1998, the PKK's only lifeline was Syria. Spurred on by its alliance with Israel, the Turkish government felt strong enough to threaten Syria with war unless it expelled Ocalan and the PKK bases in the Bekaa Valley. Unable to rule out the prospect of Israel's joining a Turkish punitive expedition, Damascus complied and expelled Ocalan in October 1998 (Cornell 2001: 42). After the PKK forces relocated to northern Iraq, they managed to deny the Turkish state an effective control of large tracts of its southeastern territory. Subsequently, a Turkish incursion dealt a severe blow to their military capabilities (Kirisci and Winrow 1997: 161-164). However, since Ocalan's capture in 1999,[8] his unreserved submission to the Turkish authorities has damaged the PKK seriously. The PKK leadership has gone to a collection of military commanders. They are less ideological and less Marxist than Ocalan. No individual has assumed a public leadership role. After 1999, the bulk of the PKK leadership moved across the frontier into northern Iraq where the Iraqi Kurds have autonomy (Wadlow 2008: 55).

When the war on Iraq broke out in March 2003, the Turkish Parliament decided to open the Turkish airspace for United States over-flights and authorised the government to send Turkish troops into northern Iraq. Turkey seemed more of a geopolitical nuisance to the Iraqi Kurds than the United States and its allies. The US also persuaded Turkey not to invade northern Iraq (Candar 2004: 48). The US made an unequivocal distinction between the PKK and the Kurdish question. On the one hand, it did not hesitate to criticise Turkey bitterly on its human rights violations, and on the other, it remained unambiguously critical of the PKK and supported Turkey's struggle against it. The United States, for a long time, listed the PKK among the terrorist groups to be monitored. For Turkish hardliners, the US position on PKK was always in a stark contrast to the ambiguous position towards the PKK taken in Europe (Kirisci 2004: 295).

Meanwhile, the Iraqi Kurds in northern Iraq became regional political actors and Turkey's interventionist posture in the Iraqi theatre for political action, which had earned itself the image of a regional power, was restricted. An article in the *Boston Globe* articulated the perceptions of Turkey at the time when Kurdish *peshmergas* (militias) entered Kirkuk violating the 'red lines' drawn by Turkey. This exclusive Kurdish control over Kirkuk served as a pretext for Turkey to consider sending its troops to northern Iraq:

> "From the outset, the behaviour of the Kurds has been the model of an ally, and the behaviour of the Turks has been the model of the opposite—unacceptable for a fellow NATO member—and borderline suicidal for a new and shaky government facing a mountain of economic woes... Turkey has no right to play sphere-of-influence games in northern Iraq, no right to block autonomy for the Kurds in a new Iraq federation, and no right to object if Kurds seek to return home in Kirkuk and Mosul from which they were brutally evicted by Saddam Hussein" (Oliphant 2003).

After the end of the PKK ceasefire in 2004, fighting became intense and this continued till the end of 2007. A sizeable Turkish military force was then deployed along the border with Iraq. The official justification was that attacks had been carried out by the PKK units operating from inside Iraq. In late October and November 2007, Turkey launched an initial phase of military operations in northern Iraq through cross-border artillery bombardments and troop deployments in the Dohuk region. In October 2007, the Turkish Parliament reserved the right to take action against the PKK inside Iraq if neither the Iraqi government nor the KRG chose or was able to do so (Rainsford 2007). In the second phase, at the beginning of December 2007, Turkey launched a series of air strikes primarily targeting villages near the Iranian border in the northeastern Sulaymaniyah governorate. Turkey hoped that the Iraqi Kurdish *peshmergas* would confront the PKK. The *New York Times* wrote that "a large-scale Turkish intervention in northern Iraq could ignite age-old ethnic hatreds between the Turks and Kurds" (Filkins 2003). However, Turkey thus violated international law. The Geneva Convention details the necessary steps that a belligerent force must take during an armed conflict. Article 48 of the First Additional Protocol of the Geneva Conventions of 1949 states:

> "To ensure respect for and protection of the civilian population and civilian objects, the Parties to the conflict shall at all times distinguish between the civilian population and combatants and between the civilian objects and military objectives and accordingly shall direct their operations only against military objectives"(Maxwell 2004: 17).

The indiscriminate targeting of villages during air strikes and artillery bombardments violates the Geneva Conventions. The principles of necessity and proportionality are undermined by the strategic futility of the nominal aim of the campaign which is to reduce the operational capacity of the PKK by targeting its bases in Iraq. Military air raids by Turkey flouted all relevant protocol and procedure required, thus showing an utter disrespect for Iraqi sovereignty and the safety and welfare of civilians. The killing of civilians and the indiscriminate destruction of their homes and property are a gross violation of the Geneva Conventions (Kurdish Human Rights Project 2008: 5).

There were more than 60,000 Turkish troops with heavy artillery stationed near the border of south Kurdistan. Turkish troops often violated international human rights and humanitarian laws during cross-border incursions into northern Iraq. There are documented cases of mutilations and killings committed by Turkish troops in northern Iraq. Kerim Yildiz, the Kurdish Human Rights Project (KHRP) Executive Director said,

> "There must be human rights monitors on the ground to observe the military's conduct. Turkish incursions into south Kurdistan would concern Kurds in Iraq, Iran, Syria and Turkey provoking further instability in the region. History has shown us that there can be no lasting peace in the Middle East without resolving the Kurdish situation. We hope that the rights of Kurds will be guaranteed and fully recognized within the new Iraq".[9]

Evidently, the United States' primary concern regarding the Turkish attacks has been related to their scale and intensity as opposed to the outright illegitimacy of military action. Its policy appears to have been governed by the strategic calculation that the Turkish military action in Iraq occurred given the strong political pressure on Ankara to act against the PKK. The United States was also concerned about maintaining Turkey's Western orientation and energetically supported Turkey's membership in the EU. It attached great importance to Turkey's close cooperation with Israel and saw it as a key player in its dual containment policy toward Iran and Iraq (Kirisci

2004: 296). Because of Turkey being a key NATO ally of the US in the region, Washington evidently felt it necessary to accommodate Ankara on this issue. On the other hand, the US has registered its concern that a more comprehensive aerial bombardment of northern Iraq or a ground invasion would destabilise the only region of Iraq which has enjoyed a modicum of stability since 2003. Similarly, the EU has also failed to condemn Turkey's actions in an outright manner. Whatever the reasoning behind the policies of the US, EU and the wider international community towards Turkey, it is clear that Turkey's behaviour has only served to undermine the KRG's autonomy, and endanger the lives and human rights of its inhabitants, whilst yielding few logistical gains in its fight against the PKK. Turkey has co-opted the language of the 'War on Terror' in order to legitimise measures that otherwise compromise international law, state sovereignty and human rights, under the pretext of its own security concerns (Kurdish Human Rights Project 2008: 6). Rather than leading to a lasting and peaceful resolution of the root causes of Turkey's conflict in the Kurdish regions, the military action that violates international law is only likely to inflame existing tensions.

PKK–Iraqi Kurdish Relationship

At a first glance, it might be expected that since they are all Kurds, the PKK and the various Iraqi Kurdish groups would be natural allies. However, there are bitter divisions in Kurdish society. In addition, the divide-and-rule strategies of the states containing Kurdish populations have reinforced these Kurdish divisions.

At one time or another, the PKK has been allied to both the Kurdish Democratic Party (KDP) and the Patriotic Union of Kurdistan (PUK). For instance in 1983, the PKK and KDP signed an accord termed 'Principles of Solidarity' under which they each agreed to a unified commitment against "every kind of imperialism with American imperialism at the top of the list, and the struggle against the plans and plots of imperialism in the region" (Gunter 1993: 304). The agreement gave PKK transit rights and rear bases in KDP territory. Turkish military pressures after September 1983 heightened the differences between the two groups that were not overcome even by 'summit' meetings between Ocalan and Masoud Barzani in Damascus. It was then that Jalal Talabani of the Patriotic Union of Kurdistan (PUK) signed a memorandum of agreement with the PKK in May 1988. The agreement was never implemented, but at least the parties maintained 'bridges' (Kutschera 1994: 74).

The establishment of a Kurdish government in northern Iraq in June 1992 brought the contradictions between the two movements to a head. In fact, the crisis between Turkey, the Kurdish Workers' Party (PKK) and the Kurdish Regional Government of Iraq (KRG) was triggered by the two Gulf Wars of 1991 and 2003. Until the 1991 War, Turkey's main partner for fighting the PKK was the central government of Baghdad, which had agreed to its periodic hot pursuit of the PKK armed units into Iraqi territory. After the war, Turkey cooperated with the Kurdish Regional Government (KRG) as the emerging de facto sovereign in the region. This was necessary in order to ensure the return of Kurdish refugees to Iraq from Turkey. Subsequently, Turkish–KRG cooperation was deemed vital in order to employ the Iraqi Kurdish card against the PKK. For the Kurds of Iraq, they needed good relations with Turkey in order to stabilise their autonomy, as Ankara was their only lifeline to the outside world (Bengio 2007: 1). The fact that the PKK trespassed on their territory also led the KRG to desire a measure of cooperation with Turkey, to both limit the PKK and avoid massive reprisals. Often, elements of the PKK increased their activity in northern Iraq and reportedly killed local residents in an effort to control a territorial base. The infighting between the two opposing Kurdish groups in northern Iraq, the KDP and the PUK, had created an environment conducive for the PKK to consolidate itself. These groups sometimes attacked civilians, foreign relief workers and journalists (Cordesman and Hashim 1997: 85; Gunter 1996: 50-56).

A change came in the aftermath of the 2003 War, whereby the dynamics of engagement gradually drifted towards estrangement. Turkey was drawn more deeply into the vortex of West Asian politics. From the outset, Turkish leaders had strong reservations about the invasion. They had no love for Saddam Hussein, but he provided stability to Turkey's southern border. They worried that his overthrow might fragment Iraq while strengthening Kurdish nationalism, thereby jeopardising Turkey's security (Larrabee 2007: 105-106). The formation of a quasi-Kurdish state in northern Iraq emboldened the PKK—which had lost its bases in Syria—to revive its anti-Turkish activities. The Kurds of Iraq, in contrast to Turkey, unreservedly supported the Americans during the war, thus dislodging Ankara from its long-held position as the United States' incontestably preferred partner in the region (Bengio 2007: 2). Since the War on Iraq 2003, the United States has refrained from taking any measures against the PKK and its policy on the issue of PKK's terrorism has changed. There was a rift between the former close allies regarding the measures to be taken against the presence of the PKK in northern Iraq (Eligur: 2006: 6). Turkey and the KRG were now pitted against one another as they sought to shape and win US favour. With the fall of Saddam, Turkish protection was no longer necessary. The Kurds unified their administration and founded a strong bloc. Eventually, the sanctions on the Kurds were lifted. The KRG also supported a political process to achieve a comprehensive political solution to the problem of the PKK. Moreover, the KRG is economically dependent on Turkey and under any political configuration would be eager to maintain good relations with a powerful neighbour at the door steps of the EU (Somer 2004: 252; Rafaat 2007b: 294). Moreover, the Kurds found alternative ways to establish relations with the outside world by travelling abroad without returning to Turkey or to other neighbouring countries as they had done in the past.

However, both Jalal Talabani and Massoud Barzani, the leaders of the PUK and the KDP respectively, understood the military risk of tackling the PKK since they had shared common platforms in the past. They have also been restrained from taking action because they enjoy a position of at least a symbolic leadership over the Kurdistan national movement across the region (Stansfield et al, 2007: 3-4). The President of Iraq's Kurdish Regional Government, Massoud Barzani, implored the PKK to disarm and the Turkish government to make democratic changes regarding the Kurdish question while underlining that this is Turkey's domestic affair. Turkey opened a consulate in Arbil following a historic visit by Foreign Minister Davutoglu.[10] The growing economic interdependence between Turkey and the Iraqi Kurds makes it unlikely that the latter may promote Kurdish separatism in Turkey. This reduces the spectre of Kurdish irredentism and the Turkish elites' fear that Kurdish cultural–political rights may facilitate future Kurdish secession (Somer and Liaras 2010). In fact, the establishment of a de facto Kurdish state in northern Iraq under Western protection gave a new impetus to Kurdish nationalism and provided a logistical base for attacks on Turkish territory by the PKK.

There were approximately 14,000 Turkish Kurds in northern Iraq who had fled the civil strife in southeastern Turkey. The UNHCR was treating these displaced persons as refugees (Cordesman and Hashim 1997: 85). However, many supported the PKK and there was no way to tell when Turkey would attack northern Iraq. Any Iraqi Kurdish effort to build ties with the PKK would alienate Turkey and possibly lead to at least a tacit military cooperation between Turkey and Iraq in suppressing all Kurdish resistance. Moreover, the Iraqi Kurds' drive for autonomy had gained momentum. The Turkish officials were concerned that the effect of the creation of an autonomous state on Turkey's own Kurdish population posed a threat to the country's territorial integrity.

Political Support for the PKK among the Kurds

The PKK had been relatively successful in perpetuating not only its own existence, but also the armed struggle against the Turkish state. Even the Kurds, who dislike its methods or its leadership style and the reality of PKK operations, have raised the Kurdish issue at the international level, focused attention on the problem and attempted to pressurise the Turkish state into reconsidering its policies.[11] Furthermore, the Kurds distrust the state rhetoric to the effect that reform is impossible while a 'terrorist' campaign is being waged. Many of the Kurds have recognised that the PKK has created a political space in which other Kurdish organisations and parties have been able to operate. Many potential alternative Kurdish political figures have also believed that it has not been feasible for them to form an alternative political movement within Turkey (Barkey and Fuller 1998: 46-48). The PKK managed to combine political activism with armed resistance and internationalised an issue that had previously received little attention.

The developments in northern Iraq have had an impact on the marginalised and dissident Kurdish population. Internationally known pro-Kurdish leaders (e.g. Leyla Zana) expressed their sympathy for Iraqi Kurdish leaders and this sentiment had a powerful impact on the pro-PKK public opinion in southeastern Turkey. Local governments under the control of the pro-Kurdish parties are financed by the European Union's funding through the European Regional Development Fund (ERDF) and the European Social Fund (ESF) (Gokalp and Unsar 2008: 107).

The Turkish government has always reacted very harshly and swiftly against any manifestation or promotion of Kurdish rights. Long prison sentences have been given to individuals who never participated in violent actions against the government, but simply defended Kurdish rights in writing and speeches. The persecution of Dr. Ismail Besikci[12] was such an incident that attracted international attention to Turkey's human rights abuses. Ismail Besikci then defended his support for the establishment of a Kurdish state:

> "The Kurds have lived in Kurdistan for 4,000 years, whereas the Turks started to move from Central Asia through Khorassan into Iran, Kurdistan, Iraq, Syria and Anatolia in the second half of the eleventh century... They have lived in these lands for less than a thousand years. They have humiliated and degraded the original owners of these lands... to wipe out the Kurdish nation, its language and its culture is barbaric... The Turkish nation does not deserve to be known as the perpetrator of such barbarism.... I want to dwell a little upon the concept of "national pride". Wanting the Kurdish people to be free, wanting them to live in equal conditions with the Turkish people is taken to be propaganda undermining the national pride of the Turks. In fact, demanding equality for the Kurdish people or the removal of bans on Kurdish language and culture definitely cannot undermine the national pride of the Turks. On the contrary, it would strengthen it since defense of human rights and freedoms strengthens national feelings."[13]

However, some Kurds argued that the emergence of the PKK worsened the situation for the Kurdish cause overall; it polarised the situation and further reduced the already limited organisational freedoms that the Kurds had gained as they sought to build national consciousness over the long term in non-confrontational ways. Governmental attempts at recruiting village guards often pitted village against village, hamlet against hamlet and tribal organisation against other tribal groupings as the PKK and the state competed for the support of individual villages (Barkey and Fuller 1998: 42-43). Despite some of the deep divisions that the insurrection generated, and notwithstanding the Kurds approval or not of all the PKK's tactics or its leadership, the PKK imposed itself upon the Kurdish political scene as the single central reality and has dominated its dialogue for many years.

The Kurds in Turkey's Election

The Kurds of Turkey are in a paradoxical position. Cultural repression in Turkey was fiercer than in Iraq or Iran, though at least, Turkey had formal attributes of democracy. Since 1983, several legislative elections have provided an arena for Kurdish politicians but with a very limited manoeuvring room. Most Kurdish-oriented parties in the 1990s have been closed by the Constitutional Court due to alleged links to the PKK (Cornell 2001: 44). The elections of October 1991 were the first to witness the emergence of a genuine and explicitly Kurdish bloc, when 18 deputies elected on the Social Democratic Party (SHP) ticket broke off to join the small People's Labor Party[14] (*Halkin Emek Partisi* or HEP). It was a mixed group where some saw themselves as close to the PKK, while others were more traditional social democrats and nationalists (Kurkcu 1996: 3). The HEP's political evolution from within the Turkish party system, its alliance with SHP, and its stated commitment to non-violent methods of solving the Kurdish problem allowed it to cultivate resistance within the political establishment and a commitment to democratisation. The Party encouraged the development of a broad debate within the Turkish political system. By participating in the Turkish political system the HEP encouraged right and left-wing politicians to articulate and defend Kurdish representations (Watts 1999: 650). On July 3, 1992, the State Security Court indicted the founders of the HEP for 'separatist propaganda'. In early 1993, the PKK declared a unilateral ceasefire. The whole ceasefire proposal gave impetus to the creation of a new Kurdish party—the Democratic Party (DEP). In December 1993, Hatip Dicle, considered close to PKK, was elected as the DEP chairperson. On March 3, 1994, the Parliament voted to lift the parliamentary immunity of seven DEP deputies. They were arrested at the door of the Parliament and charged under Article 125 of the penal code ('crime against the state'), which carries the death penalty (Kutchera 1994: 15; Bruinessen 1996: 20). The Turkish government failed to respond favourably to the PKK initiative and continued its regular military operations against them.

The December 1995 elections, which took place during the second ceasefire of the PKK and in relatively free conditions, offered an accurate picture of the political moment pertaining to Kurdistan and the Kurdish political arena. In this regard, the main event was clearly the participation of the *Halkin Demokrasi Partisi* (People's Democratic Party, HADEP), successor to the earlier outlawed parties espousing Kurdish nationalism—the Halkin Emek Partisi (Labour Party, HEP) and the Demokrasi Partisi (Democratic Party, DEP). It led to a so-called 'Bloc of Labour, Peace and Freedom' which was supported by the main Kurdish organisations and the extra-parliamentary Turkish left organisations. HADEP obtained only 4.2 percent of the vote—far below the 10 percent required by the Constitution to enter the National Assembly. Nevertheless, it has displayed new signs of dynamism in the Kurdish 'micro-space' which includes the provinces of Mardin, Sirnak and Diyarkabir; the main bastions of Kurdish nationalism since 1960s. HADEP took 46.7 percent in Diyarbakir, 22 percent in Mardin, 26 percent in both Sirnak and Siirt, 27.7 percent in Van, and 54.3 percent in Hakkari (Bozarslan 1996: 17-18).

The results of the 1999 Parliamentary elections indicated the wide popularity of HADEP. The Party received only 4.8 percent of the total votes nationally, but enjoyed as high as 60 percent of the electoral support in local elections in the southeastern provinces (Robins 2000: 64). The poor performance was related to the 10 percent threshold for representation in the Parliament. There is little chance of attaining a mandate nationwide and many voters concluded that a vote for HADEP was wasted. However, the result of simultaneous municipal elections suggested a different picture. In many towns in the southeast, including the large cities of Van and Diyarbakir, HADEP candidates won landslide victories with up to 70 percent of the vote (Cornell 2001: 44-45). The result showed that large parts of the population of the southeast strongly favour a democratic representative of Kurdish rights.

In the 2002 national elections, the pro-Kurdish Democratic Society Party scored just over six percent. The national support for the Party was between 3.8 to 4.2 percent (Hakura 2007: 27). The only political party which crossed the 10 percent threshold in the November 2002 elections was the Republican People's Party or *Cumhuriyet Halk Partisi* (CHP), self-identified as the guardian of Turkish ethnic nationalism. The Nationalist Movement Party or *Milliyetci Hareket Partisi* (MHP) was decisively defeated in the November 2002 elections and was left with no seats in the Parliament. This has also weakened the ability of the hardliners to obstruct the adoption and implementation of political reforms directly addressing the Kurdish problem. The *Adalet ve Kalkinma Partisi* or Justice and Development Party (AKP) won an absolute majority of the seats enabling it to form a government on its own. The Peoples' Republican Party (CHP) became the only opposition party in the Parliament. However, neither the single-party majority government nor the opposition in the Parliament gave full support to the aspirations of the Turkish Kurds (Patton 2003: 43; Kirisci 2004: 281-294). The Constitutional Court ban on HADEP for alleged assistance to the outlawed PKK fuelled more support for the Party which regained strength for launching further democratic Kurdish movements.

In the July 2007 Turkish elections, the pro-Kurdish Democratic Society Party (DTP) managed to secure 20 seats in the Parliament which indicated the gradual consolidation of the pro-Kurdish identity at the state level. The majority of the Kurdish electorate in southeastern Turkey chose an Islamist Party i.e. Justice and Development Party or (AKP) over the ethno-nationalist DTP, challenging the DTP's passionate conviction that their pro-PKK party represents the Kurdish population in Turkey (Cagaptay and Unver 2007: 7). The DTP won 54 mayor's seats in the largely Kurdish municipalities of the Turkish southeast. These democratically elected politicians were not PKK members. They opposed violence from the state or the rebels. They called for a state–rebel ceasefire and wanted to work with the Turkish officials to end the conflict. The AKP won 46.7 percent of the vote and secured 342 seats in the Parliament; only 18 short of obtaining the two-thirds majority. The AKP pursued a policy of trying to contain Kurdish nationalism in Turkey by policies of economic development and more government aid to the heavily-populated Kurdish region in the southeast (Olson 2007: 34). Despite the rhetoric on Kurdish language and culture, pro-Kurdish political actors have failed to develop a sophisticated political agenda dealing with the contingencies of the social and economic problems of the Kurdish population of whom they assume representation. In the absence of any viable political alternative with a social democratic agenda, marginalised segments of the Turkish population including a large Kurdish electorate have gradually resorted to the pro-Islamic AKP. Indeed, the victory of pro-Islamists in the predominantly Kurdish provinces of Turkey has proved that the Kurdish question in Turkey refers to an ever-changing socio-political contention embedded in the contingencies of political, economic, ethnic, religious, sectarian, tribal and ideological situations in the region (Gokalp and Unsar 2008: 107-108). The elected DTP officials articulated the Kurdish case separately from PKK's political agenda. In November 2007, DPT called for a decentralisation of power for the Kurdish regions; it was for the first time that a Kurdish party had presented a viable political vision. Unlike the PKK, whose demands have ranged from independence to broad cultural rights, DTP's ideas are not punctuated by violence (Marcus and Apostolou 2008).

Despite the 20 pro-Kurdish representatives in Parliament, the PKK engaged in further aggression and violence. Turkey has yet to exhibit the courage to negotiate a political solution to the Kurdish issue, while the PKK continues to rely upon guerrilla warfare in its struggle to achieve self-determination for Turkey's 15 million Kurds. The July 2007 general elections resulted in consolidating the power of the pro-Islamists which also ushered in the pro-Kurdish members of parliament (MPs) to the Turkish Parliament. The Turkish ultra-nationalist National Action Party (MHP) revealed the accelerated pace of ethno-nationalist and religious institutionalisation in Turkish politics and state structure. The pro-Kurdish parties, however, visualised the concept of the ethnic as an ideal rather than de facto reality and made it the central tenet of their platforms (Watts 1999: 649). As long as pro-Kurdish parties worked within the system and adhered to principles of non-violence, they deserved to participate in Turkish democracy.

In 2008, the Kurds formed the Peace and Democracy Party (BDP), which began to moderate the movement's ideological profile and increase its civil engagement in Turkey and abroad. In the 2011 election the BDP won some thirty seats—a clear signal that the Kurds can conduct political as well as actual warfare (Egin 2013). The Kurdish party operatives opened active and visible bureaus in Brussels and Washington advancing their political agenda in the global community.

Ankara's Response

In order to maintain stability in Turkey, the government must contain and control the Kurdish nationalist movement in the West Asian region. The Turkish military has changed its policy towards the civilian population and especially in order to crush the insurgents. The Gulf War and the War on Iraq, 2003 made Ankara's dilemma greater, but it offered some opportunities with regard to its own Kurdish problem as well as the inter-regional Kurdish question. As a result, Turkey became directly involved in the affairs of almost three million Kurds in northern Iraq. The control of the movement in Turkey was easier than in northern Iraq. In July 2003, the Parliament adopted a 'Reintegration Law' offering reduced prison sentences to combatants belonging to PKK/ KADEK and other terrorist organisations as identified by the government who agreed to lay down their weapons and provide information to the authorities. The law offered full amnesty to those guilty of providing non-lethal support to terrorist organisations. In October 2001, the Turkish Parliament adopted a series of critical amendments to the Turkish Constitution and in August 2001 it adopted a legislation which resulted in legalising for the first time in the history of Turkish Republic, the broadcasting of and education in Kurdish language. This was accompanied by a decision abolishing capital punishment, enabling Ocalan's death sentence to be commuted to life imprisonment in October 2002 (Kirisci 2004: 274). The Parliament also amended an article of the Census Law that had been used to prevent the use of Kurdish names. The amendment removed language that had prohibited the use of names contrary to the 'national culture' or 'customs and traditions'; instead, prohibiting names contrary to 'moral norms' or names that 'offend the public'. The revised wording was intended to ease the restrictions; however human rights advocates claimed local authorities failed to adjust their practices. In September 2003, the Interior Ministry issued a circular notifying the local officials of the new regulations.[15] However, the circular prohibited the use of letters in Kurdish.

The Turkish forces failed to realise the magnitude of the PKK military threat, but responded adequately. Among the most effective measures taken was the militarisation of the entire southeast. The army and the militarised police seized de facto control of daily life and managed to ingratiate with the population a tleast in part through initiatives such as education programmes for girls. The military also won support because a large portion of the Kurdish population found the protection of the Turkish government far more attractive than the terror of the PKK and its hostility to Kurds of rival clans or differing political views. The most dramatic result of the cooperation between the government and people was the 'village guards' which were local Kurdish self-defence forces especially organised to counter PKK operations (Radu 2001: 57). The effective use of Special Forces to pressure and hinder the PKK movement in the mountain strongholds often violated human rights.

However, the PKK and Ansar-al Islam, which the US government viewed as terrorists, remained active in the region. Anti-Turkish activities, demands for statehood for Kurds and rise of PKK activity in northern Iraq refuelled Turkish policy makers. New clashes occurred between the PKK fighters and the Turkish security forces inside Turkey. Meanwhile DEHAP, the Turkish–Kurdish party widely seen as the PKK's political arm, organised mass protests that demanded Ocalan's release. These circumstances renewed the armed conflict between Turkey and Kurdish nationalists. Such conflicts strained Turkey's efforts in resolving its domestic Kurdish issue through democratisation and for building cooperative relations with the Iraqi Kurds (Somer 2004: 236).

Turkey has attempted to justify its 2007 cross-border military activity as a defensive response to the PKK's activities in northern Iraq. In fact, the military incursion into northern Iraq is understood in the broader context of Turkey's long-standing strategic goals in countering regional Kurdish autonomy as well as of specific domestic Turkish political considerations which came to the fore in 2007. The deeply suspicious stance towards Kurdish autonomy in Iraq is misplaced, ignoring the positive impact that this could have in providing a model solution for the reconciliation of Turkey's own Kurdish issue (Kurdish Human Rights Project 2008: 2). During the election campaign of 2007, the governing AKP was put under significant pressure by the main opposition parties, the CHP and the MHP, to take a hardline approach on PKK activity in southeast Turkey.

Kurdish politics in Turkey has been reduced to separatism and has, therefore, been the source and outcome of state-induced securitisation. Kurdish politics was perceived as collectively preaching a violent reaction against the Turkish state and its nation while the latter were trying to assimilate the Kurdish constituency by propagating a firm belief in the unity of the Turkish people, regardless of the different linguistic, religious, ethnic and national groups in Turkey (Aras et al 2002: 14). Ankara has responded to the Kurdish question by associating all Kurdish political movements with the PKK.[16]

Since 2002, for the first time, Turkey's government began to grant greater rights to the Kurds. By 2009 this took the form of the "Kurdish Opening", which proposed granting amnesty to PKK militants, broadcasting rights to private Kurdish television networks and allowing Kurdish languages classes in schools. The AKP government also initiated secret negotiations with senior PKK operatives in Oslo. Erdogan tapped Turkey's chief of intelligence, Hakan Fidan, to represent the government in these talks, but the negotiations halted when the recordings of the secret meeting were leaked by an unknown source. Worried about jeopardising the strong nationalist vote which the AKP depends on, Erdogan quickly retreated and recommenced his anti-Kurdish rhetoric. The government launched a crackdown on Kurdish intellectuals, journalists, BDP members, mayors and political activists accusing them of being members of terrorist organisations. Between 2009 and 2011, 7,748 people were detained and 3,895 arrested. But the detention, trial and political repression of these nonviolent Kurds backfired—stirring sympathy for the PKK at home and abroad (Egin 2013).

The rise of Islamic State of Iraq and Syria (ISIS) changed the Kurdish question in Turkey as well. Following the ISIS's siege of the Syrian Kurdish city of Kobane in 2014, there were rumours that the Turkish government was aiding ISIS. Hundreds of thousands of Kurds in eastern and southeastern Turkey took to the streets in protest. Turkish fighter jets bombarded the PKK positions in southeastern Turkey for the first time since the start of the peace process in 2012. The attack on the PKK came in the wake of Kurdish factions and security forces engaging each other in several Turkish cities, as anger grew over perceived government inaction against the ISIS's attack on Kobane (Letsch 2014). The Kurds were furious at the Turkish troops for blocking them from crossing over into Syria to fight with the Kurdish militia there. The Kurdish movement has managed to survive and sustain itself in Middle East where politics is a dangerous affair. Whether in Iran, Iraq, Syria or Turkey, the Kurds are now one of the major players in the Middle East, having defeated the ISIS in Kobane (Ozkan 2015).

Forced Evacuations

War is not only about killing people and material destruction, but also about the destruction of social institutions and social cohesion in society. Mass terror becomes a deliberate strategy. Destruction of schools, houses, religious buildings, fields and crops as well as torture, rape and internment becomes common. Modern warfare is concerned with not only destruction of life but also ways of life (Bracken and Petty 1998: 3). The aim of forced evacuation and resettlement was the destruction of social and cultural cohesion among the Kurds and their subsequent assimilation as Turks. In response to their uprisings, large communities in Kurdistan were dispersed through deportation throughout Turkey in the 1920s and 1930s. The Kurds were dispersed thinly so that they could not constitute more than 10 percent of the population of any district to which they were deported (Izady 1992: 104). The first deportations were simply reprisals against the rebellious tribes. In the later years, deportations became part of the concerted effort to assimilate the Kurds (Bruinessen 2000b: 79). To break up the Kurds' social cohesion, they were not allowed to have contact with each other. It was even suggested that the Kurdish children be sent to boarding schools where they would speak exclusively in Turkish (Gunter 1997: 6). However, a lack of state resources and the size of the Kurdish population prevented these plans from being implemented.

Forced evacuations and destruction of villages started at the end of the 1980s and beginning of the 1990s and reached its peak in the mid-1990s. Between 1990 and 1992, Turkish armed forces destroyed villages and forced the local population to leave the countryside in Hakkari, Sirnak, Van and Siirt. In 1993, security forces in southeastern Turkey increasingly conducted intensive, large-scale counterinsurgency campaigns to eliminate the PKK's logistical bases of support. Village destruction and forced evacuation of the population became systematic in Bitlis, Diyarbakir and Mardin. Such operations resulted in hundreds of thousands of displaced Kurdish villagers in 1993 –1994.[17] Death squads killed thousands of Kurdish politicians, lawyers, journalists and community leaders (Bruinessen 1996: 20). Security forces burned down the homes and evicted people from villages that refused to enter the 'village guards' (*Kurucu*) system. Village guards, however, have been implicated in numerous human rights abuses, and in turn the PKK has targeted them and their families. Arbitrary detention and torture often accompanied security forces' raids on villages.[18] These reflected the course of the war between the PKK and the Turkish state.

Between 1994 and 1995, Tunceli[19] and parts of Bingol, which were inhabited mainly by Kurds of Alevi origin, were targets of successive military operations aimed at de-populating large parts of the countryside. Over a period of two months, around a third of the villages in Tunceli were evacuated under severe military pressure and many of them were destroyed and burned down by the army. In 1996, Sivas, an area which is inhabited by both Kurds and Turks, was also affected by village destruction and forced displacement (Jongerden 2001: 80-82). Large stretches of forest which had been designated as a natural reserve, were deliberately burnt down. The rationale for all this destruction was the presence of guerrillas of the PKK, believed to be hiding out in the forests of the province. The inhabitants of the destroyed villages were suspected of giving food and shelter to these guerrillas.

After the capture of Ocalan in 1999, military activities within the borders of Turkey almost came to a halt. The issue of reconstructing the evacuated and destroyed villages rose on the political agenda.

Integration of the Kurds into Turkish Society

Kurdish regions have traditionally been the most underdeveloped parts of Turkey and have experienced little economic and social improvement. The private sector, attracted by the economic opportunities in the more prosperous western regions has for the most part ignored the Kurdish provinces, often citing the inadequacy of infrastructure. This along with the insufficient state investments explains the growing divergence in per capita income between the Kurdish regions and the rest of the country (Barkey 1993-94: 68). The army had banned villagers from grazing animals and farming on the mountains into which the PKK retreated after attacks. The inflow of migrants, escaping both a lack of opportunity in the eastern provinces and the devastating effects of the continuing struggle between the military and the PKK in the southeast, brought into Ankara, Istanbul, Izmir and other cities millions of people whose ethnic backgrounds and social values were significantly different from those of the existing population of western Turkey (Salt 1999: 74). The Turkish security forces treated everyone harshly. By late 1980s, they had separated 'good' villages from 'bad' ones. If the villagers did not agree to join the village guard, a government sponsored Kurdish militia treated them severely. The PKK also attacked villages and guards that refused to support them with food and water, or which did not appear amenable to the group's Marxist–Lenininst message of liberation (Marcus 1994: 18). However, many Kurds supported the PKK's campaign for Kurdish nationalism.

A majority of Kurds, one third Alevi and two-thirds Sunni, had positively integrated into Turkish society through education, socio-economic enhancement, mass communication and military service. Over one million Turkish–Kurdish marriages have taken place. More than a hundred have served in the Parliament and they also occupy the highest echelons of government. Some Kurds (20–25 percent) feel that the Turkish state has not adequately addressed their political, economic and cultural grievances. In a comprehensive survey, Professor Dogu Ergil of the Ankara University demonstrated the dominance of enlightened thinking among the Kurds in southeastern Turkey on a range of critical issues: 75 percent support co-educational schools, 90 percent endorse secular ideals and 83 percent favour Europe over Asia. Turkey's Kurds tend to migrate to Europe and western Turkey rather than to northern Iraq (Hakura 2007: 27). However, declining religious practice is strongly correlated with higher income and educational attainment; economic impoverishment rather than culture or religion seems to be the main barrier to female emancipation.

The regime that was established in 1980 following the coup did pass the restrictive law on publications and languages other than Turkish, but that law was repealed in 1991. It is now commonly accepted that Kurdish is no longer banned in the context of cultural activities. In practice, Kurdish music, folklore and customs are all permitted. All that remain prohibited are education and television in Kurdish, but in practice the government tolerates radio broadcasts in Kurdish (Gunduz 2001: 26). A credible argument can be made that the synthesis of modern Islam, national pride and secularism could resolve the Kurdish question on the basis of civic citizenship and religious affinity. The hegemony of the PKK with its history of dogmatic Marxist–Leninism and its attachment to armed struggle is very much a reflection of the refusal of successive Turkish nationalist regimes to accommodate Kurdish aspirations for cultural and political autonomy (Kutschera 1994: 12).

During the 1990s, a poll conducted in the southeast showed that only 29 percent of the population viewed the PKK as the best representative of the Kurdish people (Poulton 1997: 245-248). Moreover, the greater part of the Kurdish population has taken Turkish identity in whole or in part. Indeed, Kurds in Turkey have three options: to reject the Turkish identity altogether; to accept it in its civic version while retaining their Kurdish identity which amounts to integration or to accept the Turkish identity signifying ethnic assimilation. A poll in 1993 showed that over 13 percent of Istanbul's population claimed Kurdish roots, while 3.9 percent considered themselves Kurds and 3.7 percent identified themselves as Turks with Kurdish parents. Apparently, the remainder consider themselves simply as Turks. Even accounting for the less-than-ideal polling conditions at the height of the conflict including the state restrictions on Kurdish identity, the outcome showed that a significant number of Kurds have integrated into Turkish society (Cornell 2001: 43).

From 1998 to 2002, the percentage of Turkish citizens who viewed 'terror and security' as the greatest threats to the country dropped from 39.3 to 5.5%. Since the PKK revolt began in 1984, dynamics other than violence and security considerations have gotten a chance to play a significant role in determining the parameters of the conflict. The Turkish Parliament passed a series of laws granting significant cultural–linguistic rights to ethnic Kurds, such as broadcasting and teaching Kurdish (Somer 2004: 236). These rights, whose implementation has so far been slow, were modest by world standards and fell short of the politically conscious ethnic Kurds' expectation for change. Nevertheless, unprecedented steps were taken by Turkey in the direction of normalisation of the Kurdish conflict via demilitarisation and liberal democracy.

Although the government implemented the most liberal legislations in Turkish history, it continued to deny the existence of ethnicity. The Kurdish areas have consistently lagged behind the rest of Turkey in terms of economic development. Demographic and socio-economic changes within urban communities encouraged new Kurdish identities to become silent. Kurdish migrant populations in Turkey were displaced throughout cities in Kurdistan and central and western Anatolia and into alternative workplaces such as automobile factories without state assistance (Cornell 2001: 35-37). Displaced populations have been conscious of Kurdish nationalism—with the diversified workforce they also become part of the working class and leftist movements and become identified in the public sphere (Natali 2005: 99). Meanwhile, uneven economic development programmes heightened ethnic distinctions between the Kurdish regions and Turkish Anatolia.

Turkey's Kurdish question which had a complex relationship with nationalism was not immune to change. Rapid urbanisation, de-tribalisation, western migration, globalisation and developments in northern Iraq affected its dynamics. The problem did not fit well with the traditional Turkish narrative, but was purely a socio-economic problem including recognition for autonomy. The urban–rural dichotomy had undermined the development of unified Kurdish nationalist organisations which were displaying intense rivalry among prominent feudal families thus affecting Kurdish unity (Brown 1995: 123). Further, a sustained PKK policy of massacring the families of Kurds including women and children who sided with the security forces also weakened support for the PKK.

In July 2009, Prime Minister Erdogan announced the "Kurdish Initiative" or "Democratic Opening". The initiative marked the achievement of several rights for Kurds: The use of formerly Kurdish titles for districts was permitted; legal barriers for speaking Kurdish during prison visits were eliminated; Kurdish language and literature departments at various universities were established; giving Kurdish names to Kurdish children was permitted; TV channels broadcasting in the Kurdish language were allowed (Gunter 2011).

Kurds, Turkey and the European Union

Turkey and European Union (EU) relations have evolved with lots of difficulties since Turkey's application for full membership on September 12, 1987. Historically, Turkey was a strategically important country for the EU. On the other hand, there were plenty of obstacles for Turkey's membership to the Union. These obstacles varied from the role of the military in the civilian government to Turkey's attitude towards minorities. Turkey's Kurdish issue, in this sense, is one of the stumbling blocks for Turkey on the road to EU accession. The Kurdish crisis came just when Turkey needed to demonstrate its democratic credentials to the EU (Taspinar 2007: 122). In October 2001, the Turkish Parliament adopted a series of critical amendments to the Turkish Constitution and in August 2002 was able to adopt the necessary legislation to give effect to these amendments. This was accompanied by a decision abolishing capital punishment, enabling Ocalan's death sentence to be commuted to life imprisonment in October 2002. These reforms have been recognised as a sign of the Turkish government's commitment to join the EU as well as a manifestation of the EU's ability to instigate political transformation in a candidate country (Kirisci 2004: 279). This development has coincided with increased pressures from the EU on Turkey to ease legal–political restrictions on non-violent Kurdish activities, within the context of the "Democratic Opening". Combined with considerably diminished direct threats to state security, the environment of the conflict has significantly changed (Somer 2002: 74).

On October 3, 2005, when the EU formally initiated accession negotiations with Turkey, more attention was focused on the Kurdish problem. In fact, "respect for and protection of minorities" is one of the principles accepted in the Copenhagen Criteria[20] which defines whether a country is eligible to join the European Union or not. Western attempts to establish—directly or indirectly—Kurdish autonomy in Turkey aroused considerable suspicion and resentment among the Turks. Turkey has accepted the Conference on Security and Cooperation in Europe's Copenhagen Document of 1990 which addresses minority rights and the Geneva Reports on National Minorities; however, subject to a reservation that reiterates the Lausanne formula. The government has refused to sign the European Framework Convention on Minorities or the European Charter for Regional or Minority Language, but it has signed the International Covenant on Civil and Political Rights which contains an article on national minorities (Gunduz 2001: 25-26). And at the Copenhagen summit in 2002, the EU promised to open talks 'without delay' provided Turkey made sufficient progress on democracy, human rights and legal reforms.

Seeing the Kurdish question as one of the biggest obstacles to the Turkish European Union membership, the EU has shown an unwillingness to adopt Turkey's ethnic conflict as an internal EU problem. Indeed, many EU states have directly and indirectly contributed to the ramifications of the Kurdish question, which has become an ethno-nationalist challenge with a violent face. While the EU reiterated its request to the legitimate pro-Kurdish actors to distance the legal pro-Kurdish politics from the PKK, the PKK continued to enjoy protection in many European countries.[21] The pro-PKK, pro-Kurdish groups including the Democratic People's Party (renamed the Democratic Society Party or DTP) were among those that experienced the highest levels of frustration with the EU's accession process. The Kurdish groups close to the PKK have been enthusiastic about Turkey's EU accession since the EU's overtures with regards to human rights and democracy opened space for political manoeuvring for Kurdish mobilisation. The Islamist and organised pro-Kurdish groups received considerable EU funding that had been made available to Turkish civil society particularly to the human rights organisations that help promote their agendas domestically and internationally (Tugal 2007: 5-10). The Kurds considered accession to the EU as the most imperative political opportunity for meeting their ethnic demands—but found that the EU is using the 'Kurdish card' not to help the Kurds, but to keep Turkey out of the EU[22] (Gokalp and Unsar 2008: 95). Many Kurds hoped that the EU might help to exert a greater pressure on the Turkish government to resolve the Kurdish issue quickly and by more peaceful means (Marguiles 1996: 27). This disillusionment led to further disorientation in pro-Kurdish circles confusing the contingencies of their goals and agenda which in turn disturbed the pro-Kurdish actors' relationship with their grassroots' constituency.

Some events deeply shook the Kurds' trust in Europe. NATO's war on Kosovo not only conveniently blotted out all developments in Turkey and Kurdistan, but also drove home the message that the West applies double standards; Western Europe and the US acted as a virtual ally of the Kosovo Liberation Army but drove the PKK into the hands of the Turkish military. Nonetheless, the capture of Ocalan allowed the PKK to see the European Union as an opportunity to transform itself from an outmoded guerrilla movement losing its international legitimacy to a civil and political organisation (Gokalp and Unsar 2008: 95). It is believed that the PKK has been put on the list of terrorist organisations by the European Union and the United States unjustly. In April 2007, the PKK and its political wing known as KONGRA-GE were removed from the European Union's terror list by the European Court of Justice;[23] The Turkish state used violence against the Kurdish people in order to terrorise them.

Turkey's EU candidacy has been diplomatically troublesome since the official negotiations began. The EU pragmatically displayed a security-minded, self-serving approach towards the Kurdish question rather than a willingness to be a facilitator in the formulation of a comprehensive political solution. The purpose was to manage the problem in the best interests of Europe rather than resolve it. In this context, the Kurdish question has become a manipulative weapon for the EU to block Turkey's accession process. The EU, on the one hand, uses the 'Kurdish card' to keep the Turkish allies out of the EU by reaffirming that Turkey suffers from a deficient democracy and a socio-politically unstable, economically underdeveloped southeastern region and on the other hand, the "Kurdish card" has enabled the EU to put pressure on Turkey to control the regional instability (Uslu 2008: 118-9; Gokalp and Unsar 2008: 103). Political opposition to the Turkish candidacy in Europe has escalated despite a staunch political commitment by Turkey to meet the Copenhagen Criteria. The former President of the European Commission, Jacques Delors, once said that the EU was a "Christian club". The view continues to be held in some European Christian Democrat parties.[24] The German Chancellor, Angela Merkel, expressed doubts about the viability of the Turkish membership in the EU. With the presence of large Turkish–Kurdish populations in EU member countries, the Kurdish problem has effectively been exported to Europe. The EU concern relates to both the human rights violations and the burgeoning Turkish–Kurdish conflict in the midst of Europe itself—especially in Germany, where some 400,000–500,000 Kurds and 1.5 million Turks reside (Barkey and Fuller 1997: 77). The French President, Nicolas Sarkozy, is another ardent opponent of Turkey's accession. The President of the European Commission, Jose Manuel Barroso, also said that any EU enlargement after the membership of Bulgaria and Romania would need to wait until all constitutional and structural issues within the EU had been worked out (Gokalp and Unsar 2008: 94). EU suspended talks with Turkey in December 2006 because of the conflict between Turkey and the Greek-majority government of Cyprus. Turkey refused to open its ports and wanted a de facto acceptance of the self-declared Turkish republic of northern Cyprus which no other country in the world recognises (Mardell 2006). Turkey's engagement with the EU and its alliance with the United States have important structural variables for its security and economic survival. Democratisation vis-à-vis the Kurdish identity and integration with the EU have facilitated a striking shift in Turkey's position from a coercive to a benign constructive regional power (Onis 2003: 10). However, more democracy did not guarantee the end of the conflict and political violence.

Regional Implications

Geopolitical shifts have had far-reaching consequences in altering the balance of power in the region affecting the Kurds as well as Turkey's foreign relations with its immediate neighbours. Throughout the last two decades, Iran, Iraq and Syria had had their own reasons for supporting

PKK activities. In the case of Iran, the motive was the concern regarding the growing Turkish influence in West Asia, especially in Azerbaijan, where a rise in Azeri nationalism could threaten Iran's territorial integrity. In the 1980s and 1990s, Iran supported PKK terrorism and tried to export its theocratic regime to secular democratic Turkey. Thus, Iran was seen by the Turkish security establishment (mainly the military) as posing a vital threat to the existence of the Turkish state. The resurgence of PKK terrorism in Turkey along with the rise of a Kurdish movement in Iran since the 2003 Iraqi war seems to have united the two countries against the commonly perceived threat. Both countries have a common interest in the protection of Iraq's territorial integrity (Eligur 2006: 3). Tehran's motivation in seeking to limit the PKK's activities in its territory stems from Iran's political and economic isolation. Turkey has long suspected Iran of secretly supporting the PKK. Tehran, in turn, blamed Ankara for allegedly offering shelter to the left-wing Kurdistan Democratic Party of Iran and a rival group, *Komala*. Yet, both have moved to cooperate on security issues. Tehran has directed a charming offensive at Ankara inviting Turkish officials to search its territory for rebel camps and offering to destroy them. Erdogan travelled to Tehran in 2004 offering the hand of friendship and sought enhanced relations based on mutual interests despite the radically different political systems of the two countries. Beyond the economic aspects of Erdogan's visit, it did appear that Iran is willing to take certain steps to curtail PKK activities. In July 2004, Iran launched a crackdown on PKK militants holed up along its border with Turkey. Turkey's NTV private television station reported that six Kurdish fighters and 10 Iranian troops had been killed in the operation. Tehran officially admitted the death of 10 Kurdish *peshmergas* and only two of its soldiers (Peuch 2004; Olson 2000: 871-75). Tehran handed over a number of PKK militants to Turkish authorities. In June 2005, Ankara congratulated the newly elected conservative Iranian leader Mahmoud Ahmadinejad for his electoral victory and expressed Turkey's willingness to improve bilateral relations with Iran. Turkey and Iran continued their security cooperation to check Kurdish aspirations for an independent state. In 2006, both sent massive contingents of troops and artillery to their respective frontiers, sealing off the borders as well as violating the sovereignty of Iraq by carrying out significant cross-border military operations and shelling the villages and mountains of Iraqi Kurdistan.

The Gulf War complicated Turkey's Kurdish problem by introducing an international dimension to the issue. The nascent Kurdish regional government developed under the leadership of Massoud Barzani of the Kurdish Democratic Party and Jalal Talabani of the Patriotic Union of Kurdistan protected by the US-led multinational force operating from Turkey. Saddam Hussein's resilience had enabled the Kurdish entity to consolidate its independent existence. The Turkish policy in northern Iraq is driven by one goal: to eliminate any influence that encourages Turkey's Kurds to seek autonomy or independence (Brown 1995: 126). Ankara has no design for absorbing northern Iraq into its territory as some have suggested.[25] Turkey was concerned that the creation of an independent Kurdish state or even a federated entity within Iraq would fuel the fires of its own restless Kurdish population. Ankara insisted that it would not countenance a threat to Iraq's territorial integrity; the KRG zone should not expand to incorporate the province of Kirkuk; the Turkmen ethnic minority in Iraqi Kurdistan be properly represented and protected and the Kurdish *peshmerga* not be allowed to retain heavy arms. Ankara also insisted that Turkey's own Kurdish separatist PKK/KADEK should not be free to use the mountains of Iraqi Kurdistan in its campaign against the Turkish state (Park 2004: 26-27). Turkey has persisted in the strengthening of the Turkoman minority in northern Iraq and of the Iraqi Turkoman Front (ITF). Moreover, Ankara's preference remains for a centralised, territorially secured and strong Sunni Arab-influenced Iraq.

Syria's support of the PKK is primarily motivated by the uneasiness with which it perceives the construction of a dam on the Euphrates River, part of the southeast Anatolian Project, which restricts the flow of the water to it. Syria also had irredentist claims over the Hatay province which was annexed by Turkey in 1939. Turkish diplomatic initiatives in the region have primarily concentrated on lobbying with the Syrian government to cease support to the PKK; Syria's support for the PKK had brought it and Turkey to the brink of war in 1998. To a certain extent the initiatives proved successful when Syria officially banned the PKK which has a strong organisational base and expelled Ocalan (Eligur 2006: 2; Brown 1995: 126). Furthermore, after the War on Iraq in 2003, both countries shared the same threat perception about the establishment of a Kurdish state in northern Iraq which could generate separatist aspirations among their own Kurdish minorities. For this reason, both the countries have supported Iraq's territorial integrity. In July 2003, Syria conducted military operations against the PKK members in its

Kurdish-populated regions along its Turkish border (Kamish, Derik, Rakka, Afrin and Deresiye) and turned them over to the Turkish authorities. In the subsequent years, Syria has maintained its military operations against the PKK (Eligur 2006: 2-4).

Turkey has legitimate reasons for being concerned with the ethnic division of power and for opposing an ethnicity-based federation in Iraq. Elevating the aim of the prevention of a Kurdish state to the level of Turkey's most important strategic interests in the region spreads the impression that Turkish and Kurdish interests are in fundamental conflict (Somer 2004: 251). The resolution of the economic problems which have caused ethnic resentment in southeast Turkey requires much more enhanced developmental policies.

Turkey's Dirty War Against its Own Kurds

United States NATO partner Turkey is rapidly expanding war against its Kurdish population in the country's southeast. The Turkish government forces continue military campaign to crush an uprising by the Kurdish Worker's Party. Since February 2016, hundreds of civilians were killed in Kurdish inhabited areas. Human rights groups report that government forces have carried out massacres of civilians and extrajudicial killings. Cizre and the old city of Diyarbakir –the defacto capital of Turkish Kurdistan have seen the most severe fighting in an urban rebellion that has spread across northern Kurdistan. The government claims that it's engaged in a war against terrorist who are destabilizing the country. President Recep Tayyip Erdogan's ruling Justice and Development Party (AKP) has little interest in discussing Kurdish demands for rights and autonomy as counterpart in Syria and Iraq. The war in Syria has had a profound military and political impact on Turkey. Turkey, blame not only the PKK but also Syrian counterpart YPG, began shelling Kurdish position across the border in the Syrian province of Aleppo (Rosenfeld 2016). Kurds blame Turkey for not doing enough to combat the ISIS, and accused Ankara of sheltering the jihadist.

Kurds accuse Turkey of using the US-led coalition against ISIS as a cover to attack the Kurdish PKK in Turkey and Iraq, and now against the YPG in northern Syria. The US and EU consider the YPG as one of their most effective allies in the fight ISIS. According to Kurdish sources Turkey's bombardment of their position is helping IS to attack Kurdish held frontline areas in Syria and Iraq. ISIS militants attacked Syrian Kurdish villages south of Kobane after Turkey began shelling the YPG. Since then, IS has increased its attacks against Iraqi Kurdish forces in the Makhur area near the city of Mosul. PKK leaders have repeatedly warned of a total civil war inside Turkey in retaliation for attacks against Syria's Kurds. On February 17, 2016, a PKK splinter group Kurdish Freedom Hawks (TAK) carried out a bombing in Ankara that killed 27 Turkish soldiers and one civilian. The PKK carried out much of the violence against government and military targets in the south–east. The Kurdish Freedom Hawks (TAK) is more hard-line and their attacks have become more deadly and focused on Ankara and Istanbul (Kirby, 2016). The TAK had been quite for few years but renewed conflict because of the failed ceasefire in 2015. The Turkey-PKK battlefield has expanded from guerrilla fighting in the mountains to urban warfare in the heart of Turkey's predominantly Kurdish cities including in Diyarbakir.[25] Many of the Kurdish targets were Turkey's military establishment. There is a sense of betrayal in Kurdish areas in Turkey. The Kurds wants to know the reason why West supports the Kurdish rebels in Syria but calls their allies in Turkey terrorists, even though they have the same leader and ideology. Meanwhile Erdogan will have no sympathy for the Kurdish population who has been demanding for autonomous region in the south. Most of the Kurdish attacks within Turkey are due to long running internal issues that have flared up since the end of ceasefire in 2015. Turkey is worried by the rise of Kurdish groups in northern Syrian particularly the Syrian Kurdish Popular Protection Units (YPG) militia and its political arm the Democratic Union Party (PYD).

July 2016 Attempted Military Coup

Turkey is theoretically powerful enough, with US backing to withstand the threats from ISIS and the PKK. But it's not clear the government has the domestic support it needs to do so. Turkish concerns over the PKK and ISIS appear to have been trumped by polarization between pro-and anti- AKP camps. The source of Turkey's dangerous polarization is Erdogan himself. Erdogan has won successive elections since 2002 and build a cult of personality, as a kind of authoritarian underdog. He has successfully targeted and politically brutalized the secular Turkish military, liberals, left wings voters, the Media and the minorities (Cagaptay 2015). The military has typically adhered to the fiercely secular founding principles set out by Turkey's first president, Mustafa Kemal Ataturk. The failed July 2016 military coup is making president Erdogan more powerful portraying him as victim and tighten group on power.

Turkey has seen its economy improve and dramatically expanded its influence during Erdogan's thirteen years power. He will use the opportunity to widen the crackdown against opponents, against state institutions and will attempt Turkey into a more presidential form of government (Bruton, 2016). The attempt coup was carried out by faction within the Turkish Armed forces that organized under a council called the "Peace at Home Council". The motive behind the attempted coup was that an erosion of secularism, the elimination of democratic rule, a disregard for human rights, and Turkey's loss of credibility in the international arena. The government accused Fethulla Gulen, a Muslim cleric who is base in US of trying to foment an uprising the military, media and judiciary (Rosenfeld etal, 2016).

Turkey has a history of military coups but Erdogan's Islamist-leaning government was believed to be in a stronger than previous administrations. During the last decade Erdogan's government economic performance outshined. He also inserted loyalists into key parts of the state apparatus and increasingly cracked down on suspected plotters. But the recent events of military coup have destabilized and bring bad image to the country, with Kurdish rebels fighting a new insurgency in the south-east of the country. The Syrian civil war has also spilt over into Turkish territory, with ISIS mounting a series of terror attacks across the Turkey (Kingsley and Ghaith 2016). Erdogan's government faced a major challenge for maintaining security in the region.

Turkey Under Attack by ISIS

As turkey pushes its campaign against Kurdish insurgents (PKK) another deadly foe is gaining momentum—the ISIS. The jihadist group is considered responsible for suicide attacks in the country; one of the most recent was July 2016 Ataturk airport attack which killed 41 and injuring more than 147 people. According to Turkey's officials and US intelligence the ISIS or an ISIS-inspired group was to blame for the deadly attacked in airport (Tuysuz and Steve, 2016). As part of the US led coalition against ISIS, Turkey allows coalition planes to fly raids on IS targets in neighbouring Iraq and Syria from its territory. ISIS is losing ground in Iraq and Syria and probably they have got to find somewhere to operate. The acceleration of suicide bombings in Turkey comes after the country increased its involvement in the US-led campaign against the Islamic State in Syria. IS attack as an outcome of Turkey's policy in Syria which has favored opposition factions striving to overthrow President

Bashar al-Assad. Ankara has largely turned a blind eye to the cross-border activities of rebels, allowing jihadists to flock to Syria and paving the way for IS to establish a so called 'Caliphate' in Syria and clandestine cells in Turkey. According to Soner Cagaptay, director of the Turkish research programme at Washington Institute for Near East policy, Turkey has singlehandedly attempt to shape the outcome of the Syrian War and now suffering due to the fallout of its ill executed policy. IS has responded with increased acts of aggression on Turkish soil and is picking soft targets, including left-wing and Kurdish populated areas and foreigners. In Syria Kurdish YPG group led by US is heading campaign against the ISIS (Soguel 2016). The 21 August 2016 attacked in a conservative Kurdish neighborhood in the city of Gaziantep near the Syrian border signaled the ISIS target against the Kurdish population. The Kurdish militia have played a central role in recent victories against ISIS in northern Syria, including driving the group from the key city of Manbij in August 2016 and cutting key supply from the Turkish border to its heartland in Raqqa (Visser and etal 2016). In the coming years, ISIS is likely to continue to attack on Turkish establishments and the Kurds. Turkey has become embroiled in a conflict on two fronts, inside Turkey and across its Syrian border.

Turkey Retaliates ISIS and Kurdish Groups

On 24 August 2016 Turkey has launched a major military intervention in Syria, sending tanks and warplanes across the border in a coordinated campaign with Syria opposition fighters. The operation code name, "Euphrates Shield" has dual purpose: to dislodge ISIS from Jarablus[26] and to contain the expansion of Kurdish militias in northern Syria (Shaheen 2016). Turkey considers Syrian Kurdish militias an equal or greater threat because of links to its own domestic Kurdish insurgents. Turkey has been deeply concerned by the advances of the main US backed Syrian Kurdish militias –YPG which poised to control nearly the entire Syrian side of the border with Turkey. But the Syrian government denounced the Turkish military incursion and called for an immediate end to what it described as a "blatant violation" of Syrian sovereignty (Arango and etal 2016). Turkey has backed rebels against Assad throughout Syria's civil war. Turkey's relations with American have also deteriorated as the latter backing of the Kurdish People's Protection Unites (YPG), which has expanded its sphere of influence in northern Syria. The YPG has conquered vast tracks of land from ISIS with the backing of American air power. The Turks fear the alliance is helping them gain territory for an autonomous zone along the Turkish border. Ankara considers the YPG as supporting the Kurdistan Workers Party (PKK) which is fighting an insurgency against the government. Turkey's operation has further complicated the already protracted Syrian civil war.

Ankara wants to force the Kurds to withdraw to the east of Euphrates River and stop establishing a corridor to link two Kurdish led areas in north western Syria. After capturing Jarablus from ISIS, the Turkish led forces have been targeting Kurdish controlled villages. Turkey enjoys tacit support from Russia, the Syrian government and Iran in acting to prevent further territorial gains by the Kurds and their allies. On the other side, US has is trying to prevent Turkey coming into conflict with its allies in the region. A Turkish campaign against the Kurds in Syria could ignite further clashes with Kurdistan Worker's Party inside Turkey. The PKK recently upped it attacks significantly in correlation with the Turkish operation inside Syria.[27] As Syrian Kurds is gaining momentum, Turkey considers Kurdish expansionism on its border a threat to national security. Turkey wants Syria to become part of its sphere of influence in the region.

Conclusion

From the beginning, Turkish nation and state-building failed to incorporate a portion of ethnic Kurds, which resulted in a series of brutally suppressed ethnic–religious rebellions during the 1920s and 1930s in eastern Turkey. Questions relating to Kurdish identity and self-perception have not disappeared but remain very much in Turkish politics. These questions stem from the fact that Turkish society has not yet found its homogeneity or stability and is split into many sub-groups with conflicting aspirations. The question of minorities has negatively affected Turkish political stability for many years and has also inflicted much damage on Turkish international relations (Kushner 1997: 223). Combined with uncertainties regarding the future of the Iraqi Kurds and Turkey's democratisation and prospects for joining the European Union, these circumstances impose various influences and constraints on the self-perception of Turkish Kurds (Somer 2004: 237). Turkey is more sensitive to European pressure on human rights than its neighbours. There are strong ideological impediments to the recognition of the Kurds as an ethnic group with its own culture, but concessions are almost unthinkable. The military and civilian elites (which include assimilated

Kurds) are deeply committed to the Kemalist dogma that the people of Turkey are one homogenous nation and they perceive each denial of unity as a vital threat to the nation.

The end of the Cold War period was marked by rising Kurdish nationalism and uncertainty at Turkey's southern border. There were high expectations for change on the part of the ethnic Kurds throughout the region. The myth perpetuated in the past that the Kurds were errant Turks who should regain their Turkishness either through assimilation or by force, however, is no longer a viable policy where ethnicity is such a potential force. Moreover, ethnic Kurdish Turks are willing and supportive citizens who are seeking greater freedom to express their cultural heritage and greater attention in the southeast from Ankara in the area of infrastructure development and security. Cultural–educational policies is an important arena in which external actors, such as the EU, can have a positive and long-run impact by helping Turks to challenge beliefs that attribute social disintegration to ethnic and cultural pluralism. State behaviour and political developments should be expected to significantly affect the self-definitions and political preferences of the large spectrum of ethnic Kurds living in Turkey. Economic privatisation programmes have impacted the Kurdish trajectory because they strengthened rural structures and reinforced the government political base in the countryside.

Turkey has a democratic form of government and public debate is a vital and necessary accompaniment to any kind of conflict. The legacy of violence and power politics between the PKK and the government is hard to overcome. Therefore, a dialogue between the Turkish government, Kurdish Parliamentarians and Turkish Kurds should begin to take place. Turkey cannot be both a democracy and a military state. The Kurds no longer want to be absorbed by the greater whole of Turkish nationalism; they want to live side by side in equality with the Turks in a pluralist and multi-ethnic society. (Schleifer 2013)

The Kurds in Syria gained more autonomy as the Assad regime began to lose its grip on power and the Iraqi Kurds continued on their road to a form of independence. The Arab Spring of the last two years gave Ankara an opportunity to assert itself as a regional leader and as a champion of democratisation and human rights; however, its efforts at doing that were being continually undermined by the Kurdish issue and the regional perception that Turkey doesn't practice at home what it preaches abroad.

Notes

1. Ataturk's famous lieutenant.
2. The motivations for the 1925 Sheikh Said revolt were a mix of Kurdish nationalist and reactionary politics. Said himself was upset by the Kemalists decision to abolish the Caliphate. For an analysis of the Said rebellion see Olson, Robert (1989), *The Emergence of Kurdish Nationalism and the Sheikh Said Rebellion: 1880-1925,* University of Texas Press: Austin.
3. The 1924 Constitution states that "without religious and ethnic difference, every person of the people of Turkey who is a citizen is regarded as a Turk."
4. Kemalists are the followers of Kemal Ataturk.
5. Dev Genc (Revolutionary Youth) also known as Dev Yol (Revolutionary Way), was active in the mid and late 1970s. It grew out of the Turkish People's Liberation Army (TPLA).
6. The Hafez Assad regime ended its support for the PKK in 1998 under threat of war from Turkey.
7. See, "Kongra-Gel, Kurdistan Freedom and Democracy Congress (KADEK), Kurdistan Wokers' Party (PKK)", (Online: web), Accessed 30 January 2008 URL: http:// www.globalsecurity.org/military/world/para/pkk.htm
8. Ocalan was arrested in Kenya by Turkish security agents and is serving a life sentence. Under the pressure from the European Human Rights Commission (EHRC), Turkey abolished the death penalty in 2002.
9. For details see, Kurdish Human Rights Projects (16 December 2006), "War in Iraq and the Kurds", (Online: web), Accessed 15 November 2008, URL: http://www.khrp.org/news/pr2003/wariniraq.htm
10. See, "Time to Rebuild Middle East: Davutoglu says in Erbil", (Online: web), Accessed 24 November 2010, URL: http://www.krg.org/articles/detail.asp?smap=02010200&lngnr=12&rnr=73&anr=32240
11. The situation is increasingly reminiscent of the Palestinian views of the PLO in the past decades—The PLO over time came to be the symbol of Palestinian resistance and the main vehicle of nationalist expression despite the existence of many Palestinians who had a quarrel with PLO methods, disliking Arafat and opposing terrorism and internecine killings among the Palestinians. Nearly all Palestinians have defended the PLO against all outside challengers. The PKK among the Kurds has not yet reached the stage of the PLO among the Palestinians but with time it is gradually moving in that direction.
12. A Turkish sociologist, who challenged the Kemalist myth about the Kurds in a book published in 1969, entitled *The Order of Eastern Anatolia: Socioeconomic and Ethnic Foundations.* He was arrested in 1990 for writing a book—*Kurdistan: An Interstate Colony,* (Alan Press: New York), where he analyses the Turkish policies for pacifying the Kurds.
13. "Dr. Ismail Besikci Defies the Turkish State", *Kurdistan Liberation,* no.2 (August-September 1990): 2
14. At this time, the Kurdish People's Labour Party was the only legal Parliamentary party espousing Kurdish rights. The Constitutional Court of Turkey ordered the closure of the Party in July 1993.
15. For details see "Kurdistan-Turkey", (Online: web), Accessed 30 January 2008, URL: http://www.globalsecurity.org/military/world/war/kurdistan-turkey.htm

16. Evidence for this can be found in Turkey's Constitutional indictments, the condemnation of legitimate Kurdish political actors (parliamentarians and mayors) as 'terrorists' by civil and military elites and the never-ending public pressure on Kurdish political actors to publicly condemn PKK activities and declare their disassociation from the PKK.
17. The total number of civilians displaced from the southeast during the decade of the conflict was estimated at a staggering two million.
18. For details see, "Turkey's Human Rights Development", *Human Rights Watch Report 2005, Helsinki*, (Online: web), Accessed 16 July 2010, URL: http://www.hrw.org/reports/1995/WR95/HELSINKI-16.htm#P655_198257
19. Dersim is the traditional Kurdish name. In the 1930s, the Turkish government changed its name to Tunceli.
20. The European Council in Copenhagen concretised the regulations for accession and passed the 'Copenhagen Criteria' in 1993; for details see Behr, Hartmut (2007), "The European Union in the Legacies of Imperial Rule? EU Accession Politics Viewed from a Historical Comparative Perspective", *European Journal of International Relations*, 13(2): 239-262.
21. See, Erdogan, Recep Tayyip (27 October 2007), "No EU country has extradited members of the PKK to Turkey, despite labeling it as a terrorist organization", in *Turkey Vexed by PKK Talks with EU and Iraq*, (Online: web), Accessed 20 November 2009, http://www.turkishdigest.com/archive/2007_10_01_archive.html
22. In a 2005 International Conference on "The EU, Turkey, and the Kurds", at Brussels; pro-Kurdish groups organised in Europe stated their resentment over the EU's failure to address the situation of the Kurds.
23. For details see, "Kurdish National Congress of North America (KNC-NA) Asking US to Remove PKK from the Blacklist", April 7, 2008, (Online: web), Accessed 10 November 2008, URL: http://www.kurdishaspect.com/doc040708KNC.html
24. See, "Q&A: Turkey's EU Entry Talk", 11 December 2006, (Online: web), Accessed 14 November 2010, URL: http://.news.bbc.co.uk/2/hi/4107919.stm.
25. For details see, "Turkey Vs Syria's Kurds vs Islamic State", *BBC News*, 19 February 2016, URL: http://www.bbc.com/news/world-middle-east-33690060, Accessed 7 August 2016.
26. A northern town in Syria, ISIS control and is critical location for supplies and other logistic support. The lost of Jarablus is major setback for the ISIS.
27. For detail see, "Syria War: Rival Claims as Turkish Strikes Kill at least 25" BBC News, 29 August 2016, URL: http://www.bbc.com/news/world-middle-east-37208941, Accessed 29 August 2016.

CHAPTER 4

Political Situation of the Kurds in Iran and Syria

Kurdish demands for autonomy or independence for Kurdistan (the land of Kurds) has been one of the most enduring sources of conflict in modern West Asia. The end of World War I and the disintegration of the Ottoman Empire created a power vacuum in the region. Moreover, the end of the Cold War augured new versions of global order and conflict management. The rise of ethnic consciousness and the political demands of many minority or ethnic groups for self-determination have run against the perceived interests of the state as the dominant actor in global politics. The history of Kurdish ethno-nationalism demonstrates the politicisation of Kurdish ethnicity coinciding with the formation of the modern nation-state system in the Middle East.

The Kurdish nation is living and suffering a particular critical conjuncture in its history. At a time when democracy and respect for human rights are making advances in many parts of Asia, Europe and elsewhere, the transgressions against Kurdish lives and liberties are getting worse. The situation of the Kurds of Iraq has strongly motivated the Iranian and Syrian Kurds to aspire to similar achievements for an autonomous Kurdistan. The outcome of the two wars i.e. the Gulf War and the American invasion of Iraq further ignited the problems and the prospects for the Kurds in the region. The transnational aspect of the Kurdish question has contributed to mutual influencing of the Kurdish nationalist movements throughout the twentieth and well into the twenty-first century in Middle East. The Kurds have manifested an independent spirit throughout modern Iranian history—rebelling against central government efforts to restrict their autonomy during Safavid, Qajar, Pahlavi and during the post-1979 Revolution.

The Kurds in Iran

A Brief Historical Overview

Iran is a country of diverse ethnic and linguistic communities. There are Kurds in the west and northwest, Baluchis in the east, Turks in the north and northwest, and Arabs in the south. Persians are situated in the central areas. Throughout the history of Iran, these ethnic groups have lived in geographically distinct regions and provinces. Along with this residential separation, social and economic distance has long persisted and it continues among ethnic communities. Iran has always been predominantly populated by people of distinct linguistic and cultural identities. Persians or Parthians (the Greeks called them "Perse" from the provinces they were usually found in viz., Pars or Fars) generally lived in the Central Plateau. Kurds lived in the ranges of the west and northwest (the Zagros Mountains) since the period of the Medes. In the valleys of Central Asia were the Turks, in the south were the Qufs and towards the southeast were another Iranian ethnic group known as the Baluchis (Aghajanian 1983: 1). There was never any mass colonisation of Iran by the Arabs, but penetration in the southwestern and southern regions continued where the climate was favourable.

Ethnic Composition

Persians (50%) may dominate Iran numerically and politically, but there are many smaller groups with their own agendas including the Arabs (3%) and the Baluchis (2%). Most Turkomans (2%), Lurs (2%), Gilakis and Mazandaranis (8% in all) are assimilated because they speak Persian dialects. But while some of the Azeris (26 per cent) are assimilated as well, many of them speak their own language and increasingly seek a united Azeri nation encompassing much of Azerbaijan. Religion further complicates matters, and the Persian Shi'a persecution of the Bahais, Christians, Jews, Zoroastrians and Sunnis has stoked resentment for the Tehran regime. Kurds make up around 10–15 percent (approximately 4 million) of Iran's population and have made repeated challenges to the Iranian state. They are the third most important ethnic group in the country after the Persians and Azerbaijanis. The area that can be described as Iranian Kurdistan stretches over three or four provinces. They are concentrated in the area of the Zagros Mountains along the western frontiers with Turkey and Iraq and are adjacent to the Kurdish populations of both those countries. The Kurdish area of Iran includes most of West Azarbaijan, all of Kurdistan, Bakhtaran (formerly known as Kermanshahan until 1979), Ilam and parts of Lorestan. The province of Kurdistan (the only province that is governmentally recognised as a Kurdish area) is populated entirely by Kurds. The Kurds in western Azerbaijan share their area with the Azeris and in Kermenshahan, the region is shared with the ethnic Lurs. The majority of the Kurds are Shi'ite. In the 1970s, there were substantial migrations of rural Kurds to historic Kurdish cities such as Sanandaj, Bakhtaran and Mahabad. There are also scatterings of Kurds in the provinces of Fars, Kerman, Baluchestan and Sistan, and there are large groups of approximately 350,000 living in a small area of northern Khorasan[1] (Hassan 2008: 4-8; Yildiz and Taysi 2007: 4). These are all descendants of Kurds whom the government forcibly removed from western Iran during the seventeenth century. Kurdistan in Iran covers an area of about 1,25,000 square kilometres. It reaches from Mount Ararat in the north to the other side of the Zagros Mountains. In the west it is bound by the Iraqi–Iranian and Turkish–Iranian borders and in the east by the Lake of Uromiah.[2] Within Iranian Kurdistan, as with greater Kurdistan, there is no geographic, economic or cultural homogeneity. Geographically, Iranian Kurdistan contains mountains, plains, villages and large urban areas (Koohi-Kamali 2003: 26-27).

Fig.4.1 Iran's Ethnic Distribution

Source: http://timesofislamabad.com/is-kusdish-rebellion-on-rise-in-irans-kurdish-region/2016/06/27/

The Kurds became pawns in the Persian–Ottoman rivalry beginning in the early sixteenth century with the coming to power of the Safavid dynasty in Iran. Taking advantage of their religious (Sunni) affinity with the Kurds, the Ottoman sultans sought to attract the allegiance of the Kurds against the Shi'ite Safavid Iran. Throughout the sixteenth century, both Ottoman and Safavid administrations embarked upon sustained programmes of creating strong centralised states; a policy that ran counter to the relative freedom of Kurdish principalities and led to Kurdish revolts (Entessar 1992: 11). Although the rebellions were crushed either by Ottoman or Iranian armies, the state leaders found it necessary to reach an agreement to control the Kurds.

The Iranian ruling powers in whatever form they may have taken, have historically demonstrated a less than accommodating stance towards the Kurds that lived within their borders. Throughout the sixteenth century both the Ottomans and Safavids emerged as regional powers. The Kurds were targeted specifically by the Safavids as they were deemed problematic to their power. This led to the formulation of treaties—such as one signed between the Ottomans and Safavids in 1639—which designated the semi-sovereign Kurdish principalities to the Ottoman and Persian Empires in an effort to control the Kurds. It marked the beginning of the strategy employed by state powers of pitting Kurdish tribes against each other. The Safavid administration engaged in a selective system of punishment and rewards that took advantage of tribal hostilities. By the mid-nineteenth century, all the Kurdish principalities had come under the direct control of the central government (Entessar 1992: 11-12).

Simko Revolts against Reza Shah

The weakness of the Persian government during World War I encouraged some Kurdish chiefs to take advantage of the chaotic situation. Ismail Agha Simko, Chief of the Shikar tribe, established his authority in the area west of the Lake Uromiah from 1918 to 1922. Jaafar Sultan of the Hewraman region also took control of the region between Marivan and northern Halabja. When Reza Pahlavi seized power in 1921 through a military coup, he adopted a zero-tolerance policy towards the Kurdish rebellions and uprisings. In 1922, Reza Khan (who later became the first Pahlavi monarch) took action against the Kurdish leader Simko. The Iranian government persuaded him and he was killed in 1930. Simko's revolt was the first major attempt by the Kurds to establish an independent Kurdistan in Iran. After the revolt, Reza Shah pursued a crude but effective policy against the Kurds (Entessar 1992: 12-13)[3]. Reza's reasoning was that tribal rebellions needed to be met with an overwhelming display of military force. As Reza consolidated his hold on power, taking on the title of Reza Shah, he initiated a new repressive period of nation-state building, creating a centralised nationalist state agenda and a uniform national identity emphasised on 'Persian Consciousness' over other ethnic or religious identities. Part and parcel of the centralisation programme was the disarming and sedenterisation of the tribes and the establishment of central control. Reza Shah's policies greatly affected the tribal people of Iran, weakening tribal relationships and changing the socio-economic characteristics of the tribal communities including the Kurdish tribal community whose leaders were forced to obey the central government. This state of affairs continued till August 1941, when the Allied forces entered Iran and Reza Shah was force to leave the country (Koohi-Kamali 2003: 92).

Much like Kemalist Turkey, Reza Shah strove for a secular, Westernised society, promoting industrialisation and economic self-assurance (Cleveland 1994: 174) and under the aegis of his society for 'Public Guidance', attempted to thwart all expression of non-Persian identity. The Kurds, as with the other non-Persian ethnic groups in Iran, suffered greatly under the enforced 'Persianification'. Textbooks, radio broadcasts and all other forms of printed work in non-Persian were banned. The use of Kurdish in education, public speech or print was forbidden. Kurdish schools were closed down and government administrative positions in Kurdish regions were given to Azeri and Persian officials. Reza Shah's emulation of Ataturk's policies continued and he referred to the Kurds as 'Mountain Iranians' coinciding with the use of the term 'Mountain Turks' used to describe the Kurds in Turkey after the establishment of the Turkish Republic. But, he stopped form banning the use of the word 'Kurd' (Bullock and Harvey 1993: 99-100).

As the Second World War broke out, German influence in Iran became increasingly marked, leading to the abdication of Reza Pahlavi under extreme pressure from the Allies in September 1941. After the abdication, the efficacy of the central government's control over tribal areas in Iran was greatly weakened. Mohammad Reza, Reza Shah's son and successor, was weak and lacking in authority; his actual power was diminished greatly by the Soviets and the British who had consolidated their control over Iran and were in the form of military occupiers, in de facto control of the country.

The Kurdish region fell under the Soviet sphere of influence and it was with their aid that the Kurds were able to form the Republic of Mahabad in 1946, taking advantage of the weakness of the central government (Yildiz and Taysi 2007: 36).

The Republic of Mahabad

In August 1941, the Allied Forces entered Iran. The British occupied the south of the country and the Soviets positioned themselves in the north. Reza Shah, suspected of having German sympathies, was forced by the British to abdicate. The Iranian army collapsed in the occupied areas. Taking advantage of the national and international situation, the Kurds stove for autonomy. The imprisoned or internally exiled chiefs established local independence and armed themselves with their own hidden arms but also with the arms that were acquired after Persian troops fled the area. In the cities, the urban intellectuals organised political groups and began to advocate Kurdish political and cultural autonomy. The result of these efforts was the establishment of the Kurdish Republic of Mahabad in 1946. The formation of the Kurdish Republic was the result of a cooperation between an educated elite represented by urban middle-class intellectuals who were promoting Kurdish cultural political nationalism and a military/political elite represented by the powerful tribal chiefs who tried to take advantage of the wartime confusion to gain independence.

However, the Republic existed only for a short period since the presence of the external forces and the Allied occupation of Iran during World War II was temporary. The West decided to back the Shah's regime and consolidate its power throughout the country. The Soviets took the side of the Iranian government with the hope of obtaining an oil concession. This sealed the defeat of the Kurdish Republic which was too weak to resist the Western-equipped, supervised, strongly supported political and military force of the Iranian regime. The Kurdish Republic lasted for 11 months and controlled about one-third of the whole Kurdish areas. Its sovereignty extended in the northeast from Saqqiz over the northern sectors of Iranian Kurdistan with a population of about one million. The rest of Kurdistan including many rich areas remained out of its control and was deprived of economic strength and manpower (Koohi-Kamal 2003: 123).

On March 31, 1947, Qazi Mohammad, his brother, Sadr-i-Qazi and his cousin, Seif-i-Qazi were hung in the Chavar Chira. The Tehran government had reestablished its authority in Mahabad and with that a long period of political repression began. Kurdish books were gathered by soldiers and burned; teaching of the Kurdish language became forbidden (Koohi-Kamali 2003: 121). After the fall of Mahabad, Mohammad Reza continued the sedenterisation programme begun by his father, attempting to reintegrate the non-Persian residents of Iran into the emerging centralised power structure of the state (Entessar 1992: 23).

By the time of the Mahabad events, Reza Shah's tribal policy had left a great impact on the Kurdish communities which were entirely sendentarised. The shortcoming of the Republic was connected with the composition of the leadership which was politically and culturally led by the urban intellectuals. The inability of the Kurdish intelligentsia to mobilise the Kurdish masses had limited the movement. Geographically and ideologically, it did not spread to all the Kurdish areas. Moreover, the Republic's programme of social and economic reforms failed to deal with the issues of tribalism. The Kurdish leaders had almost no political experience (Koohi-Kamal 2003: 123-124). The Kurdish Democratic Party was not a mature organisation. It lacked a well-organised and strong leadership to take the movement forward. Moreover, the boundaries of ideology were not clear and it was unable to offer a comprehensive programme for the Republic. The Party was neither homogenous nor unified; disagreement and division made it difficult for the Party to make decisions at crucial moments. However, in spite of all its shortcomings, the Kurdish Republic was the first modern Kurdish nationalist movement. It represented a great achievement towards the achievement of the Kurdish national independence. The Republic forwarded a historical image of the Kurds as a nation. The establishment of a briefly independent Kurdish republic at Mahabad has since served as an inspiration to nationalists.

The Constitution of the Islamic Republic was ratified in November 1979, which was a major setback for human rights in general and for the rights of women and religious minorities in particular.[4] Under the new Constitution, certain religious minorities such as Zoroastrians, Christians, Jews, and Sunni Muslims were recognised (Hassan 2008: 3).

The Islamic Revolution and the Kurds

Following the 1979 Revolution in Iran that toppled the monarchical regime, the people of Iranian Kurdistan actively participated in bringing about the collapse of the Shah regime. Kurdish political parties played a key role in rallying public support for a better future for Iran that could accommodate the various nationalities among which were the Kurds, within an integral Iran. The Democratic Party of Iranian Kurdistan (PDKI) among other political parties propagated a democratic Iran with an autonomous region in the areas belonging to various nationalities including Kurds, Azeris, Baluchis, Arabs and Turkomans. But, the newly installed clerical regime declared a holy war against the people of Kurdistan and considered the Kurdish political parties debarred including the PDKI. Ayatollah Khomeini declared *Jihad* (holy war) against the Kurdish people. Since then a massive military, economic, cultural and psychological war has been waged in Iranian Kurdistan against a civilian Kurdish population.[5] When it became clear that the new government had no intention of giving the Kurds either democracy or autonomy, the Kurds rebelled against the government. This rebellion was met with repression by the Iranian government. As a result of this systematic genocidal campaign, tens of thousands of innocent people were killed and injured and millions displaced during the 30-year reign of the Islamic regime in Iran. The Iran–Iraq war was used as an excuse by both sides to repress their own Kurds. Since then, Iranian Kurd rebels have been using Iraq, and later, the Kurdish autonomous zone in Iraq as a base for their attacks (Young 1999: 2).

The Kurdish uprising proved more deep-rooted, serious and durable. The Kurdish leaders were disappointed that the Revolution had not brought them the local autonomy that they had long desired. Scattered fighting began in March 1979 between the government and Kurdish forces and continued after a brief ceasefire. Attempts at negotiation proved abortive. One faction, led by Ahmad Moftizadeh, the Friday-prayer leader in Sanandaj was ready to accept the limited concessions offered by the government, but the Kurdish Democratic Party led by Abd-al-Rahman Qasemlou and a more radical group led by Shaykh Ezz-o-Din Hossaini demanded the inclusion of all Kurdish-speaking areas in Iran, a specified share of the national revenue for expenditure in the province and a complete autonomy in provincial administration.[6]

Kurdish was to be recognised as an official language for local use and for correspondence with the central government. Kurds were to fill all local government posts and to be in charge of local security forces. With the rejection of these demands, serious fighting broke out in August 1979. Ayatollah Khomeini, invoking his powers as commander-in-chief, used the army against other Iranians for the first time since the Revolution. No settlement was reached with the Kurds during Mehdi Bazargan's[7] Prime Ministership. However, the Islamic Revolution provided a golden opportunity to Kurdish nationalism.

Since the Mahabad Republic, the Iranian Kurds have remained active as a politico-military organisation in the form of the Kurdistan Democratic Party–Iran (KDP-I) and Komala, participating at times in regional conflicts although usually engaged in a localised, low-intensity conflict with the Iranian government. Under both the Shah of Iran and the Islamic Republic, the Kurds, like other non-Persian minorities, have suffered the general deprivation of cultural rights, economic development and political enfranchisement. After an initial surge of popular support for the removal of the Shah, the Iranian Kurdish nationalists and some left-wing opposition organisations immediately moved against the Islamist government from bases in Iranian Kurdistan. Teheran countered with bloody repressions and summary executions of the suspected opponents to the new regime, including KDP-I and the Mujahedin-i-Khalq, a leftist organisation that carried out executions of religious and political figures in the Teheran regime (Dahlman 2002: 284-85).

Kurdish Political Parties in Iran

The Kurdish political parties in Iran are weak as a result of internal disunity, political repression and the dependence of Iranian Kurds on government jobs. They lost their opportunity for more Kurdish autonomy after they failed to gain influence following the Islamic Revolution in 1979. The main Kurdish parties in Iran, the Kurdish Democratic party of Iran (KDPI) and the Marxist group Komala, fragmented into several factions after losing the war against the Iranian Revolutionary Guards in the 1990s.

Kurdish Democratic Party of Iran (KDPI)

The Democratic Party of Iranian Kurdistan (PDKI) also referred to as KDP, KDPI or DPIK, was founded in Mahabad, on August 16, 1945. PDKI replaced the 'Komalay Ziyanaway Kurd' (Council of Kurdish Resurrection). After the collapse of the Mahabad Republic and the execution of its President and KDP's founder, Qazi Mohammad, the Party went underground and shifted to the left, becoming closely allied with the (Communist) Tudeh Party. Repeated waves of arrests and reprisals in the 1950s thinned the

Party's membership; in 1959 most of the leaders, still at large, escaped to Iraq. The KDPI was the leading party during the period of the Islamic Republic. During the first years of confrontation with the Islamic Republic, the KDPI controlled large parts of the countryside. Since 1983, it has given up the idea of maintaining liberated areas (Bruinessen 1986: 17). During the Twentieth Congress of the Socialist International held at the UN headquarters in New York (September 9–11, 1996), PDKI was given the status of observer member. In 2007, PDKI's membership was elevated to a consultative status. The highest body of PDKI is its Central Committee, which is composed of 21 permanent and 10 substitute members. The Central Committee elects about 7 of its members as the Political Bureau, which includes the Secretary-General.

The KDPI defines its objectives as the following:

- The right of self-determination for the Kurdish people within Iran.
- The struggle against political, economic, military and cultural influences of imperialism.
- The establishment of a socialist society; A federal, democratic and independent Iran.
- Realisation of workers' social and economic demands.
- Equality of men and women in society and within the family.
- Separation of religion and state.[8]

The principal slogan of the KDPI since its establishment has been "Democracy for Iran; Autonomy for Kurdistan within the framework of a democratic Iran" (Bruinessen 1986: 17). The KDPI received its main support from the urban middle-class intellectuals (teachers and students), merchants and government employees and from the tribal elites.

The assassination of two KDPI leaders, Abd-al-Rahman Qasemlou in Vienna in 1989 and Sadeq Sharafkandi in Berlin in 1992, was a loss to the Kurdish struggles in Iran. The KDPI has been handicapped by internal rivalries for the past several years. Since 1994, there have been reports of internal problems existing within the KDPI that have weakened its political strength. As a result, its political activities were lessened dramatically; to the extent that the Party's viability was placed under question. A party which had been known for its democratic principles eventually became intolerant towards its own membership—to the point that division within the ranks eventually led to a split in December 2006. These problems culminated in the separation of the minority wing of Mala Abdualla Hasanzada from the majority wing of Moustapha Hedjri in December 2006. The split appeared to stem from personal, rather than ideological differences, between the two groups (Tahiri 2007).[9]

International and regional political developments have created a great opportunity for the Kurds. The Islamic Republic of Iran is facing international condemnation for its nuclear programme and its human rights abuses. An article in the *BBC News* reported that the Kurdistan Democratic Party of Iran has turned to arms only for defence and is in fact focusing on political activities. Moreover, Iraqi Kurdish officials have said that their regional government will allow groups like KDPI to operate in northern Iraq as long as they do not engage in military actions against Iran (Saberi 2007).

The Revolutionary Organisation of the Kurdish Toilers of Kurdistan (Komala)

The other major Kurdish organisation is the Revolutionary Organisation of the Toilers of Kurdistan (Komala) which became active during the Revolution. The Komala which was considered as a Marxist organisation has been acting as the Iranian Communist Party's Kurdistan branch since 1982.[10] Since its formation the Komala has been part of the Iranian National Resistance Council (a coalition of Iranian opposition groups based in Paris). The Komala has confronted the landowners and tribal chiefs in Kurdistan and has been involved in peasant uprisings. Komala's relations with the KDPI have vacillated from cooperative to conflicting (Entessar 1984: 929-930; Young 1999). Despite disagreements with the KDPI, it has supported the idea of democracy for Iran and autonomy in Kurdistan. As an independent Marxist group, Komala aims to establish a social system based on social justice and equality. It strives to end oppression and to achieve autonomy for the Iranian Kurds (Koohi-Kamali 1992: 180-181).

Komala, as a Marxist–Leninist Kurdish group, has struggled within a similar framework as that of the KDPI. However, Komala's target groups are mainly those which, despite being Kurds, do not have religious and exceedingly nationalist perspectives. They are against the existing feudalist structure which promotes KDPI sympathies among the Iranian Kurds. But, contradictory to its ideology the Komala accepts itself as a Kurdish party which has actively prioritised the rights of the Iranian Kurdish population. The Komala has given more importance to the concept of confidentiality for organising its cells. Komala and the KDPI had been involved in armed conflict in the early 1980s. But, they used their contacts for better relations with each other in the early 1990s. The development within the Komala is a split, which took place in August 2000, following their last Congress. A group led by Abdollah Mohtadi, the ex-CPI Secretary, left the Party. They formed the smaller Revolutionary Toilers' Komala of Kurdistan. They seek minority rights under a federative state. The said group had its one and only Congress in August 2001. The Komala had its Tenth Congress in July 2002 (Martin 2007). Komala has chosen to specifically target the Iranian regime until it addresses the plight of the Kurds and grants them autonomy.

Partiya Jiyana Azada Kurdistan or Party for Free Life in Kurdistan (PJAK)

Kurdish organisations such as the KDPI and Komala have carried out an armed resistance against the Islamic Republic of Iran, but they have abandoned an armed struggle in favour of a federal solution. During the late 1990s, when the traditionally established Kurdish political parties were mainly absent from Iran, the PKK received support from Iranian Kurds and many joined it. PJAK owes its legitimacy to the demands and aspirations of the Kurds, expressed following the abduction of the Kurdish National leader Abdullah Ocalan in 1999 (Rebin 2010). Iran faced armed opposition mainly from PJAK—the Kurdistan Independent Life Party—affiliated to the Turkish PKK, which reportedly began operations in 2004. The PJAK is effectively the Iranian branch of the PKK and shares its camps in northern Iraq. The group has declared a strategy of cooperation with minority groups in Iran; especially Balochis and Turkomans. PJAK has sought to adapt to military and political developments by re-branding itself internationally as a secular and primarily non-violent group seeking to stand up to Tehran's authoritarian Islamic rule (Brandon 2008). The autonomy of Kurds in neighbouring Iraq has inspired agitation for greater rights among Iran's roughly five million Kurds. PJAK as a militant separatist group conducted a number of guerrilla attacks in 2007.[11] It retained a military presence in the Qandil Mountains and other border areas of Iraq, prompting the Iranian military to periodically bombard Iraqi Kurdistan.[12]

However, PJAK has realised that the Kurdish issue can be solved in a political and peaceful way. To show its abhorrence for violence and hostility, PJAK has called on the Iranian government to stop its military operations in Kurdistan and lay the basis for negotiation of a peaceful settlement to the Kurdish issue. Nonetheless, the Iranian regime has failed to appreciate its call to solve the Kurdish question and has responded to the Kurds militarily (Brandon 2006; Rebin 2010).

Kurdish nationalism throughout the West Asian region has triggered Kurdish organisation in Iran to establish the Kurdish United Front. Iranian Kurds have created a movement aimed at peacefully promoting democracy and demanding rights that have been neglected or denied. Kurds have no share in the distribution of power and economic development; the four Kurdish provinces of Iran are not developed and are deprived. They face limitations in their cultural activities, which is preventing cultural development (Esfandiari 2006).[13] Some Kurdish activists believed that the creation of the Kurdish United Front was simply an attempt by reformist groups to regain political power.

Political Situation

The political system and governmental structure of the Islamic Republic of Iran is a unique and complex blend of theocratic and democratic government. Iran is the only Shi'ite state in the community of nations of the Muslim World and its legal framework is formulated in accordance with the precepts of religious jurisprudence and Shi'a traditions. The 1979 Revolution effectively changed the regime and established a governmental structure based on Ayatollah Khomeini's 1970 political treatise, *Islamic Government (Hukumat-e-Islami)*. The guidelines set out in this treatise emphasised support for a theocratic governmental structure and its perseverance within the political sphere. Following the Revolution, a state constitution was written to reflect these concepts. Iran's current political system and governmental structure is, therefore, based on the constitution introduced after the 1979 Revolution, which was amended in 1989 (Jones 2009: 15). The Iranian Constitution made Kurdish infiltration into the political hierarchy extremely difficult and the Kurdish population has often absented from participating in national elections. All activities by political parties are prohibited. The Islamic regime has outlawed all political parties in Kurdistan. According to paragraphs 197 to 202 of the Punishment Law, members of Kurdish parties are classified as 'evil'.[14]

The establishment of the Kurdish Regional Government (KRG) in Iraqi Kurdistan since 1991 has changed the position of the Iranian Kurds. The relationship between the KRG and Iran would not permit an armed struggle by the Iranian Kurds against Iran and the KDPI and Komala were prevented from military action against Iran by the Iraqi authorities. The Iranian government continued to make use of its good relations with the Iraqi Kurds and during the early years of 1990s assassinated a number of Kurds based in Iraqi Kurdistan.[15] During Mohammad Khatami's reformist presidency from 1996 to 2005, there was some opening of the cultural and political space in Iran. The Iranian Kurds, inspired by the achievement of the Iraqi Kurds and the escalation of PKK activities used this space/opportunity to embark on cultural activities on an unprecedented scale (Stansfield et al 2007: 6-7). The inclusion of Iran in the United States' 'Axis of Evil' and the invasion on Iraq in 2003 gave the Iranian Kurdish parties hope that the Iranian government might also fall. The Iranian Kurds responded to the election of Jalal Talabani as the Iraqi President by celebrating in the streets of Kurdish-dominated cities such as Mahabad. Similarly, there were significant demonstrations in other Iranian Kurdish cities following the passing of the Iraqi Constitution in which the federal system was approved and the Kurdistan region recognised. Following this, the main Kurdish parties of Iran adopted the idea of federalism. The political example of the Kurds in Iraq has been considerable; but, the economic and cultural achievements of the Iraqi Kurds have also influenced the Iranian Kurds significantly—especially, with the Iranian Kurds standing prominently in the flourishing artistic and cultural milieu of Arbil and Sulaymaniyah. From a nationalist point of view, they are not only happy for the achievements of the Kurds in Iraq, but also dream about enjoying similar political and cultural rights in Iranian Kurdistan (Stansfield and Ahmadzadeh 2009: 9-10).

During certain periods, relations between the government and the Kurds did improve—most notably during the Mohammad Khatami regime. Elected in 1997, Khatami publicly supported the Kurdish struggle and sought to provide a more integrated level of representation. The reformist Khatami received more than 75 percent of the Kurdish vote when he was elected President of Iran in 1997. The Kurds along with the great majority of Iranians had felt deeply unhappy with the hardline Islamic regime. They supported Mohammad Khatami and his reform movement which promised greater social and political freedom for all Iranians including ethnic and religious minorities. Khatami appointed Abdullah Ramazanzadeh, a Kurd, as the first Governor-General of Iranian Kurdistan. In his second term of office Khatami brought Ramazanzadeh to Tehran to serve as a cabinet secretary (Koohi-

Kamal 2003:175). However, this period of amicable relations was short-lived and by 1999, protests in the streets of Kurdish cities such as Mahabad, Sanandaj and Urmia had broken out in support of the imprisoned leader of the PKK, Abdulallah Ocalan. This was viewed as trans-nationalisation of the Kurdish movement. These protests were violently suppressed by the government forces. According to human rights groups, at least twenty people were killed.[16]

The 2000 Parliamentary elections prompted a backlash by hardline clerics. Eighteen Kurds were elected to the new *Majlis* after the first round of elections in February 2000. President Khatami also appointed several Sunni and Shi'a Kurds as cabinet advisors as well as two Kurdish cabinet members. Kurdish inclusion in the central government increased substantially which created some optimism for Kurdish expectations of self-governing autonomy and saw the creation of a 40-member Parliamentary faction representing the predominantly Kurdish provinces of Kurdistan and Kermanshah (Yavuz and Gunter 2001:39). Widely seen as responsible for easing tensions in the region, Ramazanzadeh's exit from the cabinet and combined with the Guardian Council progressive attack on the reformist government meant progress in Kurdistan slowed to an unacceptable pace in 2001. The Kurdish representatives like the others who demanded change realised the obstacles in achieving their goals. The most dramatic manifestation of their demands was made for equal treatment. In October 2001, Kurdish representatives—a legislator and five deputies of the *Majlis*—from the province of Kurdistan collectively resigned in protest against the Khatami government's double standards in discriminating against the Kurds. One of the main concerns expressed was their unhappiness with the appointment of a non-Kurd as the new Governor-General after the popular Ramazandeh was summoned to Tehran to become a cabinet secretary in President Khatami's cabinet (Koohi-Kamal 2003: 213-215). They accused Khatami's government of discrimination against Kurds. Many analysts believed that the Kurds, as other Iranians, cast their votes in the Presidential elections not to endorse Khatami, but to reject the hardliners.

Despite being re-elected with 78 percent of the votes in 2001, Khatami did not challenge the conservative clerics. He ignored recurrent pleas by reformist lawmakers to call a referendum to approve vetoed reform legislation and repeatedly implored citizens to refrain from demonstrating in public. Within the broader reform movement, Khatami was accused of serving as a democratic façade for an oppressive regime. Khatami's reformist administration had delivered nothing in terms of recognising the Kurdish language including education. The Kurds felt they were being discriminated against in government jobs and investment and they resented the heavy presence of the army and the Revolutionary Guard (Smyth 2014). Many Iranians abandoned hopes for a government-led reform and a record-low turnout for the 2003 municipal elections resulted in a landslide victory for the hardliners.[16]

The hardline conservatives managed to thwart the reform movement at almost every step, blocking many reform-minded Parliamentarians from the 2001 election. As a result, Mohammad Khatami lost credibility in the eyes of his supporters when he did not postpone the elections. The situation continued to deteriorate, as over half of the Kurdish Parliamentarians were prevented from participating in the February 2004 Parliamentary election. As expected, the election was boycotted by over 70 percent of the Kurds and civil unrest occurred in Kurdish cities in protest of the unfair elections. The low turnout in Kurdistan for the election was interpreted by the KDPI as a sign that the Kurds in Iran supported a policy of boycotting the election. Among the boycotting parties, Komala asked the Kurds to take part in the demonstrations and support the public movement in Iran. However, the subsequent months witnessed no serious events in Kurdistan in support of the reformists, with demonstrations in Iran against the results of the election being limited to the major cities such as Tehran, Shiraz, Isfahan and Mashhad. Other smaller cities were not involved in the demonstrations. Some of the Kurds were arguing that if the Kurds took part in these demonstrations, there would be a danger of Iranian security forces turning their attention to Kurdistan. Nevertheless, the Kurdish students who lived in Tehran were active in the demonstrations (Yildiz and Taysi 2007: 44). The Iranian Kurds expressed an overwhelming dissatisfaction with the government, believing that Khatami's reformist platform had fallen short of the promised improvement in integration and participation and had failed to engage the Kurds in a political process with the regime. Moreover, the Kurds remain frustrated with years of regional underdevelopment and cultural discrimination behind them.

Mahmoud Ahmadinejad's[18] victory in the 2005 Presidential elections capped a return to power for Iran's radical, hardline conservatives and marked a departure in Iran's domestic policy. The election that ended in run-off was widely reviewed both within Iran and in the international community as being neither fair nor free. The election was heavily boycotted by the Kurds many of whom believed that Mahmoud Ahmadinejad had been involved in the murder of the KDPI leader Abdul Ghassemlou in 1989. There was fear that his ascension would usher in a worrying roll-back of the little reform that had occurred. Soon after his presidential inauguration, reports surfaced of his 'harsh' turndown of the request from Kurdish Members of the Parliament to include Kurds in his cabinet.[19] Although ethnic riots and violations of human rights in Iran have not been uncommon in the past, incidents of ethnic unrest seem to have risen steadily after President Ahmedinejad took office in 2005

The prolonged exile/absence of the Iranian Kurdish parties and the KRG–Iranian friendship has caused strains among the parties. There are different factions and organisations that are active on behalf of the Iranian Kurdish population; the PDKI has long been seen as the central organisation for Kurdish representation. The PDKI has long withdrawn from its military struggle and has been pursuing a non-violent and diplomatic campaign. Iranian Kurdish parties have also consistently fractured and there have been major splits in both the KDPI and Komala. In early 2006, the Kurdish United Front, a movement that is not an official party but a non-governmental organisation, was formed in Iranian Kurdistan by Bahaeddin Adab, a former Kurdish Member of Parliament, who was banned along with thousands of other reformists from running in the 2004 Parliamentary elections. The KUF plans to help Kurdish representatives gain seats in the city councils and in the national parliament, as well as to raise the Kurds' awareness of their rights and to demand the implementation of the equal rights and democracy promised to them by law in Iranian Kurdistan (Yildiz and Taysi 2007: 111). In December 2006, a significant number of members in the KDPI broke away, renaming themselves KDP (removing 'Iran' from the name of the Party and returning to the original name as established in 1945). The change of name not only distinguished the new party from the old, but also related to its broadly nationalist approach. In October 2007, a number of Komala's leading figures broke away to form 'Komala—the Faction of Reform and Development'. In both cases there were physical clashes among the followers of the various factions (Stansfield et al 2007: 6-7). The main reason behind this bifurcation of the Kurdish parties in Iran is that they have not been present inside Iranian Kurdistan for the last two decades. This has meant that they have not engaged in armed struggle since

1990 and they have become increasingly isolated from the vast majority of the Iranian Kurds. Their failure in conducting an armed resistance against the Iranian government has been matched by their inability to engage with the Kurdish civil society that emerged and developed during Muhammad Khatami's presidency. In fact, the Kurdish parties of Iran never showed any interest in the policies of the reformists in Iran and viewed them suspiciously. For some of them, a reformist victory in the last election would have been viewed as quite counterproductive for the Kurds. Mustafa Hijri, the leader of the KDPI, has in an interview argued that it was a good thing that Mir Hossein Moussavi did not win the recent elections. According to him, if Moussavi had won the election, it only could have resulted in prolonging the Islamic regime. The long years of living in exile and not having to adapt to the social and political changes in Iranian Kurdistan have caused a disconnect to emerge between the parties and the Iranian Kurdish society. The socio-economic changes in Iranian Kurdistan and the rise of a young, highly educated generation with new aspirations and demands have deepened the gap with the classical Kurdish political parties. Furthermore, the introspective and self-absorbed manner that the parties have used to treat their internal conflicts and disagreements has had very negative effects on their perception by young Iranian Kurds (Stansfield and Ahmadzadeh 2009: 10-11).

The Iranian Kurdish parties are heavily divided and the Iranian government policy remains unyielding. Following decades of alienation from national political activities, Kurdish participation has improved slightly. Whilst direct Kurdish parliamentary representation has been limited by the omission of the Kurds from the Constitution, the election of Kurdish politicians to positions advising the Guardian Council, governing the Kurdish region and as a part of the cabinet have prompted premature optimism. Despite all the difficulties facing the Iranian Kurdish political parties, no policy of change in Iran, whether internal or external, can ignore them. Furthermore, the high degree of political and national consciousness among Kurds in Iran has been heightened by the establishment of the KRG in Iraq (Stansfield et al 2007: 5-6). However, the first Kurdish government since Mahabad offered an inspirational political model—but more importantly—provided a central operational base for Kurdish activities. Kurdish politics is and has been an integral part of the bigger political picture in Iran.

Human Rights Violations in Iranian Kurdistan

Iran has undoubtedly become one of the international community's most discussed countries in the world. The Islamic Republic's pursuance of nuclear technology has raised concerns, but has also overshadowed the more serious issues. Under the leadership of the Islamic Republic of Iran, the rate of executions in Iran has risen to one of the highest in the world. Although the Kurdish people consist of less than 15 percent of the Iranian population, they make up about half of the number of people executed and have been subjected to political persecution in the past 10 years. Many Kurdish political prisoners and civilians are also executed in secret. Since July 2005, over 1,500 Kurdish civilians have been killed, executed, sentenced to jail or charged to pay compensation by the security forces of the Islamic Republic. For instance, Mohammad Sadiq Kaboudvand, a well known Kurdish human rights activist who founded the Kurdish Human Rights Organization (HROK) in 2005, was arrested in July 2007 and was charged with acting against national security through HROK (Hassan 2009). During the uprising in July 2005 over 1,700 Kurds were arrested and the fate of the numerous detainees remains unknown.[20] Similarly in 2005, after the murder by Iranian security forces of the Kurdish activist Shivan Qaderi in Mahabad, six weeks of riots and protests erupted across Kurdistan and in neighbouring Baluchistan resulting in the deaths and illegal detention of hundreds of people and led to the closure of several major Kurdish newspapers.[21] The relationship between the Kurds and the government is highly fractious; as the Kurds sought a legitimate representation, religious equality and some level of autonomy.

Like elsewhere in Iran, student activists in Kurdish areas often face charges of "acting against national security." Authorities also accuse students of endangering national security by "working with opposition parties". One way by the authorities to suppress student activism is through the university disciplinary committees, which have the authority to expel or transfer students to other universities. These committees have a record of using their powers to punish students for peaceful political activities (Human Rights Watch 2006). Souren Hosseini, head of the Democratic Student Union, an organisation for Kurdish students headquartered in Sanandaj and with branches in campuses throughout Iran, is an example of a student who faced punishment and persecution for his activism. In May 2005, Hosseini and several others applied to the Kurdistan provincial government for a permit to form a student union, but they didn't receive a response. On December

14, 2006, the university disciplinary committee expelled him from campus on charges of "disturbing the public mind" for organising campus protests and transferred him to a university in the city of Dehghan (Human Rights Watch 2009: 27).

The Kurdish people in Iran have been heavily targeted by the Islamic Republic since its 1979 inception when Ayatollah Khomeini declared a fatwa against the province of Kurdistan. The Revolutionary Guard crushed the opposition unrest by sending 1,10,000 troops complete with heavy artillery, fighter jets and armed helicopters. According to the International Campaign for Human Rights in Iran, since Hassan Rouhani took office in 2013, Iran has executed more than 200 people; especially Kurdish activists. Iran's human rights violations became grotesque with the rise in executions and in the number of political prisoners inside the country (Paveh 2014).

The 15th Article of the Iranian Constitution states that the government language is Persian (Farsi), and that "the use of regional and tribal languages in the press and mass media, as well as for teaching of their literature in schools, is allowed in addition to Persian."[22] Despite the language provisions in the Iranian Constitution, the Ahwazis, Baluchis, Kurds and southern Azerbaijanis face difficulties in exercising their rights to use their own languages, both in private and in public. These minority linguistic rights guaranteed by the Constitution are not provided in practice.[23] For example, all state-schooling in Kurdish areas is conducted exclusively in Persian. The study of Kurdish language in schools is prohibited. Kurdish websites, newspaper and magazines are closed or charged for their content including several human rights organisations and periodicals such as the *Sirwan Weekly*, the Kurdish-language magazine with the largest circulation in Iran which attempted to develop linkages with the wider rights' movement, promoting dialogue rather than divisiveness. Unfortunately, in the growing climate of repression, the Iranian authorities closed down the *Sirwan Weekly* along with the other periodicals in the 2006 (Yildiz and Taysi 2007: 111). The conservative judiciary closed more than 100 reformist newspapers and jailed hundreds of liberal journalists and activists, while security forces cracked down on the ensuing student protests. Significant political and economic reforms were overwhelmingly approved by the Parliament only to be vetoed by the Council of Guardians. The economy of the Kurdish area has collapsed and the unemployment rate in Kurdistan is estimated to be 47%.[24] The human rights violation in Iranian Kurdistan is not a result of sporadic or persistent violation of some officers but it is the result of a systematic programmed policy of the Islamic Republic of Iran against the Kurds and the people of Iran. The majority of the groups and organisations operating in Iranian Kurdistan maintain a broader agenda and often couch Kurdish demands in the context of the general democratic rights for all Iranians.

Iran's Domestic Dilemmas

Iran has a unique governing framework which accords ultimate power to non-elected and unaccountable Islamic clerics—culminating power in the Supreme Leader Ayatollah Ali Khomenei. Under this regime, the Iranian government has enforced severe restrictions on all aspects of political, cultural and economic life and routinely violates even those limited protections enacted in its own Constitution and laws. The restricted scope of Iran's electoral politics was made clear in the Parliamentary elections held in February 2004 in which the clerical oversight body disqualified more than 3,000 candidates from competing including 80 sitting Members of the Parliament (Jones 2009: 23-24).

Iran's theocratic system is deeply unpopular with its citizenry. Many Iranians across a wide spectrum of age, class and ethnic and religious backgrounds are candid and scathing in their criticism of their government and its politics. Iran also expressed this ciriticism through a series of surprising electoral outcomes in the late 1990s that even within the narrow limits of permissible politics indicated resounding support for progressive reform of the governing system. Large-scale demonstrations are rare due to a fear of repression, but they have surfaced intermittently and with great intensity in various parts of the country (Brzezinski and Gates 2004: 15). Most notable were the July 1999 and June 2003 student protests—both of which were violently crushed by government security forces.

Young people comprise as much as 70 percent of the population and are positioned to serve as arbiters of the country's political order. Young Iranians are highly literate, well-educated and supportive of expanded social and cultural liberties and political participation. Approximately, one-thirds of the young job seekers are unemployed. Economic interests rank high on their list of political priorities. With the disqualification of liberal-minded candidates from Iran's 2004 Parliamentary elections, the country's reform movement has effectively been sidelined as a significant factor in formulating the domestic and international policies. Reformist leaders were largely unwilling to challenge the basic parameters of Islamic politics and their organisation which includes nascent political parties such as the Islamic Iran Participation Front (IIPF)[25] proved unable to mount an effective bid for change. Conservatives and hardliners who are committed to the preservation of the Islamic Republican's states quo remain firmly in control of all institutions and instruments of power in Iran. They represent the love for power and are the only authoritative interlocutors for any diplomatic interface. Although some may be amenable to a limited moderation of Iranian polices and rhetoric, conservatives have repeatedly demonstrated their willingness to preserve the regime by crushing anti-regime protests and imprisoning or even killing their opponents (Brzezinski and Gates 2004: 15-16).

The Kurds in Syria

The Kurds in Syria, in contrast to the Kurds of Iraq, Iran and Turkey are little known in the West, but they have similarly strained relations with the state that governs them and face human rights abuses as a minority. The Kurds in Syria have been subjected to discriminatory practices for decades. The exclusive ethno-centric Arab nation-building project also officially called the Arab Republic of Syria has denied other ethnic and cultural groups an equal and lawful existence (Yildiz 2005: 4-5). Syrian Kurds have had an almost negligible international profile compared to their neighbours as there has been much less violence in their relationship with the Syrian state. This is largely due to their smaller number and scattered geographical distribution as well as the effectiveness of the official coercion and repression.

Syrian Kurds have been greatly affected by the entanglement of inter-Kurdish and Kurdish–state relationships in West Asia. Historical, tribal and family ties with Kurds across the borders in Turkey, Iran and Iraq remain very strong. Syria's Kurds, as a less numerous and prominent group, have been recruited, abandoned and deeply influenced by the Kurdish movements. Developments in Iraq and Turkey have had a major influence on the Kurds in Syria. They have been excluded from the state's ideology and also from individual social and economic advancement—unless they are prepared to become effectively Arabs in all but ethnic origin. This requires abandoning Kurmanji in favour of Arabic and accepting Arab cultural and political values and goals (Lowe 2006: 2). However, it would be a mistake to see the Kurdish problem in Syria solely as an ethnic problem with a regional dimension; the Syrian Kurds should be seen within the context of the lack of democratic governance in Syria which affects all Syrians. The Kurds are denied basic human rights especially civil, political and cultural rights. However, the situation also offers a direction for policy work; the development of democratic governance in Syria could mitigate the Kurdish problem in Syria and in turn diminish calls for separatism by other Kurds in the region (Ziadeh 2009: 1-2).

The Kurdish Population

The Kurds constitute the largest national minority in Syria and the only one with a territorial base. The Syrian Constitution calls the country 'the Syrian Arab Republic' implying thereby that all its citizens are considered to be Arabs—their ethnic origins notwithstanding (Vanly 1992: 146). Yet, the Syrian authorities have shown intolerance to the Kurds.

Fig4:2 Kurdish Areas in Syria

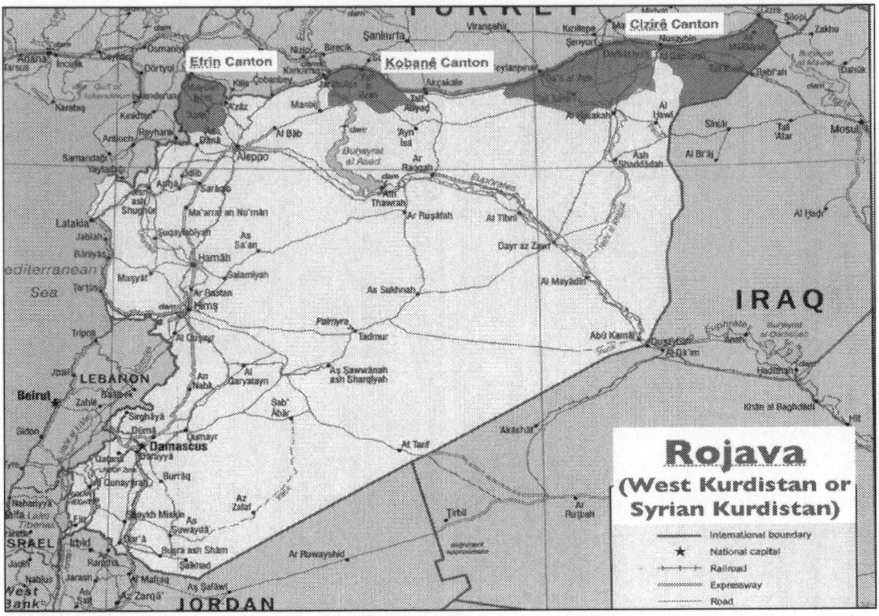

Source: "Syrian Kurdistan or Rojava". http://www.geocurrents.info/geopolitics/state-failure/isis-advances-kurds-retreat-northern-syria

The Kurdish populations in Syria are estimated to be nearly 1.5 million or approximately 9 percent of a total population of 22 million making them the largest non-Arab minority.[26] Because of the government's anti-Kurdish policies and intentional census manipulation, the actual figure is distorted (Dahlman 2002: 292). Many Syrian Kurds migrated from Turkey in the 1920s, while others have been living in areas of Aleppo and al-Hassakah province in the northeast for centuries. Figure 3 illustrates the Kurdish areas in Syria. They are also concentrated primarily in the north and northeast of the country, in Jazeera, Efrin and Ain al-Arab regions (Lynch and Ali 2006: 6). The majority of the Syrian Kurds speak the Kurdish language (Kurmanji) and identify with Sunni Islam.

Denationalisation and the Repression of Syrian Kurds

A Kurdish nationalist movement, *Khoybun,* emerged in the 1920s and vigorously lobbied for greater cultural and political autonomy but most of its demands like the establishment of the Kurdish-language schools, recognition of Kurdish as official language and the appointment of Kurdish administrators in Kurdish areas were rejected by the French (Gambill 2004). Moreover, beginning in 1956, a succession of Arab nationalist regimes came to power in Damascus and began suppressing the Kurdish minority. As a result, the Kurds in Syria continue to face obstacles in securing their basic rights. The legacy of the state's 'Arabisation' and nationalism campaigns of the 1960s and 1970s were conducted with the objective of gaining control of all internal social spheres by restricting political and civil rights in the name of internal stability. In October 1962, Syrian authorities issued a census in the al-Hassakah province, the northeastern Syrian province in which the majority of Kurds have their origin. The authorities produced statistical reports on the pretext of discovering people who may have crossed illegally from Turkey to Syria. As many as 12,00,000 Kurds (nearly 20 percent of Syria's Kurdish population) were revoked and denationalised (Kurd Watch 2009a; Yildiz 2005: 95). The government categorised them as 'stateless Kurds'. As a result, they lost all rights of citizenship, including the right to vote and participate in public life, the right to travel outside the country, the right to private ownership, right to education and the right to employment in the public sector (Lynch and Ali 2004: 4). In 1966, the Government continued the programme of 'Arabisation' whereby around 1,00,000 Kurds were moved out of 300 villages and were replaced by Arabs. This was reinforced in 1973 and the lands have not yet been returned to the Kurds. This was a tactic to separate the Kurdish population in Syria from the Kurds of Turkey and Iraq and to keep them in smaller groups. The number of stateless Kurds continued to grow and was estimated to be around 4,00,000 people.[27] Land has been an important issue between Kurds and the Syrian government. The policies of the Syrian state against the Kurds affect their land rights. The state has given land to Arabs in order to break up Kurdish geographical and cultural cohesion. They are not allowed to own property or to work within the state institution. No Kurds were issued licenses in reference to agricultural lands.

Since 1962, the Syrian state has divided the Kurds in Syria into three major demographic categories: Syrian Kurds, foreign Kurds and 'concealed' Kurds. Syrian Kurds have retained their Syrian nationality. Foreign Kurds were stripped of citizenship and registered in official archives as *Ajanib* ("foreigners" in Arabic); there were about 2,00,000 of them. Concealed Kurds are denationalised Kurds who have not been registered in official records at all and whom the Syrian authorities have characterised as "concealed". They were unregistered Kurds (in Arabic, *Muktumin*). The children of these people are discriminated against in various ways. For example, their access to education is limited. According to the Human Rights Watch, *Muktumin* are discriminated against on educational, legal and ethnic grounds (Yildiz 2005: 95). Nearly 80,000 people belong to this category. Among the concealed Kurds are persons whose fathers are classified as foreigners and whose mothers are citizens; persons whose fathers are foreigners and whose mothers are classified as concealed and persons whose fathers and mothers are classified as concealed. In addition, according to Kurdish sources, there are about 2,80,000 undocumented Kurds who reside in Syria, but have no citizenship. The official justification was that these Kurds were 'alien infiltrators' from Turkey who had crossed into Syria and hence had no entitlement to citizenship (Human Rights Watch 1996: 3). Therefore, no government statistics are available on this group. The Syrian government claimed that the Kurds have had little cause for complaint and comfortably identify with the Syrian nation because they have been included as full Syrian citizens with equal rights and opportunities like other ethnic or religious groups.

Syria's national identity has been a serious problem since the country's independence. The modernity and artificiality of Syria's borders and its multi-ethnic and religious make-up have made identity a complex affair. The struggle for Syrian independence from France was primarily fought in terms of 'Arab' nationalism. Since 1961 the official name of the country has been the 'Syrian Arab Republic', hence denying recognition of non-Arabs and instead placing Syria at the heart of a broader Arab nation. Pan-Arab nationalism continues to be the official ideology of Syria and has severe implications for the non-Arab minorities of Syria—most of all the Kurds. Syrian Arab attitudes towards Syrian Kurds must be seen within the context of the perceived threat posed by all Kurds to the 'Arab nation'—especially, given the long and bloody struggle between the Kurds and Arab governments in Iraq (Lowe 2006: 1).

The government started executing the resettlement plan in the early 1970s, but under a new terminological cover: for the 'Arab belt' the government substituted "Plan to establish model state farms in the Jazira province." Under the new justification for the plan, the government would build "model farming villages" in the Kurdish region and populate them with Arabs. The government expropriated the lands on which it built these 'model farms' from Kurdish owners, either under the guise of land reform or because the owners were Kurds whose citizenship had been withdrawn in 1962 because they had failed to prove their residency under that year's census. In 1975, the government resettled an estimated 4,000 Arab families, whose own lands had been submerged by the construction of the Tabqa dam on the Euphrates, in 'model farms' in the very heart of the Kurdish region. The government suspended the 'Arab Belt' project in 1976 but never dismantled the model villages nor returned the Kurds who had been displaced from their land (Human Rights Watch 1991: 186; Montgomery 2005: 12-13). The 'Arab Belt' was a plan for a cordon between the Syrian and neighbouring Kurds around the northern and northeastern rim of the Jazira along the borders with Turkey and Iraq. Kurdish land was confiscated and Kurds resettled in the Syrian interior to make way for Arabs. There was a strong military presence and Arab settlements were provided with superior facilities and state benefits to encourage greater economic prosperity (Lowe 2006: 3).

Kurds under Hafez al-Assad

The rise of nationalism, stemming regionally from Nasserism[28] and locally from the Baath Party's ascendancy in 1963, increased official discrimination against the Syrian Kurds. The Baathist government's Kurdish policy was intended to eradicate Kurdish presence from the Syrian public life (Ziadeh 2009: 2). The state-inspired campaign of Arabisation of the Kurds continued in the 1970s under the government of Hafez al-Assad. Under Hafez al-Assad, Arab nationalism became a founding principle of the 1973 Constitution. It became an essential component of political culture, whereas pan-Arab and socialist ideals gradually lost their significance. This meant that all Kurds were excluded from the state doctrine. Exclusion was reflected in the ban or non-admission of Kurdish political parties as well as in the repression of pro-Kurdish demonstrations and festivals by the security apparatus (Kurd Watch 2009 b: 16). Syria also emulated Saddam Hussein's policies by moving thousands of Arabs into the Kurdish regions to create a buffer between them and the Kurdish communities in the neighbouring states (Fattah 2005). Repression was one method of handling the Kurdish question under Assad. At the same time he endeavoured to integrate the Kurdish population into the 'national project' (for example, by opening up the Baath Party to non-Arabs). Moreover, the repression of the Kurdish national movement in his own country did not stop Assad from pursuing a pragmatic policy towards the Kurdish movements in Iraq and Turkey, i.e. he supported these movements when relations with their respective governments deemed it opportune. A prime example was his tolerance and support for the Turkish PKK and its leader Abdullah Ocalan in the 1980s and 1990s (Montgomery 2005: 131-132). This policy resulted in the consolidation of transnational relations between the Syrian Kurds and their 'brothers' across the border in Iraq and Turkey.

Violations of Cultural and Linguistic Rights

The Kurdish language in Syria, the Kurmanji dialect, was criminalised on several levels by decrees in the 1970s, 1980s and 1990s. As a result, the Kurdish names for hundreds of villages in both the al-Hassakah province and the Afrin region were replaced by Arabic names (Mcdowall 1998: 47-48). Syrian Kurds are under pressure to erase their cultural identity, including public celebrations and feasts as well as speaking Kurdish; the essential mechanism for the Kurds to preserve their culture in public and at the workplace. Additional ordinances penalised the use of Kurdish at the workplace. Singing non-Arabic songs at weddings and other festivals was forbidden. Businesses with non-Arabic names had to be renamed and stores that sold Kurdish videos or cassettes were closed down. Children are not allowed to study Kurdish in schools and Kurdish teachers are forbidden to employ it during classroom instruction. Children are also forbidden to learn the Kurdish language through alternative means. The ruling Baath Party has created an official singular Syrian identity for Syria as an Arab state. To achieve that identity, ethnic minorities like Syrian Kurds have been suppressed brutally. Joe Stork, who is with the Human Rights Watch in Washington, outlines how many of the Kurds have been deprived of basic citizenship rights. The main points of discrimination have to do with their legal standing. He says,

> "Many of them don't even have identification cards, which are essential for getting necessities like education, like health care and so forth. This is accentuated by the fact that they are the largest ethnic minority in the country" (Young 2005: 1).

Since the early 1990s, Damascus has issued orders forbidding Kurdish parents from officially registering their children with Kurdish names. Discriminatory regulations banned the use of Kurmanji (including in conversation, publications and place names) and cultural displays (such as playing Kurdish music). The formation of Kurdish civil and political groups was prohibited. Most publications for circulation were either brought illegally from Lebanon or printed in secret. The creation of a Kurdish autonomous zone in Iraq pushed the Kurdish issue to the forefront in Syria where stateless Kurds seek citizenship and recognition as a major group in the country (Lynch and Ali 2006: 1).

Kurdish rights to freedom of association and assembly are curtailed. Syrian authorities forbid the formation of private Kurdish forums and associations, which constrains Kurdish civic and cultural life. However, this was a typical restriction on civil society throughout Syria which experienced a major crackdown after the Damascus Spring; a brief period of liberalisation in 2001 (Ziadeh 2009: 3-5). The Kurds faced difficulties in obtaining licenses to celebrate certain cultural events such as the *Norouz,* the Kurdish New Year festival.

There have been, however, many Kurds in positions of power or influence in Syria and these are often cited by Syrian Arabs as evidence of Kurdish equality and immersion in the state. However, these Kurds tend to be urban and affluent, speak Arabic rather than Kurmanji and want to be reconciled with the 'Arabness' of their identity. As such, they command little respect among the Kurdish population, especially in the north (Lowe 2006: 2-3). The Human Rights Watch reports "various bans on the use of Kurdish language; refusal to register children with Kurdish names; replacement of Kurdish names with new names in Arabic; prohibition of businesses that do not have Arabic names; not permitting Kurdish private schools; the prohibition of books and other materials written in Kurdish" (Human Rights Watch 1996: 3). European diplomats noted in 1994 that "possession of Kurdish books is tolerated, although the distribution is very limited. Printing in Kurdish, however, seems not to be tolerated, and Kurdish books therefore are illegally imported from Lebanon and northern Iraq" (Malmisaniji 2006: 6).

Kurdish Political Organisation in Syria

During the French mandate period in Syria (1920–1946), Kurds were allowed to organise politically and permitted to publish books and periodicals in their own language. Distrustful of the majority of the Arab Sunni population, the French authorities recruited disproportionate numbers of Kurds (as well as Christians and heterodox Muslims) into the police and military (Gambill 2006: 2). During the beginning of Syria's existence as an independent state, politicians and officials of Kurdish descent occasionally boasted of a modest yet noticeable presence in many state institutions including high offices. Husni al-Zaim, who led the first military coup in Syria and became President in 1949, was Kurdish. The Kurds maintained a strong participation in political parties particularly those of the communists, whose leader, Khaled Bakdash was a Kurd. Many influential clerics, such as the former state mufti, Ahmed Kiftarro were Kurdish as well (Moubayed 2005: 3-4). The Kurds were not only active in the political life in Syria, but had their own political environment. However, the Syrian government grew increasingly authoritarian, particularly with the rise of the Baath Party[29] and adopted increasingly discriminatory measures against the Kurds.

The Kurdish community responded to the steadily growing government repression with a show of political unity. In 1957, the Kurdish Democratic Party of Syria (KDPS) was founded by a broad coalition of prominent Kurdish intellectuals calling for recognition of Kurdish national rights and an end to the marginalisation of Kurds in the administration. The KDPS recruited thousands of members and began developing a sophisticated political organisation. However, in 1960s the government launched a massive crackdown arresting the KDPS Secretary General, Nurredin Zaza and other key leaders of the group (Gambill 2006: 2). In 1965, two years after the Baath Party came to power the Kurdish Democratic Progressive Party (KDPP) was founded, supported by Jalal Talabani, head of the Patriotic Union of Kurdistan. Under the weight of a severe government repression, the Party quickly fragmented. The KDPP was headed by Abd al-Hamid Darwish, who became a member of the Syrian Parliament in 1992 (Moubayed 2005: 3).

By 1965, the Kurdish parties had fragmented into numerous organisations divided over issues such as whether to work for Kurdish autonomy or work within the Communist Party and reject any Kurdish affiliation with the Syrian government. Most of the Kurdish parties operated in two larger and overlapping political groups: the Kurdish Democratic Alliance and the Kurdish Democratic Front. The Kurdish Democratic Alliance includes four parties: The Kurdish Democratic Unity Party (Yakiti), the Kurdish Democratic Progressive Party, the Leftist Kurdish Party and the Kurdish Democratic Party (the Parti). Four other parties fall outside the two main groups: The Syrian Kurdish Democratic Party, Kurdish Party in Syria (Yakiti), the Accord Kurdish Movement in Syria and the Kurdish Future Trend, which was established in 2005 (Ziadeh 2009: 5). In addition, the Kurdish movement has remained not only divided but also isolated from wider pro-democratic circles. The Syrian state's repression and its attempts to delegitimise Kurdish mobilisation by linking any Kurdish activity inside Syria to Kurdish movements outside of the country were very effective. Under the weight of severe government repression, the Party quickly fragmented into competing factions and lost much of its support base. Since then, Kurdish groups in Syria have been plagued by divisions. The reasons for their weakness are a combination of the government's repression of any form of political mobilisation, the security services' success in infiltrating various parties, political disunity within the Kurdish community, the Assad regime's recruitment of certain Kurdish elites and Syria's support for Kurdish separatist groups in Iraq and Turkey in the 1980s and 1990s, which deflected attention from the internal situation (Lowe 2006: 3; Gambill 2006: 3). In addition, Syria does not have a legal framework such as a political parties' law that could provide a sustainable basis for the operation of political parties. The Syrian Constitution in Article 8[30] mentions that the Baath Party is the leading party in the society and the state (Human Rights Watch 2009).

However, at least 14 unlicensed Kurdish parties operate in Syria. Many of these parties are divided, and alliances between them are often short-lived and depend on personalities. The parties are fairly consistent in their calls for democracy in Syria and for recognising Kurds as an ethnic group. Unlike the response of Kurds in Turkey or Iran to government repression, the Syrian Kurdish parties never took up arms against the government. While the parties are all technically illegal, the Syrian government tolerated their existence on the condition that they remained fairly quiet, did not call for any form of self-government, and offered no unified threat. However, the Syrian Kurds have been profoundly affected by the post-2003 developments in Iraq (Barkey 2005: 10).

The Events of 2004–2005: Kurdish Reawakening

The history of the Kurds in Syria took a violent turn in March 2004. Tensions rose dramatically on March 12, 2004 between rival Arab and Kurdish fans during a football match in Qamishi, northeastern Syria, and security forces responded by firing live bullets targeted only at the Kurdish section of the crowd killing several people. Amnesty International confirmed that 36 people were killed, mostly Kurds. Over a hundred were injured. Two days of protest and riots followed in Qamishi and other adjoining towns. More than 2,000 people, almost all of them Kurds, are believed to have been arrested in the wake of the event. Kurdish detainees, including children as young as 12, women, teenage girls and elderly people were tortured and ill-treated. Dozens of Kurdish students were expelled from their universities and dormitories, reportedly for participating in peaceful protest.[31] Most of the detainees were released, including 312 detainees who were released under an amnesty announced by President Bashar al-Assad on March 30, 2005 (Zoepf 2005). However, no official investigation was carried out into how tension at a football match escalated into such widespread riots or into the use of lethal force by the security forces or the mass arrests and reports of torture and ill-treatment that followed or into any possible root causes of the events.

The Kurds demonstrated in front of the Syrian Parliament and local government offices demanding equal rights, the removal of martial law in Syrian Kurdistan, democratic reform and called for the reversal of the Arabisation policies in the Kurdish regions. A statue of Hafez al-Assad, the father of the current president Bashar al-Assad was destroyed. The offices of the police, Baath Party and town hall were burned (MacFarquhar: 2004).

Unrest flared up again in May–June 2005 after the murder of Sheik Mashuq Khaznawi, a respected leader and a Kurd. The details of Khaznawi's death are murky, but he disappeared in Damascus and was tortured and killed.[32] He was primarily a religious leader, but had been a strident advocate for the oppressed Kurdish poor. Sheikh Khaznawi's funeral in Qamishli attracted thousands of people and helped sustain the movement. At a demonstration following the funeral, the police beat protesters and as many as 60 Kurds were arrested, detained and tortured (Fattah 2005; Lowe 2006: 6).

Some Kurds treated the unrest as a major event and referred to it as the *Serhildan* (uprising). The developments of 2004–05 have been described by commentators as a Kurdish 'awakening' or 'resurgence' but the Kurds had already been awake to their identity and this kind of protest was not only resurgent, but quite unprecedented (Lowe 2006: 6). The demonstration was seen as a significant step towards emboldening of the Kurds. The extent of the involvement of the Kurdish political parties in the unrest remains unclear. Most parties strongly condemned the violence and chose not to sustain the demonstrations. During the unrest, the leaders initially liaised with one another but then issued press statements and dealt with the authorities individually.

On the eve of the anniversary of the Qamishli clashes, Amnesty International published a report highlighting cases of Kurdish rights defenders who have sought to promote rights of the Kurdish population in Syria and suffered arrest, torture and unfair trials. The Amnesty International said,

> "The Syrian authorities must set up an investigation into the apparently disproportionate response of the security forces to the March 2004 events. They must investigate the alleged unlawful killings and deaths as a result of tortures and ill-treatment in custody and the widespread reports of torture, and propose remedies to deal with the systemic discrimination against Kurds as well as other human rights violations that may have contributed to the tension and the outburst of violence."[33]

There was an unprecedented level of popular consensus in the Kurdish community, but a lack of political unity could not lead to a successful movement. No mass demonstrations have taken place since the summer of 2005. Public rallies are held at regular intervals, but participation is quite low. They are organised by the Yekiti and the Azadi, with the help of the Kurdish Future Movement in Syria and the Democratic Union Party (PYD); the latter has maintained close ties with the PKK. Relations between the Kurdish political parties and the Arab opposition have stabilised.

The Damascus Spring of 2005 was a short period of relative political freedom in Syria. Kurdish leaders tried to seize the moment to bring a greater unity among the Kurds and link up with the Arab–Syrian pro-democracy movement. It resulted in the Damascus Declaration for National Democratic Change of October 16, 2005—an umbrella statement representing all the actors in the domestic Syrian opposition, including the two main Kurdish political groupings. In a special section on national minorities and the Kurdish issue, the Damascus Declaration emphasised

> "..ensuring freedom for individuals, groups, and national minorities to express themselves and maintain their cultural and linguistic rights and making sure that the state shall respect and cultivate such rights within the Constitution and under the protection of the law.....a fair democratic solution to the Kurdish issue in Syria to guarantee full equality of Syrian Kurdish citizens with other citizens in terms of the rights of nationality(citizenship), culture and learning their national language, as well as all other constitutional, political, social, and legal rights, on the basis of a unified Syrian state and people.... The rights of citizenship and nationality must be returned to all who are deprived, to settle this matter once and for all."[34]

The Kurdish presence in the 'Damascus Declaration' has provided a good starting point for the Kurds to move out of their isolation in cities such as Qamishli, Ein al-Arab and Efrin, and be a part of the wider Syrian pro-democratic political scene.[35] The Declaration has given the Syrian opposition a national dimension as the source of its legitimacy came from both Arabs and Kurds. The drafting of the 'Damascus Declaration', which recognised the need to find a fair democratic solution to the Kurdish issue within the country's unity, was noted. In addition, the Coordination Committee, a joint Syrian Arab–Kurdish cooperation effort was formed to address the issues related to human rights in Syria (Ziadeh 2009: 5-6). The 'Damascus Declaration' formulated a democratic solution in a manner that guarantees the complete equality of Syrian Kurds with the other citizens regarding nationality rights, culture, learning the national language and other constitutional, political, social and legal rights on the basis of the unity of the Syrian land and people. However, four parties—Yekiti, Azadi, Future Movement and Democratic Union Party (PYD)—did not sign the Declaration. Their reservations were due to the absence of the passage referring to the explicit recognition of the Kurds as an independent nation along with the Arabs in Syria (Kurd Watch 2009: 21).

Government Response

In an attempt to mitigate their plight, some Kurds began to mobilise themselves and advocate their rights. Others took the tremendous risk of leaving Syria illegally and seeking opportunities abroad. However, those caught were deported back, imprisoned and subjected to harsh treatment. Individuals who had actively tried to change the situation for stateless Kurds were detained and tortured.

According to a Kurdish representative, due to the emergency law in Syria, the security services decided the court in which cases were to be tried. The cases which are considered the most serious are referred to the Supreme State Security Courts (SSSCs) or Emergency courts whereas less serious cases were referred to the military court. The events in Qamishli in March 2004 involved state security and the people arrested were tried in special courts. The Kurds were persecuted and charged with vandalism, rioting and insulting the Syrian flag. The Kurds were arrested on suspicion of membership of a Kurdish political party, collaboration with foreign powers and/or endangering the unity of Syria. Many of the Kurds were tried before the Supreme State Security Courts and were granted a penalty of five years imprisonment.[36] In this regard, the Refugees International recommended that the Government of Syria and United Nations High Commissioner for Refugees (UNHCR)

- Take immediate and concrete steps to fulfill the promise to the grant of citizenship to all individuals lacking effective nationality in accordance with Article 3 of the Syrian Nationality Act and international law;
- Repeal all laws and decrees which deny the Kurdish people in Syria the right to enjoy their own culture and language;
- Begin a programme of reparations and development for Kurds who had lost property and status in 1962 that is at the same time sensitive to the rights of Arab occupants;
- Ensure every child born in Syria has the right to acquire a nationality and is not stateless;
- Enact a legislation to permit passage of nationality from mother to child;
- Become party to the 1954 Convention Relating to the Status of Stateless Persons and the 1961 Convention on the Prevention of Statelessness;
- The Syrian government should recognise Kurdish culture and language within Syrian society;

- The UN High Commissioner for Refugees should work alongside the Syrian government to end statelessness in the country, including affected Kurds;
- The UNHCR should broaden focus and operations to include stateless persons in addition to refugees as mandated, as well as provide relief consistent with its agency mandate to address stateless people;
- The UNHCR should identify a staff team to work actively on ending statelessness in Syria and open UNHCR branch offices in regions of the country where statelessness is more severe;
- The United States and concerned governments must establish a clear policy on the Kurds in Syria, including resolution of the statelessness issue.[37]

Since, Bashar al-Assad came to power in 2000, he has held talks about openness and more democratic practices within the Syrian government. These efforts never stimulated any change in policy or practices towards the Syrian Kurds. There has been support for reform in Syria but mainly from the outside sources and activists abroad who are concerned about the Kurds. These efforts, however, have not made much progress on the ground.[38] On November 10, 2005, President Bashar al-Assad assured to resolve the issues of the Kurds and emphasised the importance of national unity in Syria. However, the government's promises about resolving the plight of stateless Kurds were not fulfilled. "Promises are made by the authorities but in practical life there are no changes", one stateless man told Refugees International (Abbas 2004; Lynch and Ali 2006).

The United States' invasion on Iraq in 2003 gravely exacerbated the Kurds' predicament and undid the progress the Kurdish community had made. It was, however, developments in Iraq that had the greatest significance. The Syrian Kurds grew in self-confidence as they followed closely the US invasion of Iraq and the fall of Saddam Hussein in 2003 and the subsequent increase in autonomy gained by the Iraqi Kurds. The US invasion heightened tension between the Kurds and Arabs in Syria as many Arabs accused Iraqi Kurds, and by association Syrian Kurds, of supporting the US-led war on Iraq (Human Rights Watch 2009). Along with other actors in the region, Damascus staunchly opposed the invasion. The Kurdish support for the highly controversial invasion created a conflict not only between the Syrian regime and Iraqi Kurds but also with Syrian Kurds. Moreover, the Syrian Kurds viewed their own predicament through an increasingly pessimistic lens as their Iraqi counterparts received political autonomy while their own government neglected to give their community a viable identity card. Government relations became particularly tense when international pressure on Syria intensified after the fall of Saddam Hussein's regime (Ziadeh 2009: 7). The international outcry over the assassination of the former Lebanese Prime Minister Rafik Hariri and an increased scrutiny of Syria's relationship with Lebanon made the Syrian regime even more suspicious of internal opposition—particularly Syria's Kurds.

The Kurds within Syria are not highly organised because of the mountainous region they live in and because they are dispersed throughout the area. There is very little communication between the different Kurdish tribal groups. The organisations that have formed restrict their activities to non-violent forms of political protest. The problems faced by the Syrian Kurds exist in a greater context of regional discord and instability that affect Kurds throughout West Asia. There was a concern that the growing number of denationalised Kurds and the worsening violations of Kurdish civic, economic, social and cultural rights threatened not only to provoke a Kurdish resistance to the Syrian state, including demands for independence, but also encouraged the state to respond to these demands with violence (Ziadeh 2009: 8-9). Kurdish grievances included equal legal protection under the Syrian Constitution, better education and economic opportunities and the cessation of Arabisation policies.

The Kurdish issue is crucial to Syrian domestic stability and reforms are required; otherwise, this increased level of Kurdish unrest is likely to continue. The Syrian government is in no position to make substantial economic improvements, but there are some signs of willingness to be slightly more conciliatory on cultural issues and to grant citizenship to at least some of the stateless Kurds. However, any real mood for change seems unlikely within a regime whose entire legitimacy is based upon an Arab nationalist rhetoric. To grant meaningful concessions to the Kurds would endanger the foundations of the state ideology (Lowe 2006: 7).

Syrian Conflict 2011 and the Kurds

The Syrian crisis has become a tough knot to untie. The anti-democratic, human-rights violating, oppressive and dangerous political attitudes of the

Syrian regime resulted in the Syrian people's rebellion. The relentless battle that Bashar al-Assad's regime is waging against the opposition is compounded by the intrigues of the regional powers that have become involved, directly or indirectly, in the conflict. Following the start of the popular mobilisation on March 15, 2011, the Syrian regime bet the house on a military solution. After the violent response, demonstrations turned into an armed struggle. The human cost of the conflict has been high: 70,000 deaths, one million refugees to neighbouring countries and another three million internally displaced persons. To halt the rebels' advance, the regime has not hesitated to use its heavy artillery—shelling entire towns and cities from both the ground and air (Alvarez Ossorio 2013). The 2011 people's rebellion supported by all parts of the society against the oppression of the Assad regime was started in the Kurdish region of northern Syria in 2004–2005. The Free Syrian Army chose to fight the violence being received from the Syrian government. However, the organised Kurds chose neither the Syrian regime nor the armed struggle but the democratic and peaceful way. The third option provided the Kurds an opportunity to establish an Autonomous Regional Administration. In this new administrative system, all sections of society in the Kurdish Region—nearly 4 million Kurds, 3,00,000 Arabs, 1,50,000 Christians, and more than 25,000 Ezidis, Assyrians, Turkomans and Alevis have found the chance to demand their rights.[39] From the start of the uprising, the Kurdish regions have kept a low profile with regard to mobilisation against the regime and have taken advantage of the power vacuum to establish a considerable degree of autonomy in the province of al-Hassakah.

The situation as it unfolds does not provide any answers but leaves questions. When we look at the position of the Kurds, the Syrian Kurdish leaders are very ambiguous about their own struggle. It is a fact that the Kurdish militias fight against the Jabhat Al-Nusra and the Islamic State in Iraq and Levant (ISIS)[40] and it is also true that al-Assad's regime is not glad with the current degree of autonomy in the northeast. The strategic choices made by the Kurdish leaders remain unclear for the time being (Messely 2014). Apart from the strategic choices the final goal remains unclear i.e. whether it is greater autonomy or greater Kurdistan. The consequences of these possible scenarios for the Kurds in Turkey and Iran and the countries themselves are impossible to calculate. Turkey's Erdogan as well as Iran's Rouhani have made it clear that they play a major role in the Middle East.

In July 2011, The Kurdish National Conference met in Qamishli. The conference proceedings led to the formation of a Kurdish National Council. The conference demanded the right to determine the destiny of the Kurdish people in the framework of a unified Syria and to change the security-based dictatorship and instituting a plural democratic state. The conference gave support to the Kurdish revolutionary youth movement and called for the adoption of a decentralised political system to administer the country. The Kurds believe that the time has come to make up for lost time and claim both their ethnic identity-based and national rights. In fact, the Kurdish parties are calling for the establishment of a federal state, modelled after the one established in Iraq after the fall of Saddam Hussein; an idea that is strongly opposed by the Syrian opposition. The Kurdish political movement is contemplating the post-Assad era and realises that the Syrian state will soon be at its weakest ebb, allowing it to impose Kurdish demands more forcefully than at any other time in the history of the modern Syrian state (Sidki 2014).

Since the outbreak of the conflict in 2011, the Democratic Administration of Rojava (the western part of Kurdistan in Syria) or the de facto autonomous Kurdish region has been formed in northeast Syria. The People's Protection Units (YPG) is the defence force of the autonomous region. While the Iraqi Kurdish forces (*peshmerga*) are receiving military assistance from Western countries including France, Germany, UK and United States, the Syrian Kurds have received little help accusing that they have remained close to the regime of Syrian President Bashar al-Assad. The Syrian Kurds are essentially operating in an isolated canton facing the ISIS fighters to the south and a deeply suspicious and hostile Turkey in the north (Stephens 2014). The YPG and the *peshmerga* took control of the long-besieged Syrian town of Kobane on January 2015 and Qamishli after months of fighting the ISIS militants.[41] Currently, the YPG is engaged against the ISIS terrorists across northern Syria and has openly called on the Kurds from outside to join the movement.

The Establishment of Rojava (Western Kurdistan) as Autonomous Region

The Kurds in Syria has played a significant role in both the Syrian Civil War and the fight against the Islamic State, which began in 2012. Since 2015 after Syrian troops pulled out of Kurdish regions and left Kurdish forces in control. Now the Kurdish region is Syria is heading towards on the model of Kurdish Regional Government in Iraq. With the US support, the Syrian Democratic Forces (SDF), an alliance of Kurdish and Arab fighters has taken control of the city of Manbij. The capture of Manbij from IS represents the worst defeat for the jihadist group in Syria. In July 2015 the ISIS lost the town of Tal Abyad on the border with Turkey. Manbij served as key transit point for the IS supply route from the Turkish border of Raqqa. An alliance of Kurdish and Arab forces has liberated the city of Manbij from the "Islamic State" militant group. But as IS militants fled the city, some reportedly used hundreds of kidnapped civilians as human shields.[42] The PYD[43] is promoting democratic confederalism, and they considers jailed PKK founder Ocalan as its ideological leader. A representation office of the Syrian Kurdistan (Rojava, Western Kurdistan) administration has been opened in Berlin. With Berlin office, the Democratic Autonomous Administration of Syrian Kurdistan has opened its fourth representative mission abroad; Moscow, Prague and Stockholm. Preparations are underway for the opening of Rojava representation offices in Paris, Copenhagen and Washington as well.[44] The Syrian Kurds is reaching out to the global community to support and fight against the ISIS. Not only battling the ISIS, they are also attempting to create a model of democracy that might actually bring stability to a war torn region.

The Syrian Kurdish Democratic Union Party and several allied groups including Assyrians have voted to create an autonomous federation in the northern part of Syria. Representatives of 200 people met at Rmeilan in Hassekeh province and declared Rojava autonomous regions. The Kurdish region of Syria or Rojava has three cantons, Afrin Canton in the West, Kobane Canton in the center, and Jazira Canton in the East. The Kurdish areas in Syria are more mixed with Arabs and Christians, while the Iraqi Kurdish region is mostly populated by Kurds only. The three Cantons are working in cooperation with many local and international players to push back the Islamic State.[45] The largest political group in the Kurdish region of Syria is the Democratic Union Party (PYD). The PYD is working along with Arabs and other minorities in the region. Military service was declared compulsory in July 2014. The PYD is the primary Kurdish forces fighting against the Syrian government and against the Islamic State. The military wing of the PYD includes both the People's Protection Units (YPG) and the Women's Protection Units (YPJ), famous for female special unit that handles crimes of domestic violence and rape. It is estimated that women represents 30-40 percent to the total of fighters.[46] However, Turkey view that YPG is as an extension of the Kurdistan Workers Party (PKK), Turkish-Kurdish rebel group fighting for autonomy since the 1980s. A ceasefire between Turkey and the PKK end in 2015 and violence clashed have since claimed hundreds of lives. While Turkey is fighting against the PKK on its soil, Syrian Kurds has declared and carve out a self-declared autonomous region. Meanwhile YPG has gained the trust of Turkey's international allies – US in the fight against Islamic State. The PKK is considered a terrorist organization by the EU and the US, but Turkey has failed to convince its Western allies to do the same of the YPG in Syria. The US department and EU pressed Turkey to stop shelling the YPG and also urged Syrian Kurds not to expand their areas of operation.[47] Meanwhile the UN has also urged Turkey to comply with international law in Syria. On March 2016, a top US military commander visited northeast Syrian to confer with Kurdish fighters in battle against the Islamic State. US support of the YPG increased subsequently as Washington sought shape a proxy ground forced to battle ISIS (Dettmer, 2016). The US support to Kurdish rebels is seen by the Syrian rebel commanders, who accused the Obama administration of giving up on the Syrian revolution. The future of the Kurdish region of Syrian is in the hands of PYD and Kurdish National Council (KNC) who are countering the Islamic State. The Syrian Kurds has been advocated for a federal democratic Syria. The establishment of Kurdish autonomous region has angered neighboring Turkey and Iran which fears that growing power in Syrian is encouraging separatism amongst its own minority.

Female Fighters of Kurdistan

The female Peshmerga guerillas of Kurdish Liberation Movement built a reputation for themselves in the 1970s and 1980s. In Iraqi Kurdistan, during the armed resistance against the regime of Saddam Hussein, Kurdish women took up arms alongside their husbands. They even formed a separate female battalion of the Peshmerga. Having secured the northern Iraq in the aftermath of the first Gulf War, the Kurds have spent the last two decades building up a stable economy and military in autonomous region of Kurdistan. For instance, the Free Life for Kurdistan Party (PJAK) has female fighters in the eastern Kurdistan (Kurdish region in Iran). Kurdish Peshmerga female fighters are trained in combat skills before deploying to fight the Islamic State at military camp base in Sulaimaniyah, northern Iraq (Cosgrove 2014). In spite of the dangers and ferocity of the battle many Kurdish women soldiers have taken the responsibility on their own to fight ISIS. Unlike the Arabs, the Kurdish believes in gender equality influenced by the Marxist-Leninist ideology, making women's liberation a key component. The Women's Protection Units or Women's Defense Units (Kurdish: Yekineyen Parastina Jin,YPJ) was set up in 2012 as the female brigade of the People's Protection Units (Yekineyen Parastina Gel, YPG) militia. The organization grew out of the Kurdish resistance movement in Syria. It has over 7,000 to 10,000 volunteer fighters age between 18 and 40. The Women's Protection Units have been hailed as a vital force re-taking Kobane with its estimated 10,000 volunteer troops. Feminist praised the YPJ for confronting traditional gender expectations in the region and redefining the role of women in conflict. According to photojournalist Erin Trieb, "the YPJ is in itself a feminist movement. They want equality between women and men, and a part of the reason they joined was to develop and advance the perceptions about women in their culture. They can be strong as men and capable of being a leader" (Cox 2015). In the recent years Kurdish women has gained equality in joining the military forces. Many Kurdish women take as an opportunity for independent and empowerment in the traditional male-dominated society. Women's participation in the armed struggle and their success as political activists has broken many taboos in Kurdish national movement.

Fig. 4:3 Kurdish female soldiers look to smoke coming from an ISIS car bomb detonation

Source: "Women wage war on Islamic State", https://widerimage.reuters.com/story/women-wage-war-on-islamic-state, accessed on 29 November 2016

Kurdish women protection units played an important role in the liberation of Kobane town from the ISIS. The female Kurdish fighters are feared by Islamic State militants, who believe that they'll go straight to hell if they are killed by a woman (Joshi 2014). Many of the women said they'll remain soldiers even after the war with ISIS is over. Many of them are patriotic and want to continue to fight for an independent Kurdistan. For instance a young Kurdish female fighter Rehana has garnered a great deal of media attention after reports emerged claiming that she had killed more than a hundred ISIS fighters single handedly. A picture of smiling beauty, wearing combat gear and toting a rifle is still making the rounds in social media. However reports claimed that she died fighting the ISIS. Kurdish women fighters treated all Kurdish parties as one homogenous group and preceded the armed struggle, which gave Kurdish women a reputation as important political actors and equal decision-makers (Dirik 2014).

The courage, audacity and resistance of Kurdish women fighters combating Islamic State in Kobane have made headlines around the world. In 2014, the Kurdish women fighters (YPJ) and the women's guerilla units (YJA-Star) of the Kurdish Workers Party (PKK) along with their male comrades were the first forces to respond to the call of the trapped Yezidis refugees fleeing Iraq from the ISIS. These fighters cleared more than a 100 km passage through northern Iraq to Mount Sinjar and broke the siege of ISIS. They provided the desperate refugees with a secure corridor into the relatively safe northern part of Syria. Syrian Kurds model of empowering women is based upon the gender liberation perspective developed by the PKK and applied by the Kurdish movement and the pro-Kurdish Peace and Democracy Party (BDP) in Turkey (Acik 2014). Kurdish women have marked revolutionary step by passing an equality decree that could guarantee their own rights in the conservative Arab region. Their active involvement in fighting has not only seriously challenged gender roles, but also altered traditional views of revolution and politics as male dominated patriarchal region. The equality decree's progressive line of female participation is seen by some as a direct challenge to Sharia law. A noted Arab feminist and writer Nawal El Saadawi observed that, "Kurdish women lead a war for freedom and democracy against oppression and subservience and tell the world that women are equal to men. They represent women throughout the world" (Begikhani 2015). Women in other parts of Kurdistan and Arab world look to the women in Kobane as evidence of new hope and an aspiration for a real transformation of gender equality. The massive participation of Kurdish women in the fight against ISIS jihadist gave an eye-opener in the conservative Arab world.

Conclusion

The Kurdish question continues to be an important factor in the Middle East and in international politics. Improved communications, nationalist struggles and even government repression have contributed to making the Kurds into more of a nation than they were before. In Iran and Syria, the state has attacked university professors, students, critics and dissenting groups who have supported the cause of the Kurds. The state also suppressed and/or violently eliminated Kurdish opposition, terrorised Kurds who spoke their mother tongue or wore their traditional dress or called themselves Kurds and punished those who did not identify themselves with the so-called totality of the whole. Individual freedoms and rights are meaningless since unity is the highest virtue; individuals must be subordinated to the whole. Wills and desires that go against the whole are 'inconsequential' and therefore to be suppressed. The state as a class institution exercises excessive force to achieve its end.[42] The policy of assimilation and homogeneity has influenced and continues to influence the forms of Kurdish resistance and is a cause of the open use of violence (Gurbey 1996:10). The Kurdish policies of Iran's post-Khomeini government are not very clear yet. Assassination of Kurdish leaders (besides Ghassemlou and his companions, many Kurdish intellectuals have been assassinated by the Iranian agents) suggests that Iran believes that the Kurdish population may be eased away from nationalist politics and co-opted with limited cultural, but not territorial, concessions. It is unlikely to grant the Kurds autonomy.

The Kurdish public opinion in Syria and to a lesser degree in Iran rejected calls for separatism, instead demanding cultural rights and the rights to political participation which a democratic system guarantees to all citizens. A success in Iraqi Kurdistan gave a boost to the cultural struggle but did not transform it into a political or military struggle. But, the invasion of Iraq and formation of the KRG gave Syrian Kurds a huge morale boost. Then came along the Syrian revolution 2011, a historic opportunity to achieve what the Kurds had never been able to achieve before, and restore the rights which were stripped from them. They have formed the autonomous region of Rojava in the northeastern part of Syria after recapturing the town of Kobane from the ISIS extremists.

The Kurdish society itself has drastically changed over the past half-century. One of the most significant changes is the movement of a large number of Kurds away from Kurdistan as migrant workers, displaced persons (due to warfare), deportees or political refugees. The armed movement of the Kurds of these countries has failed and the remnant of their leadership lives as refugees in Iraqi Kurdistan or Western Europe. These political refugees have contributed greatly to the emergence of Kurdish nationalism as a mass movement. The gradual spreading of Kurdish nationalism was answered with an increasing repression by the central governments, leading in turn to further movement of populations out of Kurdistan. Iran and Syria should take steps that would satisfy the legitimate demands of their Kurdish populations.

Notes

1. Also see, "Iranian Ethnic Groups", Iran Chamber Society, (Online: web), Accessed 15 December 2009, URL : http://www.iranchamber.com/people/articles/iranian_ethnic_groups.php
2. For details see, " Kurds", (Online: web), Accessed 05 August 2009, http://countrystudies.us/iran/40.htm
3. Also see, "Iranian Kurdistan", (Online: web), Accessed 3 December 2010, URL: http://www.absoluteastronomy.com/topics/Iranian_Kurdistan.
4. Unlike the Constitutional Revolution, in which the clergy had lost most of their powers, the Islamic Revolution brought them back in full force with unparalleled power. The first revolution (1906) had been fuelled by Western ideologies such as nationalism, liberalism, secularism and socialism. In the Revolution of 1979, a thoroughly clerical constitution with Islamic codes was created with conscious efforts to condemn nationalism and democracy as Western concepts.
5. See "Human Rights Situation in Iranian Kurdistan", (October 2009), Kurdistan Peace and Development Society, 1-20.
6. For details see "Iran after the Victory of 1979 Revolution", (Online: web), Accessed 25 February 2010,http://www.iranchamber.com/history/islamic_revolution/revolution_and_iran_after1979_4.php
7. He was the Prime Minister of Iran's Interim Government in 1979.
8. See, "Historical Background of Democratic Party of Kurdistan", (Online: web), Accessed 6 December 2010, URL: http://pdki.org/english/2010/08/19/historical-background-of-democratic-party-of-iranian-kurdistan/
9. Also see, "Kurdish Democratic Party of Iran (KDPI)", (Online: web), Accessed 6 December 2010, URL: http://www.globalsecurity.org/military/world/para/kdpi.htm
10. The Iranian Communist Party was established in 1983 through the merger of Komala and the Iranian party, 'The Union of the Communist Fighter'.
11. For details see, "Freedom in the World 2008: Iran", July 2008, (Online: web), Accessed 8 October 2010, URL: :http://www.unhcr.org/refworld/docid/487ca215c.html

12. In the early 1990s, Iran, in hunting the Kurdish Iranian political parties, regularly shelled the border areas of Iraqi Kurdistan. Since the late summer of 2007, Iran has again started shelling the border areas around the Qandil Mountains, targeting the PJAK fighters.
13. Also see, "Kurdistan Democratic Alliance Supports Kurdish United Front in Eastern Kurdistan", 01 October 2006, (Online: web), Accessed 08 December 2010, URL: http://www.kurdmedia.com/article.aspx?id=11081
14. For details see, "Human Rights Violation in Iranian Kurdistan", 12 September 2007, (Online: web), Accessed 08December 2010, http://www.pdki.org/articles1-1057-73.htm
15. Iranian Kurdish sources estimated the number killed to be more than 200.
16. For details see, "Iran: Country Reports on Human Rights Practices-1999", Released by the Bureau of Democracy, Human Rights, and Labor, U.S. Department of State, February 23, 2000. (Online: web), Accessed 8 December 2010, URL: http://www.state.gov/g/drl/rls/hrrpt/1999/409.htm
17. See, "Freedom in the World 2008: Iran", July 2008, Freedom House, (Online: web), Accessed 8 December 2010, URL: http://www.unhcr.org/refworld/docid/487ca215c.html.
18. He is the main political leader of the Alliance of Builders of Islamic Iran. He has been criticised domestically and internationally for his economic lapses and disregard for human rights. He is an outspoken critic of the United States, Israel and United Kingdom.
19. See "Iran's New President Snubs Kurds", *Iran Focus*, 7 July 2005, (Online: web), Accessed 1 December 2010, URL: http://northerniraq.info/forums/viewtopic.php?f=1&t=506.
20. See, "Human Rights Violation in Iranian Kurdistan", 12 September 2007, (Online: web), Accessed 04 October 2008, URL: http://www.pdki.org/articles1-1057-73.htm
21. For details see, "Iranian Kurdistan", Unrepresented Nations and People Organization, (Online: web), Accessed 6 March 2010, http://www.unpo.org/content/view/7882/115/
22. See, *Constitution of Republic of Iran*, adopted 24 October 1979, amended 28 July 1989, Article 15.
23. For details see, "Iran" (2010), Unrepresented Nations and Peoples Organisation (UNPO), Submission to the UN Office of the High Commissioner for Human Rights Universal Periodic Review: 7th Session of the UPR Working Group, February 2010.
24. See, "Human Rights Violation in Iranian Kurdistan", 12 September 2007, (Online: web), Accessed 04 October 2008, http://www.pdki.org/articles1-1057-73.htm
25. It is a reformist political party.
26. All figures are from the Minority Rights Group International, *World Directory of Minorities and Indigenous Peoples*, (Online: web), Accessed 5 August 2009, http://www.minorityrights.org/directory
27. For details see, "Representation Committee for Kurdish Parties in Syria-Europe Organisation", (Online: web), Accessed 3 September 2009, URL: http//www.yekiti party.org/en/print.php?id=1228140870&archive=1230778088
28. It is an Arab nationalist political ideology based on the thinking of the former Egytian President Gamal Abdel Nasser. It was a major influnce on pan-Arab politics in the 1950s and 1960s and continues to have a significant resonance throughout the Arab World.
29. For more information about the nature of the authoritarian regime in Syria, See Heydemann, Stephen (1999), *Authoritarianism in Syria: Institutions and Social Conflict 1946-1970*, Ithaca,

New York: Cornell Unversity Press and Hinnebusch, A Raymond (1998), *Authoritarian Power and State Formation in Baathist Syria: Army, Party, and Peasant,* Boulder, CO: Westview Press,

30. See, "Syria: Constitution", Adopted 13 March 1973, ICL Document Status: 13 March 1973.
31. For more details see, "Kurds in the Syrian Arab Republic One Year after the March 2004 Events", (Online: web), Accessed 03 September 2009, http// www.yetiki-party.org/en/print.phd?id=1229352764& archive=1230778088. Also see, Suri, Sanjay (11 March 2005), *Torture and Oppression of Kurds in Syria,* (Online: web), Accessed 03 September 2009, URL: http//www.antiwar.com/ips/suri.php?articleid=5142.
32. See, "Kurd", *World Directory of Minorities,* (Online: web), Accessed 13 August 2009, http//www.minorityrights.org/?lid=5270&tmpl=printpage
33. "End Human Rights Violations against the Syrian Kurds" (10 March 2005), Amnesty International Press Release, (Online: web), Accessed 03 September 2009, http:// www.yetiki-party.org/en/print.php?id=1229353408&archive=1230778088.
34. For more details of the "Damascus Declaration for Democratic National Change" see the Documents on Democracy section of the *Journal of Democracy,* Vol. 17, (1), January 2006: 181-184. Also see,.
35. After the Declaration was issued, two Kurdish parties rejected it, accusing its prescriptions of failing to consider the Kurdish issue as a matter of 'one land and one people'. The Kurdish Party in Syria (Yakiti) viewed the Declaration as having mistakenly "identified citizenship as the maximum right of the Kurds" while neglecting to address the critical issue of a Kurdish national home. The Kurdish Azadi Party argued that the Declaration "does not reflect the reality of the Kurdish situation" and that the Kurds represented a "second nation" within the Syrian state. The defining conflict remains between those who favour national reconciliation and comprehensive liberties for all (still a majority of the Kurds) and those who want to see the emergence of an independent Kurdish state totally separated from Damascus.
36. For more details see, "Syria: Kurds, Honour-Killings and Illegal Departure", Report from a fact-finding mission to Damascus, 15-22 January 2007, Danish Refugee Council, Danish Immigration Service: Copenhagen.
37. "Syria: Followthrough on Commitment to Grant Citizenship to Stateless Kurds, 2005", (Online: web), Accessed 31 July 2009, http://www.refugeesinternational.org/node/3289.
38. "Assessment for Kurds in Syria", 30 March 2005, *Minorities at Risk Project,* United Nations High Commisioner for Refugees (UNHCR, (Online: web), Accessed 15 June 2010 URL: http://www.unhcr.org/refworld/docid/469f3ad71e.html
39. See, "Syrian Kurdistan", October 2013, Prepared by the Foreign Affairs Commission of Peace and Democracy Party, URL: http://peaceandemocracy.org/information-file-on-rojava.pdf, Accessed 18 June 2014.
40. The Islamic State of Iraq and the Levant (ISIS) was born out of the ashes of Al Qaeda in Iraq, which was established after the US-led invasion in 2003. When Syria's war broke out in 2011, they flowed into Syria and joined up with the Syrians and other foreign fighters against the Assad regime. Now, the ISIS is a big threat in the region proclaiming its aim to establish an Islamic State or Caliphate.
41. For details see "Kurdish People's Protection Unit YPG", (Online: web), Accessed 20 February 2015, URL: http://www.globalsecurity.org/military/world/para/ypg.htm.

43. Democratic Union Party (PYD) is a Kurdish political party in Syria that was founded in 2003 by Kurdish activists. It is the offshoot of PKK. The party has between 60,000 and 80,000 members.
44. See, " Syrian Kurdistan's representative office opened in Berlin", *Ekurd Daily*, May 7, 2016, URL: http://ekurd.net/syrian-kurdistan-office-berlin-2016-05-07?, Accessed 29 August 2016
45. See, "Syria civil War: Kurds declare federal region in north", *Aljazeera*, 17 March 2016, URL: http://www.aljazeera.com/news/2016/03/syria-civil-war-kurds-declare-federal-system-north-160317111902534.html, Accessed 31 July 2016.
46. For details see, "Syria (Rojava or Western Kurdistan)", *The Kurdish Project*, URL: http://thekurdishproject.org/kurdistan-map/syrian-kurdistan/, Assessed 31 July 2016
47. For details see, "Turkey Vs Syria's Kurds vs Islamic state", *BBC News*, 19 February 2016, URL: http://www.bbc.com/news/world-middle-east-33690060, Accessed 31 July 2016.

CHAPTER 5

International Positions on the Kurdish Problem in the Middle East

In a region focused on the Arab–Israeli conflict, the question of the Kurds as the largest nation in the world without its own country has occasionally entered the international spotlight. The Kurdish question consists of a desire to have the cultural, linguistic and political rights that would protect their identity. Some Kurds seek autonomy or even independence from the countries in which they live; those states, however have long denied such aspirations fearing that they would challenge their territorial integrity. The result has been a constant instability in the region as the Kurds are becoming more politically aware of their cause and are growing more visible to the outside world.

Western powers, who have trumpeted their concern for human rights and national rights to self-determination whenever it has suited them, have not reacted with any vigour or consistency to the violations of rights with respect to the Kurds. An expediency with regard to political and economic interests in the region has been predominant. On the other hand, there are indications that the plight of the Kurds has struck a sympathetic chord with enlightened opinions in the media, educational institutions, political parties and parliamentary circles in the West. It is essential to maintain, inform and mobilise these sympathies to exert pressure on governments and international organisations to act more decisively in defence of the Kurds. The process of globalisation and transnational networks facilitated the movement and communication of Kurdish communities across borders. Kurds living as diasporas and in their homelands gained access to international non-governmental organisations, transnational networks and open societies in host-country settings. External influences reinforced the ethno-nationalist sentiment, while creating a greater complexity in the nationalist projects in their respective states. In such an environment, the position of the 40 million Kurds is a profoundly difficult one. Their indigenous homeland—Kurdistan—is divided against their will between four sovereign states; none of which recognises their lawful right to self-determination.

For a long time, the Kurdish question has failed to feature in the world affairs. The international community has been given little opportunity to reflect on the plight of the Kurdish nation. The Kurds—scattered between Turkey, Iran, Iraq and Syria as the largest minorities in these states—claim that their worldviews are incompatible with those of their ruling nations. Their needs and interests are coherent vis-à-vis the norms and values of the international communities and their positions match their requirements of balance of power and of threat. The regional powers perceive the Kurds as threats—historically, socially and culturally—to the stability of their authorities. The international communities, on the other hand, perceive the Kurds as an elusive element in West Asia, and as a result, use them as effective bargaining chips. Taking advantage of the democratisation efforts across the globe, and hoping to attract the political support of the West, diasporic Kurds and the Kurdish nationalist elites have tried to redefine their governments as an experiment of democracy.

The Kurds and the League of Nations

After the First World War, from the year 1918 to the year 1919, the international circumstances became beneficial to the Kurds. According to the Sykes–Picot Agreement,[1] Britain and France divided their colonies in West Asia according to their interests, which ultimately partitioned the Kurdish territory and denied the Kurds the right to self-determination (Yildiz 2005: 12). However, the Bolshevik revolution in Russia at that time, which was an event of internal struggle for power, made the new Soviet government give up all territorial aspirations on Kurdistan. This event left a political vacuum in the new Soviet government, giving way to a great possibility for Kurdistan to become independent. Before the Sevres Conference, the King Crane Commission Report had recommended the setting up of Kurdistan, which was to cover only a quarter of the Kurdish territory (Mitrovic 2009: 2).

Having tried and failed to achieve an end to the war, on January 8, 1918, the United States President Woodrow Wilson articulated the Fourteen Points programme that would consider a basis for lasting peace. Covering such principles as freedom of the sea in the League of Nations, Wilson affirmed the principle of self-determination in his 12th Point:

> "The Turkish portions of the present Ottoman Empire should be assured a secure sovereignty, but the other nationalities which are now under Turkish rule should be assured an undoubted security of life and an absolutely unmolested opportunity of an autonomous development and the Dardanelles should be permanently opened as a free passage to the ships and commerce of all nations under international guarantees."[2]

The British interest shifted to Mosul for its potential in economic and political values of Mesopotamia (Iraq). Around the same time, the fear of Arab and Turkish rule and the division of land between the imperialist powers made the Kurds organise themselves politically and negotiate with the various powers. Opinions within the Kurdish communities varied between those who supported the Western powers, those who were pro-Turkey and those who advocated complete independence. Many Kurds preferred not to commit to one particular standpoint among these different strands of thought (McDowall 2000: 129).

Treaty of Sevres

Signed on August 10, 1920 the Treaty of Sevres was a peace treaty signed between the Allied Forces and Turkey. This treaty reduced the territory of the Ottoman Sultanate, which had weakened by its dependence on the European powers for trade. In drawing up the treaty, a territory in present day southeastern Turkey and northern Iraq was explicitly designated as Kurdish territory. This territory extended north to the border of the then-envisaged newly independent Armenian state and south to the Syrian Jazira. The Treaty provided for all racial and religious minorities within the Ottoman territories. Articles 62 and 64 of the Treaty specifically dealt with the Kurds and Kurdistan and their right to independence, which would be granted by the League of Nations through a referendum, a year after the signing of the Treaty.[3] However, the Treaty of Sevres collapsed due to the Turkish War of Independence.

Treaty of Lausanne

The British were primarily concerned with protecting their interests in Mesopotamia (Iraq) and in preventing the Turks from annexing their controlled territory in the Mosul area. It became necessary to renegotiate peace with Turkey. Thus, in spite of previous British references to the Kurds as being an 'autonomous race', despite the Kurds protests to the British representatives and despite having promised Kurdish self-determination within its territory at Sevres, Kurdish representatives had no official part in the negotiations, which clearly stated that independent Kurdish and Armenian states were no longer feasible (McDowall 2000: 140). Kurdish nationalities petitioned the British party to the Treaty demanding that they respect their right for Kurdish autonomy. However, British interest in an autonomous or independent Kurdistan reduced in parallel to Turkey's gains in its War of Independence and Kurdish protests against the Treaty were consequently sidelined.

The Treaty of Lausanne was signed on July 24, 1923 following negotiations with Turkey. The Treaty granted Turkey sovereignty over the territory of Kurdistan (now within modern Turkey). Although the Treaty made provisions for the protection of the life and liberty to all the inhabitants of Turkey without distinction of birth, nationality, language, race or religion, it failed to even mention the Kurds—who comprised one-third of the Turkish population (Yildiz 2005: 15). The result of intense political manoeuvring was that by 1923, Kurdistan was divided between four different states—Turkey, Iraq, Iran, and Syria.

In 1920, Britain was awarded a League of Nations' mandate over Iraq and represented the new state in its foreign affairs. Britain also argued that Mosul belonged to Iraq. On the other hand, Turkey claimed the province as part of its historic heartland. As a result, a League of Nations' commission was sent in 1924 to study the case. In 1925, the commission recommended the attachment of the region to Iraq. In 1926, the League resolved a dispute between Iraq and Turkey over the control of the former Ottoman *vilayet* of Mosul and awarded the control to Iraq (Kilic 1959: 60-61). The intention of the British policy was to use Kurdish nationalism or independence as a threat so that their imperial policies in the region were not challenged. British policies toward the Kurds and Iraq was the reason why the Kurds in Iraq have a greater cultural autonomy, including the right to speak and publish in the Kurdish language and to participate in the provincial administration of the areas than in Syria, Turkey or Iran (Olson 1992: 476).

Although Turkey had accepted the League arbitration in the Treaty of Lausanne in 1923, it rejected its decision. Nonetheless, Britain, Iraq and Turkey signed a treaty on June 5, 1926 that mostly followed the decision of the League Council, which assigned Mosul to Iraq. This put the Mosul question to one side in that it diminished the visibility of the Kurds in the international relations as an emerging nation-state. This event also helped Turkey and Iraq to experience cooperation over the Kurdish issue and share a common perception on the Kurdish populations that had existed for a period of some 60 years (Robins 1993: 676). Although Iran holds similar attitudes towards its Kurds, its relation with Iraq was turbulent and sometimes violent due to the Kurdish and *Shatt al-Arab* water access contentions.

Regionalisation began with the Kurdish resistance movement. Reza Shah of Persia, who proclaimed the monarchical state of Iran, met with Kemal Ataturk while visiting Ankara in 1934. Both the leaders discussed the need to suppress their Kurdish populations under the pretext of 'promoting security and territorial integrity.' Such discussions expanded to include Iraq as well as Afghanistan and served as a catalyst for the emergence of the Saadabad Pact of 1937.[4] Above all, the Pact was a sign of goodwill among the signatories for preventing any Kurdish resistance (Olson 2001: 39). The goal of the Pact was to limit the potential impact of the Kurdish issue on Turkey, Iraq and Iran.

The effective participation of Iran in implementing the Saadabad Pact was reinforced by signing a new boundary treaty between the Kingdom of Iraq and the Empire of Iran. This Treaty marked the first major agreement between the two newly established states and specifically sought cooperation in settling border issues, including the Kurdish resistance movement's activities along their joint frontier. Although both Treaties did not last for long, they were effective in restraining all Kurdish cross-border skirmishes until the onset of World War II. After the advent of Republican Iraq in 1958 and the coming of the power of a 'pan-Arab nationalist' group, playing the Kurdish card became an attractive political and military weapon against the Shah's government in Iran (Entessar 1992: 116).

The Kurds fell victim to the great powers politics of the UK and the USSR; both of whom thought it in their interests to cooperate with the increasingly strong states of Turkey and Iran. Since both the UK and the USSR wanted good relations with Turkey and Iran, they acquiesced in Turkey's and Iran's suppression of Kurdish national movements. One of the reasons for good relations between Turkey and the USSR was to prevent the Bolsheviks from meddling in Kurdish nationalist forces. A priority of Turkish foreign policy was to prevent Soviet support for Kurdish nationalism, especially after Turkey had adopted a more pronounced Western-oriented foreign policy (Oslon 1991: 34). Both Turkey and Iran had crushed major Kurdish resistance and they forbade the Kurds from indulging in cultural as well as political activities.

The Kurds: From World War II to the End of the Cold War

The major geopolitical reason favouring the creation of a Kurdish state after World War I on the part of the European powers was to place a buffer between the Turks of Anatolia and the Turkic peoples of Central Asia. The creation of a Kurdish state would have a geostrategic advantage for the USSR; the European powers especially the UK or France, could utilise the Kurdish state and the population against the governments of Turkey, Iran, Iraq and Syria whenever they deemed so in their interest (Olson 1992: 479-80). World War II brought significant changes in Iran and Iraq that benefited the Kurds. The invading British forces removed both the pro-Nazi governments of Baghdad and Tehran from power.[5] Kurdistan became a main arms supply road for the Soviets. To eliminate any German-backed disruption activities on this road, the Soviets helped the Iranian Azeris and Kurds to establish their own governments. Kurdish nationalists from all parts of Kurdistan were quick to join the Republic of Kurdistan (the Republic of Mahabad), which was established in northwestern Iran in 1945. This short-lived Kurdish state signed three treaties of friendship and cooperation with the newly established Democratic Republic of Azerbaijan. However, in similar circumstances, these two Soviet-backed republics lasted for less than a year due to the end of the World War II. The government in Tehran crushed this experiment with the backing of the US and Britain. They publically hanged Qazi Muhammad, the Republic's elected President along with several other Kurdish leaders (Gaspar 2003). The significance of the Republic of Kurdistan was two-fold. First, it revived the Kurdish hope for an independent nation-state, which all regional powers hated to see materialised. Second, it became the only Kurdish state in history to draft, ratify and sign treaties in accordance with the principles of international law (2001: 40-43). The crushing of the Kurdish Mahabad Republic as well as the Democratic Republic of Azerbaijan by Iranian forces after the withdrawal of Soviet forces in 1946 made it politically incongruous for any European power including the UK or the US to advocate support for a Kurdish state in Iran. After crushing the Kurdish Mahabad Republic, the ability of any great power or strong regional state to use Kurdish nationalism for its own national interest diminished for nearly two decades (Olson 1992: 484).

The Baghdad Pact, Algiers Accord and the Kurds

In 1947, the world entered the period of the Cold War. There were creations of regional pacts and alliances to either prevent or foster Soviet or United States expansion. Some West Asian powers, with a full backing from the US, hosted the Baghdad Pact in February 1955 (known at the time as the Central Treaty Organization). Iran, Iraq, Turkey, the United Kingdom and Pakistan signed the Pact, which urged its members to "co-operate for their security and defence". While Iran and Iraq's entry into the Pact was motivated by the anti-communist ideology—especially, the 'threat of a Communist-inspired Kurdish uprising' which was seen as a possibility within their borders; for the US, its entry into the pact had more reasons—after the security of Israel, the Kurdish issue was of maximum significance to them (Kayeki 2010). Later on, Iran's entry into the Pact enabled it to become the dominant power in West Asia. However, for Iraq, the Pact was dismissed a few years later.

In July 1958, General Abdul-Karim Qasim nullified the Baghdad Pact, when he overthrew the ruling monarchy in Iraq. Qasim was under the influence of the Iraqi Communist Party, whose ties with the Soviet Union were the strongest in the West Asia. Acting in the interest of the Soviets, Qasim gloriously welcomed the exiled Kurdish leader Mustafa Barzani's return to Iraq. In 1959, Qasim's new government withdrew from the Baghdad Pact. Iran and Turkey saw these two actions as signs of regional hostility (Kakeyi 2010). The remaining members transferred their memberships to a successor alliance, the Central Treaty Organization (CENTO) with its new headquarters in Ankara. Understanding the complexity of the situation and having experienced communism first hand during his decade-long stay in the Soviet Union, Barzani distanced himself and his Kurdish cause from Qasim's totalitarian regime by demanding a democratic solution to the Kurdish question. Having found no reason to continue negotiations with Baghdad, Barzani revolted in 1960 and later solicited Iran's support in his fight against Qasim's regime. Support came; however, the US objections to it minimized its full strength.

With the assassination of Qasim in February 1963, Iran–Iraq relations took a turn for the worse. Barzani masterfully used this atmosphere for the benefit of the Kurdish liberation movement. He argued that the new Iraqi Baath Pan-Arab socialists in power are worse than the former ruling pro-communists. Increasingly, shipments of arms and equipment from Iran made their way to Kurdish fighters in order to fight the first Baath regime of

Iraq (Olson 1992: 484). It led to the fortification of the Kurdish nationalist movement as manifested in the armed eruption of the Kurds for autonomy between 1961 and 1975 (Nehme and Meho 1995: 44). Under pressure from the Soviet Union, the Baathist government in Iraq announced the recognition of the right of the Kurdish people in Iraq to autonomy (Mcdowall 1997: 328). The Kurdish rebellion, however, collapsed after Iraq and Iran signed an accord on March 6, 1975 at the meeting of the Organization of the Petroleum Exporting Countries (OPEC) in Algiers (Khergamval 1999: 11).[6] Both the countries formally settled all outstanding border differences and agreed to maintain border security and end infiltrations (Entessar 1992: 125). The Kurds were devastated by the Algiers Accord of March 1975.

Since 1946, Turkey, Syria, Iran and Iraq (under British control until 1958) re-established their policies of political and military cooperation against the various Kurdish nationalist movements. This cooperation persisted till the fall of Saddam Hussein in 2003.

The United States' Policy towards the Kurds

From World War I to the First Gulf War

The United States' involvement in Kurdistan dates back to World War I and President Woodrow Wilson's famous Fourteen Points, which supported the principle of national self-determination to other nationalities (of the Ottoman Empire) that were under Turkish rule. But the United States was not specifically associated with the abortive Allied arrangement for an autonomous or independent Kurdistan immediately after World War I. The distribution of Kurds among the four present host nations (Turkey, Syria, Iran and Iraq) took place well before the United States became involved to a significant degree with the West Asian affairs. The US was neither a signatory to the 1920 Treaty of Sevres, which had called for an autonomous Kurdish State with an option to seek independence, nor was it a signatory to the revised 1923 Treaty of Lausanne, which had dropped all references to the Kurdish state. Moreover, since the United States did not join the League of Nations, it was not party to the mandate system that had created the present state of Iraq or the arrangement that had led to the incorporation of the Kurdish-inhabited Mosul province into the Iraqi state. Nonetheless, there has been a perception among Kurdish groups over the years of an implicit US commitment based on Wilson's espousal of self-determination and endorsement of the principle by subsequent US administrations (Prados

1991:27). The United States pursued and encouraged Mulla Mustafa Barzani to revolt in the early 1970s for several reasons:

1. As a favour to its ally Iran, which hated Iraq;
2. As a gambit in the Cold War as Iraq was an ally of the Soviet Union;
3. As a means to relieve pressure on Israel so that Iraq would not join some future Arab attack on the Jewish state;
4. As a means to satisfy its own need for West Asian oil since Barzani had promised them that the United States could look to a friend in OPEC once the oil-rich Kurdistan had achieved independence (Gunter 1999: 427-428).

The emergence of a left-wing, pro-Soviet regime in Iraq in 1958 and the resumption of Kurdish insurgency against the Iraqi government altered the bases of US policy towards the Kurdish movement. There are tenuous indications of US contacts with Kurdish insurgents in Iraq during the 1960s (Ghareeb 1981: 43-44). In the early 1970s, as tensions between Iran and its neighbour Iraq increased, the US Secretary of State Henry Kissinger agreed to support a plan devised by the Shah of Iran to encourage an uprising by the Kurds in Iraq. By 1975, Kissinger had secretly channelled $16 million of military aid to the Kurds, who believed that Washington was supporting their right to self-determination (Karsh and Rautsi 1991: 75). The resulting covert aid programme was instrumental in convincing Barzani to reject the autonomy plan offered by the Baathist regime and renew his insurgency campaign in 1974. But, Barzani's doubts were confirmed when the Shah of Iran abruptly withdrew his support for the Kurdish revolt after reaching a surprise agreement with the Iraqi government to settle outstanding bilateral issues in March 1975. The US aid programme, which was contingent on the use of Iran as a conduit, was terminated at the same time. Mustafa Barzani ultimately was granted medical treatment and asylum in the US, where he died as a broken man in 1979 (Korn 1994: 12-15). The collapse of Barzani's revolt, the withdrawal of Iranian support and the publicity surrounding US covert actions as a result of the Congressional investigations of the mid-1970s were all factors that discouraged further support for the Kurds. More importantly, in the early 1980s, US–Iraq relations began to warm up to a large measure due to the growing US perception of Iraq as a counterpoise to the militant fundamentalist Islamic regime that came to power in Iran in

1979. In addition, Iraq gave several positive signals to the West, including showing a more moderate stance on the Arab– Israeli conflict (Prados 1991: 28-29). Iraq invaded Iran, beginning a bloody war that was to last until 1988. During the course of the war, both Iran and Iraq carried out brutal massacres of their own Kurdish populations. The US and other Western countries gave covert support to Saddam Hussein's regime, supplying Baghdad with the materials to create chemical weapons and providing intelligence reports that allowed their use against the Iranian forces. The improved climate of US–Iraqi relations militated against a renewal of the US–Kurdish ties during the 1980s.

The United States government tacitly supported Saddam's regime because at that time the former viewed the new Iranian regime as a major threat to their interests in West Asia. As a matter of fact, the United States barely responded to Saddam's infamous poison gas attack against the Kurdish town of Halabja in March 1988, where at least five thousand civilians, mostly women and children, were killed. Neither did the United Nations nor any of its agencies ever discuss the use of Iraqi chemical weapons from 1978 to 1988 against the Kurds; nor did they protest the heinous genocidal *Anfal* campaigns, which exterminated innocent Kurds in 1988 (Avineri 2005: 31).

The US and its Allied Forces Intervene in Northern Iraq

The situation changed with the Iraqi invasion of Kuwait on August 1990. The Kurdish crisis also intensified. Turkey's President Turgut Ozal proposed that the United Nations take over the territory in northern Iraq and establish a 'safe haven' for the Kurds, but this did not proceed. The West was reluctant to intervene on the Kurds' behalf and viewed the Kurdish question as an internal affair of Turkey, Iran and Iraq. In particular, they were afraid of upsetting the sensibilities of Turkey, a NATO ally (Bradshaw 1991: 79). However, on April 8, 1991 the leaders of the member states of the EC (European Community, now European Union or EU) approved the British Prime Minister John Major's proposal to create a UN-supervised enclave in northern Iraq for the protection of the Kurds. The resultant operation from the John Major government's proposal known as 'Operation Provide Comfort' essentially involved declaring the area of Iraq above the 36th Parallel, which includes Arbil, Mosul, Zakho and Dohuk, as a 'no-fly zone' to prohibit any Iraqi aircraft. The aircrafts from the US, Great Britain, France and Turkey—mainly from North Atlantic Treaty Organization (NATO) base in Turkey—regularly patrolled the 'no-fly zone.' The title of the initial operation was "Operation Provide Comfort," which was in time replaced by "Operation Northern Watch".[7] On April 5, 1991 the UN Security Council adopted Resolution 688, which approved the establishment of 'safe havens' north of the 36th Parallel that would be protected by the Coalition forces; Kurdish civilians were encouraged to return to these protected zones (Hashim 1992: 13, Avineri 2005: 32). The Resolution condemned the repression of the Iraqi civilian population in many parts of Iraq and demanded that the Iraqi government permit the immediate access of international humanitarian organisations to persons in need of assistance.

The unprecedented 1991 UN Security Council Resolution 688 played an important role by condemning "the repression of the Iraqi civilian population(...) in Kurdish population areas and demanding that Iraq(...) immediately end this repression" (UN 1996: 99).[8] The Secretary General announced that the UN was negotiating with the Iraqi government over the deployment of a 'UN police force' to safeguard the Kurdish enclave. By mid-June, there were reports of the UN agencies and other non-governmental organisations assuming responsibilities for the provision of essential services in the Kurdish enclave and the transition from military to UN-backed security. On the other hand, the emergence of Kurdistan's de facto autonomy forced the Kurds to set up their own administrative and legislative organs to avoid chaos and a further decline in public security (Hashim 1996: 13). But, the Kurdish experiment in freedom revealed deep-seated differences and splits within the Kurdish movement and attracted the intervention of their Turkish and Iranian neighbours.

The Kurdish zone covers 36,000 square miles (18% of the total area of Iraq), running from the river Tigris in the west to the east to the border with Iran and including the Cizre-Dohuk-Amadiya triangle that made up the original safe haven; it also extends along the Iranian border, south to Halabja and west of Suleimaniyah and Arbil. The liberated area, created by the northern 'no-fly' zone, covered about two-thirds of Iraqi Kurdistan. The rest of the Kurdish population remained at the mercy of Saddam Hussein. However, the zone remained under the UN embargo of Iraq as well as an internal Iraqi blockade (Prince 1993: 17).

The US had permitted the Turkish military to cross the border and kill Kurdish guerrillas when it so pleased. For example, in 1995, Turkey sent 35,000 ground troops backed by F16 jet fighters, paratroopers, tanks and helicopters deep into Iraqi Kurdistan, seizing a strip almost 30 miles long and 140 miles broad, and occupied the town of Zakho. Although the invasion was a flagrant intervention of an internationally protected area under Iraqi Kurdish control, the attack had the prior consent of the Allies—the US being the foremost among them. The assault was the largest military operation that Turkey had undertaken in 70 years, which resulted in civilian arrests, abductions and casualties among both Iraqi and Turkish Kurds. Another major incursion took place in 1999 following the capture of Abdullah Ocalan, leader of the Turkish-based Kurdistan Workers Party (PKK), which at that time was engaged in a guerrilla insurgency against Turkey's repression of its Kurdish population (Gasper 2003). These repeated US-backed invasions make a mockery of Washington's claim that it was concerned about the Iraqi Kurds.

US–Kurd Relation in Post-Saddam Iraq

In the post-invasion period, the Kurds gave maximum priority to the securing and consolidation of a semi-independent status. In contrast, the US policy emphasised on ensuring Iraq's sovereignty and on having a strong central government. These conflicts of interest in the region led to the differences between the Kurds and the US. On the one hand, the Kurdish Regional Government (KRG) has had a policy of keeping a balance in its relations between both Iran and US. On the other, the US has had a strategy of maintaining close links with its NATO ally, Turkey. But there was a tension between Iran and the US and Turkey was fiercely hostile to the Kurdish cause (Rafaat 2007: 79-80). This was a serious obstacle to the US–Kurdish relations.

The United States had important leverages of its own in preventing any disagreements with the Kurds from escalating. One of them was the 'Turkish card.' The United States recognised Turkish concerns, invited Turkey to participate in the US-led Coalition and remained silent about the Turkish threat of cross-border operations. In April 2003, for example, the United States pushed the *peshmerga* forces from Kirkuk, which due to Turkish concerns had entered Kirkuk as part of the Coalition forces (Gunter 2005: 120). Colin Powell, the then US Secretary of State, allowed Turkey to send military observers to Kirkuk in order to witness the replacement of Kurdish troops by American Special Forces. The United States appeased its old ally, Turkey, by reducing the Kurdish influence on Kirkuk, secured authority over the city's fate and adroitly managed to maintain its relations with the Kurds. To succeed, however, the US policy had to limit Turkish influence in northern Iraq also. In July 2003, US forces apprehended 11 Turkish elite troops, who were allegedly preparing to assassinate the Kurdish leading political figure and destabilise the de facto Kurdish government (Park 2004: 26). Turkey had threatened a much larger operation and Washington feared that the incursions could lead to a full-scale war between Turkish military units and the *peshmerga*. US officials prevailed upon Ankara to limit its military operations in exchange for US intelligence and other assistance against the PKK and commitment from Iraqi Kurdish leaders to take action against PKK activities in their territory. The US military personnel set up a centre for sharing intelligence in Ankara, which provided imagery and other immediate information gathered from US aircrafts and unmanned drones flying over the separatists' mountains (Tyson and Wright 2007). The Americans' role in aiding Turkey, its NATO ally, complicated US diplomatic initiatives in Iraq; particularly its efforts to push Iraqi political leaders to enact legislations aimed at promoting political reconciliation with the Kurds. Ankara was also not pleased with the existence of a de facto Kurdish state in Iraq.

Iran's influence in Iraq has grown dramatically since the ouster of Saddam Hussein. When Iraqi Kurds assumed control of the region, the KRG banned incursions into Iran from the armed camps of Iranian Kurdistan's opposition parties, which had their bases within the borders of Iraqi Kurdistan. Moreover, since the US invasion of Iraq, there has been an addition of an economic dimension to the KRG–Iran relationship. According to Kurdish officials, the annual trade between the two is estimated to be about $800 million. There are Iranian consulates in both Arbil (the capital of the Kurdistan region) and Sulaymaniyah (the second largest city under the KRG). Unlike other neighbouring countries, the KRG has official representation in Tehran (Carpenter 2009: 28).

The United States, in its effort to reduce Iranian influence in Iraq, has sought to undermine Kurdish–Iranian relations. For example, in January 2007, US forces, accompanied by military helicopters, stormed the Iranian consulate in the Kurdish city of Arbil, arresting five Iranian employees. Then, on September 20, 2007 the US army arrested an Iranian trade delegation on suspicion of smuggling weapons into Iraq for use against US soldiers. These actions of the United States damaged Iranian–Kurdish relations. As an act of protest against the US detention of Iranian officials, Iran temporarily closed the main border crossing to the KRG. In the words of Hoshyar Zebari, Iraq's foreign minister, "Iran is punishing the Kurdish region for the US detention of an Iranian citizen" (Rafaat 2007: 84). The closure of the border has had serious repercussions for the economy of the KRG, causing it to lose millions of dollars worth of trade each day. Moreover, many Kurds have speculated that Iran allows the Ansar al-Islam[9] to operate across the border, to project its influence and leverage in the KRG (Schangzer 2004: 41-42; Khalil 2007).

Another significant incident that contributed to a rift between the KRG and Iran was the shelling of villages by the Iranian army in August 2007, which lasted for several weeks.[10] Iraqi Foreign Minister Zebari and the KRG condemned the attack. The KRG held a special meeting on August 28, 2007 and called on the Iraqi government, the UN, and the US-led Coalition forces to pressurise Iran to stop the assault.[11] Iran confirmed the shelling in an official statement through General Yahya Rahim Safavi.[12] The US remained silent when the Iranian army had conducted its bombardment and when the Iranian government had closed its border. The failure of the occupying US forces to take the responsibility of defending the Kurds is evidence of its strategy to create a gap between the Kurds and the Iranians (Rafaat 2007: 85).

The Kosovo crisis in 1999 further illustrated the lengths to which the United States supported Turkey against the PKK. When the NATO launched its air strikes against Yugoslavia to withdraw its forces from Kosovo, so that the ethnic Albanians living there could obtain their minority rights, autonomy and independence,[13] the obvious precedents with the Kurdish situation in Turkey were aroused. As members of NATO, both the US and Turkey participated in the Kosovo operation. The US State Department spokesperson claimed that Turkey is a democratic country, which was committed to seeking peaceful solutions to the Kurdish issue (Gunter 1999: 436). The US claimed it saw no double standards in Turkey's participation in the Kosovo operation. But, the US policy was not much different when the Turkish government launched its war against the Kurdish insurrectionists within its own borders. Therefore, the PKK used assassinations and bombs in public places both in Turkey and in Europe to further enhance its cause. Its terrorism was comparable to that of the Palestinian Liberation Organisation. Yet, the United States never confronted Turkey's harsh and repressive response to the PKK's tactics for obvious reasons. The opinion of the European public was equally silent too. This is in contrast to the number of outcries that had resounded in Europe when Israel had brutally attacked Jenin (West Bank). The years of systematic Turkish counter-terrorist measures against the Kurds emptied hundreds of Kurds villages of its occupants and caused tens of thousands of casualties (Avineri 2005: 31-32). But never had the Kurds' circumstances—a dispossessed people, deprived of statehood—elicited in Europe a fraction of support that was enjoyed by the Palestinians.

The US's inability to deal coherently with the Kurds is symbolised by the US State Department's division into separate bureaus. Since Turkey is in the Bureau of European and Eurasian Affairs,[14] problems involving the Turkish Kurds fell under this bureaucracy. However, Iraq is in the Bureau of Near Eastern Affairs[15] and therefore, problems concerning the Iraqi Kurds fell under this one. In the case of Kosovo, the United States felt that it was necessary to stop ethnic violence in Europe before it escalated and expanded. The Kurds in Turkey did not present such an emergency threat did Kosovo. Moreover, one can explain the 'good' Kurds in Iraq and the 'bad' ones in Turkey in terms of the perceived national interest of the US. The US saw Turkey as a valuable geostrategic NATO ally and so, for a continuing allegiance with it, it was necessary to support it. Therefore, the US support for the Iraqi Kurds is perceived as supportive of the overall US policy against Iraq. Although it shows double standards in the attitude of the US towards the Kurds, it has made perfect sense in terms of the immediate US national interest (Gunter 1999: 437). In contrast, Washington has never openly criticised the state-sponsored terrorism inflicted on the Turkish Kurds by the Turkish army.

While Washington condemned Iraq for its treatment of the Kurds, it has supported Turkey for its even more brutal repression of its own Kurds. In Turkey, there is no permission to use Kurdish language in schools. The Turkish army has displaced two million people from their homeland in its war against the Kurdish population which is worse than the one being waged in Iraq. Yet, as a valued member of NATO and as a candidate for the European Union, Ankara does not suffer the slightest measure against it and relies on Western help for its repression. Above all these, Turkey was the third biggest recipient of the US military aid, the use of which has killed over 30,000 Kurds during the last two decades (Gasper 2003).

Despite its economic and political achievements, there are few prospects for international recognition of an independent Kurdistan. Washington has opposed such step, fearing that proclaiming Kurdish independence would not only lead to a further fragmentation of Iraq but it would antagonise all of Iraqi Kurdistan's neighbours—Turkey, Iran and Syria. The underlying problem is that the Kurds are the largest nationality in the world without an officially recognised state (Carpenter 2009: 24-25). There have been many interpretations of the United States policy towards the Iraqi Kurds. The covert involvement of US in Iraq's internal affairs is fully illustrative of the Machiavellian spirit. The US encouragement to the Kurds to resort to war has twice eliminated all possible opportunities for the Kurds to live peacefully within a united Iraqi state (Nehme and Meho 1995: 54). The Kurds did not learn the avoidance of being used in the deadly game. The West was reluctant to intervene on the Kurds' behalf viewing the Kurdish question as the internal affair of Iraq, Iran, Turkey and Syria (Bradshaw 1991: 79).

The Arab Position on the Kurdish Issue

The Arabs, rallied behind a mass-based movement espousing Arab nationalism, suffered from defeat in the 1948[16] war. During this war, the non-Arabs in Arab lands were in a peculiar position.

It is often said that the Kurds have no friends but the mountains. The Kurds in 1950s and 1960s had a limited place in an Arab world, which was marching towards Arab unity and nationalism. On another level, the Arabs expected the Kurds to assimilate in the grand movement of Arab Nationalism rather than focus on their divisive issues of identity, language, and possible secession. To be a Kurd or an Assyrian was not welcomed in an Arab world that was emerging from defeat and colonialism (Ghabra 1999). Time after time, the Kurds have certainly accepted support from countries that were opposed to the Turkish, Iraqi or Iranian governments for their own reasons. But governments, who had chosen to support the Kurds for tactical reasons, have often found themselves left high and dry when their allies, true to their own distinct interests, cut their own deals. No Arab country is eager to encourage separatism in other Arab states primarily because many of these states have ethnic, religious or linguistic minorities of their own. They fear that the arbitrary boundaries of Kurdistan and the resultant fear of separatism that is encouraged might spread to the other nations as well.

Many directions and concerns influence the Arab position as well. The classic instances of this are in the cases of Saudi Arabia, Kuwait and to a lesser extent the other Gulf Arab states. At the end of Operation Desert Storm, Saudi Arabia and Kuwait clearly had little concern for Saddam Hussein, but the uprisings in Iraq—largely centered in the Kurdish north and the Shi'ite south—alarmed them more. Both Saudi Arabia and Kuwait have substantial Shi'ite minorities. Both the countries did not want Iraq to fragment along ethnic and religious lines. Furthermore, the policies of most Arab countries—even a major country like Egypt—did not want instability and regional imbalances in the region. The Arab states tried to avoid the Kurdish problem—what they saw as a prelude to further secession in the existing Arab states. They insisted on the integrity of Arab boundaries; considered the Kurdish issues as internal affairs and emphasised on the maintenance of relationship between the Kurdish minorities and the states. Thus, in short, the broader Arab world as a whole pays little attention towards Kurdish issues with the exception of those countries which are themselves involved—Iraq and Syria—or which consider the stability of the region in their own interests. Beyond this, the Kurdish issue does not appear to resonate deeply in the Arab world, though it raises issues of the rights of cohesive minority groups, which have implications for other Arab countries.

The rest of the Arab world is less directly involved in the Kurdish question. Other than Iraq and Syria, no other Arab country has a significant Kurdish minority, though a few may be found scattered in Jordan and Lebanon. A country's interest in or concern for Kurdish issues tends to diminish with its distance from the region. Those Arab countries which border Iraq naturally are more concerned with the issue than those farther away. No Arab country has been a major supporter of Kurdish aspirations. Verbal support for greater autonomy without independence has been offered but usually without much enthusiasm. Another reason for lack of enthusiasm is that no Arab country is eager to encourage separatism. Aside from their boilerplate rhetoric about Arab brotherhood, many Arab states have ethnic, religious or linguistic minorities of their own. They fear that separatism encouraged in one place might spread (Dunn 2007: 235). For instance, when the Kurdish regional government welcomed the US Senate decision on federal Iraq in 2005, a large section of the Arab media rejected the resolution (Ridolfo 2007). On the other hand, Kurdish politicians, particularly in Iraq and Turkey, perceive the disunity of the Arabs as a blessing.

Kurdish Relations with Israel

Israel has had a long-standing relationship with the Kurds, whom they regard as one of their few non-Arab allies in the area. The Kurdish factor has played a special role in the geostrategy of Israel after the establishment of the Jewish State. The Kurds provided help in the 1950s when Kurdistani Jews were fleeing to Israel. In its search for non-Arab allies in the region, Israel has supported Kurdish militancy in Iraq since the 1960s. In 1980, the Israeli Premier Menachem Begin publicly acknowledged that besides humanitarian aid, Israel had secretly provided military aid to the Kurds in the form of weapons and advisers. Later, the relationship was kept low-profile due to Washington's alliances in the region: first, with Iran during the Shah's monarchy and then, with Saddam Hussein's Iraq when he fought Ayatollah Khomeini's Iran (Baig 2004). The distinctive relations between Israel and the Kurds manifested during the Operation Desert Storm conducted by the US and Coalition forces against Iraq in 1991. In the aftermath of the war, the Allies instigated uprisings against the Baghdad regime, in the Shi'ite South and the Kurdish North. The government troops harshly suppressed these uprisings. The subsequent reprisals in the north resulted in a humanitarian crisis, which turned tens of thousands of Kurds into refugees. Around the globe, Jewish organisations started a vigorous propaganda and lobbying campaigns to aid the Iraqi Kurds and to exert pressure on Iraq to stop the persecutions (Barron 1991: 64). Israel demonstrated its sympathy with the Kurds by means of large-scale supplies of medication and first-aid items through the Turkish–Iraqi border. The campaign was organised by the Israeli community of the Iraqi Jews. Israel also provided, through north Kurdistan, first-aid items to south Kurdistan. The Iraqi Jews organised a large-scale demonstration in Tel Aviv in support of the Kurds (Minasian 2007: 16-20).

However, the Israeli attitude towards the Kurds was largely dependent on the level of the Israeli–Turkish cooperation. As the Israeli Prime Minister Benjamin Netanyahu pointed out in May 1997, the threat of terrorism unites Turkey and Israel (Washburn 1998). Israeli–Kurd relationship further soured in February 1999, when the Kurds accused the Israeli intelligence agency Mossad of providing information that led to the arrest of the PKK) leader Abdullah Ocalan in Kenya. Kurdish protesters attacked the Israeli embassy in Berlin, resulting in the deaths of three protesters by Israeli security forces. In an unprecedented public denial, the then Mossad Chief Efraim Halevy dissociated Israel from Ocalan's capture. Despite such bumps and despite its alliance with Turkey, Israel succeeded in keeping its relationship with the Iraqi Kurds intact by keeping a safe distance from the PKK (Baig 2004).

However, the foundation of Israel's partnership with Turkey was mainly to counter threats from Iran, Syria and Iraq.

"Israel has always supported the Kurds in a Machiavellian way—a balance against Saddam", one former Israeli intelligence officer told *The New Yorker* (Younge 2004). The establishment of the Kurdish autonomy in northern Iraq after the 2003 war and the overthrow of Saddam Hussein's regime led to the commencement of a new stage in the Israeli–Kurdish relations. This was a serious limiting factor for Israel's political contacts with the other states of the region. Nevertheless, the Kurds count on the support of Israel's state structures and even more, on the hundred thousand Kurdistani Jews, who had previously resided in Kurdistan (Minasian 2007: 26-27). In the post-Saddam Iraq, Israel had dramatically chosen to escalate the nature of its involvement with Kurdish militants, and in so doing, had risked its strategic alliance with Turkey. Apparently, the comprehensive cooperation with the Kurds depended on the expanding interaction of Iran and a number of Arab states in the region.

Nevertheless, the development of the Israeli–Kurdish relations negatively affected the Israeli–Turkish relations. The invasion of the Israeli army in Lebanon in the summer of 2006, and the deployment of Turkish peacekeepers in southern Lebanon deepened the political contacts between Israel and the Kurds (Safrastyan 2007). Israel's stance on the Palestinian and Kurdish issues has induced Turkey's involvement in West Asia, which has in turn caused an imbalance in the Israeli–Turkish relations. In many respects, the development of political processes around the Iranian nuclear programme has impinged further on the imbalance, which undoubtedly has affected the Turkish–Israeli relations.

The aggravation of the Iranian factor remained a critical element in the dynamics of the Israeli–Kurdish relations. Over the years, attempts to conduct covert operations from the territory of Iraq using the organisations in Kurdish-populated areas of Iran (in close cooperation with the American intelligence services) have become a significant component of Israel's Kurdish strategy. However, in addition to the goals pursued by Israel in its relations with the Kurds (except the constant imperative i.e. the weakening of Iran, the change of its theocratic regime and the reduction of its influence in the region), a new important task has emerged—namely, to obstruct the development of the Iranian nuclear programme by all means. With the assistance of the US and Israeli intelligence agencies, fighters from the Kurdish organisations formed the United Front of the Eastern (Iranian) Kurdistan in March 2006 in Arbil (Iraqi Kurdistan) to infiltrate into Iranian Kurdistan.

Since the 1960s, Israeli intelligence and military operatives were quietly at work in Kurdistan, providing training to Kurdish commando units and—the most important in Israel's view—running covert operations inside the Kurdish areas of Iran and Syria. Israel felt particularly threatened by Iran, whose position in the region has been strengthened by the war and nuclear programme. The Israeli operatives included members of the Mossad, Israel's clandestine foreign-intelligence service, who worked undercover in Kurdistan as businessmen. According to Seymour Hersh, the Pulitzer Prize-winning reporter, Israel has built up the Kurdish military in order to offset the strength of the Shi'a militias and to create a base in Iran from which to spy on Iran's suspected nuclear facilities (Hersh 2004). In addition, Israel trained the Kurdish Special Forces for the execution of the mission the American intelligence services failed to accomplish—namely, to infiltrate into the Islamic opposition in Iraq, collect intelligence and liquidate the heads of the Sunni and Shi'ite insurgents (Younge 2004).

Israel, through its shell firms and organisations, had carried out its military and political penetration into the northern Kurdish-populated regions of Iraq and had invested in large-scale economic and infrastructure projects—for example, the construction of a large modern airport at Arbil (Younge 2004). The Kurdish–Israeli relations are a major element of Israel's policy in the Middle East; an effective leverage to exert pressure on Iraq (and to a lesser extent, Syria) in order to detract the attention of the regional governments and to prevent their active intervention in the Arab–Israeli conflict. On June 30, 2014 Netanyahu asked the international community to strengthen Jordan in the fight against "Islamic extremism" and to back the independence of the Iraqi Kurds. Tel Aviv fears that the ISIS [Islamic State of Iraq and the Levant (Syria)] may extend its control to areas of Jordan after seizing parts of Iraq thus jeopardising Israeli security.[17]

Transnational Aspects of the Kurds

The principal actors in world politics are the nation-states, but they are not the only actors. The international system consists of nation-states, international organisations and private actors. The increasing number of international organisations runs parallel to the increasing levels of economic, political, social and cultural transactions between individuals, societies and states. The growth of many kinds of non-state actors challenges and even weakens the 'state-centric' concept of international politics and replaces it with a 'transnational' system in which relationships are more complex. These organisations have changed the international environment (Miller 1994). The proliferation of non-state actors has recently led some observers of international relations to conclude that states are declining in importance and that non-state actors are gaining status and influence.

Transnational space has added a new dimension to the *Kurdayati* (Kurdish ethnic consciousness) in West Asia. The term 'transnational' is commonly used to refer to various types of social relations and political interactions that transcend national boundaries. It is obviously an appropriate term to refer to the network of contacts and the complex of activities connecting Kurdish communities across the globe (Bruinessen 2000). It also refers to externally based opportunity structures such as diasporic networks, international non-governmental organisations, host-country democratic systems and advanced telecommunication systems that provide new forms of support or constraints to the Kurdish nationalist projects. In contrast to political space inside the state, transnational space is a de-territorialised arena, where cross-border cultural flows transcend state boundaries and where Kurds can openly renegotiate or reinvent their national identity (Munch 2001: 13-17; Peteet 2000: 183-84). Transnational space has encouraged the emergence of new political identities and re-shaped the existing ones based on shared migration experiences in international organisations and ties to new community leaders in host-country settings. Resources linked to transnational space, alongside ongoing restrictions at home, have re-enforced the ethnicised sense of *Kurdayat*i that has emerged since the state-formation period. They have also established a new alliance between Kurdish groups where they did not exist before. More than one million Kurdish refugees, guest workers and asylum seekers that compose the Kurdish diaspora, have established thick transnational networks between host countries and the Kurdish homeland. Transnational linkages have merged different Kurdish communities on a political, personal and institutional level (Natali 2005: 160-161). For example, during and after Abdullah Ocalan's arrest in Nairobi, Kurdish protests manifested throughout European cities and the Kurdish regions come together as an imagined community.

Transnational space has helped institutionalise the *Kurdayati* at an international level. In contrast to a restrictive or limited political space inside the state, transnational space offers Kurdish nationalists access to a larger legal political arena to make their nationalist claims without fear of repression and for a relatively continuous period of time. Kurdish communities mobilise alongside the wide range of transnational social movement organisations that have emerged with the democratisation processes and increased public participation in international policy processes (Kriesberg 1997: 4-5). The Kurdish Human Rights Association, Amnesty International and Human Rights Watch have implemented awareness campaigns and development programmes in the Kurdish regions.

The Kurdish issues in Iraq, Turkey, Iran and Syria have been highly complex, controversial and extremely politically sensitive with periodic outbreaks of violence between the Kurds and the central governments. Except for Iraq's use of poison gas against the Kurds, Turkey, Syria and Iran have used many other techniques such as destruction and displacement of villages, intimidation, arbitrary detention and military operations against civilian populations. There have been deep divisions amongst the Kurds themselves which have been expressed through violence. Various foreign countries and their intelligence agencies had brought in these divisions. The Kurdish identity is not monolithic. Some Kurds believe in the existence of a pan-Kurdish nation; others stress on identities—tribal, religious, or national (Wadlow 2008: 52). Different forms of *Kurdayati* have evolved in Iraq, Turkey and Iran as a function of the political space in each state. Variations in political spaces have resulted in a semi-legal, fractured and changing ethno-nationalist movement in Iraq; a highly ethnicised, illegal, urban-based leftist nationalist movement in Turkey that became tied to Islam and a more adaptive form of Kurdish ethno-nationalism in Iran represented by a secular, leftist Sunni nationalist elite.

After Kurdish infighting from 1994 to 1996, the UN and US officials sponsored reconciliation efforts with the KDP and PUK representatives in European capitals and Washington DC. They negotiated political, economic and security agreements among the KRG, foreign governments and international organisations. Changing international norms and in particular the emphasis on democracy and federalism in Iraq helped legitimise Kurdish nationalist institutions. At the thirty-fourth conference of the International Federation of Human Rights in Casablanca in January 2001, a resolution was passed calling for international protection of Kurdish rights to self-determination. That same year, the Swedish Parliament reaffirmed the need to support Iraqi Kurds and protect the self-government (Natali 2005: 163-165)

The United Nations assumed a key role in rehabilitating Iraqi Kurdistan. The controversial oil-for-food programme (UNSCR 986), implemented by the UN from March 1997 to 2003, alleviated the adverse effects of the trade embargoes for the Iraqi Kurdish populations.[18] The post-Gulf War regional politics and in particular the Turkish government's quest to constrain Kurdish autonomy has framed international relief programmes. With the control of the only legal open border into Iraqi Kurdistan until 2003, the Turkish government limited the movement of personnel, goods and services to and from Kurdistan.

The oil-for-food programme continued to provide to the region substantial resources from Iraq's public oil wealth. The KRG directly cooperated with thirteen UN agencies in the region, including the management of oil-for-food programme. At its own expense, the KRG supported the programme by providing the services of thousands of government staff (teachers, health workers, electricity staff, water and sanitation workers etc). The KRG also provided warehousing and other building facilities as well as transport, security and telecommunication services. In managing the programme, the UN literally ran on KRG-built and maintained roads. KRG funds were obtained from unstable sources; mostly road taxes and taxes levied on imports.[19]

International NGOs (INGOs) had been operating in Iraqi Kurdistan since 1992. The Kurdistan Regional Government had cooperated with these organisations as much as possible to benefit from their experience and assistance. There were about 28 INGOs operating in the Kurdish areas, which were from eleven countries, such as Save the Children or Help Age International from the UK; Qandil from Sweden; and Emergency from Italy, which were involved in all types of projects. The emergency had settled down and the humanitarian needs were largely looked after under the UNSCR-986 programme. Many were also involved in various construction projects such as IDP housing, water projects, or access roads funded under the UN programme. The Ministry of Humanitarian Aid and Cooperation was responsible for overseeing the activities of INGOs operating in the region.[20] The Ministry aimed to have better coordination of services, less duplication of projects and easier operations in the area for the INGOs.

In fact, the US invasion of Iraq and the overthrow of Saddam Hussein in April 2003 have reinforced the role of transnational influences in Kurdistan. Kurdish politics remains tied to the Iraqi reconstruction and the US security agenda. Despite the disappearance of international NGOs and termination of the oil-for food programme in 2003, the transnational space for Kurds remains large. Given the deepening economic crisis and growing interference of neighbouring states, the situation of the Iraqi Kurds did not differ substantially from that of the Kurds in Turkey, whose oppression continued with the knowledge and even support of the leading NATO states (Ofteringer and Backer 1994: 41).

Kurds from Turkey, Iran and Syria have not received the same type of international recognition or political support as have the Iraqi Kurds. Whereas Iraqi leaders and organisations have been legitimised internationally, their counterparts from Turkey have been criminalised abroad and deligitimised inside the state (Fernandes 2002). External structures for Iranian Kurds have been more restrictive. The absence of a legal framework, defining the conditions under which NGOs can operate and the disinterestedness of the conservative Islamic leaders has limited the transnational penetrations in Iran and Syria. The asymmetrical nature of transnational space has created a 'good Kurds–bad Kurds' dichotomy that has inhibited the political and institutional development in the Kurdish movement.

Kurdish Diaspora

Diasporic phenomena have a long history and are not only associated with the modern world (Cohen 1997). It is a process, which, through the ease of international mobility and by facilitating transnational social relations, increases the opportunities for a diaspora formation. The concept of diaspora is clearly associated with transnationalism as Tololyan writes, "Diasporas are the exemplary communities of the transnational movement" (Tololyan 1991: 4). The concept of diaspora is used increasingly to describe any community, which in one way or another has a history of migration (Marienstras 1989). The concept has been regarded as useful in describing the geographical displacement and/or de-territorialisation of identities and cultures in the contemporary world. This approach includes writings on syncretism, 'hybridity' and cultures of resistance among groups of migrant origin (Hall 1993; Brah 1996). Thus, diaspora is used to describe the processes of transnationalism, the experience of displacement as well as the salience of pre-migration social networks, cultures and politics in a wide range of communities (Sheffer 1995: 5-6; Safran 1991: 83-84; Clifford 1994: 302).

Political mobilisation is a considerable source of resistance and organised expression used by various ethnic groups with the objective of gaining visibility in public spaces and political recognition for their identities (Vertovec and Cohen 1999). Many refugee communities display a political and social orientation towards their country of origin. In many cases, political events and conflicts in the country of origin continue to influence and often divide the communities (McDowell 1996; Valtonen 1997). In fact, the social structure of a refugee community is largely a continuation of patterns in the country of origin. In many ways, refugees continue to be part of their old social settings. Political allegiances and relations in the country of origin obviously have a special significance. It can be argued that the very strong political orientation towards the 'homeland' is different from the relations other migrants have towards their countries of origin. Thus, it can also be argued that the concepts of transnationalism and de-territorialisation are not enough if one wants to describe the specific refugee experience that distinguishes the refugee from the ordinary migrant.

The concept of diasporas encompasses the transnational and de-territorialised social relations of refugees. It conceives of the political project in the 'homeland,' which plays a fundamental role for many refugees. Seeing refugees as living in a diasporic relation is a way that has both the society of origin and the society of settlement. The diasporic consciousness of the Kurdish refugees was especially evident in the political activism of the Kurdish community. The political and social divisions and allegiances in Kurdistan greatly influence the Kurdish refugee organisations in exile. As with other refugee communities, the Kurdish community is a highly politicised community. There was an often expressed indirect support for the 'Kurdish cause' and the struggle of the Kurdish people among the Kurdish organisations. The forced displacement of the Kurds, their collective memory of their original homeland, the alienation and discrimination they experienced in Europe, their wish to return to Kurdistan, their collective commitment to the restoration of their homeland and finally their transnational social networks are features of the diasporic relations displayed by the Kurdish refugees in Europe (Wahlbeck 1998: 11).

The Kurds in Turkey and Iraq benefited from thousands of influential diasporic Kurds who had raised international consciousness and given significance to their nationalist agenda. But, Iranian and Syrian Kurds have less-developed diasporic networks. The regionalisation of the Iranian Kurdish diaspora, as opposed to the Europeanisation of Kurdish diasporic communities from Iraq and Turkey, has created a much different migration experience for the Iranian Kurds abroad and in opportunities for the nationalist communities at home (Natali 2005: 176-77).

The Kurdish diaspora have taken advantage of the transnational space by mobilising on behalf of their ethno-national identity. They have organised educational and cultural activities, including musical events, in the homeland and in Europe. Many have created internet sites and political party offices to represent the larger Kurdish communities as an oppressed minority. More than one million Kurds live in Western Europe and there are Kurdish cultural institutions in most European countries, where a significant Kurdish population is settled. The Kurdish diaspora has played a major political role in making known to the Western public their community.

The Kurdish diaspora in the past two decades has become increasingly oriented towards the situation and the struggle in their countries of origin. It has made increasingly effective contributions to developments there. The role of the diaspora has been significant in the strengthening of Kurdish culture, in organising relief efforts for Iraqi Kurdistan, and in supporting the military as well the political struggles in Turkey. The revival of Kurdish writing, at a time when the Kurdish language was banned in Turkey, could only have taken place in exile. Without the repression that forced Kurdish intellectuals out of Turkey, Kurmanji literature would probably not have experienced its present renaissance. Meanwhile, Turkey under European pressure, relaxed its laws and Kurdish books and journals were published there, though within narrow limits. Thus, books that were first published in Europe were reprinted in Turkey and debates from the diaspora were carried onto Kurdistan.

Kurdish Institutions

The Kurdish Institute of Paris, founded in 1983 by Kurdish intellectuals living in various European countries, with the support of France's then socialist government, is the first major Kurdish institution in Europe. It was created when Kurdish refugees who wished to preserve their culture came to Europe, to escape persecution in their countries of origin. It is a cultural and social centre for the Kurdish community in Paris; a study and documentation centre with a large research library and a diplomatic mission. It is not affiliated with any specific Kurdish party or association but it has facilitated meetings of Kurdish politicians of various parties with European officials and politicians. It publishes a number of journals and bulletins and it has pioneered attempts to develop a standard for northern Kurdish (Kurmanji) through a series of conferences attended by many Kurdish authors.[21] Kurdish institutes were also founded in Brussels (1989), Berlin (1994), Moscow (1996) and Washington DC (1996), as well as a well-endowed Kurdish library in Stockholm (1997). Each of these institutes differs from the others in its constituency and types of activity, but all of them have contributed to the consolidation and strengthening of the Kurdish language and culture (Bruinessen 2000). The Washington Kurdish Institute,[22] because of its location, has played an important role in political lobbying on behalf of the Kurds. Besides these institutes, two Kurdish human rights organisations, established in important European capitals, have worked very effectively in the European political arena. Both the Bonn-based International Association for Human Rights in Kurdistan and the London-based Kurdistan Human Rights Project (independent, but perceived to be close to the PKK) have effective lobbyists at various European institutions. They have initiated or supported a growing number of court cases against Turkey before the European Court of Human Rights, consistently leading to condemnations of Turkey. A number of significant Kurdish cultural projects have been located in the UK and the Kurds have received a degree of acceptance in mainstream culture. KHRP promotes awareness on the situation of the Kurds and efforts are made to bring an end to the violation of their rights in Iran, Iraq, Turkey and Syria.[23] They use reports to promote awareness of the plight of the Kurds on the part of the European Parliament, the Parliamentary Assembly of the Council of Europe, the national parliamentary bodies and inter-governmental organisations including the UN.

Kurdish National Congress (KNC)

The Kurdistan National Congress (KNC) is an unarmed organisation and as an umbrella organisation above party lines has worked in a diplomatic manner to create Kurdish unity. KNC tried to put the case of an Independent Kurdistan in the agenda of the great powers and wanted the international organisations to do away with the unfair and artificial borders that divides

Kurdistan into five countries (since the First World War). The KNC was established on April 14, 1985. In 1989, 1991, 1996 and 1998, the KNC had four General Meetings in Paris and London respectively. Every time hundreds of Kurdish politicians, scientists, writers, poets and Kurdish parties' representatives attended the KNC conferences from all parts of Kurdistan. The KNC conferences also received thousands of messages and supports from all over the globe. The KNC is unique because Kurdish organisations and individuals from the leftist to rightist ideologies and levels, all come together with the one aim to create a Kurdish state; to protect the unity, peace and settlement between the Kurds. The KNC has worked for Kurdish national security interests.[24] The Congress is designed to attract Kurds of all political persuasions and from other countries, who are dedicated to their national cause. The body has broadened the visibility of the Kurds, internationalised the movement and tried to further legitimise it.

The aim of the KNC is to carry out political and diplomatic work for the independence and establishment of a Kurdish state in the total land comprising Kurdistan. This cannot be achieved without a central authority for the Kurdish nation gathering all the Kurdish parties, organisations, political, scientific, intellectual and social Kurdish personalities, regional Kurdistan governments and parliaments under one umbrella that is the KNC. The KNC believes that the establishment of a Kurdistan government-in-exile is a practical step towards the independence of Kurdistan and a Kurdish state. Considering that the KNC is the highest legislative authority for the Kurdish people in all regions of Kurdistan, it was established and its constitution was approved during the fourth conference held in London in October 1998 (Mella 2005: 194). Among the important decisions and recommendations was the formation of a committee to follow up the formation of the Kurdistan government-in-exile.

When Ocalan was forced to leave Syria, he ended up in Italy. This speeded up the preparations for another constitutive meeting of the KNC. Ocalan met with a surprising range of Kurdish personalities, including political opponents. Many of the smaller parties and organisations indicated their willingness to take part in the planned National Congress. But the two large Iraqi Kurdish parties—PUK and KDP, which could not do without good working relations with the Turkish authorities—rejected the invitation. Also, the Iranian KDP-I and the Socialist Party of Kurdistan (Turkish)—the most important of the PKK's rivals—showed little enthusiasm. Ocalan's unexpected departure from Italy in January and his ultimate capture in February in 1999 put the PKK in disarray and thwarted further plans for inter-party cooperation. However, Ocalan's capture by Turkey unleashed strong emotions amongst the Kurds of all political persuasions and a rarely experienced-before sense of unity was developed. This was the reason that the National Congress held its inaugural session in Amsterdam on May 24, 1999 and it appeared pluralistic (Bruinessen 2000a). Both the Iraqi and Iranian Kurdistans were represented by prominent and influential personalities. Although the PKK unmistakably engineered the congress, a large proportion of the participants were men and women without previous links to this party including experienced politicians, academics and religious leaders. The National Congress proved a major step in Kurdish nation-building.

The 'Charter for the Rights and Freedoms of Women in the Kurdish Regions and Diaspora' was launched in the House of Lords on June 22, 2004. It was a collective effort between the Kurdish Women's Project and the Kurdish Human Rights Project to urge the elimination of all forms of discrimination against Kurdish women and to promote their participation in the social, political, economic and educational spheres of life.[25]

Kurdish Parliament-in-Exile (KPE)

The Kurdish Parliament-in-Exile (KPE), which was established in 1995 and held its first session in Hague, played a significant part in placing the Kurdish question on the European political agendas. The KPE is the executive authority of the KNC and has the same aim i.e. the establishment of a Kurdish state. With headquarters in Brussels, Belgium, it was established after the Kurdish Democratic Party (DEP) under the leadership of Yasar Kaya was banned in Turkey. The Parliament acted for Kurdish diplomatic representation and established contact with numerous parties and personalities in Europe. After the banning of the DEP, a number of DEP Parliamentarians fled Turkey and sought refuge in Europe. Some of its members included Leyla Zana and Ahmet Turk. The Parliament consists of 65 members elected from the exiled Kurdish (DEP) Parliamentarians, mayors, Kurdish prominent personalities, representatives from national institutions, youth organisations and trade associations (Karabat 2009). This Parliament is transnational in more than one respect and is part of the Kurdish diaspora in Europe. It is a 'trans-state'; although established by Kurds from Turkey. It includes members from Iraqi and Iranian Kurdistans and attempts to strengthen the representation from other parts of the Kurdish areas. It is transnational in nature with its members being those who have gained political asylum in different European states and it has permanent offices in Brussels. Ocalan himself declared that the body was the first necessary step towards creating federative districts for the entire Kurdish population living in Turkey, Iraq, Iran and Syria (Gunter 1997: 43-44).

The KPE also suffers from its lack of recognition by any existing government in the world. Unlike the Palestine Liberation Organization (PLO), which for years maintained embassies abroad and gained formal observer status in many international organisations, the KPE so far has not attained this status. However, it has gained the sympathy of a number of private international supporters from many European countries. The Turkish government's strong and inflexible denunciations of the PKK and the KPE have helped the Parliament to expose more to the outside nations. It has held its plenary sessions in different European countries including the Netherlands, Austria, Denmark, Norway, Russia and Italy. Ankara severely criticised both Belgium and the Netherlands for allowing the KPE to gather for meetings in their capitals. Ankara even retaliated by banning military purchase from Hague and putting it on its 'red list' (Barkey and Fuller 1998: 34-38). From its inception, the KPE's image of being an organ of the PKK has handicapped it. For this reason, it did not succeed in bridging the gap with other Kurdish political parties and its diplomatic successes remained limited as well. As a result, major states such as the US, Britain, France and Germany have refused to recognise the Parliament (Gunter 1997: 44-45). However, the establishment of the KPE in Europe has opened up many, entirely different worldviews to the Kurdish political activities.

The Kurdish Media

The emergence of satellite television and the internet has challenged the power of the sovereign state and introduced new components into the relationship between the state and the media. The convergence of media on the internet has built up new virtual geographies that offer migrants a new kind of experience. The new transnational media has merged social spheres and severed the traditional links between physical places and social meetings (Uwosomah 2008: 6). The development of these technologies has created effective channels for the distribution of media that operate outside of the borders, laws, and policies of a single sovereign state. Mass media in its various forms (newspapers, radio, television etc.) has been used both as a tool by the nation-states as well as a weapon against them. Meyrowitz says that it has created "places and cultures which offer diasporas around the world new resources and new disciplines for the construction of imagined selves and communities" (Meyrowitz 1985: 10). It is about the protection of national community and sustaining the imagined community. The crux of the diasporic media is "associated with the advent of global networks and patterns of cultural flows across global space" (Robins 2003: 190). Satellite broadcasting has changed the relationships between nation-states; economics and sources of funding affect virtual nationalism. It also shapes and controls the form of human association and action (McLuhan 1967: 8).

In the 1980s and 1990s, Turkey aggressively tried to eliminate the Kurdish separatist movement without success, leading to the rise of the PKK as well as the migration of a number of Turkish Kurds to Western Europe. The presence of these new emigrants as well as news about the guerrilla war in Turkey worked as a catalyst for Kurdish ethnic self-awareness among the Kurds already residing in Europe. This new Kurdish self-identity among the educated and wealthy Kurdish diasporas led to the development of a number of cultural activities. The activities also included the revival of the Kurdish language as a vehicle for political and literary discourse; the founding of Kurdish institutes and the establishment of MED-TV—the world's first Kurdish international satellite television—which first operated under British license from London and later, from Brussels with studios in Berlin and Stockholm (Merrifield 2005). Satellite television (MED-TV) has been an effective medium for bringing uncensored (or at least not state-censored) news and opinions to the Kurdish public in Turkey and in neighbouring countries. This television station is a good example of an extensive transnational cooperation among the Kurds in exile. MED-TV started its broadcasts in the spring of 1995 and it produces its programmes in different European countries, distributing them all over Europe, the Middle East and northern Africa. Private benefactors in the Kurdish communities all over Europe financially support the station. Besides MED-TV, many Kurds, especially from Iraq, have followed satellite programmes from various Arabic-speaking countries. However, since MED-TV uses the Kurdish language, it rapidly became popular among the Kurds in Europe (Bruinessen 2000a). Before MED-TV, the only international broadcast in the Kurdish language was the weekly news on short-wave radio aired by Voice of America.

After failing to achieve self-rule after years of armed struggle in Turkey, Iran, Iraq and Syria, many Kurds viewed the establishment of MED-TV as achieving 'sovereignty in the sky'. MED-TV had far-reaching international political repercussions. The whole project enraged the Turkish government, which was perhaps not surprising bearing in mind the oppression of the Kurds in Turkey and the discontentment of the Turkish authorities at any Kurdish cultural expression. According to the Turkish government, the station was a PKK organ and they demanded the closure of the station. Among other counter-actions, the Turkish authorities directed intensive diplomatic pressure against the channel. Iraq's Kurdish Democratic Party (KDP) established its own satellite station named KTV, which began broadcasting in 1999 (Bruinessen 2000a). Thus, the Kurdish institutes, Kurdish media and Kurdish language courses that operate in Western Europe have provided the Kurdish movement with instruments of nation building, asserting cultural and political rights.

The European Union Perspective on Kurds

Europe has a historical responsibility towards the Kurds. It also has a political and moral obligation to facilitate a just and peaceful resolution to the Kurdish issue. The European states had built the foundations of the situation in the Kurdish regions by failing to uphold an independent Kurdistan in the wake of the dissolution of the Ottoman Empire. Since Europe had washed its hands off the Kurds in the 1920s, developments in the situation further add to the European responsibility for ameliorating the situation of the Kurds. Europe has substantially failed to issue any real condemnation of Turkey's policies towards the Kurds, despite the fact that for many years a brutal armed conflict, accompanied by a high incidence of torture was occurring at its doorstep. This stems from a significant extent to the European conceptions of the Turkish regime as a Western ally, a NATO member and a prospective EU partner (Branscheidt 2008). Europe sees the Kurds in Turkey through Ankara's eyes; it portrays them in the press and elsewhere as violent terrorists, who are engaged in an illegal separatist campaign.

Far from calling Turkey to account for its treatment of the Kurds, Europe has provided raw materials for anti-Kurdish military operations in the form of assistance for developing a formidable arms industry and supplying weapons at a greatly reduced cost. For instance, the UK has supplied Armoured Land Rovers that are used in the suppression of the Kurdish civilian population (Gilby 2003: 2-5). Without the political, economic, and military support of the leading EU countries, Turkey would not have been able to carry out its crimes against the Kurds.

The politicisation of the Kurdish diasporas as well as increased efforts by the Turkish authorities to maintain or regain their control of their Kurdish subjects abroad have gradually made clear that the Kurdish question is not just Iraqi, Iranian, Syrian or a Turkish problem but it has become a problem of European politics. The presence of an increasingly effective Kurdish legal and political representation in Europe and the Kurds' use of European civil liberties have ushered in the Kurdish movement (Bruinessen 2000b). Turkey had made an effort to outlaw the Kurdish Parliament-in-Exile, which in turn compelled the European politicians to take a tough stand on the Kurdish issue. Kurdish activities were from time-to-time violently countered by the ultra-nationalist Turkish 'Grey Wolves'[26] and the Turkish hit-squads were established to fight against Turkish targets in Europe.

Turkey is not a European country or a member of the European Union. But, it is a member of the Council of Europe (CE) and the Organization for Security and Cooperation in Europe (OSCE) and is party to a number of relevant international treaties. This has made the Kurdish question almost by definition a matter of concern for various European bodies. The OSCE, for instance, has accepted a number of far-reaching recommendations on the linguistic and educational rights of minorities, which, if applied in Turkey, would help towards reducing the urgency of the Kurdish question (Bruinessen 2000c). A political stand on the Kurdish issue is ultimately a stand on minority rights in Europe.

The EU has condemned the violence perpetrated by the PKK and other terrorist groups on Turkish soil and urged the PKK to respond to the political initiative of the Turkish government by laying down its arms and putting an end to violence (Khayati 2006). The EU Commission's unwillingness to address the Kurdish problem as a cohesive issue is beset with troubles; The EU has implicitly agreed with Turkey that the Kurdish problem is just a terrorism issue or at most a limited human-rights problem. If the EU prematurely accepts Turkey as a member of its union, it will damage its own human-rights commitments and jeopardise its long-term credibility. Turkey's EU candidacy can be promoted in such a manner so as to genuinely help solve its Kurdish problem upholding its territorial integrity and by creating a healthy democratic Turkey that benefits all of its citizens, as well as the EU (Gunter 2007: 122).

On May 2, 2002, the Council of the European Union adopted by written procedure the inclusion of the Kurdistan Workers Party (PKK) in the EU list of terrorist groups. They made this decision in the face of the Turkish government's persistent demands, though in 1999, the PKK repeatedly declared a unilateral ceasefire and abandoned the armed struggle in favour of a democratic solution to the Kurdish question, which had culminated in the establishment of the Kurdistan Freedom and Democracy Congress (KADEK) and the disbanding of the PKK.[27] The implications of this move on the human rights of Kurdish refugees and asylum seekers are enormous. This is despite the fact that over the years, more than 4000 villages have been destroyed; more than three million people have been displaced and tortured and the Turkish military's routine practices of making the suspected Kurdish activists, guerrillas and sympathisers to the Kurdish cause to involuntarily disappear have continued (Wahlbeck 1999). These assaults on the Kurdish people continue unabated.

The Centre Europe-Tiers Monde or Europe–Third World Centre (CETIM) urged the EU to uphold and guarantee that fundamental rights and freedoms were not sacrificed in the formulation of policies that govern the fight against terrorism and the preservation of security. It also appealed to the EU Council to rethink its decision on including the PKK in the list of terrorist organisations in view of the implications on Kurdish refugee communities and asylum seekers in Europe.[28] The European parliamentary resolution called on the Turkish government to pursue a democratic solution to the Kurdish question following the 'encouraging statement' by Turkish Prime Minister Recep Tayyip Erdogan, who in a meeting in the Kurdish city of Diyarbakir had admitted the existence of the Kurdish problem and called for a solution. It also urged the Turkish authorities to lift restrictions on political parties, such as the pro-Kurdish political party HADEP, and to allow the Kurdish language to be used in the education system and media. Furthermore, it stressed for striking a balance between the need to control state security; avoid civil-military strains; effectively promote political dialogue, economic and social development of the 'southeast' region through a comprehensive strategy (Khayati 2006). The Parliamentary Assembly of Europe encouraged

Turkey—as a Council of Europe member state—also Iran, Iraq and Syria to acknowledge that the Kurdish language and culture are part of the heritage of their own countries. The EU as the political body of Europe has a legal responsibility to address the Kurdish situation.

The Kurds as a Stateless People

Political modernisation leads to social closure along ethnic lines and a pervasive fragmentation of political space. The tragic consequence of these developments is that the promises of modernity remain out of reach for the majority of the citizens of such states. They become excluded from and are rejected by the institution able to guarantee the minimal rights associated with the modern age—the nation-state. Equal treatment before the law, political participation and protection from arbitrary violence are goods inaccessible to the Kurds in West Asia, for the minorities in southern Sudan, the Hutu in Burundi and Tamils in Sri Lanka among many others. The case of the Kurds is especially dramatic because there is no state in the world, which would rule in the name of their nation, protect the interests of its members living on the territory of other states, or provide a shelter for refugees fleeing terror and suppression by ethnic enemies. While Hindus fleeing Pakistan were received by India, Muslims fleeing India by Pakistan, Jews from all over the world by Israel, ethnic Germans from eastern Europe by Germany—the Kurds are a classic example of stateless group falling through the net of a world with none to receive them(Wimmer 2002:195-95).

The 'Quartet' consisting of the United States, Russia, the United Nations and the European Union is committed to a Palestinian state or for a commonly phrased "Two-State Solution."[29] But the 'Quartet' is not committed to a Kurdish state. Unlike the Palestinians, who are indistinguishable from the other 22 sovereign Arab states in the region by virtue of their ethnicity, culture, religion and language, the Kurds have a distinct history, culture and language. Whereas, the totality of the people claimed to be 'Palestinians' number around six million including those in the Palestinian diaspora, there are over 30 million Kurds—excluding those Kurds who live abroad—spread throughout Iran, Iraq, Turkey and Syria. The Quartet neither has sought to add another Arab state in the region nor has committed to the issue of Kurds—or for that matter a separate Kurdish state—except for granting the Kurds autonomy in northern Iraq; where Kurds enjoy cultural autonomy but cannot speak of full political rights the way the Palestinians do.

The international community has ignored the self-determination of the Kurdish people. Before delving into the history of the past years, suffice it to say that the power and influence of Arab oil was a major factor in the interest of the international communities in this region. Western nations craved the oil of Arabia and the Persian Gulf, while Kurdistan was too remote. The Kurds have lived as a minority among the rival and expansionist Turks (Ottoman Empire), the Iranians (Persian Empire) and the Arabs; they have resisted bitterly and fought the oppressors.[30] The Kurdish fate is a reminder of the fates of the Austro-Hungarian and Ottoman empires at the end of the First World War, of which Hannah Arendt wrote:

> Nobody had been aware that mankind, for so long a time considered under the image of a family of nations, had reached the stage where whoever was thrown out of one of these tightly organised closed communities found himself thrown out of the family of nations altogether. Civil wars.... were not only bloodier and more cruel then all their predecessors in the religious wars...they were welcomed nowhere and could be assimilated nowhere (Arendt 1951: 266,291).

The Kurds and the Aftermath of the Arab Spring

The Arab Spring 2011 has realigned the political balance among Turkey, Iran, Syria and Iraq. The uprising has affected the region's Kurdish nationalist movements recreating some of the incidents of the 1990s. The upheaval in Syria has positioned Ankara and Tehran at opposite ends of the regional political spectrum. Turkey has sided with the protesters, while Iran has supported the Syrian President Bashar al-Assad. At this juncture, the Syrian situation is a zero-sum game. Either Assad or the opposition is winning. The state of affairs continues with uncertain solutions for the political conflict (Cagaptay 2012: 9). The Arab Spring and the United States' withdrawal from Iraq have transformed the dynamic of the Kurdish problem and the security environment in the region. Before the Arab Spring upheaval, Syria, Turkey and Iran cooperated in acting against the PKK. But now, Iran may reverse its policy encouraging the PKK to attack Turkey in retaliation for its support of the Syrian rebels. Turkey is at a critical juncture in its much-criticised Syrian policy failure to intervene in Kobane. Turkey would only get involved in Syria if the US-led Coalition targeted President Assad's regime and the ISIS. However, the US State Department reiterated that the Coalition is focusing for now on the ISIS alone which is a global threat (Lowen, 2014). Strained relations with the Kurds could feed the spiral of protest which can hamper the peace process.

Whether in Iran, Iraq, Syria or Turkey, the Kurds are now one of the key players in the Middle East. They fought against the ISIS to recapture towns and cities in Syria and Iraq. Secular, democratic and a champion of women's rights, the Kurdish movement has emerged as the most serious rival to radical groups like the ISIS. In this time of darkness in the Middle East, the Kurdish movement has a reason to be hopeful about its future (Ozkan 2015).

Conclusion

The post-Cold War period alone has witnessed the massacre of Kurdish villagers in Iraq by chemical weapons after the Iran–Iraq war (1980–88), a failed Kurdish uprising and massive refugee crisis after the Gulf War (1991), followed by the creation of a Kurdish enclave in northern Iraq. Further, the US war on Iraq in 2003 and the fall of Saddam strengthened the Kurdish movement in the Middle East. The communications revolution and the emergence of an organised Kurdish diaspora have also changed the nature of the Kurdish question. It is no longer a conflict of the Kurds only and the states of the region, but it has imposed itself on the political agendas of European countries and the USA as well. Although the Kurds are not united and certainly do not speak with a single voice, the international community has begun to recognise them, perhaps not as a separate nation yet, but as Kurds and not merely as citizens of Turkey, Iran, Iraq or Syria. Satellite television has given the Kurdish nationalists access to a powerful means of nation building. The complex of transnational networks discussed earlier has made the Kurds into much more of a nation than they were two decades ago. The efforts by the Iraqi and Turkish governments to suppress Kurdish nationalism by brutal military force have contributed to the process of nation building—both paradoxically and considerably. Thousands of Kurdish villages were destroyed and millions of Kurds were forced to leave Kurdistan, but this has precisely helped in making the Kurds from different regional backgrounds overcome their differences and in integrating many of them into more inclusive, non-territorial Kurdish networks. The emergence of the Kurds as actors in the international political arena is a greater challenge to Turkish, Iranian, Syrian and Iraqi states than the guerrilla struggles they have fought in the past decades. As Kurds sit on a great basin of oil and water resources, Kurdish nationalism probably will increasingly be more salient in the coming years.

Notes

1. The Sykes–Picot Agreement of 1916 was a secret agreement between the government of the UK and France, with the assent of Imperial Russia, defining their respective spheres of influence and control in West Asia after the expected downfall of the Ottoman Empire during World War I. The agreement was negotiated on behalf of the British by Sir Mark Sykes and on the behalf of the French by Francois Georges Picot.
2. Wilson, Woodrow, *Fourteen Points Speech (1918)*, (Online: web), Accessed 13 August 2010, URL: http://usa.usembassy.de/etexts/democrac/51.htm
3. The details of Articles 62 and 64 are shown in Appendix 3.
4. The Treaty of Saadabad (or the Saadabad Pact) was a non-aggression pact signed by Turkey, Iran, Iraq and Afghanistan on July 8, 1937. This Treaty lasted for five years.
5. Britain occupied a special position in Kurdish politics due to its colonial legacy. Because of the role played by Britain in delineating the frontiers of modern West Asia and Turkey, Kurdish politicians, particularly traditionalists, expected Britain as an advocate of the Kurdish cause.
6. It was an agreement between Iran and Iraq to settle the border disputes like *Shatt-al- Arab*. One of the major purposes of this agreement was to make the Shah of Iran stop supporting the Iraqi Kurds from fighting with the Kurdish leader Mustafa Barzani against Saddam. According to the Agreement, Saddam Hussein was to stop supporting the Iranian Kurds. For details of the Accord see, "Algiers Accord 1975", (Online: web), Accessed 24 August 2010, URL: http://www.mideastweb.org/algiersaccord.htm.
7. For details see, "An Introduction to the Kurdish People of Iraq and Elsewhere", (Online: web), Accessed on 25 February 2010, URL: http://www.eurolegal.org/neoconwars/kurdsiraq.htm.
8. United Nations Security Council Resolution 688, 5 April 1991. Also see Weller, M (ed.) (1993), *"Iraq and Kuwait: The Hostilities and Their Aftermath"*, Cambridge International Document Series, Cambridge, Grotius Publications Ltd. Vol.3, 12-13.
9. It is a Kurdish Sunni-Islamist group, promoting a radical interpretation of Islam close to the official Saudi ideology of Wahabism with strict application of the Sharia. The group was formed in 2001 in the Kurdish-controlled northern provinces of Iraq near the Iranian border, with bases near the villages of Biyara and Tawela, northeast of Halabja.
10. The Spokesman, Kurdistan Regional Government, "KRG Condemns Iranian Shelling of Border Areas", 28 September 2007, (Online: web), Accessed 01 September 2010, URL:,http://www.krg.org/articles/detail.asp?lngnr=12&smap=02010100&rnr=223&anr=2040
11. "Baghdad, Iraqi Kurds Protest Alleged Iranian Shelling", (29 August 2007), *RFE/RL Report*, (Online: web), Accessed 01 September 2010, URL: http://www.rferl.org/content/article/1078412.html
12. "Report: Iran Official Says Iran Shelled Kurds," *USA Today*, (Online: web), Accessed 01 September 2010, URL: http://www.usatoday.com/news/world/iraq/2007-09-25-iran-iraq_N.htm
13. For details see, "UN: Final Report to the Prosecutor by the Committee Established to Review the NATO Bombing Campaign against the Federal Republic of Yugoslavia", (Online: web), Accessed 14 September 2010, URL: http://kosova.org/post/UN-Final-Report-to-the-NATO-Bombing-Campaign-Against-Yugoslavia.aspx

14. The Bureau promotes US interests in the region on issues such as national security, NATO enlargement, coordination with the European Union and other regional organisations, support of democracy, human rights, economic prosperity, the war on terrorism and nonproliferation. For details see, US Department of State, "Bureau of European and Eurasian Affairs", (Online: web), Accessed 15 September 2010, URL: http//www.state.gov/p/eur/
15. The Bureau of Near Eastern Affairs deals with the US foreign policy and diplomatic relations with the Middle Eastern countries and regional policy issues that include Middle Eastern peace, terrorism and weapons of mass destruction and political and economic reforms. For details see, US Department of State, Bureau of Near Eastern Affairs (Online: web), Accessed 15 September 2010, URL, http://www.state.gov/p/nea/
16. The State of Israel was established after the 1948 war.
17. See, "Netanyahu Calls for Jordan Support, Kurdish Independence", *Middle East Eye*, 30 June 2014, URL: http://www.middleeasteye.net/news/netanyahu-calls-jordan-support-kurdish-independence-1830159244, Accessed 29 July 2014.
18. For details of the UNSRC 986 see, United Nations (1996), *The United Nations and the Iraq-Kuwait Conflict: 1990-1996*, Department of Public Information, Vol.9, New York: 182-183.
19. For details see, Kurdistan Regional Government (4 July 2005), "A Brief History of Iraqi Kurdistan: The Kurds and Kurdistan", (Online: web), Accessed 01 October 2010, URL: http://www.krg.org/articles/article_detail.asp?
20. For details see, "Kurdistan Regional Government" (15 October, 2002), *Kurdistan Today*, (Online: web), Accessed 02 October 2010, URL: http://www.old.krg.org/docs/KT021015_full.asp
21. For details see, "Kurdish Institute of Paris", (Online: web), Accessed 12 October 2010, URL: http://www.institutk,urde.org/en/
22. It is a non-profit research and educational organisation, established in September 1996, whose motto is "For Kurdish People Worldwide". For details see, "Washington Kurdish Institute", http://www.kurd.org/
23. For details see, "Kurdish Human Rights Project", (Online: web), Accessed 12 October 2010, URL: http://www.khrp.org/
24. For details see, "Charter of the Kurdish National Congress", The 4th Kurdistan National Congress, held in London from October 10-11, 1998. Published by The KNC Media & Communication Committee: London. Also see, "Kurdish National Congress", (Online: web), Accessed 12 October 2010, URL: http://www.knc.org.uk/
25. For details see, "Enforcing the Charter for the Rights and Freedoms of Women in the Kurdish Regions and Diaspora", Kurdish Human Rights Project: London.
26. It was founded as the youth organisation of the Nationalist Movement Party (MHP) in 1969. The paramilitary wing of the 'Grey Wolves' has been utilised by the Turkish intelligence services to assassinate PKK leaders. It is accused of terrorism and infiltration by the European policy-makers.
27. See, "EU Adds the PKK to List of Terrorist Organisations", *Statewatch News online*, (Online: web), Accessed 22 October 2010, URL: http://www.statewatch.org/news/2002/may/04pkk.htm
28. For details see, "Changing Asylum and Immigration Policies, the Threat to Democracy in the European Union after September 11 and the Situation of Kurdish Refugees in the UK",

Human Rights Sub-Commission 2002, Geneva: Centre Europe-Tiers Monde (CETIM), (Online: web), Accessed 18 October 2010, URL: http://www.cetim.ch/en/interventions_details.php?iid=186

29. The "Quartet" is a foursome of nations and international and supranational entities involved in mediating the peace process in the Israeli–Palestinian conflict. The group was established in Madrid in 2002. For further related information see, "Statement by the Middle East Quartet", 2 February 2007, Department of Information: New York, URL: htp://www.un.org/News/Press/docs/2007/sg2122.doc.htm.
30. Puder, Joseph, "Rewarding the Palestinians while Ignoring the Kurds", (Online: web), Accessed 14 March 2010, http://thebulletin.us/articles/2009/03/24/commentary/op-eds/doc49c8e03b24922735006145.txt

CHAPTER 6

The Question of Kurdish Self-Determination: Challenges and Prospects

The end of the Cold War changed the world. The process of globalisation, weakening of many central governments, drive for greater economic opportunity and political participation unleashed new powerful forces including ethnic and nationalistic forces. In the modern world of decolonisation and nation-states, the Kurds continue to suffer from a form of internal colonialism that has stunted the complete development of their nationalism. The Kurds constitute the largest stateless nation in the contemporary world. Kurdish nationalism seems stuck in a time warp from which others have already emerged more than a century ago. Independence and recogntion as a national entity have eluded the Kurds. Some of the frequent Kurdish revolts in the twentieth century have sought autonomy; others avowedly aimed at complete independence in a sovereign state. However, the fate of all these insurrections has been the same. No Kurdish movement has succeeded over the long run even in extracting major concessions. Some 30 million Kurds live in Kurdistan under the national jurisdiction of the four sovereign states of Turkey, Iran, Iraq and Syria, which in various ways deny Kurdish national identity and suppress its political and cultural manifestations by the use of force. The division of Kurdistan after World War I and the consequent structural diversity of Kurdish societies, administered by different political and economic regimes, have deprived the Kurds of political unity and cultural cohesion. Kurdish political organisations and movements, proliferating in a divided Kurdistan since 1918, have assumed different forms and pursued different objectives. Opposition to the denial of Kurdish identity and resistance to the imposed national identities remain the fundamental causes of Kurdish rebellion. This dialectic of denial and resistance defines the political form and character of the Kurdish nationalism.

Ethno-nationalists are relatively large and regionally concentrated ethnic groups that live within the boundaries of one state or several adjacent states. Their political movements are directed towards achieving a greater autonomy or an independent statehood. Most have historical traditions of autonomy or independence that are used to justify these contemporary demands. In some instances, that autonomy would have been lost centuries ago. Most people with nationalist aspirations live in the Third World, such as southern Sudan, the Palestinians and Kurds in West Asia and the Tibetans and Kashmiris in Asia. They have fought some of the world's most persistent wars of secession, but few have won political independence (Gurr and Harff 1994: 18).

The Kurds have long-contended that as a distinct ethnic group and as a nation, they are entitled to the universally recognised right to self-determination. The Kurds, like many other ethnic groups, have adhered to a set of shared principles which have shaped the course of their ethnic awareness. Nevertheless, ethnicity has been attributed to the development of ethno-nationalism and the existence, actual or perceived, of a common language, race, religion and historical experience. The development of ethnic consciousness gives an ethnic group (or nation) a sense of distinctiveness from that of the larger nation within which it lives. In most multi-ethnic Third World societies, ethno-nationalism has been suspect in the eyes of the dominant elite. They view this phenomenon as a hindrance to unity and the process of nation-building. Although not totally rejecting the appeal of ethnic identity, the Third World has remained suspicious of the disintegrative potential of ethno-nationalism in societies too fragile to withstand the barrage of demands from their ethnic groups with often contradictory or opposing objectives. Consequently, multi-ethnic Third World nations have endeavoured to ameliorate ethnic consciousness among their ethnic groups by accentuating their commonalities with the dominant sub-groups and integrating them into the larger society. Such integration has been undertaken largely through the processes of acculturation, amalgamation, and identification (Entessar 1984: 912-913).

Since the 1980s, there has been a large diaspora in western Europe that has participated in funding, promoting and shaping the nationalist movements—a powerful example of what Anderson has called 'long distance nationalism' (Anderson 1992). In terms of human rights violations, the Kurds have suffered as much as any other people in West Asia—facing massacre, poison gas, mass deportations, linguistic discrimination and a general refusal of their rights by all the four states in which they concentrated. Despite some improvements in the 1990s, the situation of the Kurds remains precarious. National self-determination in the sense of a state in all or part of Kurdistan remains elusive. Neither the conditions within these states nor the international conjuncture favours Kurdish self-determination. Faced with a combination of dramatic domestic political changes and profound international developments, the Kurds of Iraq, Iran, Syria and Turkey have entered a new phase of national awareness. Domestic assertiveness has emerged in the context of modern nation states, the spread of democratisation and human rights, increased communication among Kurds and political expectations. The emergence of Kurdish political self-awareness is a political evolution largely irreversible in character (Hallyday 2006: 12; Barky and Fuller 1998: 5).

Nationalism and Kurdish Ethnicity

Nationalism is an essentially modern development. The term nationalism reflects many usages in today's world. Anthony D. Smith argues that nationalism is seen as an ideological movement on behalf of a people some of whose members are supposed to establish a 'nation' currently or potentially with the aim of acquiring and sustaining autonomy, unity and identity. This approach involves three essential concepts within nationalism: national autonomy, national unity and national identity. In the ideological framework of nationalism, maintenance of these concepts for a nation is the major goal of nationalists. Besides that the ideological framework of nationalism "places the nation at the centre of its concerns and seeks to promote its well-being" (Smith 2001: 5-9; Smith 1981). Gellner and Anderson argue that the nation is a product of relatively recent technological and economic developments. Gellner's observations on the cultural gap that separated the elite from the rural producers in agro-literate societies are certainly relevant to the Kurdish case. Kurdish nationalism, if not endangered by the social and economic upheavals and labour migrations which have affected it, certainly owed its mass appeal to them (Gellner 1983). Modern communications, printing technology, radio and the cassette recorder contributed much to the creation of the Kurdish nation. For Anderson, the cultural roots of nationalism have a vital significance and role in understanding the source of great sacrifices for the sake of the limited imaginations. The convergence of capitalism and printing technology on the diversity of human language created the possibility of a new form of "imagined community"; a community of people whom one never meets face to face but whom one knows to exist and to be like oneself. It is imagined because its existence is contingent on its members sustaining a certain image of it that is based on their perceptions and feelings (Anderson 1991: 6, 46; Tamir 1995: 420-423). Fishman describes nationalism as a conscious or organised ethno-cultural solidarity which is directed outside of its initial sphere towards political, economic, and religious goals. So, it is first necessary for the group to become convinced that they possess in common certain unique ethno-cultural characteristics which are of importance to them (Fishman 1989: 108-109). Nationalism is merely designed to acquire political power that represents a search for political identity rather than a reaffirmation of cultural identity. But, Kurdish ethnicity is much older than Kurdish nationalism. An imagined community of Kurds—a well-defined Kurdish ethnicity—has existed for many centuries.

According to Smith, cultural, social and political values play the most important roles in the formation of ethnicity. In explaining ethnic revival, attention must be paid to the conjunction of culture and politics; economic development acts only as a catalyst in particular situations. Threats to linguistic and cultural identities can have a very strong potential for mobilising groups. In most cases of the process of ethnic revival, cultural manifestations appear earlier than political ones; political organisations are preceded by pre-existing cultural organisations or journals and newspapers. Political and cultural rights belong together, as political rights are prerequisites for making the decisions that are necessary to uphold and develop culture. The hatred that an ethnic group can develop against another group probably has less to do with competition per se and more with the risk of having to give up something of oneself—one's identity. It is a question of survival in a cultural rather than a material sense. If members believe that the very existence of the ethnic collectivity is threatened, the salience of ethnicity becomes heightened (Smith 1981: 13-14, 23: Alfredsson 1996: 73). A poor socio-economic environment may not directly contribute to ethnic revival, but rather to greater insecurity and political instability in which ethnic markers often gain increasing importance. Ethnic revival and the politicisation of ethnicity have been going on amongst many groups throughout the world. In the "global village", groups which previously were isolated have more contacts with the outside world through telecommunication, mass media, immigration and travel. Ethnic tensions in other countries have an immediate impact on them (Kallen 1996: 114).

Hobsbawm uses the term "proto-nationalism" to describe an ethnic group's development towards nationalism. Proto-nations live on large areas and even in dispersion and they feel that they belong together because of their mutual ethnicity, but, they lack a common polity. Where proto-nationalism exists, it is possible to mobilise the existing national symbols for creating a modern state (Hobsbawm 1990: 73-77). Kendal also argues that the forms of discrimination which result when people are prevented from expressing their identity culturally are often more difficult to bear than material poverty and economic exploitation (Kendal 1980: 83).

Even liberal states hostile to the idea of ethnic nationalism have promoted forms of civic nationalism that stress the importance of the 'unity of government' and seek loyalty to the key value principles and procedures enshrined in the constitution (Canovan 1996; Gilbert 1998). For civic nationalists, these constitutional values and principles override the more particular attachments of citizens. This drive for homogeneity is reinforced through a uniform legal system. A single set of constitutional principles guarantees identical rights and obligations to all citizens and in the case of federal states, ensures that the various component units are granted roughly the same rights and powers. In contrast, the constitutions of pre-modern polities were multiform—an 'assemblage' of overlapping legal and political jurisdictions based upon a variety of local customs (Tully 1995). Earlier polities recognised multiple and often cross-cutting ethnic, religious and territorial identities but the modern nation state attaches unprecedented importance to territory. Thus, the modern state is typically perceived as a self-contained unit within which the state acts 'as the sole collective spokesman' (Parekh 2000: 181).

The development of Kurdish nationalism, from the late nineteenth century onwards, was to a considerable degree a result of the rise of modernising states and of nationalism among the majority of the peoples who dominated them: Turks, Iranians and Arabs. Kurdish nationalism or the Kurdish nationalist movement, a direct consequence of the collapse of the Ottoman Empire, was neither the product of a war of independence against any occupation nor over the issue of resistance to colonialism, but an immediate and direct challenge to the newly founded or constructed nation-states. The Pahlavi regime in Iran, a product of the military coup of 1921, was for its part a product of the modernising state and Iranian nationalism served to encourage the emergence of a Kurdish nationalism in Iran. In Iraq, first the Hashemite monarchy from 1920 and then, after 1958, a succession of military regimes dominated by Arab nationalism provided the incentive and context for the rise of Kurdish nationalism (Halliday 2006: 16). Kurdish nationalism is the politics for the affirmation of national identity. Kurdish national identity is a product of modernity associated with the institution of the modern nation-state. It has its roots in the political and cultural processes and practices of the construction of the modern nation-state and national identity in the multi-ethnic and multi-cultural societies of Turkey, Iran, Iraq and Syria. The Kurdish nationalist movement has recurrently been a factor in the domestic and international politics of these countries. The denial of Kurdish ethnicity and national identities was the condition that created the conflict in the region. The dialectic of denial and resistance assigns a specifically transnational character to Kurdish nationalism (Vali 2006:49). In a context of the Kurdish society populating Ottoman territories, Kurdish nationalism was developed as a movement aiming to unite the dispersed population under one nation-state.

The dominant model of the nation-state as an administratively centralised politically and culturally homogeneous unit has its roots in the late fifteenth and early sixteenth centuries; it reflects a historically and culturally distinctive vision of the political order that has a strong liberal orientation. Whereas pre-modern polities tended to be composed of communities like castes, clans, tribes and ethnic groups, the modern state is defined as an association of individuals. Individuals are not linked to the state through the membership of a particular cultural community, but stand as singular citizens in the same direct relationship to the state. Thus, citizens relate to the state in an identical manner and enjoy equal status. This preoccupation with the relationship between the state and individual citizen is probably the most apparent in the liberal contract tradition. For contract theorists, the state is the product of a process of deliberation among undifferentiated individuals and no account is taken of the customs, traditions and institutions that may constitute a particular people prior to the social contract. On this model, to "be a citizen is to transcend one's ethnic, religious and other particularities, and to think and act as a member of a political community" (Parekh 2000: 181).

Kurdish ethnic nationalism can be categorised as a form of secessionism and irredentism. According to Smith, secessionism stems from two elements. One element is cultural homogeneity. As Bengio notes, "as far as language, race, and common history are concerned, the Kurds differ from the Iraqi Arabs" (Bengio 1999: 149-150). The other element is the existence of that homogeneous group within a larger political unit. However, in addition to their being part of Iraq as a 'larger entity', the Kurds have striven for independence. In other words, as Bengio explains, the Kurds have been challenging the territorial framework of Iraq and have sought to exclude themselves from Iraq ever since. Another distinctive feature of Kurdish ethnic nationalism is irredentism. Kurdish irredentism desires to bring together Kurdish populations that have historically become separated. "This group", Smith notes, "is both incorporated and divided up between different oppressive units" (Smith 1998: 218-223). In this regard, Chatham House explains:

> "Iraqi Kurdistan is geographically located at the heart of greater Kurdistan and shares contiguous boundaries with the Kurds in other countries: Turkey, Syria and Iran. The links between Kurds of those regions predate the formation of the four nation states. They are united by a common language and experiences of discrimination, and currently there is a resurgence of pan-Kurdish feeling across the four countries" (Chatham House 2004: 8).

The situation of national minorities (or ethno-national groups) differs in accordance with the state of cultural pluralism existing in a given state. It makes quite a difference whether a minority is part of a state with some smaller national minority groups or peoples or if there are several major peoples and ethnic groups. For the Kurds, the idea of modernity encompassing the notion of state has clashed with the desire to secure an autonomous administration for the Kurdish areas (Lukitz 1995: 108-109).

The Right of Nations to Self-Determination

The principle of self-determination by national groups developed as a natural corollary of the concept of nationalism that developed in the eighteenth and nineteenth centuries. As the central authorities of the Ottoman, Austrian, German and Russian empires pursued assimilationist policies or began to weaken militarily and politically, demands for greater autonomy or local self-government led to demands for total independence. With the disintegration of the Austro-Hungarian and Ottoman empires during World War I, the territories of the former empires became obtained their sovereignty. Self-determination was considered only for nations which were within the territory of the defeated empires; it was never thought to apply this concept to the overseas colonies. However, the success or failure of assertions of minority rights or self-determination in the late nineteenth century depended on the support of the colonisers (Pearson 1983: 25-30). But, the right to self-determination has been recognised by various international covenants of the twentieth century. Ethnic communities such as the Kurds have invoked the principle of self-determination to justify demands for autonomy or independence. Gudmundur Alfredsson has identified five different meanings for the concept of 'self-determination':

- The right of people to determine its international status, including the right to independence—sometimes referred to as external self-determination;
- The right of a State population to determine the form of government and to participate in the government, sometimes extended to include democratisation or majority rule and sometimes called internal self-determination;
- The right of a State to territorial integrity and non-violation of its boundaries and to govern its internal affairs without external interferences;
- The right of a minority within or even across State boundaries to special rights—not only protection and non-discrimination, but possibly the rights to cultural, educational, social and economic autonomy for the preservation of group identities;
- The right of a State, especially claimed by the developing countries, to cultural, social and economic development (Alfredsson 1982: 114).

In the dominant political discourse of the twentieth century, self-determination has been associated with nations: American President Woodrow Wilson's Fourteen Points', Joseph Stalin's influential writings on the national question and the Charter of the United Nations all refer to the right of self-determination of nations. Kurdish nationalists have therefore spent much effort to prove that the Kurds constitute a nation. The Kurds might have qualified for Wilson's Fourteen Points but by the end of World War I the Kurdish nationalists were too weak to press their claims effectively (Edmonds 1971: 90). The UN Charter (1948) implicitly referred to the colonised people of Asia and Africa only, or more precisely those peoples that were colonised by Western powers. Stalin did provide a definition which has had a great importance for the Kurdish movement. He defined the nation as having five characteristic features: common history, language, territory, economic life and culture; expressing a common national character. Kurdish nationalists could convincingly claim a common history and a large piece of territory associated with their people but their opponents denied their existence (Bruinessen 2000b: 27-28).

For almost a century, the right to self-determination has been acknowledged as one of the cornerstones of international law. In 1918, Woodrow Wilson declared to the US Congress that "National aspirations must be respected; people may now be dominated and governed only by their own consent. Self-determination is not a mere phrase but it is an imperative principle of action" (Nawaz 1965: 83). Self-determination as conceived by Wilson was an imprecise amalgam of several strands of thought—some associated with the notion of self-government; others newly hatched as a result of wartime developments—but all imbued with a general spirit of democracy. Wilson held that every people had the right to select its own form of government—an idea that might be termed as internal self-determination (Pomerance 1982: 1). This right has been enshrined in Article One of the UN's International Covenant on Civil and Political Rights, which reads: "All peoples have the right of self-determination. By virtue of that right they freely determine their political status and freely pursue their economic, social and cultural development."[1] The most striking development was the Draft UN Declaration on the Rights of Indigenous Peoples, which emphasises the importance of political self-government.[2]

In international law, when the right to self-determination was formulated after World War II it was meant to imply external self-determination, i.e. independence, and to apply only to traditional colonies. Because the right to self-determination was supposed to have been exhausted as most of the former colonies became independent, it was imperative to start redefining 'self-determination' in the 1970s so as to include 'internal self-determination', i.e. autonomy of some kind. Self-determination was restricted to nations or peoples, not other groups. Entities defined as minorities, populations or ethnic groups do not have the right to self-determination. When indigenous peoples want to claim the right to exist as distinct entities, it is important that they are defined as 'peoples' not 'minorities' (Skutnabb-Kangas 2000: 487).

The right of people to self-determination is frequently invoked, and in principle it is guaranteed in international law. But in practice, human beings as groups have fewer rights than individuals, unless they form a state. Because they do not have states of their own, the minorities in sovereign states, particularly in many of the Third World, do not have cultural rights (Chaliand 1980: 8).

The concept of national self-determination appears to express the idea of democracy and continues to shape the aims and ideas of political groups. The ratification of various new states in the recent past has led to instability, exclusion and war. Secession has brutal consequences and so does blocking the independence of a nation or a people who desire it. It seems hard, if not unfair, to deny a people the right to self-determination (Machin 2008: 102). The collapse of communism was at first supposed by many to entail the triumph of liberal capitalism. Global capitalism has no time for national self-determination because its project is a global market of sellers and buyers. But nation states still dominate world politics, and there are nations that seek self-determination in the face of oppressive states. The crisis of self-determination is not over and no new consensus on the meaning of the principle has emerged. The international community lacks a clear, principled and practicable policy towards self-determination. There is an urgent need to think clearly, systematically, and practically about what relations ought to obtain among the principles of state sovereignty, national self-determination and human rights (Freeman 1998).

The contemporary problem of national self-determination is that the political world is organised in a manner where the primary agents are states. This principle is problematic precisely because most of the world's states are multinational and some nations demand new states of their own. This demand threatens the integrity, status, power and wealth of the existing states. This contradiction produces either the very violence that the system is designed to minimise or the severe repression of potential violence. The status quo is not viable because it cannot achieve its own declared purposes: it cannot guarantee the territorial integrity of states; it is extremely reluctant to recognise the self-determination of peoples and consequently, it presides over massive violations of human rights (Freeman 1998). The internal aspect of self-determination means that states and their peoples have the right to independence from foreign domination. Thus, existing states which have been invaded or which are otherwise clearly controlled by foreign powers have a right to self-determination i.e. the right to overthrow the invaders and re-establish independence.

Allen Buchanan has proposed a theory of secession which combines liberalism with realism. He argues that the right to self-determination is not a fundamental right but should be derived from a complex set of moral considerations. These include both a realist concern not to undermine the states system as such and a liberal concern for individual rights. Buchanan's theory of self-determination is liberal rather than nationalist insofar as he treats culture as an object of individual choice rather than of a collective right—but, nations could benefit if they were victims of economic discrimination (Buchanan 1997: 31-35). The most radical liberal theory of secession has been proposed by Harry Beran. He assumes that the fundamental liberal value is individual autonomy. He derives from this premise the proposition that states are voluntary associations and that anyone may leave a state if he or she wishes to. The right to secession belongs to the minority in any territory that wishes to secede. It is not necessary that this minority suffer from human-rights violations (Beran 1984: 21-25). Donald Horowitz contends that the larger number of secessionist movements are found among 'backward groups' in economically 'backward regions'. A backward group is defined as one whose members have not benefited from opportunities in education and advanced non-agrarian jobs and has not been integrated into the mainstream of society (Horowitz 1985: 233-239). Horowitz places the Kurds in the groups with the highest potential for secession.

Margalit and Raz, investigating the moral justification for national self-determination, assert that the right to self-government is an entitlement in which the right to self-determination is valid only when held by an 'encompassing group'. Refusing both the terms 'nation' and 'people' for some unclear reason, an 'encompassing group' nevertheless sounds remarkably similar to a nation. An 'encompassing group' for Margalit and Raz is a collectivity that possesses a pervasive culture and is important for its members' self-identification and their welfare. Membership of such groups is of great importance to the individual well-being for it greatly affects one's opportunities, one's ability to engage in relationships and pursuits marked by the culture. Because these encompassing groups are important to the individual, they therefore must be granted the ability to protect the right that they have a moral entitlement to self-government (Margalit and Raz 1990: 449- 457).

The right to national self-determination is attractive because it appears both to recognise the right of a people to live according to their own culture and to be consistent with what is required by the principle of democracy. It is problematic, however, for two main reasons. First, in a world in which there are far more nations than states, claims to national self-determination threaten the existing state order and thereby international peace. Second, nationalism mobilises sentiments of collective solidarity and thereby tends both to threaten individual rights and to generate xenophobia (Freeman 1998).

There are no simple solutions to problems of national self-determination, either in theory or in practice. There may be cases where secession is the most just solution—as the remedy for persistent, gross human-rights violations—but it is highly vulnerable to the international heckler's veto and should be treated with caution. Short of secession, solutions to self-determination problems can involve moves down, up and across from the nation-state. Downward moves involve recognising autonomy for aggrieved nations within the state, for example by some form of federalism. Upward solutions employ supra-state institutions, such as the European Union, as the level at which structures can be created to meet the legitimate aspirations of conflicting parties. Political solutions across state borders involve recognising the rights of trans-state nations (for example, the Kurds) without establishing new nation states. None of these moves guarantees success in the face of intransigent opposition from existing members of the states' club, which unfortunately is all too likely. However, the penetration of state borders by the processes of globalisation provides the opportunity for imaginative new solutions to formerly intractable self-determination problems (Freeman 1998).

Self-Determination through Regional Autonomy

The maximum of the minority or ethnic conflicts in the contemporary world have a substantial international or transnational component. This may be because members of the minority community in one state form part of the majority community in a neighbouring state (e.g. Catholic nationalists in Northern Ireland) or because a minority or ethnic community cuts across borders and thus involves more than one state (e.g. Kurds, Basques, Nagas and Kashmiris). If ethnic or communal violence increases, geopolitical concerns often indicate the involvement of outside actors in the conflict.[3]

Ethnicity is an even more obvious basis on which to assert political power when one considers that under the guise of the nation-state, ethnicity (or linguistic affinity or religion) became the foundation of political organisation in the late nineteenth century.

The concept of 'self-determination' in relation to the concept of autonomy is an important pillar of nationalism. Every nationalist is concerned with autonomy (Smith 1998: 125). The self-determination principle holds that any people, simply because it considers itself to be a separate national group, is uniquely and exclusively qualified to determine its own political status including the right to its own state. It therefore, makes ethnicity the ultimate standard of political legitimacy (Connor 1976: 111-12). Separatist or minority assertions are made by poor regions which complain of underdevelopment (e.g. the Tamil homeland, southern Sudan) and rich regions complaining of exploitation or unequal treatment (e.g. the Basque country, Kashmir, Nagaland, Punjab) and those which are well off (e.g. Quebec, Northern Ireland). Indeed, one of the major political struggles within the ethnic minority groups is often between those who adopt a more traditional or nationalist attitude and those who link ethnic solidarity with cross-ethnic classes or economic issues. While economic interests were perhaps the primary motivating factor regarding the case of Hong Kong seeking autonomy within China, they are not as relevant to the Kurds in West Asia (Hannum 1990: 8). Moreover, not every nationalist movement gives priority to having a particular state. The majority of Catalonian and Scottish nationalists are more inclined to the issues of having autonomy in a multi-national state and cultural equality rather than acquiring full independence. It is a general perception that every nation must have its own state; however, it is not an imperative to be derived from the core doctrine of nationalism. It reflects the fact that "nationalism is primarily a cultural doctrine or, more accurately, a political ideology with a cultural doctrine at its centre" (Smith 1998: 122). A federal solution and the autonomy arrangement could provide for the regional assemblies to reorganise their own territory administratively, raise taxes and develop tourism and other infrastructure. This provision defuses conflict between a segment of the security forces and local population by integrating the locals in the functioning of law and order. Many national minorities do not need, and do not want, their own independent state. They want some form of autonomy within a larger state, rather than seeking secession. Many autonomous systems have been established to accommodate national minorities or 'smaller historic nations' or peoples within the states concerned. In most of the cases, autonomy has brought about substantial protection for the concerned ethnic minorities and equality of rights of all inhabitants of a region. In some cases, forms of cultural and local autonomy are adopted in order to ensure self-government in cultural affairs. In most cases, autonomy has provided these regions with a stable solution of peaceful coexistence and power sharing, both within the region and between the autonomous region and the central state (Benedikter et al 2008: 37).

Observers of ethnic conflict regard federalism as a solution to the problems of ethnically divided societies. Federalism allows the integration of diverse groups into a single system, permits diversity, distributes power widely and fosters the autonomy of minority groups. Different policies, laws and institutions reflect the diverse constituencies. Access points for political participation and accommodation increase opportunities for self-government (Manafy 2005: 139). The degree of federalism implemented can differ markedly from country to country. By definition, federalism requires only two levels of government: one at the national level and the remainder at subunits. Both levels rule over the same territory and each has at least one area of independent decision-making. In the case of Canada, the confederation agreement allowed the French-speaking Quebecois considerable freedom in maintaining their distinct culture, languages and legislative assembly. Kashmir has remained a litmus test for India's secular nationalism which has its understanding of its position based on the Article 370 of the Indian Constitution. Accordingly, Kashmir and Nagaland remains unique and is given a special status within the Indian union. Consequently, even violent fringes of self-determination movements, as the Irish Republican Army (IRA) in Northern Ireland relinquished the strategy of violent confrontation with the central state and a form of regional autonomy was established. In the complex case of the Basque, the armed activities of the *Euskadi Ta Askatasuna* (ETA)[4] have not ceased yet, but an overwhelming majority of the Basque population backs a democratic form of enlarging autonomy. Spain is a "state of autonomous communities"; it has elevated territorial autonomy to the very principle of state organisation not only in terms of respecting the rights of historical ethnic and national minorities but also in terms of a subsidiary in power sharing, efficiency in public administration and democracy in political participation (Benedikter et al 2008: 40-41).

Apparently, a small number of states have acknowledged that autonomy can serve to integrate national minorities into the state and stabilise the conflict in situations otherwise prone to go out of control. Regional autonomy as an aim was to defuse ethnic conflict primarily in the Basque and Catalan regions (Barkey and Graham 1998: 200-202). Northern Ireland, Catalonia, Basque and the Quebec regions were economically well-off and did not suffer like the Kurdish areas in Turkey, Iran and Syria.

The dependency theory explains the underdeveloped state of many nations in the world by examining the patterns of interactions among nations and by arguing that inequality among nations is an intrinsic part of those interactions. This theory holds that there are a small number of established nations that are continually fed by developing nations at the expense of their own resources. These developing nations are essentially acting as colonial dependencies sending their wealth to the developed nations with minimal compensation. The developed nations actively keep the developing nations in a subservient position. Most dependency theorists regard international capitalism as the motive force behind dependency relationships. Andre Gunder Frank, one of the earliest dependency theorists, is quite clear on this point:

> "...historical research demonstrates that contemporary underdevelopment is in large part the historical product of past and continuing economic and other relations between the satellite underdeveloped and the now developed metropolitan countries. Furthermore, these relations are an essential part of the capitalist system on a world scale as a whole" (Frank 1972: 3).

According to this view, the capitalist system has enforced a rigid international division of labour which is responsible for the underdevelopment of many areas of the world. The economic and political powers are concentrated in the industralised countries. Opposed to unequal distribution of social justice, when society is sharply divided into have and have- not, liberalism's individualistic autonomous values are compromised. Under the prevailing class-divided conservative world system, it is difficult to realise autonomous rights. Autonomy attends to the local needs of the people and advocates political participation. The Kurds are much dependent on the capitalist world for their economic and political rights.

The fragmented traditionalistic political culture, tribal affiliations, informal group politics and a conservative mode of thinking undermine the realisation of the Kurds' desire for autonomy. The most debilitating contradiction between the Kurdish traditionalistic leadership and the desire to liberate Kurdish society from an externally created internal domination is the Kurdish dependence on imperial forces for liberation; a reliance on the oppressors. This logic has prevented the development of Kurdish class solidarity and political consciousness. However, the Kurds' quest for political autonomy and self-determination has been consistently reactionary. This mode of behaviour and political factionalism has played a key role in defeating the idea of political autonomy for the Kurds (Manafy 2005: 138). The Kurds have been used as a policy tool by neocolonial and regional powers for their economic and political ends.

Politics of Denial

Theoretically, political authority in the new states was constitutional and democratic; it was derived from the collective will of the people and not from the whim of the reigning despot. The democratic doctrine of popular sovereignty provided the juridical ground for the making of this modern identity but the ensuing political and cultural processes were different. The Kurdish demand for autonomy from an autocratic government is not a fundamental solution. In defence of the ethnic minorities and nationalities in the former USSR, Rosa Luxemburg wrote that autonomy is an empty concept if the centralised autocracy is not democratised. Under capitalism, autonomy is not a practical solution to nationality problems. "So long as the capitalist states exist, imperialistic world politics determine and regulate the inner and outer life of nation; there can be no national self-determination in war or in peace" (Vali 2006: 54; Davis 1976: 218-219). The capitalist world system conflicts with democratic ideals. It is a system of equality rooted in the process of capital accumulation. The dominant world system perpetuates social injustices and human sufferings. Karl Kautsky feels that the problem of nationality can be solved only in a truly democratic system based on a universal franchise and equal direct participation in elections. Democracy needs to be defined in terms of both political and social components (Bridsall 2000: 25).

The political and cultural processes that created the nation-states in Turkey, Iran, Iraq and Syria differed. But, their strategic objective remained the same: to construct states whose identity is defined by the collective identity of their populations. This was deemed essential for the legality and legitimacy of the ruling power. The identity of the new states and their assumed unity with their respective nations was forged by a military power with new national ideologies. The process of territorial centralism that followed the formation of these states ensured that the popular will embodied in the executive and legislative authority was exercised throughout their designated territories uniformly and without regional and local opposition or insubordination. But, the new states realised that both authority and legitimacy required more than an effective control over their national territories. Thus, the control over territory became increasingly effective for its population, the citizens of the new state. The people became the strategic objective of political power, which sought to affirm that the state and the nation were not only coterminous but also indivisible. This assumed the unity of the nation and the state was reiterated by the principle of 'nationalism' which became the ideological component of the process of the construction of the nation-state.

It is the democratic identity of the state and nation—the ruler and the ruled—that changes the strategic objective of political power. The modern state defines the identity of its citizens by targeting and suppressing their ethnic and cultural differences, thus bringing them in line with the identity of the sovereign. However, modern identity is not always the ethnic identity of the majority. But, both nation-states and statelessness are products of modernity. They are dialectic opposites of the historical process. The institution of the nation-state and its associated political and cultural processes and practices has been widely hailed as the most impressive achievement of modernity. Statelessness is seldom accorded the same privileged position in the modern political discourse. The stateless person is seen as a relic of the past fighting against modernity or merely as an accident of modernity fighting against modernity (Kymlicka 1995: 29-30). National minorities have been vulnerable to serious injustices. To protect against injustice, national minorities require certain guarantees regarding their lands, cultural institutions and political self-government. The identity and the claims of the stateless are denied by the modern states which turns the efforts of the stateless into political upheavals.

The sovereign state that suppressed Kurdish identity claimed popular democratic legitimacy, bolstered by intensifying the use of political violence in the process of the construction of uniform sovereign nations and national identities. The perversion of modernity seriously undermined socio-cultural space and marginalised the non-sovereign/subordinate ethnicities. The

Kurdish rebellions in Turkey and Iran were precisely a reaction against this marginalisation. The modern states had constituted national political fields unrepresented by the minorities (Vali 2006: 56-57). The doctrine of popular sovereignty which defined the nature of authority and legitimacy in the constitutions of these states was seriously undermined by notions of citizenship which bore the identity of their dominant ethnicity. Those who did not qualify as ethnic Turks, Persians or Arabs were excluded from citizenship of the emergent national states unless they renounced/denied their own ethnic and cultural identities. Those who failed to do so were forced to comply but they ended up with resistance and revolt. For them, membership of the new state was far from being free or voluntary but was sanctioned by political compulsion (Vali 2006: 57). This gap between popular sovereignty and ethnic citizenship is bridged by political coercion; the main regulator of the relationship between the sovereign and the Kurds in these four national states.

Furthermore, traditional Kurdish organisations are acutely aware that adopting too moderate a stance in the face of an unmistakable rise in state repression may cause a shift in the public support in favour of the more radical groups. In the absence of a political breakthrough, particularly in the case of Kurdish communities in Iraq and Turkey, Kurdish-related terrorism sadly became the dominant form of violence in the mid-1990s (Morad 1992: 48-54).

Ideological Differences and Methods of Struggle

Ideas certainly play a role in determining the character of nationalist and other poltical movements. Ideological questions have preoccupied Kurdish intellectuals for a long time. Nationalism provided an ideology for communities, termed as the right of the nation to independence, to the right to revolt and resist, which was adopted all over the world. Since the 1920s there have been several variants of Kurdish nationalism in each of the three core states and in each case they have reflected external ideological forces: Marxism, liberalism and Islamism. Many of the factions within the Kurdish movement have scarcely claimed to separate identity beyond a vague ideological notion centered on Marxism as an instrument of political arbitration.

The ideological formation accounts for two striking features of Kurdish nationalism. One is the influence of Marxist ideas. Kurdish society has been relatively underdeveloped and the leadership has not been drawn from a proletarian social background. Marxism has served the ideological function of opposition to dominant, pro-Western states (Pahlavi Iran, Kemalist Turkey, Hashmite Iraq) and providing a basis, or at least aspirations, for uniting the struggle of the Kurds. The PKK's ideology was inspired by Marxist–Leninist political philosophy; a product of the militant left-wing culture of the Turkish student and urban guerilla movement of the 1970s. But, the PKK also employed the revolutionary theory of Mao Tse-tung which favoured liberation struggles in the countryside where the basis for social revolution could be developed. The other striking feature is the place of Islamist ideas. The revolt of Sheikh Said in Turkey in 1925 drew on his role as the leader of a Sufi order. Since then, Islamism has legitimised its role in the Turkish politics characterising a conservative democracy (Manafy 2005: 109; Gokalp and Unsar 2008: 116).

Since the beginning of the struggle, the PKK has been Marxist–Leninist in its ideology, Stalinist in its leadership style and Maoist in its strategy for the conquest of power (Radu 2001: 48). Many of the villagers looked upon the PKK as their liberator. The PKK is distinguished from other Kurdish political parties by its social base, which includes a sizable portion of workers and peasants. It advocates both socialism and independence for greater Kurdistan with a priority on armed struggle (Hassanpour 1994). But, the Party lost much sympathy as a result of its own brutal and violent behaviour. Most of its members and sympathisers were very young, poorly educated and from humble backgrounds. In its composition, the PKK was the most proletarian among the Kurdish organisations (Bruinessen 1984: 11).The PKK began with an active defence hoping to force out the Turkish army from Kurdistan. Its guerillas skillfully used Mao Tse-tung's method of confrontation with the Turkish army in spite of the latter's superiority, numbers and strength (McDowall 2000: 420). Although the PKK avoided a direct confrontation with the Turkish forces, it was indirectly able to define the limits of operation of a well-organised, highly-equipped, trained and numerically strong army of the Turkish state. However, the Maoist strategy is effective only when the guerrillas are supported and sheltered by the people. The PKK's strategy was to alter the conservative rural norms by exterminating the landlords. It was a challenge to the Turkish army that could not protect its agents. The PKK forces could not match the highly organised Turkish army, but their presence was intimidating (Entessar 1992: 98-99).

During the 1979 Revolution in Iran, the predominantly Sunni Kurds was cautious about the Islamic upheaval taking place in the society and clashed with it. The Kurdish areas remained opposed to the Islamic Republic and to the Islamisation programme introduced by the new regime. The very fact that in the name of Islamic unity Khomeini denied the political rights of ethnic minorities strengthened secular nationalism among the Kurds. In Iraq, there has been an Islamist influence within the Kurdish autonomous areas in the 1990s, in part as a result of Iranian influence. In neither the case of Iran nor of Syria are there any fixed or permanent ideological characters to the movement—rather a shifting set of ideological orientations, responding to circumstances.

In Iran and Iraq, Kurdish nationalism could only mobilise the masses under religious leadership, which turned it into a specifically Sunni movement. Unlike Iraq, Komala has maintained itself as an alternative to the KDPI with its call for socialist Iran in which Kurdish rights to self-determination will be honoured. However, Komala has not been able to liberate itself from the burden of traditionalism or to turn the nationalist movement into a social revolution or a people's war. Although both Komala and KDPI formally demand autonomy within Iran, an increasing number of Kurds in Iran and Iraq are arguing more openly in favour of independence—pointing to the failure of negotiations and numerous deals between the Kurds and various central governments, government associations of Kurdish leaders and of changing international relations (Hassanpour 1994).

In Iraq, it was the Qadiri Shaykh Mahmud Barzinji of Sulaymaniyah and the Naqshbandi Shaykh Ahmad Barzani (Mulla Mustafa's elder brother) who had mobilised poor peasants as well as tribesmen in nationalist rebellions against the British and later the royal government. In the short-lived Kurdish republic of Mahabad (1946), the religious authority of Qazi Muhammad was essential to guarantee the participation of the various urban classes as well as the tribes. The Shi'ite Kurds of southern Kurdistan stayed completely aloof from the Sunni-led Kurdish rebellions. Only during the 1960s when the Kurdish movement in Iraq was no longer led by religious authorities but by a secular party, did the Shi'ite Kurds begin to take part in it. The ideological influences of Kemalism, pan-Arabism and left-wing thought combined with socio-economic changes in fostering a secular and populist conception; ethnicity replaced the aristocratic and religious linkages. However, not all Kurds have come to identify themselves with the Kurdish nation. In the first place, there are those persons of Kurdish descent who have become completely Turkicised or Arabised (or less frequently, Persianised). In some respects, they have become Turks, Arabs and Persians, although the development of Kurdish nationalism has caused some of them to reassert their identity (Bruinessen 1992a: 53). There are many who have not entirely shed their Kurdish cultural identity but whose primary political orientation is towards Turkey, Iran or Iraq and they dissociate themselves from all forms of Kurdish separatism. In Turkey especially, there is a strong pressure to deny the Kurds their identity. During the past two decades, many people have vacillated between such an orientation towards their country and its 'national' culture on the one hand, and a more regional, ethnic or Kurdish nationalist orientation on the other.

There are those who identify themselves primarily with Islam. Most of them see themselves as Kurds as well as Muslims, but feel little sympathy for the secular Kurdish organisations. The Iranian Revolution inspired the emergence of several minor Islamic Kurdish political formations in both Iran and Iraq (Bruinessen 1986: 22-24). In Turkey, Islamic movements found much support among the Kurds. Turkey's sole Muslim party, the National Salvation Party (which after a ban in 1980, re-emerged as the National Welfare Party), saw itself forced to appeal to regional and ethnic grievances in order to win votes in Turkey's Kurdish provinces. As a political force, Islam is not very significant in Kurdistan and an Islamic orientation rarely implies a negation of Kurdish ethnicity (Bruinessen 1992a: 53-54).

The Kurds are a nation in formation at the crossroads of the Arab, Iranian and Turkish worlds. The sources of these divisions are socio-historical and have prevented the emergence of a full-fledged Kurdish identity, fragmented also by geography. The Kurds have historically tended to live in extremely rugged mountainous terrains that have often separated one community from another and also from those of the Arabs, Iranians and Turks (Yavuz and Gunter 2001: 33-34). Kurdish life remains tribally structured in most areas and is based on local, tightly-knit rural communities under a tribal–religious leader known as a sheikh. This tribal structure has played a dual role both in impeding the formation of a Kurdish unity by keeping the Kurds fragmented and in preserving a heightened Kurdish particularism toward the Turks, Iranians and Arabs. When the Kurdish question was reconstituted as an issue of reactionary politics, tribal resistance and regional backwardness it involved significant elements of Islam, traditional forms of social life, the peripheral economy and the components of the social space wherein Kurdish ethno-political identity was constituted (Yegen 1996: 217). Tribal structure has constituted the core depository of Kurdish identity that has kept a modern conception of nationalism.

However, major differences between the two ideological identities of Iraq's and Turkey's Kurds related to their socio-economic backgrounds. While the urban middle class and the landed families provided the Kurdish movement in Iraq with most of its leaders, the leaders of the Kurdish organisations in Turkey have tended to come from impoverished families. An inevitable outcome of this situation was that Turkey's Kurdish politics has been noticeably dominated by radical leftist ideologies. Furthermore, Kurdish organisations in Turkey have tended to favour uncompromising and often indiscriminately violent tactics against the state—echoing a characteristic tendency of the country's radical left.

The PKK was better organised than the Talabani–Barzani political organisations. While the PKK fought the landed classes in Kurdistan, Talabani–Barzani forces derived support from them. The feudal *aghas* were the KDPI's and PUK's political components. The PKK had a well-defined ideology, while the KDP-Iran, KDP-Iraq and PUK did not. Contrary to the KDP-Iraq and the PUK that depended on external forces—especially the United States—in their struggle, the PKK leaders considered it a capture by the imperialist forces, not liberation. The PKK was extremely progressive; even though it was not entirely compatible with the tribal/feudal cultures of Kurdistan. This incompatibility and the tribal fragmentation was reinforced by the imperially dominated conservative world system (Manafy 2005: 108-109).

Factionalism, ideological incompatibility, linguistic and cultural barriers have severely hampered successful Kurdish secessionist drives. Iranian Kurds are culturally closer to other Iranian nationalities than to Kurds in Iraq, Syria or Turkey. This, however, does not imply that they have forsaken their Kurdishness. It means that cultural factors favouring secessionists are not operative among the majority of Iranian Kurds (Entessar 1992: 280; Mcdowall 2000: 124). Kemalism, Khomeinism and Baathism— despite their differences—deny the Kurdish national identity as a prerequisite to their national sovereignty.

Challenges to the Kurdish National Movement

The Kurdish political world is deeply divided. The divisive rural social structure of Kurdistan is extremely conservative. This divisiveness blocks the creation of class solidarity and political consciousness. The Kurdish movement has failed to win the hearts and minds of the masses. The failure to enter into a class-alliance with non-Kurds especially in Iran and Turkey has led to discontentment (Manafy 2005: 142). Kurdish liberation struggles have been hindered by the reliance on colonial powers and regional governments and also by cultural rivalries and fragmentation. For instance, Zaza-speaking Kurds supported Sheikh Said's revolt because of his religious influence. Whereas, the Alavi Kurds' support to the Turkish secular government stemmed from their conflict with and a reaction against the Sunni ideology of the movement which was hostile to Shi'ism and afforded protection by the law of Ataturk's secular government (Entessar 1992: 84).

The lack of tactical and strategic planning was another disadvantage. It is impossible for tribal armies to fight against an experienced, sophisticated and modern army equipped with communication networks and rapid military deployment machinery —a fact that Kurdish leadership has repeatedly ignored (McDowall 2000: 197-198) The Kurdish leadership suffers from its own tribally defined ideology, tribal values, lack of unity and a reliance on regional and external forces that prevent the realisation of the national liberation struggle. McDowall writes that "the lack of homogeneity of the Kurdish forces and the lack of coordinated action seriously weakened the Kurds' fighting capacity" (McDowall 2000: 207).

Although most Kurdish nationalists nurture the dream of a united and independent Kurdistan, the leaders of the Iranian and Iraqi Kurds have for pragmatic reasons usually restricted their demands to self-determination within the framework of the existing states, i.e. political autonomy and culture rights. They refrained from openly embracing pan-Kurdish ideas. When in Turkey the Kurdish movement re-emerged in the 1960s, initially as a part of the left movement, its first demands were for recognition of the existence of the Kurds, their cultural rights and economic development. As Lenin's thoughts were widely known in Turkey, the concept of self-determination came to dominate political discourse and by the late 1970s it had become the professed aim of virtually all Kurdish parties and organisations in Turkey. The party that was the most successful in waging a guerrilla war against the Turkish state and building up a mass following among Turkey's Kurds, the

PKK, dropped its demands from independence to mere autonomy. It made efforts to draw Iraqi and Iranian Kurds into its orbit becoming a significant factor in both the Iraqi and Iranian parts of Kurdistan and competing notably with the Iraqi KDP. By the early 1990s, Abdullah Ocalan had moderated his ambitions and was hoping for a negotiated settlement and he envisaged a solution within the framework of the Republic of Turkey (Bruinessen 2000b: 277-88). All significant Kurdish leaders have reconciled themselves to the respective states.

The inability of the Kurds to establish their own state reflects the nature of their opponents and the tangled international situation of the twentieth century. It also testifies to the important disabilities that the Kurds have suffered from within. The elements of disunity have affected Kurdish political organisation (Harris 1977: 113). Although the Kurds are easily distinguishable from the rest of the world, they are by no means united. The Kurds are set apart from their neighbours chiefly by language. Kurdish belongs to the Indo-European family and is a close relative of Iranian. Yet, Kurdish is not at all a unified tongue. It is divided into at least three major dialects: Kurdi, Kurmanji and Zaza. Religious behaviour also divides the Kurds. The overwhelming majority are Sunnis. However, on the level of tribal religious practices and adherance to mystical orders, major tendencies come into play. Tribal struture is no doubt an important impedement to a national movement. In societies such as the Kurdish one, the unit of loyalty rarely ranges beyond the tribe; the individual is born into a series of family relationsips from which one cannot disentangle from the system. And this traditional organisation formed from aggregations of clans suffers from built-in rivalries and conflicts with neighbours. Disputes over grazing rights and marriage partners typically set adjoining tribes against each other. These feuds are so deep and hallowed with time that it takes extraordinary circumstances to band tribes of a region together even against outsiders. For instance, the Barzanis in the northern Iraq were opposed till the end by their traditional tribal rivals; the Iraqi government was able to field loyal Kurdish units.

However, the tribal organisation is gradually breaking down as the semi-nomadic, trans-humant and pastoral life becomes less prevalent among the Kurds. In the towns and cities of the Kurdish region as well as in the major urban centres of Turkey, Iran, Iraq and Syria there are now growing numbers of detribalised Kurds. The latter are generally better educated than their rural co-ethnics and are far more likely to identify with an overarching ethnic cause. A number among them have embraced reformist or radical social doctrines which at least in theory reject the traditional tribal system. Yet, it has been within the tribal structure that all major twentieth century Kurdish leaders have operated. The most successful were Sheikh Said in Turkey, Mulla Mustafa Barzani in Iraq and Qazi Mohammad in Iran who managed to go beyond their immediate tribal fame to attract confederations of tribes. The bandwagon effect of charismatic personality and the fame of success against a commonly despised central government have combined to bring allies to the cause (Harris 1977: 113-114). The movement has been broken down into their basic tribal units with great rapidity. Kurdish nationalism remains bounded by the states in which the different Kurdish communities live.

However, the Arab Spring and the reform movements that have swept the Middle East have further propelled and provided a platform to Kurdish nationalism. The Kurds have taken advantage of the regime change or calls for change by linking with the democratic and minority movements. Kurdish nationalism also coexists with other emerging regional issues including sectarianism, border instability and economic development (Natalie 2012). This increasing salient and complex Kurdish problem will continue to challenge governance within states while shifting in regional and global politics.

Kurdish Internally Divisive Problems

From the 1920s onwards and especially during the 1930s and 1940s a genuine Kurdish nationalism developed. The concept of a Kurdish nation united by the bonds of language, common history, culture and the ideal of political autonomy or even independence was gaining more and more currency especially among the urban sectors of the population. The spread of these ideas was closely linked to the Arabisation of the state and to the corresponding processes of social closure that left persons of Kurdish origin at a disadvantage. During the second half of the 1920s, urban intellectuals of Suleymaniyah founded a series of literary and cultural clubs. They were dedicated to what countless nationalists did and continue to do in other places during the first phase of nationalist awakening: they developed the Kurdish script and historiography, purged Kurdish vocabulary of Arab words, rediscovered long-forgotten Kurdish authors etc. However, the Kurdish intelligentsia of Suleymaniyah did not participate in the various rebellions by Sheikh Mahmud (Wimmer 2002: 186).

During the 1930s, a young generation of Kurdish officers of the newly founded Iraqi army came under the influence of Kurdish nationalism. This generation had not served under the Ottomans and was educated at the Military Academy of Baghdad. They founded organisations such as the Hizbi Hiwa (Party of Hope), in order to counter the Pan-Arabic parties and groups that were enjoying more and more popularity among their collegues of Arab origin. The left-wing faction of the Hizbi Hiwa later joined the Kurdish section of the Communist Party and founded the Hizbi Rizgari Kurd (Party for the Liberation of Kurds) which formed a kind of reservoir for the young Kurdish intelligentsia (Wimmer 2002: 186).

Kurdish nationalism further spread after the revolution of 1958 when the Arabisation of the state apparatus was advanced quickly. Kurdish nationalism increasingly spread among the urban Kurdish middle classes, especially those with college or university education who depended on a state whose power and economic potential increased enormously after the Second World War and the oil boom. The lawyers and left-wing officers who led the movement in the urban areas added a new element to Kurdish nationalism. Their vision of a better future implied not only liberation from Turkish, Arab and Persian domination but also emancipation from the power of religious notables and tribal leaders who were seen as symbols of an outdated 'feudal' order to be overcome by a revolutionary catharsis. In fact, many Sheikhs and *Aghas* had become large landowners during the second half of the nineteenth century. The urban nationalists depended on the support of these 'feudal elements' because the urban middle classes still represented only a tiny fraction of the overall population in the largely rural areas. The largest part of the territory to be included in a liberated Kurdistan was controlled by the tribal leaders and religious notables who continued to command the respect of their followers and who could mobilise large numbers of armed men in times of conflict or war. In order to give their movement a mass basis, the urban nationalists had to rely on the tribes of the Kurdish hintherlands.

The Kurdish movement did not turn away from the Left; almost all Kurdish organisations claimed to be Marxist–Leninist—however little the ranks knew about Leninism. All considered the Kurds a nation apart and demanded the right to self-determination, although this did not mean for all the establishment of a separate state. One by one, they all also adopted the thesis that Kurdistan is a colony of the ruling classes. They began to look for inspiration to the liberation movements elsewhere in the world such as in South Africa and the PLO movement. Most of the Kurdish organisations claimed to see the struggle against class oppression inside Kurdistan as equally important although they frequently accused each other of failing to address this issue. Some made a connection between the national and the class struggle: the chief exploiters—landlords and tribal or religious leaders—were often allied, through the various political parties, with their respective central state. The leftist organisations therefore labelled them collaborators and proclaimed that breaking their power was one primary aim in the "anti-feudal and anti colonial struggle". One organisation, thinking that the time was ripe for the armed phase in this struggle, actually opened the offensive in 1979 against some particularly powerful and oppressive chieftains. This precipitated a minor civil war between the supporters and opponents of these chieftains with the government forces taking the latter side (Bruinessen 1984: 10).

Frequent factionalisation took place within the Kurdish political movement. In order to obtain support from the Iranian revolutionary leadership and strengthen its forces against the Talabani–PUK faction, the KDP–Barzani group sided with Tehran, attacking the KDP-Iran. Seeking autonomy from the emerging revolutionary Iran, the KDP–Barzani group played a key role in defeating the Kurdish insurgency in Iran, despite the PUK support for the Iranian KDP (Manafy 2005: 93). Due to the division of Kurdistan into different parts, the leadership in the various regions was divided. South Kurdistan, despite its backwards social structure and relatively small geographical area, represented the leadership and the potential for all of Kurdistan. But the leadership there caused great damage and losses and the national liberation struggle in this region has not had any results. This stagnating situation improved following the rise of the national liberation movements in other regions of the world.

Kurdish political organisations are mainly dominated by traditional forces such as Sheikhs, *Aghas,* religious leaders or their family-related clientele loyalists. Although the traditional forces have criticised the power structure of feudal lords and their class priviledges, they have never attempted to abolish the class interests of these dominant forces in Kurdistan (Bruinessen 1992a: 316). It can be argued that the PKK has adopted a radical agenda in comparison to the KDP and the PUK. Although Syria provided a training haven for the PKK forces, the Party did not rely on imperial powers for the liberation of the Kurds.

The Kurdish political struggle is not in accordance with the theories of national liberation movements. The Kurdish political ideology is not consistent. At times, the Kurdish leadership seeks solutions and strives for the acquisition of more democratic rights within their own respective countries. The Kurdish movements have lacked national solidarity and have been dominated by tribal and parochial values. Their leadership has lacked sophistication in political and educational knowledge. The leaders and masses (with few exceptions) have suffered from the lack of action-driven educational expertise. Tribalism has constituted the core of the Kurdish forces. The Kurds follow their tribal and religious leaders and the existence of their tribal loyalty has deprived them of creative and pragmatic initiatives (Kinnane 1964: 206-207). For the purpose of their own economically oil-motivated interests, the colonial and neocolonial powers have imposed on the Kurdish tribes the culture of divide and rule in order to further enfeeble a unified Kurdish front. For instance, in Turkey, where there is no oil, the Kurds have been placed on the terrorist list of the US Department, but the Kurds in Iraq are seen as freedom fighters. The Kurds in Iraq are better off than the Kurds in Iran, Syria and Turkey. In comparison to the Kurds in Turkey and Syria, the Kurds in Iran have more political, economic and cultural rights. As a result of external interventionism and divisiveness, the Kurdish liberation movements have failed in many aspects. They have failed to forge a national unity and have suffered from deep divisions and treachery within their leadership. The Kurdish leadership has cooperated with external forces, which has been responsible for the failure of the Kurdish cause. The leadership has been parochial and possesses little political knowledge of the dynamics of the 'world system'. The leaders have failed to realise that the fate of the nations is decided behind closed doors at the core of the 'world system' and beyond the confines of the West Asia (Randal 1999: 12-13). The Kurds in Iraq, Iran, Syria and especially Turkey have traditionally had the option of assimilating into the dominant society, rather than pursuing their interests as Kurds.

The Kurdish Search for a Solution

There has been much debate on the question of the self-determination of Kurdistan as an independent nation-state as promised in the Treaty of Sevres. But there is a widespread realisation among political Kurds and their friends that under present circumstances, this is a utopian dream. It is not so much the divisions of the Kurds along tribal, class, religious and even linguistic lines which would impede the formation of a Kurdish nation-state. Such divisions are common and natural in a complex society and the Kurds are no different in this respect from other nations. Other states in the region have faced and continue to confront similar problems. The state forges the nation with different degrees of success. Rather, it is the realities of power in the region and the world which make a Kurdish state an unlikely outcome. It is only imaginable under conditions of simultaneous weakness, even a near collapse of all four states of Iraq, Iran, Turkey and Syria. It would require an active sponsorship and support by the US and EU or a consortium of world powers. In any case, a separate Kurdish state does not seem to feature at the present time on anyone's agenda as the Iraqi Kurds are committed to a programme of autonomy within a democratic Iraq (Zubaida 1992: 4-5).

The solutions and policies offered by those countries that occupy Kurdistan are driven by their ambitions for buying resources and selling manufactured products. In addition, the numerous Kurdish and non-Kurdish organisations, all take the same line which is negative for a liberated independent Kurdistan. Although some of those disagree on some tactical questions, in practice, the plots to dissolve the nationality (ethnic cleansing) are happening continuously by displacing the Kurdish people and dispersing them into other nationalities. The Kurds have been subjected to such policies in all parts of Kurdistan for many years by all those countries that are occupying them (Mella 2005: 148).

The Kurdish problem requires a solution based on the regional realities of the countries involved and on the reality of the prevailing world system. The prevailing political order attempts to preserve the status quo at any cost while the Kurds are determined to achieve their politico-economic and cultural rights. In ethnic and class-divided societies of West Asia, the Kurds are victims of the prevailing status-quo politics sustained by an anachronistic divisive world system whose continuity relies on the exercise of divide-and-rule policies. In all three countries (Iran, Turkey and Syria), hegemonic control prevails (Manafy 2005: 142). A solution to the Kurdish problem could be the granting of autonomy to Kurdistan. This was advocated by the late KDPI leader, Ghassemlou—as democracy for Iran; autonomy for all minorities. This solution, in the form of political autonomy, occurs within the context of the nation-states. It does not mean independence, secession or separatism but the implementation of internationally recognised autonomous territories. The military solution variously practiced by the states is irrational and unsafe.

According to Herbert Marcuse, neither the rational use of resources nor workers' ownership in the means of production can abolish the structurally created problems. A bureaucratic welfare state can be a state using force and repression (Marcuse 1969: 4). Hence, the socialism advocated by the Kurdish Left cannot be a viable solution to Kurdish problems. In Marcuse's words, the chain of subordination and exploitation must break at its strongest link and not at its weakest one (Marcuse 1969: 3-6). This is why a universalisation of human rights and social democratic transformation of the globalised world order is important (Sklair 2002: 322-325). The concept of human rights has been used as a political tool by the core of the world system in defining its own state interests. Conflict between the rights of selfish interests and human rights are generally settled in favour of the states' self-interest. The core countries promote division between the various factions in the peripheral regions in a deliberate effort to create friction (Manafy 1996: 120-122). For instance, the core countries supported Saddam Hussein during his eight years of bloody war against Iran and did not condemn the use of gas in Kurdistan. The West also did not take action against Turkey's atrocities against the Kurds. The Kurds in Iraq, Turkey, Iran and Syria have the same culture, the same identity and the same desire for an autonomous Kurdistan. However, years of control, political socialisation and indoctrination have failed to alter or assimilate the religiously and culturally different nationalities.

A radical democratic solution is problematic in Iran, Iraq, Syria and Turkey due to the fear of dismemberment and political disintegration. In these ethnic and class-divided societies, the security and continuity of the systems depend on a degree of centralised but legitimate political sovereignty. In severely divided societies democracy is not a viable option. John Stuart Mill maintained that democracy would be "next to impossible in a country made up of different nationalities". Exclusion of the ethnic minorities in elections would trigger separatist and violent political movements (Horowitz 1985: 681,615). The relationship between political space and national-identity formation provides a framework for managing ethno-national conflicts.

Since the fundamental solution to an ethnic conflict is riddled with theoretical and practical problems, conflict resolution theorists endorse a consociational democracy[5] as a way to manage ethnic conflict. This is an alliance of all ethnically divided groups and all ethnic groups have a mutual veto power. Resources and the distribution of opportunities are allocated based on ethnic proportionality and autonomy exists for each group. These measures mitigate the negative outcome of majority decisions in the ethnically divided societies. In heterogeneous states where ethnic boundaries have become institutionalised, it becomes increasingly difficult to weaken ethno-national sentiment. Ethnicity, unlike religious, civic, linguistic or socio-economic identities, is an unchanging aspect of group identity that does not necessarily lose its salience with modernisation or secularisation.

The Swiss model is regarded as another successful approach to ethnic conflict resolution. Swiss federalism has been effective in diminishing progressive ethnic conflict. The democratic tradition and effective homogeneous canton system characterising Switzerland's approach appear promising for countries plagued with serious conflict at the centre and with territorially separate groups and significant sub-ethnic divisions (Young 1976: 234; Enloe 1973: 98). There then remains the solution of autonomy—cultural and political, recognition of Kurdish identity and institutional provision for its cultivation and expression. The 1970 autonomy decree in Iraq is an example of such a procedure. Indeed in so far as this decree is applied, it did provide for the cultural and educational (including linguistic) elements of the Kurdish identity. The patchy and ambivalent recognition of Kurdish identity by various Iraqi regimes since the years of the British mandate, together with the territorial institutionalisation of the Kurdish resistance have made Iraqi Kurdistan an important centre for the development of modern Kurdish politics and culture for the whole region. However, the scope and form of the application for autonomy provisions as well as the definition of Kurdish territory and populations have depended on the whims and interests of the government; It has also not prevented that government from committing savage atrocities against the Kurdish population while maintaining some broadcasting in Kurdish and teaching that language in some schools. The Iraqi case showed clearly that autonomy only makes sense in states where the government is subject to the rule of law and where political and institutional constraints can be applied to the rulers. This is good reason why political Kurds should make common cause with the democratic forces in their respective countries as many of them have done and continue to do. However, the prospects for democratic formation in the region are dim (Carapico 2002: 379). The American invasion of Iraq has opened up possibilities for political transformations.

With the American intervention and overthrow of the Saddam Hussein regime changing opportunity structures encouraged have new political-economic organisations and linkages in the Kurdish regions. However, the period following the withdrawal of American forces has rather created more of a confusion in the sectarian Iraqi society. The future for the stable nascent democratic government in Baghdad is a big challenge for the Iraqis.

Kurdish demands for self-rule constitute a democratic pursuit that is incompatible with the despotism and ethnic-based nationalism of the West Asian states. As for many of the democratic and revolutionary movements in the region, Kurdish rights to self-determination continue to be a blind spot (Hassanpour 1994: 23). In any circumstances of uneven political and economic development, Kurdistan has offered valuable opportunities as a base for liberation that goes beyond the region. But, the opportunities have not been seized and demonstrate the weakness of these movements as well as the problems of Kurdish nationalism.

Conclusion

The Kurds, along with the other discontented minorities, are the victims of foreign intervention (colonial/neocolonial), economic and political deprivation and political repression. The conflict of ethnic nationalists, the clash of identities and loyalties and the exclusive visions over strategic issues are all source of conflict between the Kurds and the other groups in West Asia. For several decades, the Kurdish secessionist and irredentist movement has been in conflict with Turkish, Arab or Persian nationalism. A Kurdish independent state is not a realistic solution because it could trigger a wider conflict in the region and there are also serious geopolitical barriers that could hamper its creation. In the light of the ethnicised political spaces and unchangeable role of ethnicity and identity formation, managing the contemporary Kurdish problem requires readjusting the political threshold in the region. Instead of trying to create a false sense of ethnic homogenisation, the state elites in Iraq, Turkey, Iran and Syria should emphasise ethnic diversity within decentralised political systems that guarantee protection of minority-group rights. Managing the Kurdish problem requires recognising the distinct Kurdish ethnicity as an integral part of the state's nationalism. The idea of a distinct Kurdish ethnic identity and the right to some form of political and cultural autonomy within each state have become undeniable and undisputed facts among Kurdish communities across the borders despite the aims otherwise of various Kurdish nationalist organisations.

Kurdish ethno-nationalism and the drive for self-determination represent dilemmas faced by most multi-ethnic societies in terms of conflict management. Historically, autonomy demands by ethnic groups like the Kurds have elicited complete or near rejection of such demands, followed by a period of a varying degrees of repression by the dominant ethnic cultural group. For better or worse, ethnic affirmation has been largely identified with separatist tendencies, disintegration of the political system and the concomitant disorder and chaos. This has been historically true in the case of the Kurds in the concerned regions.

But globalisation has made the myth of a culturally homogenous state even more unrealistic, and has forced the majority within each sate to be more open to pluralism and diversity. The nature of ethnic and national identities is changing in a world of democratic states but the challenge of multiculturalism is to stay. Within a democratic framework, minorities could surely attain their socio-political ideals.

Notes

1. For details see, "International Covenant on Civil and Political Rights", Adopted and opened for signature, ratification and accession by General Assembly Resolution 2200A (XXI) of 16 December 1966, entry into force 23 March 1976. Office of the United Nations High Commissioner for Human Rights, (Online: web), Accessed 24 January 2011, URL: http://www2.ohchr.org/english/law/ccpr.htm
2. It was drafted by a UN Working Group on Indigenous Populations between 1985 and 1993 and approved by the UN Sub-Commission on the Protection of Minorities in 1994 (an independent body of experts) but has several barriers to overcome before ratification by the General Assembly. For details see, "Unrepresented Nations and Peoples Organization", (Online: web), Accessed 11 February 2011, URL: http://www.unpo.org/
3. For details of the conflict discussions see, Ayres, R. William (Jan 2000), "A World Flying Apart? Violent Nationalist Conflict and the End of the Cold War", *Journal of Peace Research*, 37(1): 105-117.
4. An armed Basque nationalist and separatist organisation. The group was founded in 1959 and has since evolved from a group promoting traditional Basque culture to a paramilitary group with the goal of gaining independence for the Greater Basque country from a Marxist–Leninist perspective.

CHAPTER 7

Conclusion

In the early twentieth century the colonial forces freely imposed their own arbitrarily defined boundaries on the peoples of the West Asian region. They created political and cultural problems. Following World War I, the Allies drew the boundaries through Kurdistan rather than create a separate buffer state for the Kurds. The abuse of Kurdish rights has been systematic. Kurdish aspirations for independence have been strengthened as a consequence of the history of oppression and brutality at the hands of the Arabs, Turks and Iranians. Iraq, Iran, Turkey and Syria have problems with their Kurds and therefore, a common interest in suppressing the Kurdish separatist hopes for independence. They have at times assisted one another in countering the threat of Kurdish nationalism. The pro-Western defence alliances, the Saadabad Pact (1937) and the Baghdad Pact (1955), in which they took part, enabled them to develop common Kurdish policies. The Kurds constitute the major topic of discussion in the regular meetings between Iraq, Turkey, Syria and Iran. The end of Cold War, the weakening of the Left and the process of globalisation have unleashed new forces in many countries. Of these the return of nationalism—almost with a vengeance—is probably the most notable. Although it predates the dissolution of the Soviet Empire and the ensuing nationalist scramble in Europe and elsewhere, the Kurdish crisis in the Middle East gained momentum from these events. The collapse of the multi-ethnic Ottoman Empire and the formation of ethnically based nationalist regimes are the root causes of the politicisation and radicalisation of Kurdish identity.

In the aftermath of the 1991 Gulf War, circumstances for the Kurdish uprising developed within Iraq. Following the uprising, the US closed its eyes to millions of Iraqi Kurds. Iraqi Kurdistan became the target of suppression. Hundreds of thousands of innocent people fled their villages and cities and the tragedy that followed was captured by the international community. Pressure from the international community to deal with the tragedy resulted in the United Nations' passing the Security Council Resolution 688. In the context of a humanitarian campaign by the United Nations and various international non-governmental organisations, the Security Council passed Resolution 986 for setting up the Oil-for-Food Programme to help the Iraqi people. 13% percent of the revenues were allocated to the Kurds in Iraqi Kurdistan. The embargo-related hardships led to bitter animosities and fighting between the two primary factions in northern Iraq—Massoud Barzani's KDP and Jalal Talabani's PUK—over resources and the control of trade routes. Active mediation by the United States and other outside parties helped keep the two main Kurdish parties working together for their shared goal of ousting Saddam Hussein despite occasional setbacks and outbreaks of intra-Kurdish violence. The Kurdistan Regional Government has compromised on the distribution of Iraq's oil revenue sharing law—on sharing the revenues from its unexploited oil and gas fields. Kurdistan cannot be expected to contribute to Iraq without having Baghdad honour its constitutional commitments. Furthermore, the country is overcoming its own violent past, which included a civil war during the 1990s. For that reason the region is divided, with the administrative and institutional structure divided between the two big opposing parties—the PUK and the KDP.

The two Kurdish parties have dominated Iraqi Kurdistan for the last three decades. They control maximum economic activity and communication networks as well as the *peshmerga* or Kurdish militia, which is used to both defend their territory and impose order. Having patched up their differences, the PUK and KDP have done a reasonably effective job of providing for their constituents and the modalities of sharing power in the regional parliament. As democracy in a unified Iraq takes root, they have worked out modalities to be constituent part of federal Iraq.

The fall of Saddam Hussein's regime in 2003 brought about numerous changes for the Kurdistan Autonomous Region. Since 1991, the area had enjoyed de facto autonomy within an area defined by the 36th Parallel. The military intervention by the Coalition forces in 2003 marked a turning point. For the first time, the Kurds participated in the central government and were brought into the public domain after many decades. The brutality of the Baath Party regime was on a scale that still remains visible. The use of chemical weapons against the population of Halabja in 1988, which killed

5,000 people, embodied Saddam's policy of annihilation of the Kurdish people. While the Kurdistan Regional Government took the lead in this new era for the region, 2003 saw the beginning of large-scale and hugely lethal conflict in the rest of Iraq which submerged the country in a spiral of violence. Since the 1991 Gulf War, the 2003 invasion has created one of the biggest humanitarian crises in the world with two million people already seeking refuge in other countries—principally Syria and Jordan —and two million more having fled to other parts of the country—many of them to Kurdistan.

The presence of democratising nationalist institutions has encouraged a compromise between Kurdish nationalists and Baghdad. After the US intervention in 2003, Kurdish officials attempted to renegotiate Kurdish autonomy within the Iraqi state. Barzani drew up a constitution based on a federal structure, recognising Baghdad as the political centre. Even the political sensitive issue of Kirkurk became open to negotiation. Although they consider Kirkuk as essentially a Kurdish city, Barzani and Talabani stressed its multinational aspect. After the 2003 intervention, they started advising Kurds to coexist in the spirit of fraternity with Assyrian, Arab, Chaldean, and Turkoman communities. In the provisional Iraqi constitution (transitional law for the administration of Iraq signed in March 2004), the Kurdish elite agreed to share Kirkuk's oil revenues with the future Iraqi central government.

Precedents have already been established wherein federal structures have been combined with elite accommodation within the political decision-making process, which ultimately produced stable political structures existing alongside a vibrant national economy. Such examples include Switzerland, the Netherlands and Belgium wherein each of these cases, the checks and balances implicit within a system protected heterogeneity and cultural diversity. In a country which has been devastated by decades of authoritarian rule, it would seem to be distinct, humane and possible to learn and build upon the good and bad experiences of the Kurdish political system since the 1990s. A system characterised by the inclusion of the major ethnic groups of the country could be an attempt to rid the political system of some of the inhumanity which has been its characteristic since inception. An extremely important consequence of the Kurdish safe haven's existence was that considerable portions of the Iraqi population (the Kurds) got an actual experience of self-rule, civil rights and a transition to democracy. In the context of violence, the situation in the Kurdistan Autonomous Region is extremely positive. From a security standpoint, there have been hardly any attacks or violence in the region. The Kurds, under difficult circumstances that have prevailed for the last decade, managed to carry out parliamentary elections in 2005 and establish a regional government. The success of the Kurds in Iraq as represented by the federal structure written into the new constitution offers hope for the Kurds in other states too.

Regionally, Iraq, Turkey, Iran and Syria have used the Kurds as tools against their neighbours whilst working together on the shared interest of preventing Kurdish gains in one state on the grounds that they would necessarily affect the demands and aspirations of the Kurds in another. The unique historical and geopolitical events of the separate states that comprise the 'rule of four' over the Kurds nevertheless demonstrated recurrent and parallel themes. They have each tried to depopulate Kurdistan whether to disrupt the feudal and tribal structures that sustain the traditional Kurdish society or to commit genocide against a population for whom the ruling authority wishes to make no provision. Kurdistan's demographic structure has been repeatedly altered by regional and internecine conflict, forced migration and oppressive economic and social underdevelopment. Some regimes have sought to break up Kurdistan by forcibly removing villagers to towns outside Kurdistan; therefore, some Kurds have unwillingly sought opportunities outside Kurdistan or outside the region. Iraqi Kurds supported the US-led invasion of Iraq. The inclusion of the Iraqi Kurds as the centre of political process for determining the future of Iraq have increased anti-Kurdish policies and sentiments within the ruling regimes of Iran, Syria and Turkey.

The end of the Cold War entailed a series of problems for the PKK. The Coalition against Iraq and 'Operation Provide Comfort' for all practical purposes removed northern Iraq from Baghdad's jurisdiction and the American-backed Kurdish 'Federated State' was created there. At the heart of the new entity was a power-sharing agreement between Barzani's KDP and Talabani's PUK; an arrangement achieved partly through the efforts of the Turkish government, which stepped in as a patron of the deal in order to keep the PKK out of the area. However, conflicts between the KDP and PUK prevented the scheme from being implemented and northern Iraq became a power vacuum—which coincided nicely with the aims of the PKK. Abdullah Ocalan's organisation soon based its operations there and by 1994 it had managed to deny the Turkish state effective control of large tracts of its southeastern territory. At the same time, the Turkish army's lack of preparation for mountain and guerrilla warfare undermined discipline in its ranks. As soldiers continually failed to differentiate between civilians and rebels, the PKK continued to enjoy increasing popular support. But, the situation began to change in the mid 1990s. The Turkish army, having apparently realised the importance of not alienating the civilian population, emphasised discipline within the ranks and initiated a public relations campaign that included the introduction of health and educational facilities. Meanwhile, the Turkish military eventually adapted successfully to guerrilla warfare and gathered enough strength to strike the problem at its roots in northern Iraq. Since 1995, regular and massive troop incursions (some involving up to 35,000 troops) and the establishment of a security zone have caused the PKK's position in northern Iraq to wither away. By 1998, the PKK's only lifeline was Syria. Spurred on by its alliance with Israel, the Turkish government felt strong enough to threaten Syria with war unless it expelled Abdullah Ocalan and the PKK's bases in the Bekaa Valley. Damascus complied and expelled Ocalan in October 1998. After the PKK's forces relocated to northern Iraq, a subsequent Turkish incursion dealt a severe blow to their military capabilities. Since Ocalan's capture, his unreserved submission to Turkish authorities has damaged the PKK's role.

The seizure of Ocalan in 1999 represented a change in the struggle between Turkey and the PKK. The PKK's armed struggle was weakened dramatically. The Turkish Kurds now look beyond the use of force to pursue interests through the rule of law—especially as the accession process continues for Turkey to join the EU. Turkey's move to become a member of the European Union began in April 1987 with its application to the then European Community. Turkey became an official candidate for membership in December 1999. It started formal negotiations for accession to the European Union in October 2005. At the heart of the negotiations, the EU evaluated Turkey's internal policies. Positive policy changes and revised laws have led to a better treatment of the Kurds. Nevertheless, despite major progress, the US State Department indicates that torture and other human rights issues continue to be reported in Turkey. The Turkish government maintains a hardline policy against the PKK's armed struggle. Turkey has pursued a military solution and reacted harshly against it. While some PKK forces remain active, civil strife in the southeast declined after the arrest of Ocalan. Many Western countries including the US suggested that Turkey pursue a political solution to solve the Kurdish problem. The Kurds in Turkey have a long history of opposing their government. Tension between the military and Kurdish parties in Turkish Kurdistan is growing as Turkey becomes increasingly concerned about the trends in Iraqi Kurdistan.

The PKK promoted Kurdish ethnic identity by reminding the people of the incidents of how they were threatened of their status and of the existence of Kurdish values and identity. By doing this, the PKK leadership constructed a Kurdish ethnic identity based on the hostility against the Turkish state. Hence, it developed an ethnic war based on violence and terror. But, the PKK's intrinsic weaknesses shrank its base of popular support. The Turkish military's change of policy toward the civilian population and especially its growing ability to crush the insurgents stamped out its sources of foreign support all of which combined to defeat the insurgency. In late 1999, the PKK declared to withdraw its violent activities and in early 2000, it publicly laid down its arms—apparently emulating the PLO by trying to gain recognition as a political movement instead. In addition, the capture of Ocalan allowed the PKK to see the role of European Union as an opportunity to transform itself from an outmoded guerilla movement—thus, losing its international legitimacy to a civil and political organisation.

The Turkish government recognises only a Turkish nationality and not ethnic groups such as the Kurds. Kurds who assert their ethnic identity publicly are in danger of being arrested or persecuted. Turkey continues to limit the use of the Kurdish language in the media, unlike in Iraq, where Kurdish is an official language. While the Kurds are given equal rights under the law as Turks, their Kurdish identity continues to be seen as distracting from the unity of Turkey. The Kurds were perceived to constitute a threat to the state itself. Although many Kurds are now assimilated and some have intermarried with Turks, the Kurdish identity remains alive.

The multifaceted Kurdish question is central to Turkey's future, including its relations with the European Union. The Kurdish problem has seriously constrained Turkey's foreign policy and has become the main obstacle in Turkey's drive for full membership in the EU. Its international ramifications, moreover, make it an issue of utmost importance in the regional politics of the Middle East. A deeper understanding of the matter must take into account the tribal character of the Kurdish society, the dynamics of the PKK rebellion's rise and fall and the larger context of Turkey's interest. The Turkish state must therefore take advantage of the opportunity created by its victory over the PKK. Conditions have never been better to address the Kurdish question constructively to bring an end to the political instability and economic backwardness of southeastern Turkey. The Turkish state needs to act in accordance with its own rhetoric stipulating that the Kurdish issue is distinct from PKK terrorism. The time has come for Turkey to accelerate its democratisation including the removal of restrictions on cultural rights.

The Turkish armed forces have repeatedly invaded northern Iraq and maintain a low-key presence in the territory, allegedly to wipe out the PKK bases there but probably as much to impose its will on the Iraqi Kurdish parties and to prevent Iran and Syria from extending their influence. Iran has supported the Iraqi Shi'a opposition and the Kurdish Islamic parties for ideological reasons and it has had various strategic alliances—first with the KDP and later with the PKK. From time to time, it has carried out raids far into the region in an unsuccessful attempt to capture the oppositional Iranian Kurds. Syria has been projecting its influence both through the PKK and through a balanced patronage of the Iraqi parties. One important reason the fighting between the Iraqi Kurdish factions has been so persistent is that each of these neighbouring states (as well as Iraq) has attempted to change the balance of power to its own advantage through this conflict.

Tehran and Damascus also opposed Iraqi Kurdish aspirations and have cooperated with each other and with Turkey to stymie Kurdish advances in Iraq. Although Iranian and Syrian Kurds have not received as much attention as their counterparts in Turkey and Iraq, they too have been influenced by the regional events. Increased Kurdish mobilisation and instances of violence in both Iran and Syria have alarmed these two regimes. They too may choose to intervene if Iraqi developments are perceived to threaten their territorial integrity.

In Iran, as in Turkey, the principal Kurdish nationalist organisation, the Kurdish Democratic Party of Iran (KDPI), sought more autonomy. Since the end of the Republic of Mahabad in 1946 and the targeted killings of KDPI leaders, the Iranian Kurds have proved to be a significant opposition to the government of the Islamic Republic of Iran. Nevertheless, Iranian military forces remain stationed in Kurdish areas to check anti-national elements. Although Iranian Kurds moved to end armed struggle in 1996 and participated in the Iranian political system by participating in elections, they remain victims of human rights violations. Iranian Kurdistan remains in a situation of underdevelopment. The Kurds' status as Sunni Muslims is an aggravating factor for the Shi'a-dominated government. Kurds often are suspected by government authorities of harbouring separatist or foreign sympathies. These suspicions have led to sporadic outbreaks of fighting between the government forces and Kurdish groups. The Kurds are no longer a challenge to the central government of the Islamic Republic but they represent a challenge for the central government. The Kurdish demands are made within the Iranian political system. The Kurdish identity in Iran has merged with that of the Iranian identity in some areas. Kurds are found throughout Iranian society including in the military. Kurdish culture and Iranian culture are similar. But despite their similarities, the Kurdish community in Iran faces repression and discrimination.

The 1997 victory of the Iranian reformist President Mohammad Khatami brought new hope to the Iranian Kurds. Iranian Kurdish politicians working within the system garnered a significant budget increase for the Kurdish region. But the success of the Kurdish region proved to be short-lived, with the hardliners able to block reformist candidates and recapture the Parliament in 2004. In March 2004, Iranian Kurds demonstrated in support of the Iraqi Kurds, who were granted a special status as a federal region in the new constitution for Iraq. The Iranian security forces responded violently. The election of a hardline president Mahmoud Ahmadinejad in 2005 further marginalised the Kurds. The KDPI continues to raise issues concerning the status of the Kurds in Iran. Iran has maintained the Kurdish region in a situation of underdevelopment and has failed to provide industries to Kurdistan. It refused to recognise the extent of the Kurdish region. It has had a policy of eliminating Kurdish leaders. The Kurds seek greater autonomy from the central government and continue to suffer from government discrimination.

In Syria, the Kurdish situation remains problematic. The Syrian government's harsh treatment of Kurds is unusual. The Kurds are a minority that did not represent a threat to the Syrians. As a whole, Kurds in Syria continue to face obstacles to securing their basic rights. The legacy of the state's 'Arabisation' and nationalism campaign of the 1960s and 1970s was conducted with the objective of gaining control of all internal social spheres by restricting political and civil rights in the name of internal stability. Discriminatory regulations like bans were imposed on the use of the Kurdish language Kurmanji (including in conversation, publications, the names of children and place names), cultural displays (such as playing Kurdish music) and the formation of Kurdish civil and political groups. Violent clashes broke out in spring 2004 in the Jazeera region bordering Iraq and thousands of Kurds were detained. In May 2005, when a Kurdish sheikh was murdered, the government used police and military to break up a demonstration calling for an investigation. The government also removed the Syrian nationality from about 1,20,000 Syrian Kurds, who became stateless people. Stripping off the Kurds of their citizenship and land has had a negative socio-economic effect on the Kurds in Syria. Kurds affected by these policies, both directly and inheriting their consequences, became largely impoverished. They are unable to alter their economic, legal or social status. The creation of a Kurdish autonomous zone in Iraq pushed the Kurdish issue to the forefront in Syria where stateless Kurds sought citizenship and recognition as a major group in the country.

The main obstacle to a solution of the Kurdish nationality question in Syria is political in nature. Over the years, the government has failed to recognise the Kurdish problem in order to preserve the domination of political and social life by the ruling party of the al-Assad family and its allies, who represent the interests of the Arab majority. The denial of citizenship is part of a broader effort to prevent any legal expression of Kurdish nationalism on Syrian soil. Syrian officials deny that any problem exists, maintaining that only a small number of families live without nationality. Only when the stateless Kurds in Syria have been fully nationalised and the broader issue of the Kurdish place in Syrian political, social, and economic life has been addressed, will peace and security within Syria be realised. The Kurds in Syria are still facing uncertain times.

Turkey, Iran and Syria are vulnerable to any Kurdish developments and this comes from three interconnected factors. First, these states are bound by strict ideological foundations: pan-Turkism or Kemalism in Turkey; pan-Arabism of the Baath Party in Iraq and Syria and the pan-Shi'ite Islamism of Khomeini in Iran. These ideological foundations make them feel that they are under constant threat from internal and external changes. The implications of these ideologies have resulted in constant deprivation of the minorities—particularly the Kurds. Among those deprivations are Turkey's denials of the Kurdish identity by reclassifying them as 'Mountain Turks', Iran's ethnic and sectarian repression of the Kurds and Syria's refusal to grant citizenship to more than 1,00,000 indigenous Kurds since 1962. The vulnerability of these countries is their unhappy past experiences with the nationalism-inspired Kurdish violence. These countries have been hostage to the Kurdish issue much before the US invasion on Iraq or the emergence of the Iraqi Kurdistan Region in 1991. Kurdish nationalism has been a challenge to the governments of the countries in which they live. The Americans supported for a degree of Kurdish autonomy in Iraq verging on de facto independence which has strengthened Kurdish assertiveness against central governments in Iran, Syria and Turkey.

Four irreversible factors have further exacerbated those countries' vulnerability. Firstly, factors such as globalisation, the emergence of a new world order, the telecommunication revolution and increased international attention to human rights issues have contributed to an awakening of Kurdish self-awareness. In other words, the borders that isolated Kurds from one another are no longer effective. Secondly, the American occupation of Iraq has abetted the secessionist desire of the Kurds by opening the Pandora's box of Kurdish nationalism in Turkey, Iran and Syria. The third factor is the heightening of Kurdish identity in Iraq and the Kurds' achievement of greater political, cultural and social rights, the formation of a Kurdish bloc in Parliament and the official use of the Kurdish language. Lastly, the rise of ISIS has given new opportunity to the Kurds for reasserting self-determination. All these factors have advanced the Kurdish nationalist movement throughout the region. The 'world system' as an external activating variable has played a critical role in politicising ethnic differences and the resulting political conflicts in the region.

Sixty years after the decolonisation and liberation of ethnic groups, the Kurds remain as the largest minority in the world without a state. Having the misfortune to be squeezed in the midst of four strong authoritarian states—Syria, Iraq, Iran and Turkey (which is considered to be democratic but for the larger period of time when Kurdish prosecution was taking place, it was an authoritarian regime)—the Kurds have been struggling for decades to obtain autonomy or independence.

The double standards as applied to the Kurds are explained by the perceived national interest of the US. In the case of Kosovo, the US felt that it was necessary to stop violence in Europe before it escalated and expanded. The Kurds in Turkey however do not present such an immediate threat. Therefore, the Kurdish problem can be left to fester. Moreover, 'good' Kurds in Iraq and the 'bad' ones in Turkey are explained in terms of the perceived US national interest. Turkey is seen as a valuable geostrategic NATO ally.

Saddam's Iraq on the other hand, has held the position as one of the enemies of the US since the ill-conceived invasion of Kuwait in 1990. Support for the Iraqi Kurds, therefore, is perceived as supporting the over-all US policy. However, many of the Kurds have lately realised the double-standard policy of the US. In Iraq, the Kurds were more or less left alone. In Turkey and Iran, however, the Kurdish question became a matter of national survival and henceforth the Kurds were to be either assimilated or eliminated wherever possible. The Kurdish problem, that earlier had languished on the backburner of international concerns, has now been internationalised. It would be impossible politically for the United States, the United Nations or Turkey to turn their backs on the Kurds after all that has happened. In addition, with the breakup of the Soviet Union, Yugoslavia and Czechoslovakia, the creation of a Kurdish state in Middle East no longer seems so politically questionable. The Kurds want the international community to accept their demands for a fair and just treatment. They want the international community to take the necessary action for putting right their situation.

By 2005, it was becoming clear that the American invasion of Iraq and the violence that was used demonstrated a superpower's occupation of a multi-ethnic, multi-religious state and its favour of one ethnic or religious group over another was a powerful instrument of state formation. The process involved the inclusion of the ethnic minority (Kurds) that were favoured in strategies to solidify them into a semi-autonomous state, while at the same time efforts were being made for trying to incorporate that ethnic group (Kurds) into a 'unified' multi-religious and multi-ethnic state.

For most of the twentieth century, Kurdish issues in Iraq, Turkey, Iran and Syria were isolated from each other. De-territorialisation also implies re-territorialisation, which for the Kurds has often meant asylum outside Kurdistan. As much as one-fourth of the Kurdish population lives outside the historical Kurdish homeland. The Kurds now are remarkably different from those in the late 1980s and early 1990s; links between the different Kurdish societies and their diaspora extensions have thickened. The emergence of regularised migration paths, especially to Western European countries, has re-territorialised Kurdish communities. Comprising of refugees, undocumented labourers and political exiles, the Kurdish diaspora brings the 'Kurdish question' placing it at the centre of the European public debate. Moreover, Kurdish organisations like the Kurdish National Congress have restructured to include members living in Europe and North America. Many

Kurds in the diaspora express a desire to return to a free and independent Kurdistan. The influential and highly educated diaspora of more than a million Kurds in the West represents a positive factor for the cause. The diaspora is carrying out an important lobbying role both in the West and in the Kurdish homeland. It facilitates the transfer of human and technical resources back to the homeland. The diaspora has acted as a catalyst for the development of inter-societal bonds. For instance, an Iraqi or Iranian Kurd could join Turkish–Kurdish organisations in Germany and mobilise the Kurds to hold demonstrations against the Turkish government. The Kurdish Parliament-in-Exile, which was established in 1995 in the Netherlands (The Hague), played a significant part in placing the Kurdish question on the European political agenda. It acts for Kurdish diplomatic representation and has established contacts with numerous parties and personalities in Europe. Kurdish satellite television networks like MED-TV which broadcasts from Europe has picked up everywhere in Kurdistan. One may speculate that the democratically socialised disapora will also begin to further the democratisation process in Kurdistan. Freed from the state struggles that divide greater Kurdistan, the Kurdish diaspora is expected to become more pan-Kurdish in outlook.

The emergence of globalisation and transnational process adds a new element to the political space. In each setting after the early 1990s, the Kurds became highly ethnicised across Kurdistan regardless of the different political spaces inside each state. The Kurdish problem has spread from four West Asian countries to most of Europe. It has become part of an increasingly complex transnational space including regional and international actors. Kurdish communities reconfigured their nationalist projects in relation to the external mobilising structures and in particular the changing international norms and transnational spaces. The continued volatility of the Kurdish regions and diasporas have created new security, economic and political problems outside Kurdistan while fuelling nationalist agendas at home. The Kurdish political status remains a function of the political realities of where the Kurds are located. The Kurds seek to protect their communities and have their human rights respected. The Kurds pursue their self-interests in the political systems in which they find themselves. Kurdish nationalist sentiment and organisation have become linked to democracy, human rights and self-determination and ideological currents which are imported from outside the states' territorial borders. The Kurdish identity remains a mix of the aspirations of Kurdish nationalism and the Kurdish desire to find peace, stability, respect and human dignity in the particular state in which they live.

The Kurdish right to self-determination will be realised when the artificially drawn boundaries are re-defined in the Middle East. However, re-definition of the boundaries in the region would be a radical structural transformation of the prevailing conservative and status quo order. It is unlikely that this change would be acceptable to current political cultures and structures due to the conflict between the Kurdish autonomy, the continuity of a world system and the balance that favours the dominating internal and external political structures. Najmaldin Karim, President of the Washington Kurdish Institute, a non-profit organisation that promotes the rights of the Kurdish people worldwide, stated that the Kurds will not press for an independent Kurdistan as some elements in Iran and Turkey fear. But, he strongly endorsed the creation of a democratic federal Iraq that respects the rights of its citizens and which is at peace with its neighbours. Iraqi Kurds have had a consistent political movement despite measures taken by the central government. Moreover, Iraq has recognised Kurdish national rights to a greater extent than Turkey, Syria or Iran. The changing political realities in Iraq, Turkey, Iran, and Syria have created constant challenges for the Kurds. The Kurds are pursuing their self-interests and have the right to determine their own future.

The example of the Iraqi Kurds to the Kurds of Turkey, Iran and Syria is powerful and is responsible for a resurgence of pan-Kurdish feeling across the region. With a common threat to their identity and experiences of discrimination, the Kurds of these countries have linkages. The Iraqi Kurds are the trailblazers of the greater transnational movement, buoyed by the success of their 'democratic experiment' since 1991. They are also geographically at the heart of greater Kurdistan, being the only one of the four components to share contiguous boundaries with all the three others. Thus, the potential for events in Iraqi Kurdistan affect developments across the whole of Kurdistan.

The Kurdish issue transcends the borders of the states and is intrinsically related to the stability of West Asia. However Iran, Syria and Turkey maintain a common policy towards the development of Kurds and are clear that neither do they want to see an autonomous Kurdistan within their own borders nor an independent Kurdistan rising out of the ashes of Iraq. The Kurds however, are becoming increasingly savvy in their political and economic affairs, and are no longer allowing themselves to be the unwilling pawns of the states in the region.

The Kurds are systematically oppressed according to the demands of capital accumulation. The 'world system' as system has betrayed the Kurdish struggle for political rights. The wealthy in the core and semi-peripheral nations have benefited from the weaker nations and have expanded their own economic relations. The 'world system' as an external variable has played a critical role in politicising ethnic differences and the resulting political conflicts of the Kurds. The 'dependency theory' also proved competent that poverty in the Kurdish areas is partially attributed to the fact that the Kurds have been exploited by the colonisers for their economic and political ends. The Kurds have also found out the significance of economic resources in Kurdistan. They have learnt their lessons from the past and recognise the need to control their own political affairs no matter what pressure is placed upon them by the outside forces. The Kurdish situation continues to change and the future remains unknown. Until the Kurdish political problems are resolved the Middle Eastern region will be in a state of constant instability. When people are denied their rights, it is necessarily a destablising influence as the people will be engaged in fighting state powers in order to gain the rights they deserve. The Kurds will continue to push forward for their independence. The geopolitics of Kurdistan will play a major role in the outcome of Middle Eastern politics and stability.

References

Abbas, Sherkoh (July 2004), "Plight of Kurds in Syria", (Online: web), Accessed 31 July 2009, URL: http://worldpress.org/print_articles.cfm?article_id=2021& dont=yes

Acik, Necla (2014), "Kobane: The struggle of Kurdish women against Islamic State", *Open Democracy*, 22 October 2014, URL: https://www.opendemocracy.net/arab-awakening/necla-acik/kobane-struggle-of-kurdish-women-against-islamic-state, Accessed 31 August 2016.

Aghajanian, Akbar (May 1983), "Ethnic Inequality in Iran: An Overview", *International Journal of Middle East Studies*, 15(2).

Akcali, Emel (2009), "Ethnic-Territorial Conflict", Interview by Leonhardt van Efferink, (Online: web), Accessed 03 August 2009, URL: http://www.exploringgeopolitics.org/Interview_Akcali_Emel_Ethnic_Territorial_ Conflicts_Globalisation_World_Systems_Theory_Environmental_Peacemaking_Mental_Maps_Eurasianism.html

Alfredsson, Gudmunder (Spring-Summer 1982), "International Law, International Organisations and Indigenous Peoples", *Journal of International Affairs*, 36(1): 113-124. (1996), "Different Forms of and Claims to the Right of Self-Determination" in Donald Clark and Robert Williamson (eds) *Self Determination: International Perspectives*, London: McMillan Press Ltd., 58-86.

"Algiers Accord 1975", (Online: web), Accessed 24 August 2010, URL: http://www.mideastweb.org/algiersaccord.htm.

Al-Khafaji, Isam (Oct.-Dec.1996), "The Destruction of Iraqi Kurdistan", *Middle East Report*, No. 201: 35-42.

Alvarez-Ossorio, Ignacio (May 2013), "Evolution and Outlook of the Syrian Crisis", (Online: web), Accessed 17 June 2014, URL:http://www.iemed.org/observatori-en/arees-danalisi/arxius-adjunts/anuari/iemed2013/Alvarez%20Ossorio%20Syrian%20Crisis%20EN.pdf

Amin, Samir (1980), "The Future of Socialism", in William L. Tabb (ed) *Perspective from the Left*, New York: Monthly Review Press "An Introduction to the Kurdish People of Iraq and Elsewhere", (Online: web), Accessed 25 February 2010, URL: http://www.eurolegal.org/neoconwars/kurdsiraq.htm.

Anderson, Benedict (1991), *Imagined Communities: Reflections on the Origin and Spread of Nationalism*, London: Verso

_(1992), *Long Distance Nationalism: World Capitalism and the Rise of Identity Politics*, Center for German and European Studies, University of California: California.

Andrews, P. A. (1989), *Ethnic Groups in the Republic of Turkey*, Ludwig Reichert: Wiesbaden.

Atacan, Fulya (July 2001), "A Kurdish Islamist Group in Modern Turkey: Shifting Identities", *Middle Eastern Studies*, 37(3): 111-144.

Arango, Tim and etal (2016), "Turkey's military plunges into Syria, enabling rebels to capture ISIS stronghold", *The New York Times*, 24 August 2016, URL: http://www.nytimes.com/2016/08/25/world/middleeast/turkey-syria-isis.html, Accessed 25 August 2016.

Aras, Bulent et al (March 2009), "State and Anti-System Party Interactions in Turkey and Lebanon: Implications for European Policy", *Euro-Mediterranean Study Commission* (EuroMesco).

Arendt, Hannah (1951), *The Origins of Totalitarianism*, New York: Harcourt, Brace.

Arnove, Anthony (ed) (2003), *Iraq under Siege: The Deadly Impact of Sanctions and War*, New Delhi: Viva Books Private Limited.

"Assessment for Kurds in Syria", *Minorities at Risk Project*, 30 March 2005, United Nations High Commisioner for Refugees (UNHCR), (Online: web), Accessed 15 June 2010, URL: http://www.unhcr.org/refworld/docid/469f3ad71e.html

Avineri, Shlomo (Summer 2005), "Self-Determination and Realpolitik: Reflections on Kurds and Palestinians", *Dissent*, 29-33.

Ayres, R. William (Jan 2000), "A World Flying Apart? Violent Nationalist Conflict and the End of the Cold War", *Journal of Peace Research*, 37(1): 105-117.

Baker, L. (2004), "Returning Kurds, Turkmen Threaten Iraq Crisis", *Reuters*, 28 January, (Online: web), Accessed 6 June 2010, URL: http://www.irak.be/ned/nieus/hotnewsJanuary 04.htm.

"Baghdad, Iraqi Kurds Protest Alleged Iranian Shelling", 29 August 2007, *RFE/RL Report*, (Online: web), Accessed 01 September 2010, URL: http://www.rferl.org/content/article/1078412.html

Baig, Sadi (2004), "Middle East: A Clean Break for Israel", *Asia Times*, 30 June (Online: web), Accessed 16 October 2010, URL: http://www.atimes.com/atimes/Middle_East/FF30Ak07.html

Barkey, Henri J. (Winter 1993-94), "Turkey's Kurdish Dilemma", *Survival*, 34 (4): 53-68.

_(January 1997), "Kurdish Geopolitics", *Current History*, 96 (606): 1-5.

_(Winter 1997), "Turkey's Kurdish Question: Critical Turning Points and Missed Opportunities", *Middle East Journal*, 51(1): 59-79.

_(2005), "Preventing Conflict over Kurdistan", *Carnegie Endowment for International Peace*: Washington DC.

_and Ellen Laipson (Winter 2005), "Iraqi Kurds and Iraq's Future", *Middle East Policy*, 12(4): 76-90.

_and Graham E. Fuller (1998), *Turkey's Kurdish Question*, Oxford: Rowman & Littlefield Publishers Inc.

Barron, A. (May-June 1991), "US and Israeli Jews Express Support for Kurdish Refugees", *Washington Report of Middle East Affairs*, 64-80.

Barzani, Massoud (2005), "A Kurdish Vision of Iraq", *Washington Post*, Washington, 26 October 2005, (Online: web), Accessed 21 December 2010, URL: http://www.washingtonpost.com/wp-dyn/content/article/2005/10/25/AR2005102501390.html.

"Barzani: America, Turkey will not Block Kurdish Independence", *RUDAW*, 6 July 2014, Accessed 28 July 2014, URL: http://rudaw.net/english/kurdistan/060720141.

Begikhani, Nazand (2015), " Why the Kurdish Fight for Women's Rights Is Revolutionary", *The World Post*, Jan 24, 2015, URL: http://www.huffingtonpost.com/dr-nazand-begikhani/kurdish-women-rights-fight_b_6205076.html, Accessed 2 September 2016

Behr, Hartmut (2007), "The European Union in the Legacies of Imperial Rule? EU Accession Politics Viewed from a Historical Comparative Perspective", *European Journal of International Relations*, 13(2): 239-262.

Benedikter, Thomas et al (2008), *Europe's Ethnic Mosaic: A Short Guide to Minority Rights in Europe*, Europaische Akademie Bozen (EURAC).

Bengio, Ofra (1998), *Saddam's World: Political Discourse in Iraq*, Oxford: Oxford University Press.

_(1999), "Nation Building in Multiethnic Societies: The Case of Iraq", in O. Bengio & Gabriel Ben-Dor (eds.) *Minorities and the State in the Arab World*, Lynne Rienner Publishers: Boulder, 149-169.

_(Summer 2003), "Iraqi Kurds: Hour of Power?" *Middle East Quarterly*, 10(3): 40-50.

_(December 16, 2007), "The Turkish-Kurdish-American Triangle: Between Engagement and Estrangement", *Tel Aviv Notes*, Moshe Dyan Center, Tel Aviv: V. Sorell Foundation.

Beran, Harry, (1984). "A Liberal Theory of Secession", *Political Studies*, 78: 21-31.

Berawri, Azad (2008), "The Kurdistan Referendum Movement: Political Opportunity Structures and National Identity", *Democratisation*, 15(5): 891-908.

Bozarslan, Hamit (April-June 1996), "Turkey's Elections and the Kurds", *Middle East Report*, 199: 16-19.

Bracken, P.J. and C. Petty (eds.) (1998), *Rethinking the Trauma of War*, London: Free Association Books.

Bradshaw, David (May 1991), "After the Gulf War: The Kurds", *World Today*, 47 (5): 78-79.

Brah, A. (1996), *Cartographies of Diaspora*, London: Routledge.

Bramsted, E.K. and K.J. Melhuish (eds.) (1978), *Western Liberalism: A History in Documents From Locke to Croce*, London: Longman.

Brandon, James (15 June 2006), "Iran's Kurdish Threat: PJAK", *Terrorism Monitor,* 4(12), Accessed 9 December 2010, URL: http://www jamestown.org/programs/ gta/single/?tx_ttnews[tt_news]=805&tx_ttnews[backPid]=181&no_cache

_(November 2008), "Iran's Kurdish Militants under Pressure from Joint Turkish-Iranian Assaults", *Terrorism Monitor,* 6(21), (Online: web), Accessed 8 December 2010, URL: http://www.jamestown.org/single/?no_cache=1&tx_ttnews[tt_ news]= 34111 =1

Branscheidt, Hans (5 June 2008), "The EU, Turkey and the Armed Conflict with the Kurds", (Online: web), Accessed 18 October 2010, URL: http://www. zimbio.com/Ankara+Turkey/articles/5/EU+Turkey+armed+conflict+Kurds.

Brass, Paul R (1991), *Ethnicity and Nationalism: Theory and Comparison,* New Delhi: Sage Publication.

Bridsall, Nancy (2000), "Life is Unfair: Inequality in the World" in Robert Griffiths (ed) *Developing World,* McGraw Hill: Connecticut.

Brown, James (September 1995), "The Turkish Imbroglio: Its Kurds", *Annals of the American Academy of Political and Social Science,* 541: 116-129.

Bruinessen, Martin van (February 1984), "The Kurds in Turkey", *Middle East Research and Information Project Reports,* 121: 6-14.

_(July-August 1986), "The Kurds between Iran and Iraq", *MERIP Middle East Report,* 141: 14-27.

_(1992a), *Agha, Shaikh and State,* London: Zed Books.

_(1992b), "Kurdish Society, Ethnicity, Nationalism and Refugee Problems", in Phillip G. Kreyenbroek, and Stefan Sperl (eds.) *The Kurds: A Contemporary Overview,* London: Routledge.

_(April-June 1996), "Turkey's Death Squads", *Middle East Report,* 199: 20-23.

_(2000a), *Transnational Aspect of the Kurdish Question,* Robert Schumen Centre for Advanced Studies, European University Institute: Florence.

_(2000b), *Kurdish Ethno-nationalism versus Nation-building States: Collected Articles,* Istanbul: The Isis Press.

_(2000c), "Shifting National and Ethnic Identities: The Kurds in Turkey and Europe", in Guney Goksan Ozdogan and Gul Tokay (eds.) *Redefining the Nation, State and Citizen,* Istanbul: Eren, 91-108.

Bruton, Brinley F (2016), "Analysis: Turkey Coup Attempt Sees Erdogan Tighten Grip on Power" CNBC news, July 18, 2016, URL: http://www.nbcnews.com/ storyline/turkey-military-coup/turkey-coup-erdogan-tightens-grip-power-after-failed-putsch-n611496, Accessed 6 August 2016. Brzezinski, Zbigniew and Robert M. Gates (2004), "Iran: Time for a New Approach", Report of an Independent Task Force Sponsored by Council on Foreign Relations, 15-16.

Buchanan, Allen (1997), "Theories of Secession", *Philosophy and Public Affairs,* 26(1): 31-61.

Bullock, John and Morris Harvey (1993), *No Friends but the Mountains: The Tragic History of the Kurds,* New York: Penguin Books.

Candar, Cengiz (2004), "Turkish Foreign Policy and War on Iraq" in Lenore G. Martin and Dimitris Keridis (eds.) *The Future of Turkish Foreign Policy,* Cambridge: MIT Press.

_(5 Febuary 2015), " Will Kurdish Spring Redraw Middle East Map"? *Almonitor,* (Online: web), Accessed 25 February 2015, URL: http://www.al-monitor.com/pulse/originals/2015/02/turkey-kurds-kurdish-spring-david-phillips.html#

Canovan, M (1996), *Nationhood and Political Theory,* Brookfield: Edward Elgar Pub.

Cagaptay, Soner (July 2008), "The Future of the Iraqi Kurds", Washington Institute for Near East Policy, No.85.

_(January 2012), "Arab Spring Heats Up Kurdish Issue", *Jane's Intelligence Review,* 8-10.

Cagaptay, Soner and H. Akin Unver (July 2007), *July 2007 Turkish Elections: Winners and Fault Lines,* Washington Institute for Near East Policy, No.14.

Cagaptay, Soner (2015), "Turkey Is in Serious Trouble", *The Atlantic,* October 5, 2015, URL: http://www.theatlantic.com/international/archive/2015/10/turkey-isis-russia-pkk/408988/, Accessed 7 August 2016

Carapico, S (2002), "Foreign Aid for Promoting Democracy in the Arab World", *Middle East Journal,* 56(3): 379-395.

Carpenter, Ted Galen (Fall 2009), "Middle East Vortex: An Unstable Iraq and its Implications for the Region", *Mediterranean Quarterly,* 22-31.

Carver, Natasha (Spring 2002), "Is Iraq/Kurdistan a State such that it can be Said to Operate State Systems and thereby Offer Protection to its 'Citizens'?" *International Journal of Refugees Law,* 14(1): 57-84.

Chaliand, Garard (1980), "Introduction" in Gerard Chaliand (eds.) *People without a Country: The Kurds and Kurdistan,* London: Zed Books, 8-18.

_(1994), *The Kurdish Tragedy,* London: Zed Press.

_(ed.) (1980), *People Without a Country: The Kurds and Kurdistan,* London: Zed Books.

"Changing Asylum and Immigration Policies, the Threat to Democracy in the European Union after September 11 and the Situation of Kurdish Refugees in the UK", *Human Rights Sub-Commission 2002,* Geneva: Centre Europe-Tiers Monde (CETIM), (Online: web), Accessed 18 October 2010, URL http://www.cetim.ch/en/interventions_details.php?iid=186

"Charter of the Kurdish National Congress", The 4th Kurdistan National Congress, held in London on 10-11 October 1998, published by The KNC Media & Communication Committee: London.

Chatham House (September 2004), *Iraq in Transition: Vortex or Catalyst?* Middle East Programme BP 04/02.

Clairmont, Frederic. F (20-26 Sept. 2003), "Iraq: The End of Empire", *Economic and Political Weekly*, 38 (38): 3978-83.

Cleveland, William (1994), *A History of the Modern Middle East*, Boulder: Westview Press.

Clifford, J. (1994), "Diasporas", *Cultural Anthropology*, 9(3): 302-338.

Cockburn, Andrew and Patrick Cockburn (2000), *Saddam Hussein: An American Obsession*, Verso: London.

Cohen, Robin (1997), *Global Diasporas: An Introduction*, London: UCL Press.

Connor, Walker (1976), "The Political Significance of Ethnonationalism within Western Europe", in Abdul Said and Luiz R. Simmons (eds.) *Ethnicity in an International Context*, New Brunswick: Transaction Books.

"Constitution of the Republic of Iran", Adopted 24 October 1979, Efffective 3 December 1979, Amended 28 July 1989.

"Constitution of Federal Republic of Iraq", Official Documents, (Online: web) Accessed 11 July 2010, URL: http://www.krp.org/eng/documents/default aspx?gid=1&sm=7

Cordesman, Anthony H. and Ahmed S. Hashim (1997), *Iraq: Sanctions and Beyond*, Boulder: Westview Press.

Cornell E. Svante (Winter 2001), "The Land of Many Crossroads: The Kurdish Question in Turkish Politics", *Orbis*, 45(1): 31-46.

Cortright, David and A. Lopez (Spring 1999), "Are Sanctions Just? The Problematic Case of Iraq", *Journal of International Affairs*, 52(2): 735-755.

Cox, Savannah (2015), "Meet the Kurdish Women Fighting ISIS", August 26, 2015, URL: http://all-that-is-interesting.com/female-isis-fighters, Accessed 29 August 2016.

Cosgrove, Richard (2014), "Kurdish Peshmerga's Female Fighters" *International Business Times*, September 20, 2014, URL: http://www.ibtimes.co.uk/kurdish-peshmergas-female-fighters-1466422, Accessed 30 August 2016

Dalhman, Carl (2002), "The Political Geography of Kurdistan", *Eurasian Geography and Economics*, 43(4): 271-299.

"Damascus Declaration for Democratic National Change" appears in the Documents on Democracy section of the *Journal of Democracy*, Vol. 17, (1), January 2006: 181-184.

Davis, Horace. B (1976), *The Nationality Question: Selected Writings by Rosa Luxemburg*, Monthly Review Press: New York.

Dawisha, Adeed and Karen Dawisha (May/June 2003), "How to Build a Democratic Iraq", *Foreign Affairs*, 82 (3): 36-50.

Dettmer, Jamie (May 2016), "US General's Surprised Visit to Kurds Prompts Syrian Rebels Fury", *Voice of America* 23 May 2016, URL: http://www.voanews.com/content/us-generals-surprise-visit-to-kurds-prompts-syrian-rebels-fury/3341868.html, Accessed 31 July 2016.

Dirik, Dilar (2014), "Western Fascination with 'badass' Kurdish women", *Aljazeera,* 29 October 2014, URL: http://www.aljazeera.com/indepth/opinion/2014/10/western-fascination-with-badas-2014102112410527736.html, Accessed 1 September 2016

Dosky, Shilan (June 2013), "The Evolving Situation in Kurdistan: Conflicts, National Identities and Regional Perspective", *Atlantic Voices,* 3(6): 1-9.

"Dr. Ismail Besikci Defies the Turkish State", *Kurdistan Liberation,* no.2 (August-September 1990): 2.

Dunn, Michael Collins (2007), "The Arab World and the Kurds" in Charles G. Macdonald and Carole A. O' Leary (eds.) *Kurdish Identity: Human Rights and Political Status,* Gainesville: University Press of Florida.

Eagleton, William (1963), *The Kurdish Republic of 1946,* London: Oxford University Press.

Edmonds, C. J (1957), *Kurds and Arabs: Politics, Travel and Research in North-Eastern Iraq 1919-1925,* London: Oxford University Press.

_(1971), "Kurdish Nationalism", *Journal of Contemporary History,* 6(1): 87-97, 99-107.

Egin, Oray (2013), "The Game Changer: Syria, Iran, and Kurdish Independence", *World Affairs,* May/June 2013 (Online: web), Accessed 17 June 2014, URL: http://www.worldaffairsjournal.org/article/game-changer-syria-iran-and-kurdish-independence

Elgebeily, Sherif, "Kurdistan: Federalism, Sovereignty and Independence", Interview by Leonhardt van Efferink, September 2009, (Online: web), Accessed 7 June 2010, URL: http://www.exploringgeopolitics.org/Interview_Elgebeily_Sherif_Kurdistan_Sovereignty_Independence_Kurdish_Regional_Government_Federalism_Constitution. html

Eligur, Banu (August 2006), "Are Former Enemy Become Allies? Turkey's Changing Relaitions with Syria, Iran and Israel Since the 2003 Iraqi War", *Middle East Brief,* Crown Center for Middle East Studies: 1-8.

Elphinston, W. G (1946), "The Kurdish Question", *Journal of the British Institute of Internal Affairs,* 22: 91-103.

"Encyclopaedia Britannica", (Online: web), Accessed 14 July 2010, URL: http://www.britannica.com/EBchecked/topic/372077/Mede

"End Human Rights Violations against the Syrian Kurds", Amnesty International Press Release (10 March 2005), (Online: web), Accessed 03 September 2009, URL: http://www.yetikiparty.org/en/print.php?id=1229353408&archive=1230778088.

"Enforcing the Charter for the Rights and Freedoms of Women in the Kurdish Regions and Diaspora", Kurdish Human Rights Project: London.

Enloe, Cynthia H. (1973), *Ethnic Conflict and Political Development,* Little Brown & Company: Boston.

Entessar, Nader (October 1984), "The Kurds in Post-Revolutionary Iran and Iraq", *Third World Quarterly*, 6(4): 911-933.

_(October 1989), "The Kurdish Mosaic of Discord", *Third World Quarterly*, 11(4): 83-100.

_(1992), *Kurdish Ethnonationalism*, London: Lynne Rienner Publishers.

Erdogan, Recep Tayyip (27 October 2007), "No EU country has extradited members of the PKK to Turkey, despite labeling it as a terrorist organization" in "Turkey Vexed by PKK Talks with EU and Iraq", (Online: web), Accessed 20 November 2009, URL:http://www.turkishdigest.com/archive/2007_10_01_archive.html

Esfandiari, Golnaz (January 2006), "Iran: Kurds Form Front to Demand Rights", *Radio Free Europe Radio Liberty*, 03 January 2006: Prague, (Online: web), Accessed 08 2010, URL: http://www.rferl.org/content/article/1064384.html

"EU Adds the PKK to List of Terrorist Organisations", *Statewatch News Online*, (Online: web), Accessed 22 October 2010, URL: http://www.statewatch.org/news/2002/may/04pkk.htm.

Fattah, Hassan M. (2005), "Kurds, Emboldened by Lebanon, Rise Up in Tense Syria", *New York Times*, New York, 2 July 2005.

Fearon, James D (1999), *What is Identity (As We Now Use the Word)?* Department of Political Science, Stanford University, Stanford, pp. 2-3.

Fernandes, Desmond (Jan-March 2002), *The Targeting and Criminalization of Kurdish Asylum Seekers*, London: Peace in Kurdistan Campaign, (Online: web), Accessed 4 October 2010, URL: http://www.ncadc.org.uk/archives/filed%20newszines/oldnewszines/Old%201-50/news25/kurd.html

Filkins, Dexter (2003), "Threats and Responses; Ankara: Turkey Expected to Vote on G.I. Presence Tuesday", *New York Times*, New York, 24 February 2003, (Online: web), Accessed 12 November 2008, URL: http://www.nytimes.com/2003/02/24/world/threats-and-responses-ankara-turkey-expected-to-vote-on-gi-presence-tuesday.html

Fishman, Joshua A. (1989), *Language and Ethnicity in Minority Socio-Linguistic Perspective*, Clevedon, Philadelphia: Multilingual Matters Ltd.

Forrest, Caitlin (2016), "ISIS Sanctuary Map: July 1, 2016", *Institute for the Study of War*, July 1, 2016, URL: http://www.understandingwar.org/backgrounder/isis-sanctuary-map-july-1-2016, Accessed 20 August 2016.

Frank, Gunder Andre(1972), "The Development of Underdevelopment", in James D. Cockcroft, Andre Gunder Frank and Dale Johnson (eds) *Dependence and Underdevelopment*, Garden City, New York: Anchor Books, 3.

"Freedom in the World 2008-Iran", (July 2008), Freedom House, (Online: web) Accessed 8 December 2010, URL:http://www.unhcr.org/refworld/docid/487ca215c.html

Freeman, Michael (June 1998), "National Self-Determination, Peace and Human Rights, *Peace Review*, 10(2), (Online: web), Accessed 17 January 2011, URL: http://www.mtholyoke.edu/acad/intrel/freeman.htm

Gambill, C. Gary (April 2004), "The Kurdish Reawakening in Syria", *Middle East Bulletin*, United States Committee for a Free Lebanon and the Middle East Forum (Online: web), Accessed 28 August 2009, URL:http://www.Meib.org/articles/04404_sl.htm

Gasper, Phil (April 2003), "The Betrayal of the Kurds", *International Socialist Review*, (Online: web), Accessed 16 October 2010, URL: http://www.thirdworldtraveler.com/Global_Secrets_Lies/Betrayal_Kurds.html.

Gellner, Ernest (1983), *Nations and Nationalism*, Basil Blackwell: Oxford.

"Genocide in Iraq: The Anfal Campaign against the Kurds" (July 1993), *Human Rights Watch and Middle East Watch, Report*", New York, (Online: web), Accessed 13 June 2010, URL: http://www.hrw.org/reports/1993/iraqanfal

Gerber, Martina (2007), "Iraq: The Socio-Economic Situation in the KRG Administrated Provinces: Sulaimaniyah, Erbil and Dohuk", 10 July 2007, Schweizerische Flüchtlingshilfe (Swiss Refugee Council): Bern.

Ghabra, Shafeeq (1999), "The Kurds: An Arab Perspective" (Online: web), Accessed 12 October 2010, URL: *www1.american.edu/cgp/pdf/ArabKurdPerspective.pdf*

Ghareeb, Edmund (1981), *The Kurdish Question In Iraq*, Syracuse: Syracuse University Press.

Gilbert, P. (2000), *Peoples, Cultures and Nations in Political Philosophy*, Washington: Georgetown University Press.

Gilby, Nicholas (March 2003), "Turkey and the Arms Trade 1998-2002: A Precis Nurturing Turkey's War Machine", *Campaign Against Arms Trade (CAAT)*: London, 1-12.

Gokalp, Deniz and Seda Unsar (Winter 2008), "From the Myth of European Union Accession to Disillusion: Implications for Religious and Ethnic Politicization in Turkey", *Middle East Journal*, 62(1): 93-116.

Gunduz, Aslan (Winter 2001), "Human Rights and Turkey's Future in Europe", *Orbis*: 15-29.

Gunter, M. Michael (1990), *The Kurds in Turkey: A Political Dilemma*, Westview Press: Boulder.

_(1993), "A De-Facto Kurdish State in Northern Iraq", *Third World Quarterly*, 14 (2): 295-319.

_(1996), "Kurdish Infighting: The PKK-KDP Conflict" in Robert Oslon (ed) *The Kurdish Nationalist Movement in 1990s: Its Impact on Turkey and the Middle East*, Lexington: The University Press of Kentucky.

_(1997), *The Kurds and the Future of Turkey*, New York: St. Martin Press.

_(1999), "United States Foreign Policy toward the Kurds", *Orient*: 427-437.

_(April 2003), "Kurdish Futures in a Post-Saddam Iraq", *Journal of Muslim Minority Affairs*, 23(1): 1-15.

_(2005), "Federalism and the Kurds: The Solution or the Problem?" *Orient*, (1): 45-66.

_(September 2006), *The Changing Dynamics in the Kurdistan Regional Government (KRG) of Iraq*, World Congress of Kurdish Studies: Irbil.

_(Spring 2007), "Turkey's Floundering EU Candidacy and its Kurdish Problem", *Middle East Policy*, 16(1): 117-123.

_(November 2011), "Kurdish Nationalism in the Aftermath of the Arab Spring", *Foreign Policy*, (Online web), Accessed 10 March 2013, URL, http://foreignpolicy.com/2011/11/08/kurdish-nationalism-in-the-aftermath-of-the-arab-spring/

Gunter, Michael M. and M. Hakan Yavuz (Spring 2005), "The Continuing Crisis in Iraqi Kurdistan", *Middle East Policy*, 12(1): 122-133.

Gurbey, Gulistan (1996), "The Development of the Kurdish Nationalism Movement in Turkey since the 1980s", in Robert Olson (ed) *The Kurdish Nationalist Movement in 1990s: Its Impact on Turkey and the Middle East*, Lexington: The University Press of Kentucky.

Gurr, Ted Robert and Barbara Harff (1994), *Ethnic Conflict in World Politics*, Westview Press: Boulder.

Hakura, Fadi (April 2007), *Emerging Identity*, Chatham House Publications, 25-27.

Hannum, Hurst (1990), *Autonomy, Sovereignty and Self-Determination: The Accommodation of Conflicting Rights*, Pennsylvania: University of Pennsylvania Press.

Hall, S. (1993), "Cultural Identity and Diaspora", in P. Williams and L. Chrisman (eds.) *Colonial Discourse and Post-Colonial Theory*, New York: Harvester Wheatsheaf, 392-401.

Halliyday, Fred (2006), "Can We Write a Modernist History of Kurdish Nationalism?" in Faleh A. Jabar and Hosham Dawod (eds.) *The Kurds: Nationalism and Politics*, London: Saqi.

Harris, George S. (September 1977), "Ethnic Conflict and the Kurds", *Annals of the American Academy of Political and Social Science*, 443: 112-124.

Hassan, Hussein D. (25 November 2008), "Iran: Ethnic and Religious Minorities", *Congressional Research Service (CRS) Report for Congress*, Washington.

Hasan, Omar and Ben Lando (16 November 2007), "Iraqi Kurd Oil Deals Provoke Conflict with Baghdad", *Middle East Online*, (Online: web), Accessed 13 June 2010, URL: http://www.alternet.org/world/68140/

Hassan, Sayeh (June 2009), "The Persecution of Kurdish Political Activist in Iran", *Kurdish Herald*, 1(2), (Online: web) Accessed 3 December 2010, URL:http://Kurdishherald.com/issue/002/article05.php

Hassanpour, Amir (July-August 1994), "The Kurdish Experience", *Middle East Report* No. 189, 2-7, 23.

Hashim, Ahmed (Jan 1992), "Iraq, the Pariah State", *Current History*, l9(561): 11-16.

_(Jan 1996), "Iraq: Fin de Regime?" *Current History*, 95(597): 10-15.

Held, David (1991), *Political Theory Today*, Stanford: Stanford University Press.

Heraclides, A. (1991), *The Self-Determination of Minorities in International Politics*, London: Frank Cass.

Hersh, Seymour M. (2004), "Seymour Hersh on Israeli Operatives in Kurdistan", *The New Yorker*, 21 June 2004, (Online: web), Accessed 17 October 2010, URL: http://www.fromoccupiedpalestine.org/node/1324

Heydemann, Stephen (1999), *Authoritarianism in Syria: Institutions and Social Conflict 1946-1970*, Ithaca, New York: Cornell University Press.

Heywood, Andrew (2004), *Political Theory: An Introduction*, Hampshire: Palgrave Macmillan.

Hinnebusch, Raymond A. (1998), *Authoritarian Power and State Formation in Baathist Syria: Army, Party and Peasant*, Boulder, CO: Westview Press.

Hirschler, Konrad (July 2001), "Defining the Nation: Kurdish Historiography in Turkey in the 1990s", *Middle Eastern Studies*, 37(3): 145-166.

"Historical Background of Democratic Party of Kurdistan", (Online: web), Accessed 6 December 2010, URL http://pdki.org/english/2010/08/19/historical-background- of-democratic-party-of-iranian-kurdistan/

Hobsbawm, E. J. (1990), *Nations and Nationalism since 1780: Programme, Myth and Reality*, Cambridge: Cambridge University Press.

Horowitz, Donald L. (1985), *Ethnic Groups in Conflict*, Berkeley: University of California Press.

"Human Rights Situation in Iranian Kurdistan", October 2009, Kurdistan Peace and Development Society, 1-20.

"Human Rights Violation in Iranian Kurdistan", 12 September 2007, (Online: web), Accessed 08 October 2010, http://www.pdki.org/articles1-1057-73.htm

Human Rights Watch (1991), *Syria Unmasked: The Suppression of Human Rights by the Assad Regime*, New Haven: Yale University.

_(October 1996), *The Silenced Kurds*, Vol. 8, No.4 (E), (Online: web), Accessed 17 September 2009, URL: http//www.hrw.org/reports/1996/Syria.htm.

_(October 2006), *Denying the Right to Education*, (Online: web), Accessed 6 March 2010, URL:http://www.hrw.org/backgrounder/mena/iran1006

_(January 2009), *Iran: Freedom of Expression and Associations in the Kurdish Regions*, New York: USA.

_(26 November 2009), *Group Denial: Repression of Kurdish Political and Cultural*

Rights in Syria, (Online: web), Accessed 6 March 2010, URL: http://www.hrw.org/en/node/86735/section/4

_Ignatius, David (2015), "Kurds Have Challenges beyond ISIS", *Herald Net*, 16 February 2015, (Online: web), Accessed 05 March 2015, URL: http://www.heraldnet.com/article/20150216/OPINION04/150219448

"International Covenant on Civil and Political Rights", Adopted and opened for signature, ratification and accession by General Assembly resolution 2200A (XXI) of 16 December 1966; entry into force 23 March 1976. Office of the United Nations High Commissioner for Human Rights, (Online: web), Accessed 24 January 2011, URL: http://www2.ohchr.org/english/law/ccpr.htm

"Iran" (2010), Unrepresented Nations and Peoples Organisation (UNPO), Submission to UN Office of the High Commissioner for Human Rights Universal Periodic Review: 7th Session of the UPR Working Group, February 2010.

"Iran: Country Reports on Human Rights Practices-1999", Released by the Bureau of Democracy, Human Rights and Labor, U.S. Department of State, February 23, 2000, (Online: web), Accessed 8 December 2010, URL: http://www.state.gov/g/drl/rls/hrrpt/1999/409.htm

"Iran after the Victory of 1979's Revolution", (Online: web), Accessed 25 February 2010, http://www.iranchamber.com/history/islamic_revolution/revolution_and_iran_afte r1979_4.php

Iranian Ethnic Groups", Iran Chamber Society, (Online: web), Accessed 15 December 2009, URL: http://www.iranchamber.com/people/articles/iranian_ethnic groups.php

"Iranian Kurdistan", Unrepresented Nations and People Organization, (Online: web), Accessed 6 March 2010, http://www.unpo.org/content/view/7882/115/.

"Iranian Kurdistan", (Online: web), Accessed 3 December 2010, URL: http://www.absoluteastronomy.com/topics/Iranian_Kurdistan

"Iran's New President Snubs Kurds", *Iran Focus*, 7 July 2005, (Online: web), Accessed 1 December 2010, URL: http://northerniraq.info/forums/viewtopic.php?f=1&t=506.

"Iraqi Kurdish Civil War", (Online: web), Accessed 3 March 2007, URL: http://en.wikipedia.org/wiki/Iraqi_Kurdish_Civil_War

"Iraq's Kurdistan Islamic Group to Join Mainstream Kurdish Bloc", (Online: web), Accessed 7 June 2010, URL: http://www.mowr.krg.org/article/detail.asp?lngnr=12&smap=02010200&rnr=73 &anr=1278

Izady, Mehrdad (1992), *The Kurds: A Concise Handbook*, Washington DC: Taylor & Francis, Inc.

Jones, Stephen (2009), "The Islamic Republic of Iran: An Introduction", Research Paper, 11 December 2009: The House of Commons Library.

Jongerden, Joost (September 2001), "Resettlement and Reconstruction of Identity: The Case of Kurds in Turkey", *The Global Review of Ethnopolitics*, 1(1): 80-85.

Joshi, Priya (2014), " Syria: Kurdish Women Protection Unites Wage Battle Against ISIS for Kobani", *International Business Times*, October 11, 2014, URL: http://www.ibtimes.co.uk/syria-kurdish-women-protection-units-wage-battle-against-isis-kobani-1469569, Accessed 30 August 2016.

Kajjo, Sirwan (2014), "The Rise of ISIS, a Golden Opportunity for Iraq's Kurds", *Carnegie Endowment for International Peace*, (Online: web), Accessed 2 January 2015, URL:http://carnegieendowment.org/sada/2014/06/19/rise-of-isis-golden-opportunity-for-iraq-s-kurds/he37

Kakeyi, Saeed (2010), "The Kurds in the Bilateral and the Multilateral Treaties", 11 June 2010, (Online: web), Accessed 24 August 2010, URL: http://www.kurdishaspect.com/doc061110SK1.html

Kallen, Evelyn (1996), "Ethnicity and Self-Determination: A Paradigm", in Donald Clark and Robert Williamson (eds.) *Self Determination: International Perspectives*, London: McMillan Press Ltd, 113-123.

Karabat, Ayse (2009), "Trial of Kurdish Parliament in Exile to begin in Ankara", *Today's Zamam*, Ankara, 22 April 2009.

Karadaghi, Rashid (13 October 2007), "The US Senate Resolution on a Federal Iraq: The Road to Freedom", (Online: web), Accessed 14 June 2010, URL:http://kurdishaspect.com/doc101307RK.html

Karsh, Efraim and Inari Rautsi (1991), *Saddam Hussein: A Political Biography*, New York: Free Press.

Katzman, Kenneth (1 September 2009), "The Kurds in the Post-Saddam Iraq", Congressional Research Service (CRS) Report for Congress, 1-14.

Katzman, Kenneth and Alfred B. Prados (14 March 2005), *The Kurds in Post-Saddam Iraq*, Congressional Research Service (CRS) Report for Congress, The Library of Congress.

"KDP", (Online: web), Accessed 23 December 2010, Accessed 15 June 2010, URL: http://www.globalsecurity.org/military/world/para/kdp.htmrkey.

Kendal, Nezan (1980), "The Kurds under the Ottoman Empire", in Gerard Chaliand (ed) *People without a Country: The Kurds and Kurdistan*, London: Zed Books, 19-26.

Khalil, Lydia (2007), "The Hidden Hand of Iran in the Resurgence of Ansar al-Islam", *Terrorism Monitor*, 5(11), (Online: web), Accessed 28 September 2010, URL: http://www.jamestown.org/terrorism/news/uploads/TM_005_011.pdf.

Khayati, Khalid (2006), "Kurdish Question in the European Parliament", 17 October 2006, *Kurdish Globe*, No.79, (Online: web), Accessed 24 October 2010, URL: http://www.kurdishaspect.com/doc1017101.html.

Khergamvala, F.J. (4 May 1991), "Behind Misfortune of Hapless Kurds", *Mainstream*, 29(28): 9-12.

Kilic, Altemur (1959), *Turkey and the World*, Washington: Public Affiars Press.

Kingsley, Patrick and Ghaith Abdul- Ahad (July 2016), "Military Coup attempted in Turkey against Erdogan government", *The Guardian*, 16 July 2016, URL: https://www.theguardian.com/world/2016/jul/15/turkey-coup-attempt-military-ankara-istanbul, Accessed 18 August 2016.

Kinnane, Derk (1964), *The Kurds and Kurdistan*, Oxford University Press: Oxford.

Kirby, Paul (2016), "Turkey Violence: How dangerous is Instability? *BBC news*, 29 June 2016, URL: http://www.bbc.com/news/world-europe-34503388, Accessed 22 August 2016.

"Kirkurk: Kurds' Bottomline in Coalition Talks", *Middle East Online*, (Online: web), Accessed 14 June 2010, URL: http://www.middle-east-online.com/english/?id=12896.

Kirisci, Kemal (2004), "The Kurdish Question and Turkish Foreign Policy" in Lenore G. Martin and Dimitris Keridis (eds.) *The Future of Turkish Foreign Policy*, Cambridge: MIT Press.

Kirisci, Kemal and Gareth Winrow (1997), *The Kurdish Question and Turkey*, London: Frank Cass.

Koohi-Kamali, Farideh (1992), "The Development of Nationalism in Iranian Kurdistan" in Philip G. Kreyenbroek and Stephen Sperl (eds.) *The Kurds: A Contemporary Overview*, London: Routledge, 180-181.

_(2003), *Political Development of the Kurds in Iran*, Hampshire: Palgrave Macmillan.

Korn, David A. (June 1994), "The Last Years of Mustafa Barzani", *Middle East Quaterly*, (1): 12-27.

"Kongra-Gel, Kurdistan Freedom and Democracy Congress (KADEK), Kurdistan Wokers' Party (PKK)", (Online: web), Accessed 30 January 2008, URL: http://www.globalsecurity.org/military/world/para/pkk.htm

Konuralp, Emrah (2009), *"Ecevit's Conception of Nationalism: A Unique Position or a Syncretic Vision?"* Master of Science Thesis, Ankara: Middle East Technical University.

Kriesberg, Louis (1997), "Social Movements and Global Transformation" in Jackie Smith et al (eds.) *Transnational Social Movements and Global Politics: Solidarity Beyond the State*, Syracuse University Press, 3-18.

Kurd Watch (2009a), "The Kurdish Policy of the Syrian Government and the Development of the Kurdish Movement since 1920" European Center for Kurdish Studies: Berlin, Germany: 1-22.

_(2009b), "Stateless Kurds in Syria: Illegal Invaders or Victims of a Nationalist Policy?", (Online: web) Accessed 3 September 2009, URL: http://supportkurds.org/reports/stateless-kurds-in-syria-kurdwatch-report/

"Kurdish Institute of Paris", (Online: web), Accessed 12 October 2010, http://www.institutkurde.org/en/

"Kurdish National Congress", (Online: web), Accessed 12 October 2010, URL: http://www.knc.org.uk/

"Kurdistan Regional Government", (Online: web), Accessed 15 June 2010, http://www.worldlingo.com/ma/enwiki/en/kurdistan_Regional_Government#KRG_role_in_Iraq

"Kurdish Regional Government" (21 May 2009), UK Border Agency: Country of Origin Information.

Kurdistan Regional Government (KRG), "About the Kurdistan Regional Government", (Online: web), Accessed 5 June 2007, URL: http://www.krg.org/articles/article_detail.asp?RubricNr=93&AricleNr=48&Lang Nr=12&L...

"Kurdistan Regional Government, Kurdistan Regional Government Unification Agreement" (21 January 2006), (Online: web), Accessed 15 June 2010, URL: http://www.krg.org/articles/article_detail.asp?LangNr=12&RubricNr=107&ArticleNr=8891&LNNr=28&RNNr

"Kurdistan Regional Unification Agreement" (21 January 2010), (Online: web), Accessed 15 June 2010, URL: http://www.unhcr.org/refworld/docid/469cdd7a2.html

"Kurds", (Online: web), Accessed 05 August 2009, URL: http://www.countrystudies.us/iran/40.htm

"Kurds in the Syrian Arab Republic One Year after the March 2004 Events", (Online: web), Accessed 03 September 2009, URL: http//www.yetiki-party.org/en/print.phd?id=1229352764& archive=1230778088

"Kurd", *World Directory of Minorities*, (Online: web), Accessed 13 August 2009, URL: http//www.minorityrights.org/?lid=5270&tmpl=printpage

"Kurdish Democratic Party of Iran (KDPI)", (Online: web), Accessed 6 December 2010, URL: http://www.globalsecurity.org/military/world/para/kdpi.htm

"Kurdish Human Rights Project", (Online: web), Accessed 12 October 2010, URL: http://www.khrp.org/

Kurdish Human Rights Project (2008), "Turkish Attacks on Kurdistan, Iraq: 2007-2008: Background, Motives and Human Rights", Impact, London: 1-9.

Kurdish Human Rights Project (16 December 2006), "War in Iraq and the Kurds", (Online: web), Accessed 15 November 2008, URL: http://www.khrp.org/news/pr2003/wariniraq.htm

"Kurdish Institute of Paris", (Online: web), Accessed 12 October 2010, URL: http://www.institutkurde.org/en/

"Kurdish National Congress of North America (KNC-NA) Asking US to Remove PKK from the Blacklist" (April 7, 2008), (Online: web), Accessed 10 November 2008, URL: http://www.kurdishaspect.com/doc040708KNC.html

"Kurdish People's Protection Unit YPG", (Online: web), Accessed 20 February 2015, URL: http://www.globalsecurity.org/military/world/para/ypg.htm

"Kurdish Regional Government" (15 October 2002), *Kurdistan Today*, (Online: web), Accessed 8 June 2007, URL: http://www.old.krg.org/docs/KTO21015_full.asp

"Kurdish Regional Investment Law (July 2006)", (Online: web), Accessed 15 June 2010, URL:http://www.krg.org/articles/detail.asp?lngnr=12&smap=04030000& rnr=107 &anr=12626

"Kurdistan Democratic Alliance supports Kurdish United Front in Eastern Kurdistan" 01 October 2006, (Online: web), Accessed 08 December 2010, URL: http://www.kurdmedia.com/article.aspx?id=11081

"Kurdistan Region Economic Development Assessment", Final Report December 2008, Local Government Project. The publication was produced for review by the United States Agency for International Development. It was prepared by RTI-International.

"Kurdistan Regional Government, Kurdistan Regional Government Unification Agreement" (21 January 2006), (Online: web), Accessed 15 June 2010, URL: http://www.krg.org/articles/article_detail.asp?LangNr=12&RubricNr=107&ArticleNr=8891&LNNr=28&RNNr=70

Kurdistan Regional Government (KRG), "About the Kurdistan Regional Government", (Online: web) Accessed 5 June 2007, URL: hhtp://www.krg.org/articles/article_detail.asp?RubricNr=93&AricleNr=48&Lang Nr=12&L....

Kurdistan Regional Government (4 July 2005), "A Brief History of Iraqi Kurdistan: The Kurds and Kurdistan", (Online: web), Accessed on 22 October 2006, URL: http://www.krg.org/articles/article_detail.asp?

"Kurdistan-Turkey", (Online: web), Accessed 30 January 2008, URL: http://www.globalsecurity.org/military/world/war/kurdistan-turkey.htm

"Kurdistan's Economy: Its Potential and its Challenges", (Online: web), Accessed 5 July 2010, URL: http://www.krg.org/articles/detail.asp?lngnr=12&smap=02010200& rnr=73&anr=31571

"Kurdistan Regional Government", *Ministries and Departments*, URL: http://www.krg.org/p/p.aspx?l=12&s=030000&p=228, Accessed 31 July 2014.

Kurkcu, Ertugrul (April-June 1996), "The Crisis of the Turkish State", *Middle East Report*, 199: 2-7.

Kushner, David (April 1997), "Self-Perception and Identity in Contemporary Turkey", *Journal of Contemporary History*, 32(2): 219-233.

Kutschera, Chris (July-August 1994), "Mad Dreams of Independence: The Kurds of Turkey and the PKK", *Middle East Report*, 189: 12-15.

Kymlicka, Will (1995), *Multicultural Citizenship*, Oxford University Press: Oxford.

Lahoud, Lamia, (April 1991), "We Never Give Up Hope," *The Middle East*, (198): 15-20.

Laitin, David (1998), *Identity in Formation: The Russian-Speaking Populations in the Near Abroad*, Ithaca: Cornell University Press.

Larrabee, Stephen F. (July-August 2007), "Turkey Rediscovers the Middle East", *Foreign Affairs*, 86(4): 105-106).

Leezenberg, M (2000). "Humanitarian Aid in Iraqi Kurdistan", CEMOTI, No. 29, (Online: web), Accessed 14 July 2010, URL: http://www.cerisciencespo.com/publica/cemoti/textes29/leezenbe.pdf)

_(June 2005), "Iraqi Kurdistan: Contours of a Post-Civil War Society", *Third World Quarterly*, 26(4-5): 630-35.

Letsch, Constnze (14 October 2014), "Turkish Jets Bombard Kurdish Positions", *The Guardian*, UK, (Online: web), Accessed January 2015, URL: http://www.theguardian.com/world/2014/oct/14/turkish-jets-bombard-kurdish-positions-pkk

Lijphart, Arend (1969), "Consociational Democracy", *World Politics*, 21(2): 206-225.

_(2003), "Consociational Democracy" in Robert Dahl et al (eds.) *The Democracy Source Book*, Massachusetts: MIT Press, 142-146.

Lowe, Robert (January 2006), *The Syrian Kurds: A People Discovered*, Chatham House Middle East Programme.

Lowen, Mark (8 October 2014), "Turkey's Fear of a Reignited Kurdish Flame", *BBC News*, Istanbul, (Online: web), Accessed 20 January 2015, URL: http://www.bbc.com/news/world-middle-east-29542040

Lukitz, Liora (1995), *Iraq: The Search for National Identity*, London: Frank Cass.

Luxemburg, Rosa (1964), *The Accumulation of Capital*, New York: Monthly Review Press.

Lynch, Maureen and Perveen Ali (2006), "Buried Alive: Stateless Kurds in Syria", *Refugees International*, (Online: web), Accessed 5 August 2009, URL: http://www.refugeesinternational.org/print/2470

MacFarquhar, Neil (24 March 2004), "Gains by Kin in Iraq Inflame Kurds' Anger at Syria", (Online: web), Accessed 15 June 2010, URL: http://www.nytimes.com/2004/03/24/world/gains-by-kin-in-iraq-inflame-kurds-anger-at-syria.html?pagewanted=1?pagewanted=1

Machin, Amanda (2008), "Defining the Nation? Dissolving the Problem", *In-Spire Journal of Law, Politics and Societies*, 3(2): 102-109.

Malmisaniji. M (2006), *The Past and the Present of Book Publishing in Kurdish Language in Syria*, Research paper commissioned by Next Page Foundation.

Manafy, A. (Spring 1996), "The State and Human Rights: Critical Perspective", *The Iranian Journal of International Affairs*, 1(8):120-139.

_(2005), *The Kurdish Political Struggles in Iran, Iraq and Turkey: A Critical Analysis*, Oxford: University Press of America.

Marcus, Aliza (July-August 1994), "City in the War Zone", *Middle East Report*, 189:16-19.

Marcus, Aliza and Andrew Apostolou (26 February 2008), "Talking to Turkey's Kurds",

The Boston Globe, (Online: web), Accessed 25 November 2010, URL: http://www.boston.com/bostonglobe/editorial_opinion/oped/articles/2008/02/26/talking_to_turkeys_kurds/

Marcuse, Herbert (1969), *An Essay on Liberation*, Beacon Press: Boston.

Mardell, Mark (11 December 2006), "Turkey's EU Membership Bid Stalls", (Online: web), Accessed 14 November 2010, URL: http://news.bbc.co.uk/2/hi/europe/6170749.stm.

Margalit, Avishai and Joseph Raz (September 1990), "National Self-Determination", *The Journal of Philosophy*, 87(9): 439-461.

Marguiles, Ronnie (April-June 1996), "Turkey and the European Union", *Middle East Report*, 199: 27.

Marienstras, R. (1989), "On the Notion of Diaspora" in G. Chaliand (ed) *Minority Peoples in the Age of Nation-States*, London: Pluto, 119-125.

Martin, James (2007), "Lunch with Komala", *Jerusalem Post*, 27 August 2007 (Online: web), Accessed 6 December 2010, URL: http://www.jpost.com/Features/Article.aspx?id=73033

Maxwell, Mark David (September-October 2004), "The Law of War and Civilians on the Battlefield: Are We undermining Civilian Protections?" *Military Review*, 17-25.

Mazarr, M. J. et al (eds.) (1993), *Desert Storm: The Gulf War and What We Learn*, Boulder: Westview Press.

McDowall, David (1992), *The Kurds: A Nation Denied*, London: Minority Publications.

McDowell, C. (1996), *A Tamil Asylum Diaspora*, Oxford: Berghahn.

_(1997), Modern History of Iraq, New York: I.B. Tauris.

_(1998), The Kurds of Syria, London: Kurdish Human Rights Project.

_(2000), A Modern History of the Kurds, New York: IB Tauris.

McLuhan, H.M. (1967), *The Medium is the Message*, Bantam: New York.

Meho, I. Lokman and Kelly L. Maglaughlin (2001), *Kurdish Culture and Society: An Annotated Bibliography*, Westport: Greenwood Press.

Mella, Jawad (2005), *Kurdistan and the Kurds: A Divided Homeland and a Nation without State*, London: Western Kurdish Association Publications.

"Members of the Kurdish Regional Government", (Online: web), Accessed 15 June 2010, http://www.krg.org/articles/detail.asp?rnr=159&lngnr=12&anr=10938&smap=04 060000

Messely, Mattijis (2014), "The Kurds in Syria: On the Road to Independence?" *MEDEA Institute*, (Online: web), Accessed 18 June 2014, URL: http://www.medea.be/2014/04/the-kurds-in-syria-on-the-road-to-independence/

Merrifield, William (2005), "MED-TV: Kurdish Satellite Television and the Changing Relationship between the State and the Media", Transnational Broadcasting Studies, *Adham Center for Television Journalism*, (Online: web),

Accessed 18 October 2010, URL: http://www.tbsjournal.com/Archives/Spring05/merrifield.html

Meyrowitz, J. (1985), *No Sense of Place: The Impact of Electronic Media on Social Behaviour*, Oxford University Press: New York.

Military, "Kurdistan Democratic Party (KDP)", (Online: web), Accessed 27 February 2007, URL: http//www.globalsecurity.org/military/world/para/kdp.htm/

Miller, L. H. (1994), *Global Order: Values and Power in International Politics*, Boulder: Westview.

Minasian, Sergey (2007), "Israeli-Kurdish Relations", *21st Century*, (1), 15-32.

Mir-Hosseini, Z. (1994), "Inner Truth and Outer History: The Two Worlds of the Ahl-e Haqq of Kurdistan", *International Journal of Middle East Studies*, 26: 260-269.

Mitrovic, Olga (15 March 2009), *Kurds: History of Oppression and Future Prospects*, (Online: web), Accessed 8 August 2010, URL: http://siiga.org/articles-and-interviews/kurds-the-history-of-oppression-and-future-prospects.en.html

Montgomery, Harriet (2005), *The Kurds of Syria: An Existence Denied*, Berlin: Europaisches Zentrum fur Kurdische Studien.

Morad, Munir (1992), "The Situation of Kurds in Iraq and Turkey" in Philip G. Kreyenbroek and Stephen Sperl (eds.) *The Kurds: A Contemporary Overview*, London: Routledge: 48-54.

Moubayed, Sami (April 9, 2005), "US Designs on Syria's Kurds", (Online: web), Accessed 05 August 2009, URL: http//www.atimes.com/atimes/Middle_East/GD09Ak01.html

Muir, Jim (12 July 1991), "How Can They Trust Saddam?" *Middle East International*, (404): 8-15.

Munch, Richard (2001), *Nation and Citizenship in the Global Age: From National to Transnational Ties and Identities*, London: Palgrave.

Natali, Denise (2005), *Kurds and the State: Evolving National Identity in Iraq, Turkey and Iran*, New York: Syracuse University Press.

_(2012), "The Persistent Boundaries of Kurdish Nationalism", World Politics Review, 9 May 2012, (Online: web), Accessed 25 January 2015, URL: http://www.worldpoliticsreview.com/articles/11926/the-persistent-boundaries-of-kurdish-nationalism

Nawaz, M.K. (1965), "The Meaning and Range of the Principle of Self-Determination", *Duke Law Journal*, (1): 82-101.

Nehme, Michel G. and Lokman I. Meho (1995), "Pawns in a Deadly Game: Iraqi Kurds and the United States, 1972-1975", *International Studies*, 32(1): 41-55.

"Netanyahu Calls for Jordan Support, Kurdish Independence", *Middle East Eye*, 30 June 2014, (Online: web), Accessed 29 July 2014, URL: http://www.middleeasteye.net/news/netanyahu-calls-jordan-support-kurdish-independence-1830159244.

Ofteringer, Ronald and Ralf Backer (March-June 1994), "A Republic of Statelessness: Three Years of Humanitarian Intervention in Iraqi Kurdistan", *Middle East Report,* 40-45.

Oliphant, Thomas (2003), "A Lesson for Turkey from Kurdish Allies", *Boston Globe,* 13 April, (Online: web), Accessed 26 November 2010, URL: http://old.krg.org/docs/reports-papers/bostobGlobe-lesson-for-turkey-apr03.asp.

Olson, Robert (1989), *The Emergence of Kurdish Nationalism and the Sheikh Said Rebellion, 1880-1925,* Austin: University of Texas Press.

_(1991), The Emergence of Kurdish Nationalism 1880-1924, Austin: University of Texas.

_(1992), "The Kurdish Question in the Aftermath of the Gulf War: Geopolitical and Geostrategic Changes in the Middle East", Third World Quarterly, 13(3): 476-499.

_(October 2000), "Turkey-Iran relations, 1997 to 2000: The Kurdish and Islamist Question", Third World Quarterly, 21(5): 871-90.

_(2001), The Kurdish Question and Turkish-Iranian Relations, (Arabic) Translated by Dr. Mohammad Ihsan. Erbil: Aras Publishing.

_(Fall 2007), "From the EU Project to the Iraq Project and Back Again? Kurds and Turks after the 22 July 2007 Elections", Mediterranean Quarterly, 18(4): 17-35.

Onis, Ziya (Winter 2003), "After 9/11: The Importance of the EU Dimension," *Turkish Policy Quarterly,* 2(4): 10-25.

Ozkan, Behlul (March 2015), "Amidst the Medieval Darkness of ISIS, the Kurds Stand for Secularism and Democracy in the Middle East", *The Huffington Post,* 7 March 2015, (Online: web), Accessed 7 March 2015, URL: http://www.huffingtonpost.com/behlal-azkan/isis-kurds-democracy_b_6817244.html?ir=India

O'Leary, Brendan (2005), "Power-Sharing, Pluralist Federation and Federacy" in Brendan O'Leary et al (eds.) *The Future of Kurdistan in Iraq,* Philadelphia: University of Pennsylvania Press, 83-87.

O'Leary, Carole A. (December 2002), "The Kurds of Iraq: Recent History, Future Prospects", *Middle East Review of International Affairs,* 6 (4):1-13.

Paley, Amit R. (2008), "Strip of Iraq on the Verge of Exploding: Kurds Extend Role beyond Autonomous Borders, Angering Arabs", *Washington Post,* September 13, 2008, (Online: web), Accessed 23 December 2010, URL: http://www.washingtonpost.com/wp-dyn/content/article/2008/09/12/AR2008091203584.html.

Parekh, Bhiku (2000), *Rethinking Multiculturalism: Cultural Diversity and Political Theory,* London: Macmillan Press Ltd.

_(2008), A New Politics of Identity: Political Principles for an Interdependent World, Hampshire: Palgrave Macmillan, 11-13.

Park, Bill (February 2004), "Turkey Concerned by Kurdish Autonomy in New Iraq", *Jane's Intelligence Review,* 24-27.

Patton, Marcie J (Summer 2003), "Voices from Turkey's Southeast", *Middle East Report*, (227), 42-45.

Pavi, Shadi (2014), "Iran: Kurds Tortured, Hanged", 13 March 2014, *Gatestone Institute International Policy Council*, (Online: web), Accessed 18 June 2014, URL: http:// www.gatestoneinstitute.org/4213/iran-kurds-tortured-hanged.

Pearson, Raymond (1983), *National Minorities in Eastern Europe, 1848-1945*, London: Macmillan.

Pelletiere, Stephen C (1984), *The Kurds: An Unstable Element in the Gulf*, Boulder: Westview Press.

Peteet, Julie (2000), "Refugees, Resistance and Identity" in John A Guidry et al (eds.) *Globalization and Social Movements*, Ann Arbor: University of Michigan Press, 183-209.

Peuch, Jean Christopher (29 July 2004), "Turkey/Iran: Kurdish Issues Dominate Turkish Prime Minister's Visit to Iran", *Radio Free Europe Radio Liberty*, (Online: web), Accesssed 15 November 2010, URL: http://www.rferl.org/content/article/ 1054084.html

Pomerance, Michla (1982), *Self-Determination in Law and Practice*, The Hague: Martinus Nijhoff Publishers.

Poulton, Hugh (1997), *Top Hat, Grey Wolf and Crescent: Turkish Natinalism and the Turkish Republic*, London: C. Hurst.

Prados, Alfred B. (May 1991), "Kurdish Seperatism in Iraq: Developments and Implications for the United States", *Congressional Research Service (CRS) Report for Congress*.

Prince, James M. (Jan.1993), "A Kurdish State in Iraq?" *Current History*, 92 (570): 17-23.

Puder, Joseph, "Rewarding the Palestinians while Ignoring the Kurds", (Online: Web), Accessed 14 March 2010, URL: http://thebulletin.us/articles/2009/03/24/ commentary/op-eds/doc49c8e03b24922735006145.txt

"Q&A: Turkey's EU Entry Talk" (11 December 2006), (Online: web), Accessed 14 November 2010, URL: http://www.news.bbc.co.uk/2/hi/4107919.stm.

Radu, Michael (Winter 2001), "The Rise and Fall of the PKK", *Orbis*, 45(1): 47-63

Rafaat, Aram (December 2007), "US-Kurdish Relations in the Post-Invasion Iraq", *Middle East Review of International Affairs*, 11(4): 79-89.

_(Fall 2007b), "An Independent Kurdish State: Achievable or Merely a Kurdish Dream?" The Journal of Social, Political and Economic Studies, 32(3): 267-304.

Rainsford, Sarah (20 October 2007), "Turkey in Tense Border Stand-Off", (Online: web), Accessed 15 November 2008, URL: http://news.bbc.co.uk/2/hi/europe/ 7053246.stm

Randal, Jonathan C (1999), *After Such Knowledge, What Forgiveness? My Encounters with Kurdistan*, Westview Press: Boulder.

Rebin, Alan (October 2010), "Once More PJAK Showed Willingness for Peaceful Solution", (Online: web), Accessed 08 December 2010, URL: http://www.pjak.org/english.php?id=1106

Refugees International (21 November 2003), "Iraq: A Status Report on Refugees and Displaced Persons, (Online: web), Accessed 11 June 2010, URL: http://www.refugeesinternational.org/content/article/detail/1552/

"Report: Iran Official Says Iran Shelled Kurds," *USA Today*, (Online: web), Accessed 01 September 2010, URL: http://www.usatoday.com/news/world/iraq/2007-09-25-iran-iraq_N.htm.

"Representation Committee for Kurdish Parties in Syria-Europe Organisation", (Online: web), Accessed 3 September 2009, URL: http//www.yekiti-party.org/en/print.php? id=1228140870&archive=1230778088

Ridolfo, Kathleen (04 October 2007), "Iraq: Criticism of US Senate's Partisan Resolution Echoes across Arab World", (Online: web), Accessed 14 June 2010, URL: http://www.rferl.org/content/article/1078866.html

Robins, Kelvin (2003), "Beyond Imagined Community? Trans-National Media and Turkish Immigrants in Europe", in Harvard (ed) *Media in a Globalized Society*, Copenhagen: Museum Tusculanum Press.

Robins, Philip (Oct 1993), "The Overlord State: Turkish Policy and the Kurdish Issue", *International Affairs (Royal Institute of International Affairs 1944-)*, 69(4): 657-676.

_(2000), "Turkey and the Kurds: Missing Another Opportunity?" in Morton ramowitz (ed) Turkey's Transformation and American Policy, New York: The Century Foundation Press, 61-93.

Romano, David (2005), "Whose House is this Anyway? IDP and Refugee Return in Post- Saddam Iraq", *Journal of Refugee Studies*, 18(4): 430-453.

Rosen, Armin (2016), "ISIS' territory in Syria and Iraq is shrinking but there's a catch", *Business Insider*, January 6 2016, URL: http://www.businessinsider.in/ISIS-territory-in-Syria-and-Iraq-is-shrinking-160but-theres-a-catch/articleshow/50461132.cms, Accessed 20 August 2016.

Rosenfeld, Everett and etal., (July 2016), " Turkey's attempt to oust Erdogan fail, leaving scores dead and roiling the country", 16 July 2016, CNBC news, URL: http://www.cnbc.com/2016/07/15/gunfire-heard-jets-seen-flying-in-turkish-capital-of-ankara.html, Accessed 7 August 2016.

Rosenfeld, Jesse (2016), "Turkey Is Fighting a Dirty War Against Its Own Kurdish Population", The Nation, March 9, 2016, URL: https://www.thenation.com/article/turkey-is-fighting-a-dirty-war-against-its-own-kurdish-population/, Accessed 7 August 2016.

Rubin, Michael (3 March 2007), "Enabling Kurdish Illusions", *Weekly Standard*, (Online: web), Accessed 14 June 2010, URL: http://www.meforum.org/1670/enabling-kurdish-illusions.

Saberi, Roxana (May 2007), "Iraqi Kurds Split between Iran and US", (Online: web), Accessed 6 December 2010, URL: http://news.bbc.co.uk/2/hi/middle_east/6638255.stm

Safran, W. (1991), "Diasporas in Modern Societies: Myths of Homeland and Return", *Diaspora,* 1(1): 83-99.

Safrastyan, Ruben (2007), "Turkey as Mediator and Peacekeeper during Middle East Conflict: Analyzing Events of Summer 2006", *Global Politician,* (Online: web), Accessed 16 October 2010, URL: http://www.globalpolitician.com/22934-turkey

Salih A, Muhammed (2014), "Kurdish President Calls for Referendum on Independence", *Middle East Eye,* 3 July 2014, (Online: web), Accessed 29 July 2014, URL: http://www.middleeasteye.net/news/kurdish- president-calls-referendum-independence-604264937,

Salt, Jeremy (February 1999), "Turkey's Military Democracy", *Current History,* 72-78.

Sandel, Michael (1984), "The Procedural Republic and and the Unencumbered Self", *Political Theory,* Vol. 12, 1984, pp.81-96.

Schangzer, Jonathan (Winter 2004), "Ansar al-Islam: Back in Iraq", *Middle East Quarterly,* 11(1): 41-50.

Schleifer, Yigal (2013), "Turkey: Jailed PKK Leader Gives Kurdish Peace Talks a Major Boost", *Turko-file,* Accessed 10 June 2014, URL: http://www.eurasianet.org/node/66729,

Shaheen, Kareem(2016), "Turkey sends tanks into Syria in operation aimed at ISIS and Kurds", *The guardian,* 24 August 2016, URL: https://www.theguardian.com/world/2016/aug/24/turkey-launches-major-operation-against-isis-in-key-border-town, Accessed 25 August 2016.

Sheffer, G. (1995), "The Emergence of New Ethno-National Diasporas", *Migration,* No. 28/95 (1995-2): 5-28.

Shifrinson, Joshua R. Itzkowitz (December 2006), "The Kurds and Regional Security: An Evaluation of Developments since the Iraq War", *Middle East Brief,* No. 14, Crown Center for Middle East Studies: Brandeis University.

Sidki, Bakr (March 2014), "The Kurds and the Syrian Revolution: Statehood & Participation", *Heinrich Boll Stiftung Middle East,* (Online: web), Accessed 18 June 2014, URL: http://lb.boell.org/en/2014/03/03/kurds-and-syrian-revolution-statehood-participation.

Sklair, Leslie (2002), *Globalization Capitalism and its Alternative,* Oxford University Press: New York.

Sluglett, Marion Farouk and Peter Sluglett (2001), *Iraq since 1958: From Revolution to Dictatorship,* London: I.B. Tauris.

Smith, Anthony D. (1981), *The Ethnic Revival,* Cambridge: Cambridge University Press.

_(1983), Theories of Nationalism, New York: Holmes & Meier.

_(1991), National Identity, Nevada: University of Nevada Press.

_(1998), Nationalism and Modernism: A Critical Survey of Recent Theories of Nations and Nationalism, Routledge: London.

_(2001), Nationalism: Theory, Ideology, History, Cambridge: Polity Press.

Smith, D. Anthony and Julia Kristeva, "National Identity: Nations Without Nationalism", *Foreign Affairs*, September/October, 1993.

Smith, Joan (Summer 2001), "In the Shadow of Kurdish: The Silence of Other Ethnolinguistic Minorities in Turkey", *Middle East Report*, 219: 45-47.

Smyth, Gareth (2014), "Iran Plays a Complex Game with the Kurds", *The Daily Star*, 12 May 2014, (Online: web), Accessed 17 June 2014, URL: http://www.dailystar.com.lb/Opinion/Commentary/2014/May-12/256069-iran-plays-a-complex-game-with-the-kurds.ashx#axzz34siY4deg

Somel, Selkuk (2003), *Historical Dictionary of the Ottoman Empire*, London: Scarecrow Press Inc.

Somer, Murat (June 2002), "Ethnic Kurds, Endogenous Identities and Turkey's Democratization and Integration with Europe", *The Global Review of Ethnopolitics*, 1(4): 74-93.

_(Spring 2004), "Turkey's Kurdish Conflict: Changing Context and Domestic and Regional Implications", Middle East Journal, 58(2): 235-53.

Somer, Murat and Evangelos G. Liaras (2010), "Turkey's New Kurdish Opening: Religious versus Secular Values", *Middle East Policy Council*, (Online: web), Accessed 24 November 2010, URL http://www.mepc.org/journal/middle-east-policy-archives/turkeys-new-kurdish-opening-religious-versus-secularvalues? print

Soguel, Dominique (2016), "IS Threat growing as Turkey focuses on Kurds", *Associated Press*, April 1, 2016, Istanbul, URL: http://bigstory.ap.org/article/c2cd24bd0e4f4629a8d56d3feb7996e7/turkey-sees-islamic-state-emerging-foe-over-kurds, Accessed, 22 August 2016.

Stansfield, Gareth (2003), *Iraqi Kurdistan: Political Development and Emergent Democracy*, London: Routledge Curzon,

Stansfield, Gareth et al (December 2007), *The Kurdish Policy Imperative*, Chatham House, Middle East Programme, Chatham House, 1-8.

Stansfield, Gareth and Hashem Ahmadzadeh (December 2009), "On Iran's Kurds", Interview by Michael Collins Dunn, *Middle East Institute Bulletin*, 60 (4): 1-19.

"Statement by Middle East Quartet" (2 February 2007), Department of Information: New York, URL: http://www.un.org/News/Press/docs/2007/sg2122.doc.htm

Stephens, Michael (2014), "Analysis: YPG—The Islamic State's Worst Enemy", Jane's Defence Weekly, 11 September 2014, (Online: web), Accessed 25 January 2015, URL:http://www.janes.com/article/43030/analysis-ypg-the-islamic-state-s-worst-enemy.

Suri, Sanjay (11 March 2005), *Torture and Oppression of Kurds in Syria,* (Online: web), Accessed 03 September 2009, URL: http//www.antiwar.com/ips/suri.php?articleid=5142

Susser, Bernard (1995), *Political Ideology in the Modern World,* Boston: Allyn and Bacon.

"Syria: Kurds, Honour-Killings and Illegal Departure", Report from a fact-finding mission to Damascus, 15-22 January 2007, *Danish Refugee Council,* Danish Immigration Service, Copenhagen.

"Syria- Constitution", Adopted 13 March 1973, ICL Document Status: 13 March 1973.

"Syria: Followthrough on Commitment to Grant Citizenship to Stateless Kurds, 2005", (Online: web), Accessed 31 July 2009, URL: http://www.refugeesinternational.org/node/3289.

Tahiri, Hussein (2007), "The Kurdistan Democratic Party of Iran: Which One?" (Online: web), Accessed 7 December 2010, URL: http://www.kurdmedia.com/article.aspx?id=14085.

Talabany, Nouri (Winter 2007), "Who Owns Kirkuk? The Kurdish Case", *Middle East Quaterly*: 75-78.

Tamir, Yael (April 1995), "The Enigma of Nationalism", *World Politics* (47): 418-440.

Taspinar, Omer (November/December 2007), "The Old Turks' Revolt: When Radical Secularism Endangers Democracy", *Foreign Affairs,* 86(6): 114-130.

Taylor, Charles (1989), *The Sources of Self,* Cambridge: Cambridge University Press "The Damascus Declaration for Democratic National Change", 16 October 2005: Damascus, (Online: web), Accessed 18 August 2009, URL: http://www.demdigest.net/damascusdeclaration.html.

"The Kurdish Regional Government Representation in Austria", *Inauguration of* Eight Cabinet, 26 June 2014, URL: http://www.krg.at/en/achtes-kabinett-angelobt/, Accessed 31 July 2014.

"The March 16 Chemical Attack on Halabja", (Online: web), Accessed 13 May 2010, URL: http://hrw.org/reports/1993/iraqanfal/> ANFAL3.htm.

"The Members of the Previous and Fourth Cabinet, Which was in Office from 1999 to Early 2006", (Online: web), Accessed 15 June 2010, URL:,n http://www.krg.org/articles/detail.asp?rnr=159&lngnr=12&anr=10938&smap=04 060000

The Minority Rights Group International, *World Directory of Minorities and Indigenous Peoples,* (Online: web), Accessed 5 August 2009, http://www.minorityrights.org/directory.

"The Damascus Declaration for Democratic National Change", 16 October 2005: Damascus, (Online: web), Accessed 18 August 2009.

The Spokesman Kurdistan Regional Government, "KRG Condemns Iranian Shelling of Border Areas", 28 September 2007, (Online: web), Accessed 01 September 2010, URL:http://www.krg.org/articles/detail.asp?lngnr=12&smap=02010100&rnr=223&anr=20405.

"Time to Rebuild Middle East, Davutoglu says in Erbil", (Online: web), Accessed 24 November 2010, URL: http://www.krg.org/articles/detail.asp?smap=02010200&lngnr=12&rnr=73&anr=32240

Tololyan, K. (1991), "The Nation State and its Others: In Lieu of a Preface", *Diaspora*, No. 1: 3-7.

Tomas, Nuria and Ana Villellas (July 2009), "The Kurdistan Autonomous Region: Risk and Challenges for Peace", Peacebuilding Papers, School for a Culture of Peace (Escola de Cultura de Pau), Universitat Autònoma de Barcelona, Spain.

Torchia, Chritopher (2007), "Kurdistan Tries to Rebuild Economy", (Online: web), Accessed 05 July 2010, URL: http://www.usatoday.com/news/world/2007-09-25-1223407209_x.htm

Tripathi, Deepak (2014), "Why Israel is backing Kurdish Independence", *Middle East Eye*, 8 July 2014, Accessed 31 July 2014, URL: http://www.middleeasteye.net/columns/whats-behind- netanyahu-s-support-kurdish-independence-1536584149.

Tugal, Cihan (March- April 2007), "NATO's Islamists: Hegemony and Americanization in Turkey", *New Left Review*, 44: 5-34.

Tully, J. (1995), *Strange Multiplicity: Constitutionalism in an Age of Diversity*, New York: Cambridge University Press.

"Turkey's Human Rights Development", *Human Rights Watch Report 2005*, Helsinki, (Online: web), Accessed 16 July 2010, URL: http://www.hrw.org/reports/1995/WR95/HELSINKI-16.htm#P655_198257

Tuysuz, Gul and Steve Almasy (2016), Istanbul airport attack: 36 deaths, 147 injured, Turkish officials say", *CNN News,* July 6 2016, URL: http://edition.cnn.com/2016/06/28/europe/turkey-istanbul-airport-attacks/, Accessed 22 August 2016

Tyson, Ann Scott and Robin Wright (18 December 2007), "US Helps Turkey Hit Rebel Kurds in Iraq", *Washington Post,* (Online: web), Accessed 01 September 2010, URL:http://www.washingtonpost.com/wpdyn/content/article/2007/12/17/AR2007 121702150_2.html.

"UN: Final Report to the Prosecutor by the Committee Established to Review the NATO Bombing Campaign against the Federal Republic of Yugoslavia", (Online: web), Accessed 14 September 2010, URL: http://kosova.org/post/UN-Final-Report-to-the-NATO-Bombing-Campaign- Against-Yugoslavia.aspx.

UNSRC 688(1991), Adopted by the Security Council at its 2982nd Meeting on 5 April 1991 (Online: web), Accessed 2 June 2007, URL: http://www/fas.org/news/un/iraq/sres/sres0688.htm

United Nations (1996), *The United Nations and the Iraq-Kuwait Conflict, 1990-1996*, Department of Public Information, Vol.9, New York.

"Unrepresented Nations and Peoples Organization", (Online: web), Accessed 11 February 2011, URL: http://www.unpo.org/

UNSC Resolution 1511(2003), Adopted by the Security Council at its 4844th Meeting on 16 October 2003: New York, URL: http://www.un.org/Docs/sc/unsc_resolutions03.html

UNSC Resolution 1546(2004), Adopted by the Security Council at its 4987th Meeting, on 8 June 2004, New York, URL: http://www.un.org/Docs/sc/unsc_resolutions04.html

U.S. Department of State, "Bureau of European and Eurasian Affairs," (Online: web), Accessed 15 September 2010, URL:http//www.state.gov/p/eur/

U.S. Department of State, Bureau of Near Eastern Affairs (Online: web), Accessed 15 September 2010, URL: http://www.state.gov/p/nea/

Uslu, Emrullah (Spring 2008), "The Kurdistan Worker's Party Turns against the European Union", *Mediterranean Quarterly*, 99-121.

Uwosomah, Austen Uche (2008), "The Role of the Media in the Rise and Demise of Nation-States", at the Department of Information and Media Studies, Aarthus University: Denmark.

Vali, Abbas (2006), "The Kurds and Their 'Others': Fragmented Identity and Fragmented Politics" in Faleh A. Jabar and Hosham Dawod (eds.) *The Kurds: Nationalism and Politics*, Saqi: London.

Valtonen, K. (1997), *The Societal Participation of Refugees and Immigrants*, Turku: Institute of Migration.

Vanly, Cheriff Ismet (1992) "The Kurds in Syria and Lebanon", in Philip G. Kreyenbroek and Stefan Sperl (eds.) *The Kurds: A Contemporary Overview*, London: Routledge, 146.

Vertovec, S. and R. Cohen (eds.) (1999), *Migration, Diasporas and Transnationalism*, Cheltenham: Edward Elgar.

Visser, Steve and etal, (2016), " Ergdogan: ISIS prime suspect in deadly Turkish wedding blast", *CNN*, August 22, 2016, URL: http://edition.cnn.com/2016/08/21/asia/turkey-wedding-explosion/, Accessed 22 August 2016.

Vos de George (1975), "Ethnic Pluralism" in George de Vos and Lola Romanucci Ross (eds.) *Ethnic Identity: Cultural Continuities and Change*, California: Mayfield Publishing Co.

Wadlow, Rene (January 2008), "Turkey-Iraq-Iran and Kurdish Insurgencies", *Aakrosh*, 11(38): 51-57.

Wahlbeck, Oesten (1998), *Tansnationalism and Diasporas: The Kurdish Example*, Institute of Migration, Finland.

_(1999), *Kurdish Diasporas: A Comparative Study of Kurdish Refugee Communities*, London: Macmillan.

Wallerstein, Immanuel (1974), *The Modern World System: Capitalist Agriculture and the Origins of the European World Economy in the Sixteenth Century*, New York: Academic Press.

Watts, Nicole F. (November 1999), "Allies and Enemies: Pro-Kurdish Parties in Turkish Politics, 1990-94", *International Journal of Middle East Studies*, 31(4): 631-656.

Washburn, J. (December 1998), "Power Bloc: Turkey and Israel Lock Arms", *The Progressive Magazine.*

"Washington Kurdish Institute", (Online: web), Accessed 12 October 2010, URL: http://www.kurd.org/

Washington Kurdish Institute (November 2007), "The Territorial Status of Kirkuk", Washington, 1-13.

Washington Post Company (1999), "Who are the Kurds?" (Online:web), Accessed 30 October 2005, URL: http://www.washingtonpost.com/wp-srv/inatl/daily/feb99/kurd profile.htm

Weller, M (ed.) (1993), *Iraq and Kuwait: The Hostilities and their Aftermath,* Cambridge International Document Series, Cambridge: Grotius Publications Ltd. Vol.3.

Wendt, Alexander (1992), "Anarchy is What States Make of it", *International Organization,* 46: 391-426.

Wilson, Woodrow, *Fourteen Points Speech (1918),* (Online: web), Accessed 13 August 2010, URL: http://usa.usembassy.de/etexts/democrac/51.htm.

Wimmer, Andreas (2002), *Nationalist Exclusion and Ethnic Conflict: Shadows of Modernity,* Cambridge: Cambridge University Press.

Yaphe, Judith S. (Jan 2003), "Iraq before and after Saddam", *Current History,* 102 (660): 7-12.

Yavuz, Hakan M. and Micheal M. Gunter (January 2001), "The Kurdish Nation", *Current History,* 100(642): 33-39.

Yegen, Mesut (April 1996), "Turkish State Discourse and the Exclusion of Kurdish Identity", *Middle Eastern Studies,* 32(2): 216-29.

_(October 1999), "The Kurdish Question in Turkish State Discourse", *Journal of Contemporary History,* 34(4): 555-568.

Yildiz, Kerim (2005), *The Kurds in Syria: The Forgotten People,* London: Pluto Press.

Yildiz, Kerim and Tanyel B. Taysi (2007), *Kurds in Iran: The Past, Present and Future,* London: Pluto Press.

Young, Crawford (1976), *The Politics of Cultural Pluralism,* University of Wisconsin Press: Wisconsin.

Young, Iris Marion (1990), *Justice and the Politics of Difference,* Princeton, New Jersey: Princeton University Press.

Young, Jeffrey (September 2005), *Syria's Kurds Struggle for Rights,* Washington D.C (Online: web), Accessed 05 August 2009, URL: http// www. Voanews.com/English/archive/2005-09/2005-09-02-voa15.cfm?renderorprint...

Young, Kathie (June 1999), "Kurds in Iran (Islamic Republic of Iran)", (Online: web), Accessed 26 February 2010, URL: http://www.bsos.umd.edu/cidcm/mar/irnkurd.htm

Younge, Gary (June 2004), "Israelis using Kurds to Build Power Base", *Guardian,* New York, 21 June 2004, (Online: web), Accessed 17 October 2010, URL: http://www.guardian.co.uk/world/2004/jun/21/iraq.syria.

Ziadeh, Radwan (April 2009), "The Kurds in Syria: Fueling Separatist Movements in the Region?" Special Report, United States Institute of Peace, Washington.

Zoepf, Catherine (2005), "World Briefing: Middle East Syria: Assad Pardons Kurdish Rioters," *New York Times,* March 31, 2005, (Online: web), Accessed 04 September 2008, URL: http://query.nytimes.com/gst/fullpage.html?res=9A02EED9 133FF9 32A05750C0A9639C8B63

Zubaida, Sami (1992), "Introduction" in Philip G. Kreyenbroek and Stefan Sperl (eds.) *The Kurds: A Contemporary Overview,* London: Routledge, 4-5.

Chronology of the Kurdish National Movement

1918 President Woodrow Wilson's Fourteen Points: Woodrow Wilson (President of the United States) was committed to the ideal of self-determination for all people. The Twelfth Point stated that non-Turkish nationalities living under Ottoman control "should be assured an undoubted security of life and be given opportunity of autonomous development". British forces had occupied the oil-rich Ottoman *vilayet* (province) of Mosul, bringing extensive Kurdish-populated areas under the British rule.

1920 The Treaty of Sevres: At the end of World War I, the Allied powers met to determine the political future of lands and peoples in the defeated Ottoman Empire. The Treaty provided for independence from Turkey in those parts of Anatolia where Kurds were in a majority and set forth a political mechanism for the establishment of a Kurdish state that was to have encompassed the *vilayet* of Mosul. The Treaty of Sevres was signed but never ratified.

1923 The Treaty of Lausanne: The Treaty of Lausanne superseded the Treaty of Sevres. The Kurds were not given autonomy and the areas where they lived were distributed between Turkey, Iran, Iraq, Syria and the Soviet Union. Their greatest number found themselves either under the control of the Turkish state or under British rule in the newly created state of Iraq.

1932 Iraqi Independence: In 1932, Iraq was granted full independence by the British and the Kurdish question was left unresolved.

1946 Republic of Mahabad: In Iran, the Kurds established a short-lived Republic of Mahabad, which survived from January 1946 until December 1946.

1946 Creation of the Kurdish Democratic Party of Iraq: This party changed its name to the Kurdistan Democratic Party of Iraq in 1953 to emphasise the inclusion of the non-Kurdish communities of Iraqi Kurdistan.

1975 Creation of the Patriotic Union of Kurdistan (PUK): It was established in June 1975 in Damascus, Syria after the collapse of the Kurdish rebellion the same year.

1978: PKK (Partiya Karkeren Kurdistan or Kurdish Workers' Party) was founded by Abdullah Ocalan in Turkey.

1980 The Iran–Iraq War: While many Kurds fought against the Iranians during the war, others continued the rebellion against the central government often with Iranian support.

1988 Halabja: In March 1988, the Iraqi government attacked the town of Halabja using a mix of chemicals that resulted in the deaths of around 5,000 civilians immediately and many more over the next few years.

1991 The Gulf War: The Kurds were encouraged by the United States to rise up against the government and overthrow Saddam Hussein. The uprising began in March 1991 but Coalition forces did not help the Kurds. At first, the Kurds were successful in driving out the Iraqi army from their territory but the Iraqi army regrouped and crushed the rebellion. The United Nations adopted Resolution 688, which stated that the human rights of the Kurds must be protected. A 'safe haven' with a no-fly-zone above the 36th Parallel was established.

1992 May: Elections held in areas under Kurdish control gave KDP candidates 50.8% of the vote, while the PUK took 49.2%. The two parties were equally balanced in the new Kurdish government.

1994 KDP–PUK Split: The fifty–fifty (50–50) government split between these two parties fell apart and fighting broke out between them.

1995 April: The first Kurdish Parliament-in-Exile convened at The Hague in the Netherlands.

1996 UNSCR 686: The UN agreed to an "Oil-for Food" programme with Baghdad; 13% of the implementation of the Oil-for-Food programme was for ensuring development in Iraqi Kurdistan.

1998 The Washington Agreement: KDP and PUK representatives met in Washington in the fall of 1998. Both the parties accepted the Accord. However it has not been fully implemented.

2002 Reconvening of the Kurdish National Assembly: The Joint session of the Kurdish Parliament convened in Arbil. The KDP and PUK Parliamentarians agreed to work together.

2003 March: The United States-led Coalition forces invaded Iraq which led to the downfall of the Saddam Hussein regime in Iraq.

2005: The first session of the Kurdish Regional Parliament was held in Arbil; KDP's Massoud Barzani is elected President of the Autonomous Region.

2007: The Turkish Parliament gave the go-ahead for military operations in Iraq in pursuit of the Kurdish rebels. Turkey came under international pressure to avoid an invasion.

2007 December: Turkey launched air strikes on fighters from the Kurdish PKK movement inside Iraq.

2009: Massoud Barzani was re-elected as the President of the Autonomous Region.

2011: Turkey launched air and ground attacks against the PKK in Iraqi Kurdistan. The Arab Spring began from Tunisia.

2012: Influx of Syrian refugees into Iraqi Kurdistan began.

2013: March: The jailed Kurdish rebel leader Abdullah Ocalan called for an immediate ceasefire and for thousands of his fighters to withdraw from the Turkish territory; a major step towards the end of one of the world's bloodiest insurgencies.

2014: January: The Kurdish region in Iraq unilaterally started sending its crude oil to Turkey without the approval of the central government in Baghdad.

2014: September: Kurdish troops launched offensives against the Islamic State of Iraq and Syria (ISIS) in northern Iraq.

2015: January: Syrian Kurdish fighters of the People Protection Units (YPG) reclaimed the Kobane town from the ISIS.

2015: July-Turkey joined the US-led military alliance against Islamic State but insists that air-strikes against IS should go hand-in-hand with operations against Kurdish PKK militants in northern Iraq.

2015: August- The Iraqi Kurdistan leadership urges the Turkish government to exercise restraint and calls the PKK to move its bases away from populated areas in order to reduced the risk of civilian casualties.

2016: March- Syria's Kurds declared a federal region in Syrian Kurdistan, Rojava

2016: August- An Arab- Kurdish alliance with support from US airstrikes retakes Manbij from ISIS.

Appendix 1

Table 2.2 The First Cabinet of the Kurdish Regional Government (July 4, 1992)

Name	Position	Party
Fuad Massoum	Prime Minister	PUK
Roj Nuri Shawaise	Deputy Prime Minister	KDP
Amin Mawlud	Industry and Power	PUK
Amin Abdulrahman	Deputy	KDP
Sherko Bekass	Culture	PUK
Ahmed Salar	Deputy	KDP
Mohammad Tawfiq	Humanitarian Aid	PUK
Kamal Kirkuki	Deputy	KDP
Idris Hadi Saleh	Transport and Communication	KDP
Feyeradim Rafiq	Deputy	PUK
Younadim Yousif	Housing and Public Works	ADM
Tayyib Jabir Amin	Deputy	PUK
Nasih Ghafour	Education	KDP
Uthman Hasan	Deputy	PUK
Qadir Aziz	Agriculture	KTP
Akram Izzat	Deputy	KDP
Kamal Mufti	*Peshmerga* Affairs	PUK
Azad Fattah	Deputy	KDP
Marouf Rauf	Justice	Independent
Salah al-Din Hafidh	Finance and Economic Affairs	PUK
Salah Dalo	Deputy	KDP
Kaffia Suleiman	Municipalities and Tourism	PUK
Salih Ahmed	Deputy	KDP

Kamal Shakir	Health and Social Affairs	KCP
Abd al-Ahad Afram	Deputy	KDP
Mohammad Mullah Qadir	Islamic Affairs (*Awqaf*)	KDP
Mohammad Salih	Deputy	PUK
Maamoon Brifkani	Reconstruction and Development	KDP
Husssein Sinjari	Deputy	PUK
Younis Rosebayani	Interior	KDP
Ahmed Sharif	Deputy	PUK

Source: F. Kakai, "The Kurdish Parliament",1992, pp. 123-4, cited in Stansfield, Gareth R.V. (2003), *Iraqi Kurdistan: Political Development and Emergent Democracy*, London: Routledge Curzon, 147.

List of Ministers in the Kurdistan Regional Government, Fifth Cabinet from 7 May 2006. This was the first unified Cabinet formed following the January 2006 Unification Agreement that merged the Erbil/Dohuk and Sulaymaniyah administrations of the KRG.

Nechirvan Idris Barzani	Prime Minister
Imad Ahmad Sayfour	Deputy Prime Minister
Abdul Karim Sultan Sinjari	Minister for the Interior
Sarkis Aghajan	Minister for Finance & Economy
Bayiz Saeed Mohammad (Bayiz Talabani)	Minister of the Region for Finance & the Economy; Acting Minister
Farouq Jamil Sadiq	Minister for Justice
Jafar Mustafa Ali	Minister for *Peshmerga* Affairs
Burhan Saeed Sofi	Minister for Transport
Dilshad Abdul Rahman Mohammad	Minister for Education
Abdul Rahman Osman Yones	Minister for Health
Adnan Mohammad Qadir	Minister for Labour and Social Affairs
Mohammad Ahmad Saeed Shakaly	Minister for Religious Affairs
Tahsin Qadir Ali	Minister for Water Resources
Imad Ahmad Sayfour	Minister for Housing and Reconstruction
Osman Ismail Hassan (Osman Shwani)	Minister for Planning

Yousif Mohammad Aziz	Minister for Human Rights
Idris Hadi Salih	Minister for Higher Education and Scientific Research
Abdul-Aziz Tayeb Ahmad	Minister for Agriculture
Ms Chnar Sa'ad	Minister for Martyrs and Victims of Anfal
Falakaddin Kakeyi	Minister for Culture
Hoshyar Abdul Rahman Siwaily	Minister for Electricity
Dr Ashti A. Hawrami	Minister for Natural Resources
Ms Nazanin Mohammad Waso	Minister for Municipalities
Taha Abdul Rahman Ali (Taha Barwary)	Minister for Sport and Youth
Dr Mohammad Ihsan	Minister for Extra-Regional Affairs
Mohammad Raouf Mohammad	Minister for Trade
Widad Khurshid Osman	Minister for Industry
Dara Mohammad Amin	Minister for the Environment
Nimrud Baito	Minister for Tourism
Haydar Sheikh Ali	Minister for Communication
Abubakir Ali	Minister for the Region
Dr Jinan Qasim	Minister for the Region
George Yousif Mansour	Minister for the Region
Dr Dakheel Saeed Khudhur	Minister for the Region
Mohammad Haji Mahmoud	Minister for the Region
Mahmoud Eido	Minister for the Region
Madhat Mandalawy	Minister for the Region
Sa'ad Khalid Mohammad Amin	Minister for the Region
Nouri Othman	President, Divan of the Council of Ministers
Mohammad Qaradaghi	Secretary of the Cabinet
Sarbaz Hawrami	Prime Minister's Chief of Staff
Herish Muharam	Chairman of the Investment Board
Falah Mustafa Bakir	Head of the Department of Foreign Relations

Appendix 2

Article 140 of the Iraqi Constitution

First: The executive authority shall undertake the necessary steps to complete the implementation of the requirements of all subparagraphs of Article 58 of the Transitional Administrative Law.

Second: The responsibility placed upon the executive branch of the Iraqi Transitional Government stipulated in Article 58 of the Transitional Administrative Law shall extend and continue to the executive authority elected in accordance with this Constitution, provided that it accomplishes completely (normalization and census and concludes with a referendum in Kirkuk and other disputed territories to determine the will of their citizens), by a date not to exceed the 31st of December 2007.

Appendix 3

Extract from the Treaty of Sevres

Section III: Kurdistan

Section III of the Treaty of Sèvres, entitled 'Kurdistan' composed of three articles spelling out the details:

Article 62: "A Commission sitting at Constantinople and composed of three members appointed by the British, French and Italian Governments respectively shall draft within six months from the coming into force of the present Treaty a scheme of local autonomy for the predominantly Kurdish areas lying east of the Euphrates, south of the southern boundary of Armenia as it may be hereafter determined, and north of the frontier of Turkey with Syria and Mesopotamia, as defined in Article 27, II (2) and (3). If unanimity cannot be secured on any question, it will be referred by the members of the Commission to their respective Governments..."

Article 63: "The Turkish Government hereby agrees to accept and execute the decisions of both the Commissions mentioned in Article 62 within three months from their communication to the said government".

Article 64: "If within one year from the coming into force of the present Treaty the Kurdish peoples within the areas defined in Article 62 shall address themselves to the Council of the League of Nations in such a manner as to show that a majority of the population of these areas desires independence from Turkey, and if the Council then considers that these peoples are capable of such independence and recommends that it should be granted to them, Turkey hereby agrees to execute such a recommendation, and to renounce all rights and title over these areas. If and when such renunciation takes place, no objection will be raised by the Principal Allied Powers to the voluntary adhesion to such an independent Kurdish State of the Kurds inhabiting that part of Kurdistan which has hitherto been included in the Mosul Vilayet."

Index

A

Abdullah Ocalan's organisation, 240
Abdul Rahman, Sami, 33
Ahl-i-Haqq, 11, 12
Ahmadinejad, Mahmoud, 130–131, 244
Al-Assad, Bashar, 145, 149, 151, 152
Al-Assad, Hafez, 140–141
Alfredsson, Gudmundur, 210
Alevism, 11
Ali, Kosrat Rasoul, 43
Algiers Accord, 169–170
al-Maliki, Nouri, 66
al-Qaeda, 27
Amnesty International, 145, 146
Ankara peace process, 51
Arabisation programme, 53
Arab League, 55
Arab partrimony, 53
Arabs, 178–179
Arab Spring, 198–199, 227
Article 140 of Iraq's constitution, 63, 288
Assyrian Democratic Movement, 41

B

Baath Party, 141–142
Baghdad Pact, 169–170
Barzani, Massoud, 22, 40, 88
Barzani, Mustafa, 171
Barzani, Nashirawan, 33
Begin, Menachem, 180
Beran, Harry, 213
Besikci, Ismail, 89
British imperialism, 1
Buchanan, Allen, 213
Bureau of Near Eastern Affairs, 177

C

Capital accumulation process, 23
Capitalist system, 217
Central Treaty Organization (CENTO), 169
Christian Assyrians, 41
Christian community, 12, 27, 29
Christianity, 11
Coalition forces, 63
Coalition Provisional Authority (CPA), 55
Constitution of the Islamic Republic, 121
Constitutional Court, 90

D

Damascus Declaration, 147
Democracy, 18
Democratic Republic of Azerbaijan, 168
Democratic Union Party (PYD), 153, 154
Dependency theory, 217

E

Economic sanctions, 34
Erdogan, R.T.
Ethnicity, 17
Ethno-nationalism, 115
European colonisation, 18

F

Federalism, 54
Frank, Andre Gunder, 217
Free Syrian Army, 151
Fund-al-Islam, 50

G

Geneva Convention, 84
Globalisation, 248
    globalisation, 19
Gulf War, 237

Gurani, 12

H

Hersh, Seymour, 182
Horowitz, Donald, 213
Humanitarian crises, 27
Human rights, 246, 248
Human Rights Watch, 139, 142–143
Hussein, Saddam, 5–6, 47, 52, 141, 180, 186

I

International Campaign for Human Rights in Iran, 134
International NGOs (INGOs), 36, 185, 186
Iran, 237, 240, 243
Iran, Kurds
  electoral politics, 135
  ethnic distribution, 117
  German influence in, 119
  history, 116
  human rights violations, 133–135
  Islamic Revolution, 121–123
  Kurdish diaspora, 188
  Kurdish political parties, 123–127
  non-Persian ethnic groups, 119
  Ottoman and Safavid administrations, 118
  political situation
    Ahmadinejad, Mahmoud, 130–131
    governmental structure, 127
    Guardian Council, 129, 132
    Hijri, Mustafa, 132
    human rights groups, 129
    Iranian Constitution, 127
    Khatami, Mohammad, 128–129, 130, 132
    KRG, 127
    Kurdish civil society, 132
    Kurdish parties, 131, 132
    Kurdish representatives, 129
    Parliamentary elections, 129, 130
    political and national consciousness, 132
    reform movement, 130
    social and political changes, 132
    socio-economic changes, 132
    trans-nationalisation, 129
  Republic of Mahabad, 120–121
  Reza Shah's policies, 119
  ruling powers, 118
  Simko's revolt, 118–119
  zero-tolerance policy, 118
Iranian culture, 244
Iranian political system, 244
Iranian Revolution, 22
Iran-Iraq War, 81
Iraq, 237, 240
  post-Saddam Iraq, US–Kurd relation in, 174–178
  pro-Soviet regime in, 171
Iraqi army, 27, 33
Iraqi Governing Council (IGC), 55
Iraqi-Kurdish rapprochement, 33
Iraqi Kurdistan, 242, 249
Iraqi Kurds, 240
Iraqi National Congress, 46
Iraqi National Congress (INC), 46
Iraqi national policy, 60
Iraqi National Turkoman Party (INTP), 41
Iraqi Security Forces (ISF), 58, 67
Irish Republican Army (IRA), 216
Islamic extremism, 182
Islamic and tribal laws, 8
Islamic Movement of Iraqi Kurdistan (IMIK), 50
Islamic Revolution, 121–123
Islamic State of Iraq and Syria (ISIS), 24, 96, 151, 152, 153, 154, 155, 246
Israel
  Israeli–Kurdish relations, 179–182
  Kurdish Special Forces, 182

J

Jihad, 122
Judaism, 11

K

Karim, Najmaldin, 249
Kautsky, Karl, 218

Khatami, Mohammad, 128–129, 244
Khomeini, Ayatollah, 122
Khoybun, 138
Kosovo, 246
Kosovo crisis, 176
Kurdi, 12
Kurdish culture, 244
Kurdish Democratic Alliance, 144
Kurdish Democratic Party (DEP), 191
Kurdish Democratic Party (KDP), 121
Kurdish Democratic Party of Iran (KDPI), 123–125, 126, 128, 130, 131, 222, 243
Kurdish Democratic Party of Syria (KDPS), 143
Kurdish Democratic Progressive Party (KDPP), 143–144
Kurdish diaspora
  collective commitment, 187
  ethno-national identity, 188
  international mobility, 186
  KNC, 189–191
  KPE, 191–192
  Kurdish culture, 188
  Kurdish institutions, 188–189
  Kurdish Media, 192–194
  political mobilisation, 187
  refugee communities, 187
Kurdish ethnicity, 205–209
Kurdish ethnic identity, 242
Kurdish Human Rights Organization (HROK), 133
Kurdish Human Rights Project (KHRP), 189
Kurdish Mahabad Republic, 168
Kurdish Media, 192–
Kurdish minorities, 6
Kurdish National Conference, 152
Kurdish National Congress, 247
Kurdish National Council (KNC), 154
Kurdish National Movement, 281–284
  capital accumulation, 20
  capital accumulation process, 23
  Creation of the Kurdish Democratic Party of Iraq (1946), 281–282
  Creation of the Patriotic Union of Kurdistan (1975), 282
  ethno-territorial conflict, 19
  globalisation, 19
  Gulf War (1991), 282
  Halabja (1988), 282
  hegemony, 21
  imperialism, 21
  Iranian Revolution, 22
  Iran-Iraq War (1980), 282
  Iraqi Independence (1932), 281
  KDP-PUK government split (1994), 282
  Partiya Karkeren Kurdistan/Kurdish Workers' Party (1978), 282
  peripheral states, 21
  1918 President Woodrow Wilson's Fourteen Points, 281
  Republic of Mahabad (1946), 281
  Soviet Union, 22
  Treaty of Lausanne (1923), 281
  Treaty of Sevres (1920), 281
  1996 UNSCR 686, 282
  violence and destruction, 23
  Washington Agreement (1998), 282
  'world system' approach, 19
Kurdish Parliament-in-Exile (KPE), 191–192
Kurdish political institutions, 48
Kurdish problem
  Middle East, Kurds (*see* Kurds)
  with Turkey (*see* Turkey, Kurdish conflict in)
Kurdish Regional Government (KRG), 127, 131, 132, 157, 174, 184, 185
  economy of, 176
  INGOs, 185
  KRG–Iran relationship, 175
  UN agencies, 185
  Kurdish Regional Government, in Iraqi Kurdistan
  behaviour and political factionalism 26
  chemical weapons 26
  civil war 45–47
  constitutional system 26

democratic autonomy 25
division of Iraqi Kurdistan 47–49
economy post-2003 War 61–63
eighth Cabinet of KRG 2014 44–45
fall of Saddam Hussein's regime 26
First Cabinet of the KRG 42–43
Gulf War
Allied Campaign 31
depopulation of Kurdish areas 32–34
Iraq Kurdistan Front (IKF) 30
Operation Al-anfal 30
pro-government tribal militias 31
UN Security Council Resolution 687 32
Islamic Movement of Iraqi Kurdistan 49–51
Islamic State of Iraq and al-Sham (ISIS) 65–67
Kurdish, role in Iraqi constitution 55–57
Kurdistan National Assembly 38, 52–53
Kurdistan National Assembly Election 2005 57–58
Kurdistan Parliament 39–40
parliamentary elections 39
physical geography 27–29
political decision-making 25
Post-Saddam Iraq 53–55
post-Saddam political struggle 27
power-sharing system 41–42
referendum vote 58–60
sanctions and humanitarian intervention 34–38
Second Cabinet of the KRG 43
Status of Kirkuk 63–65
structure and programme 38–39
US military forces 27
Washington Agreement 51–52
Kurdish self-determination
Buchanan's theory of, 213
concept of self-determination, 210, 212
democratic identity, 219
domestic political changes, 205
encompassing group, 213
ethnic consciousness, 204
ethno-nationalism, 204, 235
global capitalism, 212
human rights violations, 204–205
ideological differences and methods of struggle, 220–224
internal aspect of, 212
international law, 211
Kurdish internally divisive problems, 227–230
Kurdish national movement, challenges to, 225–227
Kurdish search for a solution, 230–234
modern identity, 219
moral justification, 213
nationalism and Kurdish ethnicity, 205–209
political authority, 218
principle of self-determination, 209
regional autonomy, 214–218
right of people, 212
territorial centralism, 219
traditional Kurdish organisations, 220
UN Charter, 210–211
Kurdish Socialist Party (KSP), 40
Kurdish Special Forces, 182
Kurdistan
British imperialism, 1
colonised areas, 1
concept of identity and representation, 17–19
economy, 5–6
ethnic conflict and fragmentation, 1
in Iraqi Kurdistan, 2
Kurdish life, 2
Kurdish struggle and aspirations, 2
language, customs and culture, 1
language diversity, 12–14
nationalism, 14–17
origin of, 3
Ottoman Empire, 2
physical geography, 4–5
policy of Arabisation, 3

political contours, 1
population, society and stratification, 6–10
Islamic and tribal laws, 8
lack of industrial enterprises, 9
migrant labourers, 9
non-Kurdish minorities, 6
Ottoman and Persian Empires, 10
Ottoman government, 8
social and economic negligence, 9
social relations, 10
socio-economic and political changes, 8
Sunni Muslims, 8
tribalism, 6
principle of national self-determination, 2
religious minorities, 10–12
Sevres-Lausanne period, 2
Treaty of Sevres, 2
Versailles Peace Conference, 2
Kurdistan Autonomous Region, 239
Kurdistan Democratic Party (KDP), 229
Kurdistan Democratic Party of Turkey (KDPT), 77
Kurdistan Iraqi Front (KIF), 40
Kurdistan National Congress (KNC), 189–191
Kurdistan Referendum Movement (KRM), 58
Kurdistan Regional Government, 238
Kurdistan Regional Government (KRG), 67
Kurdistan Workers Party (PKK), 153, 154, 156, 174, 190, 191, 195, 196, 224
ideology, 221
public places, assassinations and bombs in, 176
revolutionary theory, 221
strategy, 221
Kurds
Arab position, Kurdish issue, 178–179
and Arab Spring, 198–199
Baghdad Pact, Algiers Accord, 169–170
capital accumulation, 250
economic resources, 250
European Union perspective, 194–197
geopolitics of, 250
in Iran
electoral politics, 135
ethnic composition, 116–118
history, 116
human rights violations, 133–135
Islamic Revolution, 121–123
KDPI, 123–125
Komala, 125–126
PJAK, 126–127
political situation, 127–132
Republic of Mahabad, 120–121
Simko revolts against Reza Shah, 118–120
theocratic system, 135
Israeli–Kurdish relations, 179–182
Kurdish diaspora (*see* Kurdish diaspora)
and League of Nations, 164–165
Treaty of Lausanne, 165–168
Treaty of Sevres, 165
political rights, 250
Republic of Kurdistan, 168
as stateless people, 197–198
in Syria, 136–137
cultural and linguistic rights, violations of, 141–143
denationalisation and repression, 138–140
establishment of Rojava (Western Kurdistan), 152–154
female fighters of Kurdistan, 154–157
government response, 147–150
under Hafez al-Assad, 140–141
Kurdish political organisation, 143–145
Kurdish population, 137–138, 158
Kurdish reawakening, 145–147
public opinion in, 157
Syrian conflict 2011, 150–152
transnational aspects of, 182
INGOs, 185, 186
Kurdayati, 183, 184
Kurdish nationalists, 184
non-state actors, 183
oil-for-food programme, 185

political identities, 183
United Nations, 185
United States' policy (*see* United States' policy)
'world system,' 250
World War II, 168
Kurmanji, 13
Kuwait, 247

L

League of Nations, Kurds, 164–165
Treaty of Lausanne, 165–168
Treaty of Sevres, 165
Liberation of Kirkuk, 63
Luxemburg, Rosa, 218

M

madrasas, 10
Mahmoud, Sheikh, 2
Manichaeanism, 11
Marcuse, Herbert, 232
Marxism, 221
Menderes, Adnan, 76
Middle East, 242
Ministers, in Kurdistan Regional Government, 286–287
Ministry of Humanitarian Aid and Cooperation, 37
Mohammed, Qazi, 2
Muslim sheikhs, 16

N

Nationalism, 14–17, 205–209
Nestorianism, 11
Netanyahu, Benjamin, 66, 180
Non-Kurdish minorities, 6
Non-state actors, 183
North America, 247
North Atlantic Treaty Organization (NATO), 172, 174, 175, 176, 177

O

Oil and gas sub-sectors, 5
Oil-for-Food Programme, 238
Oil-for-food programme, 35
Operation Provide Comfort, 172, 173
Organization for Security and Cooperation in Europe (OSCE), 195
Ottoman Empire, 2, 237
Ottoman government, 8
Ozal, Turgut, 172

P

Paganism, 11
Pan-Arab nationalism, 140
Partiya Jiyana Azada Kurdistan/Party for Free Life in Kurdistan (PJAK), 126–127
Party of Socialism in Kurdistan (PASOK), 40
Peace and Democracy Party (BDP), 94
People's Democratic Party (HADEP), 91–92
People's Protection Units (YPG), 152, 153, 154
Political community, 15
Powell, Colin, 174
Proto-nationalism, 207
Pro-Western defence alliances, 237

Q

Qasim, Abdul-Karim, 169

R

Ramazanzadeh, Abdullah, 128, 129
Regional autonomy, 214–218
Republic of Kurdistan, 168
Republic of Mahabad, 120–121
Revolutionary Cultural Society of the East, 77
Revolutionary Organisation of the Toilers of Kurdistan (Komala), 125–126
Right to self-determination, 249

S

Saadabad Pact, 167
Saddam Hussein's regime, fall of, 238
Security Council Resolution 688, 238
Self-determination, 248
sheikh/*seyid*, 16
Shi'a-dominated government, 244
Smith, A.D., 205
Smith, Anthony, 15
Socio-economic and political changes, 8

Sorani, 13
Sulaymani, 12
Sunni Islam, 10
Sunni Muslims, 8, 243
Supreme State Security Courts (SSSCs), 148
Syria, Kurds, 136–137, 243
  cultural and linguistic rights, violations of, 141–143
  denationalisation and repression, 138–140
  establishment of Rojava (Western Kurdistan), 152–154
  female fighters of Kurdistan, 154–157
  government response, 147–150
  under Hafez al-Assad, 140–141
  KDPP, 143–144
  KDPS, 143
  Kurdish Democratic Alliance, 144
  Kurdish population, 137–138
  Kurdish reawakening, 145–147
Syrian conflict 2011, 150–152
Syrian Democratic Forces (SDF), 153
Syrian Kurdish Democratic Union Party, 153

T

Talabani, Jalal, 33, 88
Transitional Administered Law, 55
Treaty of Lausanne, 165–168, 170
Treaty of Sevres, 165, 170, 289
Tribalism, 6
Tribal system, 16
Turkey
  Islamic movements, 223
  Israeli–Turkish relations, 181
  post-Gulf War regional politics, 185
Turkey, Kurdish conflict in
Abdullah Ocalan's political vision, 79
  Ankara's response, 94–97
  civil war, 73
  cultural and linguistic expressions, 74
  cultural expression, 78
  economic development, 74
  electoral system, 74
  ethnic problem, 75
  and European Union (EU) relations, 101–104
  forced evacuations, 97–98
  government's policy of assimilation, 76
  human rights violations, 74
  integration of Kurds, Turkish society, 98–101
  ISIS attack, 109–111
  July 2016 military coup, 108–109
  Kurdish nationalist movement, 78
  Kurdish political identities, 77
  Kurdish population, 73
  Kurdish Workers' Party, 78–79
  Kurdistan Democratic Party of Turkey, 77
  Lausanne Conference, 75
  military regime and resurgence
    PKK goal, 81–86
    PKK-Iraqi Kurdish relationship, 86–89
    political and legal institutions, 80
    political support, PKK, 89–90
  principles of Kemalism, 76
  regional implications, 104–107
  socio-economic problem, 73
  socio-political leaders, 73
  socio-political liberalisation, 77
  state policy and discourse, 73
  Turkey election, Kurds in, 90–94
  Turkey's parliament and economic investment, 77
  universal education, 77
  war against Kurdish population, 107–108
Turkish army, 241
Turkish Constitution, 94
Turkish Kurdistan, 242
Turkish Kurds, 241
Turkish nationality, 242
Turkish political system, 91

U

United Nations Children's Fund (UNICEF), 34
United Nations High Commissioner for Refugees (UNHCR), 148–149

United Nations (UN) Resolution, 55
United Nations sanctions, 36
United States' policy, Kurds
  Allied Forces intervene, Northern Iraq, 172–174
  US–Kurd relation, post-Saddam Iraq, 174–178
  World War I to First Gulf War, 170–172
UN Security Council Resolution 688, 173

V

Versailles Peace Conference, 2

W

Wallerstein, Immanuel, 20
Washington Accord, 52
Washington Kurdish Institute, 189
West Asian countries, 248
Wilson, W., 170
Women's Protection Units (YPJ), 153, 154–155
World Health Organization (WHO), 34

Y

Yezidis, 11

Z

Zaza, 13
Zoroastrianism, 11